The Enthusiast

The Enthusiast

A Life of Thornton Wilder

Gilbert A. Harrison

Ticknor & Fields
New Haven and New York 1983

Library of Congress Cataloging in Publication Data

Harrison, Gilbert A.
   The enthusiast.

   1. Wilder, Thornton, 1897–1975.   2. Authors, American — 20th century — Biography.   I. Title.
PS3545.I345Z694   1983   818'.5209   [B]   83-5076
ISBN 0-89919-197-5

818.5209

H24e

128724

may 1984

Printed in the United States of America

V 10 9 8 7 6 5 4 3 2 1

Unless otherwise credited, all photographs are from the Thornton Wilder Archive, Collection of American Literature, Beinecke Rare Book and Manuscript Library, Yale University.

Material quoted from previously unpublished writings of Thornton Wilder copyright © 1983 by Union Trust Company, Executor and Trustee of the Will of Thornton Wilder. Published by permission of Union Trust Company and Donald Gallup, Literary Executor for Thornton Wilder.

Acknowledgment is made to the Collection of American Literature, the Beinecke Rare Book and Manuscript Library, Yale University, for permission to reproduce hitherto unpublished material from the Thornton Wilder Archive.

Acknowledgment is made to Harper & Row, Publishers, Inc., for permission to quote from the following copyrighted works by Thornton Wilder: *The Bridge of San Luis Rey,* copyright 1927 by Albert and Charles Boni, Inc., copyright renewed 1955 by Thornton Wilder; *The Long Christmas Dinner,* copyright 1931 by Yale University Press and Coward-McCann, Inc., copyright renewed 1959 by Thornton Wilder; *Pullman Car Hiawatha,* copyright 1931 by Yale University Press and Coward-McCann, Inc., copyright renewed 1959 by Thornton Wilder; *The Skin of Our Teeth,* copyright 1942, 1970 by Thornton Wilder; *The Ides of March,* copyright 1948, 1976 by Thornton Wilder; *The Merchant of Yonkers,* copyright 1939 by Thornton Wilder; *The Cabala,* copyright 1926 by Charles and Albert Boni, copyright renewed 1954 by Thornton Wilder; *The Woman of Andros,* copyright 1930 by Albert and Charles Boni, copyright renewed 1958 by Thornton Wilder; *The Happy Journey to Camden and*

For Nancy

Now a little before it was day, good Christian, as one half amazed, broke out in this passionate speech: what a fool, quothe he, am I thus to lie in a stinking Dungeon, when I may as well walk at liberty! I have a key in my bosom, called Promise, that will, I am persuaded, open any lock in Doubting Castle. Then said Hopeful, that is good news; good Brother pluck it out of thy bosom and try. . . .

— John Bunyan, *The Pilgrim's Progress*

You can always accomplish something by giving witness to joy. . . . Just as the scripture says that faith and hope without love are only sounding brass and tinkling cymbal, so also the joy proclaimed without mentioning the pain is only sounding brass and tinkling cymbal; unheeded, it whistles past the ear of the suffering one; it sounds on the ear but does not resound in the heart; it agitates the ear but is not treasured within. But this voice which quivers with pain and still proclaims joy — yes, this forces its way in through his ear and descends into his heart and is treasured there.

— Søren Kierkegaard, *Journals and Papers*

Contents

The Enthusiast

Letters

First, three letters written in the summer of 1910 by Amos Parker Wilder, U.S. consul general in Shanghai, to his "Dear Children," who with their mother are living in a rented house several blocks from the campus of the University of California:

I am following events at Berkeley with great interest these days and I like to read that you are helping Mama. I am sending her money as freely as I can. We are so fortunate in having a good income these years, that I am not disposed to find fault with this separation. You children are getting an education and we are saving a little for the future. Thornton says nothing of the $1.00 I sent for his birthday. Can I be mistaken about that? Let us all make much of each others' birthdays and each give a gift, even if it is not big. Charlotte's is the next (August 28). Let us be a loving, united family. I am getting on very well at this end, as far as I can see. Life is full of uncertainties and Christian-folks are not to worry about the future: we are to do each day's work cheerfully, in faith. Most of the things we dread never happen, and those that do are for the best, if we look to God, the loving, wise One. I hope you are reading *Pilgrim's Progress.* I am also sending *The Boy's Life of John Wesley.* He was the founder of the Methodist denomination; he lived to be 85, his life just spanned the 18th Century (1703–1788). He was a college man but threw in his lot with the humble — a tireless worker (rose at 4:00 A.M., went to bed early) and a man of piety and sense. Amos: I note your marks are pretty good. I should be glad if you are in all the debates you can get in; speak everytime you get a chance even if it is pretty poor stuff.

Thornton: you must write your best when you take pen in hand. For a 13-year-old your handwriting is faulty. Even as you grow older you may remain "a little boy" in heart. The Chinese have a saying, "A great man has the heart of a boy." There is a great truth here. Keep your thoughts pure and aspiring, rejoice in God's beautiful world, love your fellows and animals — be kind, and you will always be a boy even if you wear long pants and your whiskers come to your knees.

Charlotte: are you very kind these days to all? Are you thoughtless in playing with little girls, and do you do good things *they* want to do, and finally grow to have a good time because they do the things *they* want? When you put your pretty head down in prayer at night — you and black-haired Isabel — forget everything except that you are in the presence of the Great, Loving Father. . . .

Isabel: all of this previous letter is for you. Never let a brother's or sister's birthday go by again without giving a present, even if you have to go and pick a leaf from a tree! A spanking was not enough for Thornton tho he used to like those with a hairbrush I used to give him. With his artistic temperament, he used to insist on a silver back before he would permit the performance to go forward. But happily those days have gone forever.

I am reminded of the happy years we had at Maple Bluff [Wisconsin]. When your Papa is "gone before" remember that in our little cottage with my wife and children they were the happiest years of his life. He had heavy burdens in the city but when he walked along the lake shore in the early evening and saw the "lights of home," the cares slipped off like a harness — sweet children awaited him at the gate, or ran down to meet him, the mother with supper spread on the veranda; the pleasant converse, the reverent quiet, worship, each one joining in — the "all still and quiet," Papa's few moments alone under the stars, with the wind murmuring through the forest — the restful sleep — those were precious years!

Amos writes me that his name gets in the papers as a tennis "sharp." I hope you will be upset by publicity. Every man who is a part of community life has his name in the papers to some extent; I should be disappointed if my children when they grow up do not do things that get their names in the paper; but Amos will lay no stress on it. "Forget it," my boy. The thing that you do is more important than the telling about it.

I enjoy pictures of my children in the Greek play. Thornton looks like a discus thrower! . . . As for Greek plays, you know Papa has only a limited admiration for "art." Some of it — pictures, drama, music — is good as an incidental and diversion in life, but *character* is the thing in life to strive for. There are people who know all about pictures and Greek tragedy and the latest opera who are not interested in the poor and know little about kindness. If you should go to some of them and ask a subscription for famine sufferers or a hospital, they would be unsympathetic because of not being interested, but they would enthuse over something that happened a long time ago and classical music gives them a comfortable feeling! Abraham Lincoln and Marcus Aurelius would be good friends if they met, for both had pure, stout hearts, but Lincoln knew more about slaves than he did of art, and so did John Brown. I want you to appreciate all good, wholesome things of every age, but don't get sidetracked by dramatic art or Wagner music or postage-stamp collecting from present day, living, throbbing problems and needs.

We did have a big tennis party yesterday, about 40. I led them up to the lemonade trough (of course we had tea, etc. also) and looked them right in the eye. Men love to be led, and they saw I was master of the situation and not ashamed; even the men of vine-kissed France and big-stomached Germans from the far off beer country put their snouts into the cooling beverage and pronounced it good. I do hope my boys and girls will grow up to be, not timid, time-serving, mucilage-backboned men and women who are afraid that unless they do as everyone else does they will be out of fashion or laughed at — but big, gracious, jolly, sympathetic, commanding men and women who do not follow the fashion but make it — the whole man and woman touched with the quiet dignity that in a way detaches him or her without breaking the bond of sympathy.

If one believes that the world is growing better; that humanity, even common folk, are full of strong, heroic qualities that need only to be aroused; that the kingdom of Heaven is to be brought to earth, the bad fiends yielding — then it fills a youth with ardent aspirations to be in the midst of the fight — to give his fellow man the best that is in him. He knows that when he is right he is on sure ground — that the right must conquer.

When *Pilgrim's Progress* is finished I want you to read some of Thomas à Kempis — and then the marked Whittier poems. Let the hearing be reverent, each child grasping the thought.

I hope Thornton will not lay too much stress on Greek or any other plays. I must even hold that the man who does a thing is more important than the fellow who shows how it is done. "Things that are pure and wholesome and of good report" we will encourage — but there is such a mass of poor, silly men and women rushing to see plays of all kinds to get a thrill of excitment, that I beg you to regard it as an incidental of life. We will get some gray whiskers for Thornton and let him play old King Lear — meanwhile turning on the hose to represent a sure enough storm.

I rejoice that Thornton is able to water an occasional lawn. I shall not be content, however, until both my boys work in a grocery store for awhile so that they may distinguish Timothy seed from bar soap.

Thornton, age eighteen and working on a farm at the Mount Hermon School in Massachusetts, writing to his older brother, Amos, in the summer of 1915:
The principal alleviations of my life have been the evenings, my reading, and my thoughts. I am sure that you have as beautiful a place as this, although you may not have the last hours of the day free to enjoy it as I have. But steal an hour from sleep if necessary and walk along the sides of some pond or brook. And try to get a little reading in. I will send you the *Religio Medici* which is a "devotional" book but written in the most exquisite style. The marks are father's and refer to the sentiment not the style. The discussions of the supernatural especially are written in the most stirring eloquence I ever read. My chief interest here however has been Boswell's *Life of Johnson* which I read every hour I can. I'd send it to you, only it weighs a ton. I am often

able to be by myself "hoeing a row" or "turning the hay" and look forward to such jobs as chances to think over everything and anything.

Please do not think me any the less sincere because of the frightful wording of this letter. All the stiffness is the sign that Boswell has me all over. I see myself writing down an archaism or Latin construction and I have to howl at myself, but *I cannot help it*. My style will either come out from this ordeal saved or ruined. Wash out your eyes, remember that life's a kind of illusion and this pain and disease is merely funny, and that you are tenderly loved by

Thornton N. Wilder

Thornton, a junior at Oberlin College in Ohio, to his family, December 3, 1916:
My new propaganda for projecting myself among the "fellas" goes on fast. I have the most shamelessly ingenious way of introducing myself. I drop in on the rooms of boys I admire without knowing them, and take them by surprise. But I have never suffered the humiliation of their not knowing my name. Sometimes they start right off with "come in Thornton." And wait respectfully to hear *what on earth* brings me. I pretend to be profoundly interested in what [one boy] thought about going in the gospel team or not; another I had heard worked in a bank and would he help me with my Assets and Liabilities problems for Economics class? Just tonight I called on Howard Curtis, my gym teacher last year. The man fairly staggered with surprise when he saw me — the drag of the class — but we had a long talk in which he warmed up more and more, and at last he walked home with me and came up to see my room. The emanations from the personalities of gym teachers are tonic.

Thornton to Papa, February 14, 1917:
I want to go away to Italy but not to relieve suffering — though while I'm there by all means let me do it — not to seek pictures and classical landscapes — not to get away from the uninspired complacency of Oberlin. Let me go to have some time to myself. Not just a day, or a weekend, or a week — but half a year. A

person like me has got to keep writing things. When we think
we have written a good thing we need to feel as though it had
justified our existence and we don't know what "plain" people
do to satisfy that self-demand. I do not need your faith in me. I
know by what Catholics call their "vocation" that I can now, with
time, "trespass among superlatives." This elation and confidence
follows the completion of *The Little Turtle,* a play in five scenes,
brooded upon for years, but written in a month of Chemistry
lessons, imperfect and skimpy to the point of tears; but authentic
in parts.

Thornton to Papa, two months later:
My real life is abstract and moves along at its own will and caprice,
and all these outer things are a shrugging-of-the-shoulders, a quirk-
on-the-stream. So do what you like: a hoe or a hospital pail or a
bayonet in my hand are phantom, for my hand holds always a
fountain pen.

Thornton to Amos, May 26, 1917:
Your religious self-examination I cannot duplicate. I am a less
conscientious nature and do not examine my faith. I fling myself
on my knees as though at a divine compulsion, mostly when I'm
happy, though also in extremis. I am happiest in loving and being
loved by human people, and next to that in writing words and
being commended for them, and next to that in mysteries of the
spirit, into which I penetrate more every year, until God will be
my whole life. I suppose that everyone feels that his nature cries
out hourly for it knows not what, but I like to believe that mine
raises an exceedingly great voice because I am a twin, and because
by his death an outlet for my affection was closed. It is not affection
alone but energy, and in it I live and because of it I believe I
seem to see my life as more vivid, electric and marvelous than
others so placidly do. I am continually surprised at people's luke-
warmness; I am perpetually enthusiastic over some composition
or book, some person or some friend.

Thornton to Papa the following year, from Yale University:
Sometimes I get so annoyed by your desperation over a chance
cigarette or a frivolous word that I have a good mind to give

you a real jolt, such jolts as other fathers get from their sons, the real griefs of Old Eli. I am too good for you, that's all, and you make a luxury of martyrdom to yourself out of my slightest defection. Likewise [sister] Charlotte's friends consider her an amazing, rare personality, such as New England is only able to cast up once in an age, but you wear us all out with your instigations to Napoleonship and fame [and] look upon the first YMCA secretary or Settlement House directress as more interesting than Charlotte. Do try to console and comfort your declining years with the incredible news that you have produced at least two children that are the amazement and delight and amused despair of their circles (the more finely grained the spectator the greater the appreciation). Let others produce obscure devoted women and faithful Assistant Pastors; you have fathered two wild fowl flying in the storm of the 20th century.

Finally, as assistant housemaster at the Lawrenceville School in New Jersey, Thornton writes to his mother in New Haven, November 6, 1923:
Dear Wun:

If the school knew I spent so much time writing to my mother, I should be fired. From the viewpoint of the schoolmaster a mother is a tiresome nuisance. Just as we begin to shape a plaintive or remorseful or rebellious boy, his mother descends on him for a weekend and with her pitying and indulgence spoils all our plans. We have the worst opinion of you all. Shoo! It would be useless for me to represent to them that you are a very superior one, that you do not drink or smoke, wear a dog-collar or keep endless copies of *Screen Topics* among the cushions of your limousine. We only know one kind of mother; others occur in fiction.

Just a word to say that I am coming to call Saturday afternoon, November 17th — although I am told it is unchristian to make appointments so far ahead. If you have any socks to darn or waists to alter I will do them for you at that time, for I am well in the third degree of bachelorhood and a work-basket is always by my tea table. I shall arrive about 3:00 and leave about 6:00 on Sunday. Accustom yourself to the mustache before I come, so that we shall have time to talk of other things, of flashlights and Abbesses, and pale rose quartz.

How long is it since dark men have traveled 100 miles to see you, thinking about you excitedly every minute of the trip? And let their business go to rack and ruin through composing letters to you? And testify that they understood some of the most delightful corners in international literature in the light of your personality?

Madame, although I doubt whether you are old enough to be my mother, I solemnly propose it to you: will you be my mother? "Do you take this man to be your importunate son, to scold and indulge, to tease and provoke, so help you, Madame de Sévigné?" Consider well; this is the most solemn step in a matron's life: are you sure we are compatible? Is my face one that you could endure at a thousand breakfasts? Divorce in this matter is not so easy as it was. Many wretched mothers are tied for life to unseeing sons.

As for me, my mind is made up and I hereby — under a miraculous rainbow — do affix my name

Your loving son,
Thornton

Imprint of the Past

I can remember sitting on the floor with a group of people until five o'clock in the morning, just listening to Thornton. And it didn't come out of a bottle. No one was drinking. It just came out of that man's mind and heart. Why was he what he was? I'd love to know about his ancestors, because I believe you are your ancestors, your background. Where did that healthy spirit come from?

— Lillian Gish

HIS GRANDFATHERS and their fathers were not what Thornton said they were. He called them "yeoman farmers," an imaginative description, like his account of Peru in *The Bridge of San Luis Rey,* "all made up." They were merchants or ministers, unless one excepts the Theophilus Wilder who fought in the American Revolution, was given a land grant in Maine and might have farmed. Perhaps Thornton took yeoman to mean simply a man born free; all his forebears were that, the English Wilders and the Scotch Nivens, well established by the eighteenth century in New England and New York. Arthur Tappan, the grandfather of Thornton's mother, Isabella, was an abolitionist and first president of the American Anti-Slavery Society; his business failed when Southern customers repudiated their indebtedness.

Thornton's maternal great-grandfather, Thornton McNess Niven, was a contractor, engineer and builder. His son, the Reverend Thornton McNess Niven, Jr., attended a Southern seminary, served as a chaplain to General "Stonewall" Jackson in the Civil War, went to Dobbs Ferry as minister of the Presbyterian church, married a granddaughter of Arthur Tappan and was the father of Isabella.

On the paternal side, the first Wilder in the New World was Edward, who settled in New England in the early part of the seventeenth century. Amos Lincoln Wilder, Thornton's grandfather, born in 1824, went West for gold, found none, but later prospered from more prosaic ventures. He returned to Baltimore to study dentistry, practiced it in Calais, Maine and in 1869 bought an oilcloth factory and a house in Augusta two doors from the "Plumed Knight," James G. Blaine. He died at seventy, a respected businessman who regarded himself as something of an authority in spiritual matters. Amos Lincoln's wife and Thornton's grandmother, Charlotte Topliff Porter, was, in family legend, a paragon of good sense and good deeds. She came from New Brunswick, across the river from Calais. Her father, George Marks Porter, who died at ninety, had been a lumber merchant and shipowner in the Saint Croix valley. Her grandmother (and Thornton's great-great-grandmother) was the alien graft on this Protestant tree. Betsy Marks Porter of Halifax smoked a pipe in her old age, was a loyalist during the war for American independence, lived to be ninety-six and was a Jew.

There they are, plain but not undistinguished folk, rooted in northeast American soil, carriers of Christian burdens, earners not inheritors, ambitious though not avaricious, neither rich nor poor and not a poet or a painter in the lot. We see them dimly, as in a fading daguerreotype.

Parents are another matter. Here the personalities are sharply etched. Zealous for their children's health, virtue, education and security, Thornton's parents were not demonstrative. This was especially true of Amos Parker Wilder, although he may have hungered for a warmth he could not inspire. "There is the milky, sensuous, even slovenly side of affection," a dreamy fourteen-year-old Thornton wrote his forty-nine-year-old father, "in which I cannot imagine you partaking — the face-gazing and silly part of it, which is too weak and light for big, powerful people."

As a boy in Calais, Maine, Amos had peddled, carried water for elephants in the circus, learned telegraphy and worked in a grocery. His sons would hear quite a bit about the value of experience in a grocery or on a farm. He prepared for college at Augusta High School in Maine and at the Worcester Military Academy and went on to Yale, where he became editor of an undergraduate publication, a member of the glee club, a sought-after speaker, a member of Skull and Bones ("the highest honor at Yale," he informed his father), class orator in his freshman and sophomore years, a member of two fraternities and indisputably one of the top men in his class. For two years he taught school in Lyme, Connecticut and there made his first political speech, on behalf of the presidential candidacy of the Wilders' old neighbor, Republican James G. Blaine. After a brief teaching stint in Minnesota, he entered journalism, first in Philadelphia, then in Albany, New York, where he was telegraph editor of the local paper. Moving to New Haven, he accepted the editorship of the *Palladium,* taught Sunday School, earned a Ph.D. in political science, lectured and wrote on municipal reform and used the *Palladium* to crusade against poolrooms and other vices. He lost the editorship when he attacked prominent political figures who turned out to be part owners of the paper, but found work in New York as an editorial writer. In retrospect, he thought that even though he had been in terror at times of being dropped by the Right Set at Yale, his association with "choice men . . . made a rich legacy to which I cling," and he emerged with the feeling that he "need not be inferior unless I so elect."

The year of his marriage to Isabella Niven, 1894, he went to Wisconsin and bought a quarter interest in the *Wisconsin State Journal,* to which he had contributed articles on municipal and state problems. The first four children — Amos, Thornton, Charlotte and Isabel — were born in Madison between 1895 and 1900, during Papa's tenure on the newspaper.

Steely-eyed, with a high forehead and receding hairline, Amos was a bit too scholarly to be an editor-owner, and according to an account in the *Wisconsin State Journal,* "his reputation as a writer increased while the profits diminished." His editorials were not without humor and heart-tugs, and when he warred against evil they could be vitriolic; the world that did not march to his beat was a world out of step. As a man of principle he was upheld and harassed by uncompromising oughts and shoulds, "a sort of Don Quixote," his younger son came to think, who never had an aesthetic notion in his life. Still, Thornton took from him a desire to shape and improve lives, a facility with language, a histri-

onic virtuosity, moral energy, nostalgia for small towns and respect
for anonymous multitudes.

Isabella Niven was twenty-one and Amos Parker Wilder thirty-
two when they married. It was an incompatible union, and time
brought no reconciliation of their dissimilar natures. In their first
week together, she wore a dress that had a neckline he considered
too daring. When he suggested she change costumes, she reminded
him that she was the daughter of a Presbyterian minister and that
if her father had not thought the dress suitable he would have
told her so. She had wanted to become a physician, but because
doctoring was not thought proper for women, her father withdrew
her name after she had been accepted by Barnard College. She
married rightly suspecting that she was not her husband's first
love; he had been engaged to another, the girl backed out, and
on the rebound he became engaged to someone in his boardinghouse. That, too, was called off, and Isabella Niven was next.
Twenty years later, she wrote her elder son, Amos: "When awfully young, I allowed your father (who was not and never was
a good judge of anything) to make the decisions. So now I have
a ruthless dictator." Three days before their wedding, too late
to turn back, Amos Parker had told her that he was a widower
at heart and that he had no tenderness left in him after a
long seven years of courting that had come to nothing. She had
been stunned but hoped he would forget the past. "He never
did. Never has." They could have "rubbed along comfortably
enough," she thought, if it had not been for long separations,
but "there was *not enough understanding* between us to survive
that strain."

Isabella grew up in Dobbs Ferry, New York and attended the
Misses Masters School, which her father helped found. She was
a superior student, went to concerts, danced at the New York
home of the Henry Villards on West Fifty-eighth Street, sketched
in ink and water colors, learned French, gardened, had three of
her poems published in the Misses Masters *Almanac,* enjoyed theater, played the piano and was versed in the new authors and
dramatists — Verhaeren, Carducci, Ibsen, Maeterlinck. In the
1920s she became the first woman elected to public office in
Hamden, Connecticut, winning a seat on the school committee.

To Thornton she was "like one of Shakespeare's girls — 'a star danced and under it I was born.' "

Isabella's concern for her children's well-being was less intrusive then her husband's. She was not a cosseting hen and liked them best when they got old enough to be people; then she would ask what they were staying around for. "Look at birds — *thrown* out of the nest." Her religious sentiments were broader, more mystical than Amos Parker's. She was fascinated by William James's *The Will to Believe,* and her range of belief included the possibility of communication between seen and unseen worlds.

Twenty-eight months after her marriage, a second son, Thornton Niven, was born. Long after her death he would say that for a growing boy a mother must be envisaged as "pure" or the whole world collapses — "for America anyway, and I suspect every-where." It is that boy's story that we follow.

2

Wisconsin to China

MADISON, WISCONSIN at the time of Thornton's appearance on April 17, 1897 — nineteen months after the birth of his brother Amos — had eighteen thousand inhabitants, of whom eighteen hundred were students and faculty. It was the first of three "our towns" in Thornton's boyhood, and it is indicative of Wilder interests that each was academic — Madison, Berkeley, New Haven. But Madison was also a state capital, and the opinions of Wilder Senior as editor of the *Wisconsin State Journal* had weight. His duty and his pleasure was to pronounce on public questions, and it was said of him that his only rival as a mesmerizing orator* was the Republican senator from New York, Chauncey DePew, who, in 1900, boasted that there was no American who didn't feel 400 percent bigger than he had in 1896, "bigger intellectually, bigger hopefully, bigger patriotically, bigger in the breast from the fact that he is a citizen of a country that has become a world power for peace, for civilization and for the expansion of its industries and the products of its labor." The slump of 1893–1895 had almost been forgotten. President McKinley had promised a full dinner pail, and although the pail was only half full for many and empty for some, the general sentiment among 76 million Americans was that better days had never been. This was God's country and over the horizon were countless marvels — electricity, the automobile, the Caterpillar tractor, the gramophone, the pianola.

---

* "He'd rather make a speech than eat dinner, but he had humanity and warmth," Archibald MacLeish recalled. MacLeish knew Thornton's father in New Haven in the 1920s; they both frequented the Yale Graduate Club.

Thornton was the child of a confident father in a confident age, but the first months of his life gave little reason for confidence. Born prematurely and a twin, he had a precarious start. His identical brother, though perfectly formed, was stillborn, too frail to be cried or patted into life, and there was doubt whether Thornton himself would survive. For weeks during that first hot summer he was carried about on a pillow and fed limewater.

The Wilders then occupied the Kerr house on Langdon Street and soon had a summer cottage near Lake Mendota, a four-mile ride from Madison. Todger, as Thornton was called, quickly outgrew his frailty, and by the age of three he was an animated, active boy. All the Wilders were lively; indolence was as alien as luxury. Although Mother had a "slavey" and a nurse for Thornton's two baby sisters, Charlotte and Isabel, if she wasn't cooking, cleaning, sewing, laundering or looking after her small children she was reading, visiting or off on civic errands.

At his *Journal* office, on the first floor of the Piper brothers' grocery store, Papa was engaged in a circulation war with the hated *Madison Democrat,* both papers having lowered their price to two cents a copy. Along with fighting the *Democrat,* corruption and drink (the *Journal* refused liquor advertisements), he monitored the morals and health of his underlings. He would grab a reporter, force open his mouth and, if he saw a defective tooth, promptly propel the man to the dentist. In his columns, he railed against the "ignoramuses, thugs and ex-convicts in command of the department of city hall" and attacked the "degenerate status of our American municipal system . . . rooted in the domination of the saloon." He did whatever he could to save his children from the dreadful fate of his brother, Julian, an alcoholic. Thornton was fifteen and sister Charlotte a year younger when they affixed their signatures to a two-page solemn pledge, written in their father's hand and witnessed by him, that they would forever "abstain from all distilled, fermented and malt liquors as a beverage."

Crusaders have their rewards, but a large income is rarely among them. The five thousand dollars saved before Amos's marriage had gone into the purchase of part ownership in the *Journal.* Seven years later and in control of the paper, Wilder Senior was seriously in debt and forced to look elsewhere if he was to support his family. But it was not only the financial insecurity of journalism and the looming demands of four children's education that prompted his decision in 1905 to seek other work. He wanted a larger arena in which to display his talents and to that end wrote his Yale friend William Howard Taft, then secretary of war in the cabinet of Theodore Roosevelt, that he would be gratified if Taft called Senator John Spooner of Wisconsin "to ask how my matter is coming on; I believe he now has me in mind as a 'commercial attaché.' " Eight months later, after Wilder had tactfully reminded Taft that an appointment now would be better than "by-and-by when I do not need it," the Senate confirmed President Roosevelt's appointment of Wilder as consul general in Hong Kong.

The post was an honor and a financial boon to Papa. But to his wife? To be uprooted after twelve years? To give up her friends and the pleasant summer days by the lake? To have to pack, store, take two boys and two girls, the eldest barely eleven, out of school? To shepherd them across the continent and three thousand miles of ocean to a strange land? And this volatile Thornton, was it wise to interrupt his education and deprive him of familiar surroundings? She had no choice; Papa's word was law. They reached the British crown colony of Hong Kong on May 7, 1906, three weeks after Thornton's ninth birthday.

Wisconsin was never like this. Tireless servants could be hired for six to ten dollars a month — superb cooks, inspired gardeners, tailors able to copy the latest Paris or London styles. Mama hired an amah and a tailor by the week. A house was leased for $112.50 a month in gold and Thornton placed in a local school where only German was written and spoken. There the foundation was laid for mastery of Goethe's language, so valuable in Thornton's intellectual and artistic development. He was carried about in a sedan chair, returning from school at noon for "a jolly meal" with Wong, the number one boy. Bible readings and bed followed supper and a game of croquet.

Papa was to spend seven absorbing years in China promoting the new Open Door policy, for with the suppression of the Boxer rebels in 1900 the way had been cleared for expanded foreign investment, and it was American policy to win trading privileges equal to those of the already established Europeans. The twenty-five-foot bar at a club frequented by the international set of Hong Kong was crowded much of the time, but Amos Parker Wilder was absent. Nor, offered a drink by the bank manager at eleven in the morning, did he find it awkward to refuse: "One realizes at many points," he wrote his mother, "that our American life has achieved much. Our standards are higher in many ways." Nearly every night the elder Wilders were dined and wined, no one telling Papa there was a "stick" in the dessert, a dash of rum or brandy. He did not find the social obligations onerous, and it was agreeable to have an $8,000 salary and be able to send $1,000 to his creditors in Madison. It was also a pleasure to report to his mother that his wife was "in rapport with the best women of the place," but then, she always did "train with the Best People, even in far-off Madison days." He did not mention that she was unhappy.

The social demands tired her. There were other demands just as tiresome, and after six months her husband had to accept the fact that she would "never be *real* happy until she gets to her beloved Europe." Yet he rejected her suggestion that she and the children go to Switzerland. In principle, he approved of becoming world-educated, but his children must not be "harmed in the process," and if he and his loved ones had to be parted he wanted them in America. On October 30 Mother and the four youngsters sailed on the *Siberia* for San Francisco. They would have $1,500 a year from Papa, more if needed, and Thornton could be educated in English.

Friends were told that Isabel had gone to California to put the youngsters in school. "Everyone agrees," Amos Parker explained, "that Hong Kong is no place for children over nine years of age." His chief worry was that they would suffer from his absence; however, he trusted heaven and his weekly letters to keep them on the narrow path until he could join them. In his judgment, Thornton most dreaded leaving — "the little fellow's distress is terrific" — but Papa reasoned with him and diverted him at the last moment with a one-dollar watch.

Berkeley was like Madison — a bigger Madison with hills and without icy winters. Mrs. Wilder rented a small house on the corner of Parker Street and College Avenue, a half mile from the public school where Thornton was enrolled and near the university, with its tall eucalyptus trees. Model T Fords would be on the streets within two years, but the Wilders made do on foot, bicycles and the electric trolley. Papa had arranged for a Chinese boy to follow them and help keep house, and, as in Madison and Hong Kong, Mrs. Wilder quickly made friends and introduced her children to the cultural life around them. When the Greek Theater at the university put on plays, she saw to it that they had walk-on parts and helped sew or stencil gold borders and leaves on costumes. Thornton had violin, and later piano, lessons and learned the two-step and waltz at a dancing class in a neighbor's home. His Emerson Grammar School teacher seems to have appreciated that the new boy was unusual, for she allowed him to leave his seat and pace up and down the classroom when he became restless. He joined the choir of Saint Mark's Episcopal Church and for faithful attendance and deportment was presented by the bishop with two gold pins. Religious duties were not as exacting as in Madison or Hong Kong, but daily prayers were said, and on Papa's instruction sister Charlotte read aloud from *Pilgrim's Progress,* Thomas à Kempis, Woolman's *Journal,* or Whittier's poems.

Nearly three years passed pleasantly, until June of 1909, when Papa, having recently taken up a new post as consul general in Shanghai, wrote that he was looking forward to home leave and a family reunion. It had been too long since he had had "a hand on my dear children," particularly Thornton with his "dreaming dreams; . . . at least he can lean on me." He paid two short visits to Berkeley, the second in the fall (a third daughter, Janet, was born nine months later), but the togetherness was strained. His offspring had become accustomed to turning to their mother for permission, and here was this not quite a stranger, but not a familiar, everyday figure either. They had grown into their cussed selves, not the far-off angels to whom he wrote every Sunday. And Thornton was almost grown up, a lean, black-haired, blue-eyed twelve-year-old who read French and Italian dictionaries. Not handsome, perhaps; none of the Wilders had that handicap, but what a talker, and what comprehension in those luminous eyes. He might be poetic, but there was nothing Byronic about him.

He was eager, full of fun and not about to lean on his father. Yet Papa was sure that his son needed a protective arm. It's a cruel world, he would say, and Thornton would have no way of defending or supporting himself; the rest of the family would have to carry "this dear boy" (he was always "dear boy").

If he could not shape his children's lives by being with them, Papa counted on the persuasive power of the written word and on his return to Shanghai did his best to guide them by exhortation. Thornton should hear some earnest preacher and speakers on re-form topics and not go "gadding about to hear some new thing." Singing in the Episcopal choir was not as wholesome as regular attendance at one's own place of worship (Congregational). The children should shun bad books, bad pictures, bad stories and instead read *The Vicar of Wakefield*. As for the Greek Theater, playacting was unreal and unsettling and often put silly thoughts into young people's heads. High emotions were all right, but Papa inclined to homely things. He had enjoyed the concert his family gave him on his Berkeley visit — music brightened and refined life — but there were more earnest endeavors to pursue, such as carrying the banner on the temperance question. Amos was sent a "Purity" book with instructions to read it reverentially; Thornton's attention was not to be called to these sins until he was older. A letter carried the instruction: "Read this *two* days in succession. I wonder if the person who reads this will speak clearly. And distinctly and bring out the meaning?"

Papa's anxieties notwithstanding, the family separation probably benefited Thornton, for it was during the free, formative Berkeley years of 1906 to 1909, with their books, music, plays and mother's encouragement that the first hints of creative potential were visible. For Mrs. Wilder, however, the sole stewardship became too heavy a burden, especially after the birth of Janet in 1910, and whatever the tensions between herself and her husband, she came to feel the need for more than financial support, an urgency underscored by the family doctor in a letter to Shanghai. So once again trunks were brought out, clothing and household goods packed or stored, the children taken from school, and in December 1910 the family set out on their third month-long voyage across the Pacific, leaving behind young Amos, who was sent to the

Thacher School in the Ojai valley in California. Thornton and
Charlotte, thirteen and twelve, were placed in the China Inland
Mission Boys and Girls School at Chefoo in Shantung Province,
450 miles north of Shanghai and reached by postal steamer up
the Yellow Sea. Within months of their arrival in Shanghai, revolution broke out in central China and a republic was proclaimed
with Sun Yat-sen as its president.

Most of the parents of Chefoo students were Christian missionaries,
and years afterward Thornton would warn, "Beware of sharks
and missionary's children." All the teachers and administrators
were Scottish or English, as were most of the 120 students, with
only about a dozen Americans, including Henry Luce, a missionary's son, and two sons of Dr. George Wilder (no relation), who
was a medical missionary in Peking. Thornton was assigned to a
four-bed room on the second floor, from which he could look
across a whitewashed stone and rubble wall to the girls' school
and the mountains beyond. Uniformed in white pith helmets and
white suits with knee-length pants, the boys were marched on
Sundays through hot, dusty streets to attend Church of England
services, seeing on all sides goiters, tumors, abscesses, stumps of
lepers' arms and legs, the blind, the skeletal Chinese children. It
was Thornton's first sight of omnipresent misery — untended, ignored, endured.

Fagging was minimal at Chefoo, although the three boys with
the lowest grades on a test were thwacked on the palm of the
hand with a ruler, and there were many opportunities for Thornton
to compare his rising welts with those of others. Not having begun
early the study of Greek, Latin, algebra, geometry and the history
and geography of Great Britain, the Americans were at a disadvan-
tage and were often rebuked for their ignorance or for speaking
the English language incorrectly. The last boys to fall in line when
the bell rang for meals were publicly chastised. Charlotte and
Thornton were permitted each other's company for several minutes
once a week.

The Americans tended to stick together and there was considerable discussion of where they would go to college — Oberlin,
Berea, Claremont. Harry Luce and Thornton already had their
eyes on Yale. As in Berkeley, Thornton was soon marked as singu-

lar. His solemn reserve would suddenly give way to a giggle, a gay truancy, a rush of words. It was as if he were standing on tiptoe mentally, waiting to spring at the first signal from anyone willing to listen. Soccer and cricket were compulsory, but he was permitted to substitute a three-mile cross-country run along the seacoast of Shantung. At the mile-and-a-half turnaround point of his course, a row of sycamores and gingko trees enclosed a semicircle of noble tombs called the Grove of the Ancestors. Already Thornton had the notion that he would be a writer, and it was well known that writers require long stretches of time alone — to think. He thought throughout the entire run, but he thought best in the Grove.

Studies went well enough in subjects that interested him. Struggling with first-year Latin declensions, he translated Horace into English, using vocabulary he found in the back of a textbook. Later he recalled, "I peered and probed and guessed at almost impossible *arcana*. Like a beginning mountain climber I only attempted the highest peaks. Nothing is learned save with passion." A roommate observed: "He knows a great deal about the various authors and composers [but] hates spinach and sent up word to me at the end of the table asking 'just a little spinach please.' I said certainly, if you can name six Hungarian composers and five Spanish authors! Of course I knew he could do it and he rattled them off. Later he said to me 'Do it again when I ask for just a little of anything.'"

It was in the dining hall that Thornton earned the nickname "Fish." He had explained (he would be an explainer all his life) that humans need and like salt in their food because life originated in the sea, and humans trace back to *fish*. Oh no, howled the sons of the missionaries, maybe *you* but not us, and we're not descended from monkeys either! "I had a long talk with Thornton Wilder on Darwinism," Harry Luce reported home. "He says that it is quite the thing in the U.S. He says that until he came here he thought everybody accepted it."

The foreignness of Chefoo quickened rather than intimidated this mercurial adolescent. "We Wilders," he would say in 1918, "never know we are happy until the period has faded almost out of memory. How blissful I must have been at Chefoo — and how wretched."

3

"Freak"

WHATEVER SUPPORT from her husband the wife of the American consul general thought she needed when she'd been in Berkeley she either did not get in Shanghai or did not relish, and within a year it seemed best to Papa that she leave China, taking the two youngest daughters — Isabel, eleven, and baby Janet — with her. Thornton and Charlotte were to remain at Chefoo, Amos in the Thacher School. We don't know what led to this second separation — a yearning for Europe, the strain of entertaining, incompatibility, fear of another pregnancy. In any event, early in 1911, baggage and cases of condensed milk were put on the ship, and Mother, the two girls and Nurse Donaghue embarked for Italy to join Charlotte Niven, Mother's younger sister.

A plaintive letter from Papa awaited her in Florence. He would not give up hope that someday she might be sweet to him, "for a fellow in absence must have some beautiful thing to cling to." She could go where she wanted, he told her, "only get well and serene; let us so live that we shall have the minimum to reproach ourselves with when the end comes." If she had any new feelings in her "sweet breast" and was willing to be hugged and kissed, he hoped she would come back to him and that they could "do the Shanghai life normally as other people do." Thornton, he reported, was in good spirits, but Charlotte's uncontrolled swings of mood were an anxiety, for which his remedy was sound principles and earnest thinking.

Mother and girls had been met in Florence by Aunt Charlotte, then twenty-three and at the beginning of an extraordinary and long career. (She died at ninety-seven.) A volunteer settlement-house worker in New York in 1910, she had gone to Italy to see for herself the background from which the immigrants to America had come. She became interested in a center for students in Naples and now was running an international student hostel. Aunt Charlotte was a Grand Marshal of good works whose zeal and organizing talents would be fictionalized in the Abbess of Thornton's novel *The Bridge of San Luis Rey* and in the girl in *The Eighth Day* who goes to India as a missionary.

What a dispersed family they were — Papa in Shanghai, Amos in California, Mother and two daughters in Italy, Thornton and sister Charlotte at the China Inland Mission School. And what a lot of correspondence that required of Thornton. At least two sets of letters had to be written each week: those to Shanghai (one in particular asking Papa to look up some quotation about Alcibiades from Herodotus, Xenophon or Thucydides, for Papa maybe had "some unbusy scholars for friends") and, at far greater length, those to Mother, to say that dinner that day had been a crust of bread eaten with "dishwater" (vegetable soup), lamb, rice, potatoes and "weeds" (greens). A gift for narrative and dialogue shows itself in his 1911 description of bath night:

> Mr. Taylor, one of the masters, called out:
> "All those who have not had a bath lately come up here."
> I went forward to my great embarrassment. There were a few others too.
> "All right," he said, I was to have a bath.
> The bathroom is a great hall made into stalls in which is a tub of boiling hot water one honest inch high. I went down and tried it. From all parts of the room came shrieks of pain. "Ow! Ow!" I was told that these were from unfortunates who had projected their toes into the brimstone. Later, after fifteen minutes for dressing, undressing and bathing, a prefect calls out,
> "One minute more!" While shrieks of protest greet this proposal.
> "Aw, Wobbles (one of the prefects), give me some more time."

Wobbles with a watch in his hand howls out: "Half a minute."

Screams.

"All out."

Silence. Wobbles never knows which people are in which bath and the doors are shut. By and by boys rush out of their doors and run past the prefect who gives a resounding spank as the fugitives pass. This is their bath.

For his fifteenth birthday, Mother sent him a copy of *A Little Journey to Italy.*

Although Thornton had the privilege of running cross-country,* he was not excused from gym class, where Indian clubs were swung, one of which flew across the room and hit him on the head. He was carried off to the infirmary, more dead than alive, he thought. The swelling rose to the size of an egg and the authorities were in doubt as to whether to summon Papa. "Oh, Dr. McCarthy!" the nurse exclaimed to the headmaster, "Wilder is talking very strangely, very strangely indeed. I'm afraid we must fear the worst." From that moment, the headmaster knew that all was well. "If you had begun talking sense," he told Thornton, "I would have been obliged to telegraph your father."

Each student was expected to write Sunday letters to his parents, read by a teacher before mailing for conformity to approved style and content. One such letter of Thornton's to "Ma Caro Donna" described a strike. The fledgling republic's revolutionary headquarters in Chefoo had offered eighteen dollars a month to all men who would join the army, ten dollars more than the Chinese servants at the school were earning. "Result: boys work; result: Wilder washes dishes and cleans carrots, serves table and carries water for other people (boys) to wash in (not himself! Oh no!)." At the bottom, his teacher commented: "Too fantastic," to which Thornton added, "Evidently our Master does not think this to be the 'desired thing,' maybe he would have liked me to tell

---

* "I was a track man," he told publisher Cass Canfield in 1967, "and my event was long distance running . . . over hill and dale . . . blithe . . . left-foot, right-foot . . . distant of those who put all their soul into a short sprint, slaves to a graduated stopwatch. I trained to be an endurance runner."

you about 'how Evan's Bunny died' and 'how I lost my book' and such trash." The giddy correspondence with his mother was sprinkled with literary allusions. Did she remember their reading *The Odyssey* together, and how wonderful it was when Herod contemplated building his temple: "And I will think in gold and dream in silver, imagine in marble and in bronze conceive." He had been playing Beethoven sonatas on the piano and was learning by heart a Chopin prelude. And by the way, was she lonely? "I am there, I *am*," he assured her. "Before long you will see me — know I will see *you*."

Another year would pass before Mother, Isabel and Janet returned to America. Meanwhile, Thornton and Charlotte, accompanied by Papa, were to leave China on the steamship *Nile*. Thornton was to join Amos at the Thacher School; Charlotte would be lodged with family friends in Claremont, California. "How hard and callous the Wilder family gets," Thornton remarked, "through all the bi-monthly and even weekly leavetakings."

Thacher did not normally attract the sons of unaffluent families; the consul general's sons were exceptions. They were probably not charity boys, but allowance doubtless was made for the Wilders' stringent finances. Headmaster Sherman D. Thacher was a Skull and Bones brother of Papa's; they had been a year apart at Yale. Fundamentally, however, the Wilder boys were there because Papa believed he could not afford not to give his children the best education. As Thornton later put it, "He not only dreamed big, he demanded complicated refinements of his dream; he made it as hard for himself as possible. Above all, the teaching was to be first-class, tending to develop (it was a favorite phrase of his) 'noble Christian men and women.' By God, it would be impossible to dream more extravagantly than that, on a small salary." Amos and Thornton were destined for Oberlin and Yale; Charlotte, Mount Holyoke; Isabel, the Misses Masters School in Dobbs Ferry; Janet, the University of Chicago and a Ph.D.; and Amos would pursue advanced studies at Montauban, Louvain and Oxford.

A later generation would deride the Thacher School as "preppy." Undoubtedly it had a snobbish reputation. The boys dressed for dinner two nights a week. Each had his own room and own horse. One tame enough, named White Mule, was found for Thornton, and along with fifty-nine other boys, he had to feed, water and curry his horse and muck out its stall, which he minded less than getting on White Mule's back.

What sort of a fifteen-year-old was he? Thin, about five feet eight inches tall, with a straight nose, firm chin, thick eyebrows, nicely shaped ears, a high forehead like his father's, and still enough wavy dark hair to part it on the side. But what a contrast to brother Amos, the Thacher tennis star, who had preceded him by a year. "Everybody was amazed that a boy like Thornton could be a relative, a brother in fact to a boy like Amos," said classmate W. Herbert Allen. In baseball Thornton was put into right field, the dumping ground for duds, where he stood with his legs wide apart, waiting. When told that the first rule of fielding is to get your legs together, so that if you miss with your hands the ball will hit your legs and you can stop it, Thornton looked blank. "Oh yes," he said. By Papa's account, in a note to Mr. Thacher in 1912, his son was inclined to be quick-tempered, found few boys congenial, was sensitive, self-conscious but radiantly happy when he was with those he liked and who understood him. His interests were music, art, drama and literature; not sports, though he could swim. He liked Latin and regarded history, geography and mathematics as drudgery. Care had to be taken that routine that was easy to others did not terrorize him. Still, he had nerve in emergencies. Should he be permitted to have a gun or a rifle?, Mr. Thacher asked. "Delighted," Papa replied. "Thornton knows nothing of such things, am eager he should."

Two of Thornton's friends, sixty-five years after they first met him at Thacher, used the same word for him: "freak." If the boys had had to vote, Amos would have been picked as the man most likely to succeed and his brother the one most likely to fail. Wilmarth ("Lefty") Lewis, a classmate and future authority on Horace Walpole, considered himself something of a literary boy at Thacher, but he said Thornton made him look like a dunce. "He would be prattling about Synge and Yeats, all the current literary people of whom I had never heard. And he knew what he was talking about." Nevertheless, he was "the most elaborately hopeless boy I'd ever seen in everything." He didn't shine academically, athletically or socially. "You couldn't have had a less satisfactory boy than poor Thornton." Teachers were irritated by his jumpiness and what they took to be a certain pretentiousness; he seemed aesthetic, silly.

Thornton could not have been unaware of his reputation. He was sure that Mr. Thacher "despised" him, indeed, "shuddered at the very sound of my high voice." He withdrew to the little-used library across from the study hall and read Arnold Bennett, the Brontës, Jerome K. Jerome, Yeats, Browning's letters. "The most miserable kid ever seen," said Wilmarth Lewis. "We left him alone, just left him alone. And he would retire to the library, his hideaway, learning to distance himself from humiliation and indifference."

A contemptuous arrogance sometimes fills the void left by rejection, feeding fanaticism and rebellion, but Thornton's was a more tolerant and accepting nature. If he was an oddity, it did not strike him that the crowd, not he, was peculiar. In Chefoo he hadn't resented mild corporal punishment, dormitory Latin slang he hardly understood or molasses and sulfur in the spring. He could be hurt, but wounds didn't fester. Thacher was simply another challenge, different because the school was classy.

To Thornton's delight, Thacher had a dramatic club, and in the tryouts for Oscar Wilde's *The Importance of Being Earnest* he was cast for one of the leading roles, Lady Bracknell. His joy was short-lived. In the parlor one evening, Mr. Thacher, standing against the mantel with his back to the fire, informed him that Papa would rather not have him play female roles, and although it hadn't been absolutely ordered, it would be best to respect his father's wishes. Thornton was in the dumps for at least twenty-four hours, but he didn't give up the stage. "Last Wednesday evening," Thacher School notes of May 30, 1913, reported, "the little school presented *The Russian Princess,* an extravagant and uproarious extravaganza; Thornton Wilder as the villain and Jack Drummond as the heroine made a tremendous hit and in addition wrote the play." As Grand Duke Alexis of Russia, Thornton proudly strode about in a fur coat, during and after the performance.

Christmas was spent with Charlotte in Claremont, where they

attended astronomy classes and Thornton pegged away at his Latin,
hoping to win a school prize of fifteen dollars for an essay on
his beloved Augustan poets. He wrote his father regularly, apologizing for the brevity of four-page letters (he had thirty others
to write) . . . "So adieu my dear Poppy, with lots of love from
Thornton Wilder Nifty Niven, the petrified sloth." An odd boy,
eagerly awaiting the return to America of "our Lady of Florence."

At last, in early spring of 1913, Mother took leave of Italy,
and with her arrival in Berkeley the Thacher days were over.
She collected her young and brought them to a house at 2350
Prospect Street, two and a half miles from Berkeley High School
and up the block from the home of a prominent San Francisco
art dealer, Frederic Cheever Torrey. No more White Mule, trail
riding, dressing for dinner or languishing in right field.

Thornton belonged to no gang in Berkeley, preferring books
and the Torreys' player piano to playgrounds. When the children
were younger, Mother had been a spectator at family dress-ups,
Isabel and Charlotte and Amos costuming themselves in the basement, where Thornton rehearsed them in scenes he had written.
Now, she read him Molière in French, and on Wednesdays, when
he walked her home from her French circle, he came early to
hear the ladies recite Racine. He took drawing lessons at the California School of Fine Arts, and on Sundays there were concerts,
Greek plays, picnics at Mount Tamalpais. A Chinese helper, Kwong
Ling, cooked and cared for little Janet. All in all, thought sister
Isabel, Berkeley was a wonderful place to be a child.

Mr. Torrey, a decorator and art dealer, achieved notoriety when
he purchased Marcel Duchamp's *Nude Descending a Staircase* at
the 1913 Armory Show in New York. Thornton spent hours reading in the living room of the two-story, hillside Torrey house,
with its oriental slanted roof, large fireplace and Japanese prints.
A Torrey daughter, Dorothea, several years older than Thornton,
remembered a straggly-looking boy who needed a haircut coming
up the steps to the front door, entering without knocking, inspecting the shelves and sinking into a comfortable couch with a book.
"Thornton was more congenial with my father than with his contemporaries," she said. In the Torrey library he found Robert
Louis Stevenson, Henry James, Dickens, Kipling, Conrad and German classics.

The professional theater came upon Thornton like a trumpet blast, as if the heavens had parted, revealing a pageantry dreamt of but never seen. Maude Adams in *As You Like It,* Sarah Bernhardt in *Phèdre,* Sidney Howard in *The Countess Cathleen,* a thrilling performance in Oakland by Sir Johnston Forbes-Robertson of *The Passing of the Third Floor Back.* He was enthralled by *The Stranger* although, judging from Max Beerbohm's review, he shouldn't have been. His everyday, go-to-class, do-the-chores existence was like sleepwalking. Real life was in this mounting excitement over ideas stimulated by staged drama and books. After school, he read aloud Henry James's *A Small Boy and Others* to a blind widow and from time to time visited an artistic lady who lived opposite the office of the Wilder family physician, Dr. Snook, in a room all burlap screen and smudgy charcoal sketches. She gave him cocoa and interminable accounts of where she'd been, who was there, what they wore and what they said. Fascinating. A valuable friend for an incipient author, Thornton reported to his mother.

He was doing passably well in school, though his heart was not in Berkeley High. It was in the university library where, many late afternoons, he researched and copied out the repertoires of theater companies in Europe, especially those in Berlin and Vienna associated with Max Reinhardt. He would arrive home late, eat a bowl of stewed fruit, accompany his mother as far as the home of friends, go back to the library, then pick her up and, as they walked, engage her in animated conversation about the latest in literature. Willa Cather's *O Pioneers!* had just been published, as had Thomas Mann's *Death in Venice* and the first part of a strange book by Marcel Proust, *Remembrance of Things Past.* He and Mother read to each other (Thornton now wore glasses), played piano duets, sang their favorite hymn, "Art Thou Weary?" discussed Thornton's newest play, *The Advertisement League,* which had been selected for a Berkeley High vaudeville show. He respected his father's wish that if he *had* to engage in theatricals he dress in masculine clothes, but wrote, "When you have changed your mind as to it, please notify."

Notification of another kind came from China at the close of his first school term. He was to work that summer of 1913 on a farm in San Luis Obispo, doing things, Papa wrote Amos, that "will give him *sense,* though he will never follow them in full.

His *critical* disposition is somewhat to guard against and I caution him. We will hope he will not make 'a great actor,' though like many a youth of genius he might easily enough."

If Papa wanted him to perspire, Thornton asked, why couldn't he have found some bric-a-brac farm, something on the scale of Marie Antoinette's at Versailles, rather than one in San Luis Obispo?

Farmer Ellwood Varney, Jr., inexplicably called his sixteen-year-old summer boarder "Stickery," and Stickery, in his judgment, was absolutely worthless in terms of practical, everyday usefulness. For instance, when handed an apron that had shoulder straps and rear buckles similar to overalls, he was unable to get the apron on because the shoulder straps were unfastened. Washing milk cans required stripping off one's coat, rolling up sleeves and pitching in with a will, not minding greasy hands. Stickery didn't seem to get the idea. Nor could Stickery appreciate that a cow was a thing of intense interest and the smell only a trifling annoyance to be overlooked. Simply put, Mr. Varney wrote Papa, the boy was a physical incompetent.

Stickery didn't *feel* incompetent. He was up at quarter past four; ate breakfast cooked on an oil stove; milked cows in the half-dark; fed the calves, bulls and horses; cleaned the stalls; washed the bottles, cans, pails and parts of the separator; fed the pigs buttermilk, bran and water; had lunch at noon and was back at work at one. Given time out to go to town, he sat in the public library and read "for the thousandth time" Arnold Bennett's *The Old Wives' Tale*. His chief solace was a typewriter he had been allowed to rent for two weeks, so that he could type his notes and stories. Forty-three years later, remembering the summer and how he had endured it by his reading and writing, Thornton wondered whether he had been hurt by having been sent to "the craziest places." On the whole not, he decided, for he never saw himself as "abandoned in a totally unrelatable world."

That fall, Amos was seen off on the train to Oberlin College, a perplexing choice to Thornton. Why hadn't Papa sent his first son to Yale? Still, he wrote archly, "we have heard that Oberlin is well spoken of in that portion of Ohio," for which sarcasm he was sharply rebuked by his father.

The year ended with commendable grades in geometry, German, Latin and English. Batches of candy were made to send Amos for Christmas. The weather was splendid. No one foresaw a world war just ahead, or that 1913 would be the last year of Papa's service in China.

For many months the consul general had been listless, unable to summon the vigor and humor that had made him a popular after-dinner speaker. Asian sprue, a debilitating tropical disease then of uncertain cause or cure, brought with it diarrhea, an ulceration of the mucous membrane in the digestive tract and a smooth shiny tongue. Feeling that he was not up to his job, he resigned and, at a flurry of farewell parties in Shanghai, was feted by the business and missionary communities, neither at ease with the other. The Chinese government decorated him and presented him with a set of silver valuable enough to help defray part of his sons' college expenses. He returned to Berkeley in the spring of 1914.

The reunion was as unsatisfactory as before. Papa took Charlotte on a three-day trip to Yosemite but was not up to outdoor exertion. He was disconsolate, difficult to talk to. He would say to a child, "Don't you know me? I'm your father," and blamed his wife for "weaning the children away" from him. He left for a hospital in New York and from there returned to the scene of his youthful successes, New Haven, where he accepted a part-time position as director of the Yale-in-China program. Insofar as his health permitted, he was expected to promote the China work by speeches and fund raising, primarily among Yale alumni. But he was a spent man and, despite treatments at Battle Creek, Michigan and elsewhere, never recovered his strength.

Mother, meanwhile, had made up her mind to remain in Berkeley at least until June 1915, when Thornton and Charlotte would graduate from high school. Anyway, none of them wanted to miss the Panama-Pacific Exposition, scheduled to open in San Francisco that year, a thrilling prospect to Thornton, who had never seen a great painting in the original.

When war broke out in Europe in August 1914, Mrs. Wilder sewed garments for Belgian children, worked with the Red Cross and attended lectures on a Women's Peace party. There were

reasons enough to linger in Berkeley, aside from seeing two youngsters through high school and not having to be on Papa's nerves.

Tables and drawers of the Prospect Street house were filling
up with Thornton's compositions. The shortest walk in the country
was sufficient to inspire the theme, plan and title, especially the
title, of a book; such fragments as a young writer is finally able
to commit to paper, he would say in retrospect, "are a mass of
echoes, awkward, relative clauses and conflicting styles. In life
and in literature mere sincerity is not sufficient, and in both realms
the greater the capacity the longer the awkward age."* The awkwardness is indisputable. A story titled "Simplicity" begins: "Mrs.
Codesky had been up until 1:00 on the previous evening as patron-
ess to a dance of the 'younger Smart Set.' It was not the hour
that made her now so tired, though she was 53 and 'not strong,'
but the dance, that kind of dance! The self-centered, high-pitched
glare of that kind of dance; with the aroma of meanness in the
making; of jealousies and spyings out; the cruelty of youth. It
had thrown high, heavy webs over her brain, good lady; but she
had touched her pillow at 2:00, which was something accomplished. She had told Gerald, her chauffeur. . . ."

He would do better than that, though the Smart Set and its
chauffeurs held him captive for another few years. "A Fable about
Flora" describes a bored, fashionable girl who is proposed to every
twenty-four hours. In a three-act play, *Captain Cecilia,* several high
school lads at a seaside boardinghouse compete for the favor of
flirtatious Cecilia. Only one of them (Thornton?) resists her
charms, preferring her sister, who plays Bach and Beethoven. An
essay in dialogue on Albrecht Dürer provoked a teacher's gratuitous comment on its unoriginality: Plato, Goethe and many others
had used dialogue! Every one of Thornton's pages was read aloud
to his mother.

He had begun keeping a notebook, for which he complimented
himself. Hadn't Samuel Butler in *The Way of All Flesh* said that
anyone with a real literary turn would always jot down his
thoughts? "But it was *before* I read this that I carried paper around
in my pockets," he noted. If he wasn't writing, he had no "right

* Preface to *The Angel That Troubled the Waters* (1928).

to breathe." And having registered that conviction in his notebook, Thornton labeled it strained rubbish. He began speculating about how he might earn his keep. Teaching? Probably not: "It's hard to be a queer pupil without being a queer teacher." However, he wouldn't have to decide that yet. A smaller decision was made. He took $14.50 out of the bank to buy a book, two pieces of modern music and a theater ticket.

When Thornton learned of Papa's decision to enroll him at Oberlin following June graduation, he consoled himself with the thought that at least he would not have to apologize at Oberlin for being fatally interested in the arts. However, something had to be done to improve his appearance. He had a friend, he wrote Papa, who wouldn't be seen on the street with him in daylight hours:

> My queer walk and my old deformed clothes soon do the work. For suits and hats and underwear I have: yours, Amos', Mr. O'Connor's, Rea Haina's, Sidney Vincent's. I have an awful revulsion against wearing anyone else's underwear, but when some of mine from Thacher becomes too thin and ragged, Mother takes it away and leaves nothing but Mr. O'Connor's, for instance, and [an] old blue suit of his. It makes me sick all over. Mr. Thacher gave Amos a check and told him to take me to a store and fit me out in long trousers. And Amos got me two pairs of the wide trouser style that was just then on the wane. And now two years later, I have to wear them up and down the back streets of Berkeley, without any confidence and walking alone. I am enough of a by-word here at school as it is. My unconscious periodic sentences and hunting-for-the-right-word and my manner make that. A person can only be himself with ladies of 85 and with real artists of some kind.

Music was the restorative for these teenage glooms — an evening playing with the school orchestra at a young people's church banquet, a service at the largest synagogue in San Francisco. (Oh, the singing! By comparison, every other church was "millinery.") There was a concert of Moszkowski at the First Congregational

Church, a recital by soprano Alma Gluck, an Easter choral performance at the Panama-Pacific Exposition.

And yet, the closer Thornton came to leaving high school, the greater his anxiety, and not just because of dress. Shouldn't a boy, if possible, have some say about the life he was to lead? Why must he "fall into the folding-of-the-hands attitude about doing what father says at the time?" Why couldn't he travel steerage in boats and live and write in boardinghouses or in European attics and get out of that feeling that he was "always being hurt by father and always hurting him"?

Papa was unmoved. *Anything* should be done to get Thornton to Oberlin, he wrote Amos. "He needs supervision, someone to look after his clothes. He is a most helpless kid. Refrain from throwing [him] too many bouquets; he's almost impossible now. And I don't know as he delivers the goods in many instances."

Several days before graduation, it occurred to Thornton, while sky-gazing on his way to school (he ran into a telephone pole), that he would like a college roommate, but the idea was immediately dismissed as impossible. He had hoped that at eighteen he might outgrow his impediments, but admitted that "every now and then I get scared again and remember what it was like at Berkeley High." As he stepped aboard the Santa Fe in late June, he was unable to repress the fear that he would not fit in at Oberlin. Here was his brother, "so much the real thing, with testimonials from everyone," whereas he was a misfit. "Sometimes," he wrote, "I wish I were a Japanese or a Chinese in America"; he wouldn't so much mind *that* sort of humiliation.

Off he went.

4

Awakening at Oberlin

IN THOSE DAYS, there were said to be over two hundred colleges
in Ohio. Oberlin students were convinced that theirs was the best
among so many. It had been an important station on the Underground Railway; it was among the first colleges for men to accept
women students, to enroll blacks and to build a music conservatory.
Many of its undergraduates looked forward to careers in teaching
or the ministry. "What a good parson I would have been!" Thornton wrote in 1933. "How diligent, and how I would have loved
it. How anxiously I would have watched them gather; and how
concerned I'd have been, visiting them in their homes. It would
have played squarely into all my faults."

To his surprise, Oberlin and he took to each other. What a
fantastic freshman he seemed to Frederick Artz, then a senior and
future chairman of the history department: "He spoke in an excited
and exotic manner, highly punctuated with epigrams. Everything
about him — appearance, dress, speech and manner — was precise,
even precious . . . something *gamin* about him — the mischievous
boy." Yet the college was the opposite of mischievous: no drinking,
dancing, card playing, coarse language. The bobbed-hair craze
that was beginning to sweep the nation bypassed Oberlin. Everything was sensible, soothing, high-minded, and although the school
had a religious foundation there was no morbid wrestling with
souls to save them from damnation.

Teaching was of a high order, and almost at once Thornton
won a friend and mentor in Professor Charles H. Wager, English
department chairman. Thornton practiced on the organ; discovered
Edgar Lee Masters's *Spoon River Anthology,* published that year;

cut chemistry to copy the score of Elgar's *Enigma Variations;* flour-
ished on conversation ("feverish supper where I monologize for
an hour to an amused and dazzled table"); and before long was
wholly absorbed in studies, meals eaten in a bower of delightful
girls in Dascomb Hall, and the *Oberlin Literary Magazine.*

Before leaving Berkeley, he had drawn up a list of three-minute
plays, each with a cast of three, many of which got no further
than a title or, having been written, were thrown away. At Oberlin
in 1916 he completed *Brother Fire* and *Prosperino and the Devil,*
subsequently included in *The Angel That Troubled the Waters,* a
collection of his playlets published by Coward-McCann in 1928.
Each of these short plays is a fantastical fireworks of magic and
myth, set in times and places known to their author only through
an imagination stimulated by books. *Nascuntur Poetae* begins, "We
are gazing into some strong, incomprehensible painting of Piero
di Cosimo." *Childe Roland to the Dark Tower Came* opens, "The
sun has set over the great marsh, leaving a yellow-brown Flemish
light upon the scene." In *And the Sea Shall Give Up Its Dead,* "the
clangour of Judgment Day's last trumpet dies away in the remotest
pockets of space, and time comes to an end like a frayed ribbon."

Intended as poetic exercises and influenced by his reading of
Theodore Dreiser's *Plays of the Natural and Supernatural,* some
forty of these playlets would be written by Thornton's thirtieth
year, no more than a handful worthy of publication and all of
them religious allegories "in that dilute fashion that is a believer's
concession to a contemporary standard of good manners." He
doubted that they would find an audience, for "there has seldom
been an age in literature," he wrote in the introduction to *The
Angel That Troubled the Waters,* "when such a vein was less welcome
and less understood." Nevertheless, he was committed to trying
to express a spirit that was not "unequal to the elevation of the
great religious themes, yet which does not fall into a repellent
didacticism."

Lofty sentiments were congenial to Oberlin, and if Thornton's
views now diverged from his father's, it was not in their loftiness
but in their repudiation of that repellent didacticism. "We are a
poor disappointing lot in our time," Papa thought. Not at all,
said Thornton. If Papa would only *listen.* Were all fathers like

that? The tall, handsome president of his Oberlin freshman class, Robert Maynard Hutchins, the most promising boy on campus, said they were, that *his* father didn't care to listen to *his* son's opinions, and whatever Bob Hutchins said about anything had Thornton's respect.

Father and mother were again together, six miles from New Haven in Mount Carmel, living in an old Cape-Codder with an earthen basement, rotting beams, a parlor, large family room, several small bedrooms on the second floor, a bath, and cold running water in the kitchen. Fifteen-year-old Isabel and five-year-old Janet were at home, but with Thornton and Amos at Oberlin, Charlotte at Mount Holyoke and Papa often away on a cure or fund raising for Yale-in-China, except for comings and goings at holidays the family group had broken up for good. At Christmas when Papa was there, a small cart was loaded with cheap presents and he and Janet set off for the slums of New Haven. "We lived on the fringe of the slums ourselves," Janet remarked. The amenities of Hong Kong and Shanghai were a distant memory. "I can't tell you the slights Mother had to endure," Isabel recalled. Fortunately, the Wilders knew they were as good as others, and when Isabel regretted not being able to attend a reception given by the president of Yale, because she had nothing stylish to wear, her mother shot back, "Of course we're going!"

Style of another kind was on Thornton's mind — sentence structure, the sequence and sound of words. Oscar Wilde, Sir Thomas Browne and George Moore had been discarded as prose models, supplanted by Henry James, who died that year. But there was no one to tell him whether his compositions were immature or not. Even Professor Wager was not a dependable judge of the modern atmosphere. Nor was Thornton's boardinghouse audience. After all, he was a freshman; amusing, but not to be taken too seriously. And he did amuse them, reading aloud a fantasy (is it his dream for himself?) about a young lady from a well-to-do family in Chicago who disturbs her conservative family with a violent attack of ideals:

> Anabel. (*In exhalted strain, impressively*) I'm beautiful, I'm brilliant, I'm rich, what can I do? I wish to surround

myself with famous men and women. I'll form a new
school of literature, a new circle of art and music.
Why do I have to stay in a little, ugly, dark house
in Chicago? I will live in a temple in New York.
(*Challengingly*) Now, Phil.

Phil. (*Her brother, deeply moved and disturbed, getting up
and pacing the floor*) You may be able to do a little
along that line, but you mustn't hope to go very
far.

Anabel. (*To the world*) Why not?

Phil. You may not have the personality, the magnetism.
I don't like the idea of your voting yourself into the
place.

Anabel. But it's *small* to be afraid to be conceited. Let me
call out again: I'm beautiful, clever, rich — the new
Madame Récamier, Lady Wortly Montague; with
something of Cleopatra, Sappho . . .

Mother. (*Shocked*) Cleopatra!

Anabel. How little I've been until this came! I'll wear striking
gowns and have a marvelous house. It will be all
graciousness, all distinction, all charm. My very ambition will give me dignity. I will appear in the public
eye. I will learn to speak in public.

Phil. (*Almost trembling*) Stop, Anabel. Maybe you can't do
any of these things and there will be nothing left
of the colossal foolishness — a sentimental schoolgirl.
You've begun too high.

Anabel. I won't plan any lower.

Phil. (*Burning*) If you could! If you can!

Anabel. You'll be along with me. You will write it down —
the new Boswell — but not my glory — but what my
own idealism lends me!

Mother. Well, the hairdresser's waiting for you upstairs.
               END OF ACT ONE

This dialogue was mailed to Papa with a reminder that it was
not at all cynical. In acts two and three, Anabel, in her Room of
Honor, will receive her first call from a famous novelist. She will

try to be brilliant, will be misunderstood, will fail and retire to a small farmhouse in Illinois.

In the magazine room of the university library at Berkeley, Thornton had come across a publisher's announcement of *Half Hours: Four One-Act Plays by J. M. Barrie.* He had stared at the ceiling, his heart soaring. He had the same sensation at Oberlin when he read that Elsie Ferguson was to appear in Cleveland in a new play. Oh, "the sight of Elsie Ferguson in distress [or] Maude Adams pretending to be merry when her heart is breaking!" Back he went to his own short plays, punching them out like sums on an adding machine. In *The Acolyte,* there is this interchange:

> *Donna Anna.* What is your greatest wish, Jeronimus?
> *Jeronimus.*   (*Quietly, without hesitation*) To kiss the hands of my mother and to see Christ in a vision.

The Marriage of Zabbet, based on Shakespeare's *A Winter's Tale* and brooded over since Chefoo, tells of a young girl who chooses God over marriage and founds a convent. The *Oberlin Literary Magazine* printed it, which encouraged the author to send it to the *Little Review,* which rejected it. "When shall I begin to be acceptable?" he groaned. Under a pseudonym, Cosmo Davies, he wrote a preface for his Oberlin audience to four paraphrased comedies by Menander, the third-century B.C. Athenian dramatist; that was followed by prefaces to twelve imaginary papal bulls, a book for children and an essay on Viennese waltzes. He conceived of an elevated extravaganza, "Every Student," a satire on student traditions, and wrote a highly epigrammatic play as a stunt for Thanksgiving. In the parlor of the men's building, he staged an original drama about an artist at an exhibition, acting all the roles himself. Chefoo's boy, he reported home, was "doing a great deal of aesthetic Missionary Work. Very important."

The undergraduates published two periodicals — a biweekly newspaper and the *Oberlin Literary Magazine.* The latter was Thornton's lodestone. Within three weeks of his arrival at Oberlin, he was submitting pieces, all of them finger exercises, and was soon one of the magazine's most prolific contributors. The January 1915 issue carried his play *Flamingo Red,* the March issue his prize essay,

"The Language of Emotion in Shakespeare." A one-act comedy about unselfish love appeared several months later. He was going nonstop with his short plays, his cross-country running (he twisted his ankle and was in bed four days), the First Church choir, Wager's lectures on Homer, Professor Lord's on Lucretius, Professor Mosher's on Faust, enchanted by everything, including the weather, and overflowing with ideas. The very busy author even found time to advise his younger sister Isabel on how to appear older: "Open your mouth wide when you talk and let the words be long and full of real grown-up bluff talk without wrinkling your forehead or lisping or smiling. Just stare Mother in the face and say 'did they guarantee the poppy seed?' Or, 'I have just discovered that my stationery has a translucent watermark.' " A ridiculous brother, but nice.

He was being recognized on campus, for which he gave Professor Wager half credit; his new coat was responsible for the other half. "Oh, Thornton, you've got a new suit!" "No, it's only a coat. Like it?" "Turn around." "Well?" "Oh, I do."

He joined the editorial board of the *Literary Magazine* in April 1916 and the following term was made archivist of the CYMOC Club, whose members took an oath not to reveal the significance of its initials — Johnson's reply to an interlocutor: "Clear your mind of cant." One evening a month they met for two and a half hours to read papers and discuss such topics as "A Portrait of God Deduced from the Prayers Addressed to Him in Oberlin Chapel" or "The Ten Best-Selling Novels in America — 1850 to the Present" or perhaps D. W. Griffith's *The Birth of a Nation*, which had just been released. Membership in the club came at a crucial moment for Thornton, supplying sympathetic listeners and the stimulation of intellectual discourse. In addition, he fell "fathomlessly in love" with the club's president, five years older than he, a light-haired girl with a tawny complexion and large mouth. It took some perseverance, but eventually she trusted him not to make demands on her — demands like walking her home on Wednesday or Thursday nights and having a few words of conversation. He was also "fathomlessly in love" with Nina Trego, with whom he corresponded after graduation. Twelve years later, when he wrote *The Bridge of San Luis Rey*, he asked her to contribute several Spanish translations and in gratitude sent her manuscript pages of the novel, which her brother sold to the University of Nevada in the seventies for $100.

Going with a young man was a solemn business at Oberlin. Parental approval was obligatory. There was no coquetry. Such attachments never occurred to Thornton, for whom love, as he put it, was an expression "solely of delight and wonder, as it is in literature." He walked the girls home from choir practice or the library and called on them in the sitting room of the residence hall. His seriousness took the form of gallantry and talk; they were so *interesting*. Now, take this girl everyone called a grind. He was the only one to discover what a delightful, varied personality she had. However, "I must be remorseless in describing her," he wrote his mother. "She is 'large' — I used to think that her face looked a vulgar Italian — the kind with little curls greasily fingering the forehead. But now I know she is like a handsome Roman matron. When we are together she is like a little girl; we're both willing to laugh at the humblest and most ridiculous jokes in the world. Or else we're as sober as reformers. Poor girl." But she read Dante. If love were compassion and conversation, he would have been "fathomlessly in love" with her as well.

Thornton would come to discern the hand of fate in his having gone to Oberlin. "When I assert that I believe that lives are planned out for us I am always thinking of the fact that my father, by the most inexplicable accident, sent his two sons to Oberlin where the younger could get the nourishment without which he would have remained a bright, blundering hysteric." He could not tell what made for happiness, but at Oberlin he walked on air.

Under protest, he was placed by his father the summer of 1916 on another farm, this one adjoining the Mount Hermon School in Massachusetts, where he worked ten hours a day, six days a week for fifteen cents an hour, with four dollars deducted at the end of each week for room, board, electricity and laundry. He weighed 135 pounds, was in good physical condition and, between hoeing and haying and picking strawberries, read or reread *The Odyssey, Hedda Gabler, The Master Builder, Religio Medici, The Return of the Native,* Boswell's *Life of Johnson,* and *Caliban* by Percy Mac-Kaye. *The Greek Woman,* a very short play he wrote at the farm, was mailed to Professor Wager on the back of a postcard, and Wager responded to this "young witch" by urging him to trust his prophetic soul, adding, unfairly, that "your Father and Amos have evidently formed a league for the thwarting of your higher nature. I'm all for the higher nature, *moi.*"

With some pride, Thornton informed his father that he had acquired a few firsthand notions about farming that he intended to put into one of his plays. If he could only make Papa understand that he was striving for something nobler than the lighter forms of literature. And if Papa would not insist that Thornton visit relatives when he left the Mount Hermon farm in August. It was not to be; life, he sighed, was a "series of events to train the spirit of fatalism." After several days with Amos at a YMCA center on Plum Island off the coast of Connecticut, he dutifully visited various aunts and cousins.

He did have one week of real vacation that summer, however, on the island of Monhegan in Maine, where he walked, climbed, drafted a schedule to live by (three and a half hours a day for writing) and met some Germans he was "mad about." One of them, Dr. Adolf Kommer, was an assistant to Max Reinhardt, knew personally many of the principal novelists and playwrights in Europe and England and was much struck by the Oberlin student's acquaintance with modern German drama. Influenced by his German friends, Thornton pictured himself living in a large European city and mixing with sophisticated exponents of the Newest Thought.

The image faded his first week back at Oberlin; he was "too much of an American and a middlewestern," he decided, "to ever really go for the Continental Method in earnest." There was no conviction stronger in him than that, when he stood under Professor Wager, it was right for him to be there. In his ardor, he wrote a poem honoring his teacher:

> Oh, let me list on the saving word
> That brings to leaf the branches of my mind,
> Enriched and freed from fear,
> They face toward mine,
> As Virgil led the hooded Florentine.

Such romantic flights were disquieting to Papa. Was it possible that Oberlin was not as earnest and down-to-earth as he had been led to believe? Perhaps he should see for himself.

Not necessary, Thornton countered. Nor was there any reason to sound so pathetic about whether Thornton read his Bible or prayed, or to be upset by a teasing reference to "well-fed Congregational churches" or to having "missed a vocation in not having been brought up thoroughly in the Episcopal church."

Papa, however, was not amused by teasing of this sort and announced that he would make a personal inspection in December, Oberlin being not far from the Battle Creek sanatarium, where he would be paying one of his periodic visits. He came and was reassured; Oberlin was still praying and reading scripture.

They did not discuss religion, which was just as well, for Thornton had by now given up Papa's moralizing Protestant ethos; it had gone before he missed it, like a worn-out handbag left in some railway station. He formulated for himself the phrase "Religion is the emanation from an extinct star" and perceived its light as affecting each person differently, hardening some to pride and bigotry, softening others to sentimentality and a refusal to confront life's sterner demands. Later, he would imagine religion as an extinct sun whose rays still continued to warm and inspirit mankind. But however defined, true or false, it was ingrained in the human mind. Parents of strong religious faith were seldom able to transmit it to their children, but "in that charged cell which is family life — in that enclosed space of finely tuned acoustics — they transmit the concept of scale. Their children learn to think big, to make large demands on life, on themselves and on others. This scale has not necessarily any spiritual qualifications; it's enough that it's big, big." That, however, was the reflection of the mature man. At Oberlin, Thornton could do no more than defend himself against paternal dogmatism and distrust, replying to Papa's fear that his son would fail in class by pointing out that his father had been surprised that he didn't fail the first year, that he had honestly expected it, and had been wrong.*

In any event, nothing Papa said could upset Thornton's dawning

* Shortly before his death, in a letter to Robert Maynard Hutchins, Thornton spoke of his father's "all too freighted unshakeable obtuseness."

faith in his vocation. Two of his sketches, *A Fable for Those Who Plague* and *The Last Word about Burglars,* had been staged by students in Finney Chapel, and the large audience laughed and applauded and congratulated him. By the end of the year he had performed in four college plays and had had a "beautiful story" in the *Oberlin Lit.* He was no longer ashamed of his father's knowing that he cut classes to write, and when he asked himself whether he had done anything of merit so far, he answered by listing thirteen essays and short plays completed by July 4, 1916. Furthermore, he had two plays in rehearsal, a role in the YMCA follies, and act four of his never-finished magnum opus was in progress.

It should be said that these 1916 efforts, many about royalty or the rich, were not as sparkling as he imagined. One uncompleted four-act deals with an old New England family:

> *Ellen.* Brewster has the best collection of wooden cigar store Indians in the world.
>
> *Mario.* Who has the next best?

A short story, "The Miracles and Death of Dona y Benuzio," features lighted candles, dwarfs and an infanta of Spain stricken with fever.

In the midst of all this febrile activity, there recurred from time to time that half-buried doubt whether he ought to be at Oberlin, with its "pat Christian optimism," or in college at all; whether, instead, he shouldn't isolate himself on a desert. He never resolved the question in favor of one or the other. Over the next half-century, the pendulum swing would carry him from society to solitude and back again. He was not unique in this, only in the intensity of his need for both.

On one of his Oberlin blue days he was miserable because he couldn't think of a beautiful thing to write, and, having hit bottom, he rebounded by bidding himself to aspire to nothing, to be just ordinary, to eat and study and wash and be full of polite attentions to other people. Within hours his mood brightened; someone spoke to him, snow fell, he wrote a story and was up in the clouds again. He couldn't tell whether he suffered more than other boys from these lows and highs.

The tumult of the outside world in 1916 seems hardly to have entered Thornton's consciousness. Suffragettes, prohibitionists, peace and preparedness advocates were marching. In Europe the slaughter was shocking — nearly a million French and British killed in the battles of Verdun and the Somme, a million Russians dead after the offensive in Galicia. The only reference to any of this in his letters is an ironic "what I know about the wurrrld!" Not until Amos quit college and joined the American Ambulance Corps in France did the war seem real. Amos had done the noble thing; now Thornton had to examine his conscience. Could he kill?

Christmas vacation was almost upon him, and Papa allowed him to spend it at Oberlin. ("I don't want to go away, I'll be good, I'll be good.") Only six men were left in the dormitory. They went to bed "about 50–50 o'clock, having played cards and smoked (my dears!) since half past ten." Thinking of Amos, wondering whether he could ever harden himself to fighting, he entertained his far-off brother with a genre portrait of life "where wars are remote":

Table VI at Dascomb [Hall]

Mrs. Tritschler.	Say you're sorry.
Me.	I'm sorry. Slip me the yeast plants.
Miss Anita T.	*No slang* at all!
Me.	I'm sorry.
Anita.	Stop playing with my napkin ring.
Me.	Wait till I squeeze it out straight again.
Nita.	Now talk sensibly.
Me.	Then let's go back to the intelligence of women.
Nita.	No; you don't know anything about that. You should ask it to me first. No, thank you — you must not stare. It's not nice.
Me.	Your left eye is greenest!

"Tell me about the brave French," he wrote Amos. "Give anecdotes of nobility in young men. Stir me up over the war." He was all tenderness and warmth toward Amos, wanting to "chant a little ode of love" for the splendid brother on the battlefield.

On a spring day in 1917, Thornton joined in military drill on campus, taking it as solemnly as a young priest officiating at mass for the first time. He was promoted to corporal, surprising his father: "I confess this is power in an unexpected direction." Thornton could not bring himself to report that he was later demoted from his corporalship through sheer incompetence. Sent home to Mount Carmel the end of April to recover from water on the knee, he found the domestic atmosphere piteous but would not allow blame to be thrown on his mother, though her "undemonstrative temperament wreaks greater havoc than she knows." He confided to her that he had tried to enlist and been informed by the recruiting officer that his poor eyesight would exclude him from the first and second drafts. "Hurrah for bad vision and spectacles," he said. She was thankful; one son under shellfire was all she could abide.

Thornton's hurrah camouflaged a wracking irresolution. On one hand, he doubted whether he could shoot anyone and asked whether his country ought not to have "more splendid reasons" for fighting. On the other hand, the example of Amos made him ashamed of being so easily reduced to acquiescence by Papa, who was advising him to continue his Oberlin studies and stand "rock-like amid the storm." What should he do? He told himself that in his sensitive way of being distressed and despairing over his fitness, he was always at odds with life. "I am a personality peculiarly isolated. And to me in my dark (and true) mood, the simplification of a soldier's life offers sweet compensations. But let no one mistake my acquiescence for the positive fire of patriotism. I suppose I am built along the lines of the Artistic Temperament (oh, perilous sea!) and for such the stress and tossings of wars, domestic and national, can be shut out as secondary." A week later, he acceded to Papa's request that he spend the summer on the Berea College farm in the mountains of Kentucky, where, Papa trusted, his "comparative lack of experience" would give "the minimum of trouble."

Returning to his family after seven weeks of sorting blackberries, skinning beets and poking at arid soil, Thornton shared his shifting moods about the war with his mother. Now that the United States was in it, more and more of his classmates were slipping off to Cleveland to enlist, and he wished he might be made over into someone like Rupert Brooke. But when he thought of the moment of combat, his mystical vagueness hardened into a decision not to fight. He would return to Oberlin in the fall. Two years of study there were behind him, and if he had any regret, it was that he seemed fated to take the initiative in friendships, seldom being sought after himself. Still, he had learned a hundred tricks of getting to know people, of making them say things illuminative of themselves. He had invented "a kind of conversation method of insisting on saying sudden significant things in order to bring others to contributing sudden significant things, and becoming restless unless the conversation darkens with revelation." He was content to stay at Oberlin.

Papa, however, had a different future in mind. Thornton was to enter Yale. Why? Why? If he had to quit Oberlin, why not give up college altogether? He could take half the money Yale would cost and turn it into a year of writing in New York's Washington Square, "up all night talking with the young blood of American literature instead of the corrected and sandpapered from the prep schools." Or if not Washington Square, why not the Cincinnati Little Theater, which had invited him to join its repertory company?

Yale it would be, and in early September he rode the trolley from Mount Carmel to New Haven for a conference with the dean. It was decided that Thornton would live in a double room in Berkeley Oval for the fall semester. Perhaps he could snare Bob Hutchins, who was also transferring from Oberlin, as his roommate.

How Papa covered the costs of two sons at Yale (Amos returned when the war was over) is as baffling as his financing of their schooling at Thacher. Since he was a classmate and close friend of Yale dean Frederick Jones, it is a reasonable guess that the Wilder boys received whatever scholarship aid was available. Also, it was a Skull and Bones tradition to do some quiet subventing whenever any of the brothers was financially embarrassed, and some help may have come from that quarter. Thornton never knew how it was contrived. He concluded that to the impassioned will nothing is impossible, and was grateful. He also came to understand that the sacrifices his father made and the delinquencies Papa saw in him had a hidden significance: "The crown of a patriarchal father's life is the possession of an erring child. Fathers whose sons are a shining credit to them are like aging provincial actors who have never had the chance to play Broadway. Think of that wonderful progression from wounded majesty to tender forgiveness. Not a dry eye in the house." That summer, Thornton had ventured the hope that Papa would think well of him. "You have referred to me as noisily expressing my love to you; it is what I have so often intended to do and never felt it was reaching you with sufficient intensity. You must gather my depth from the short declarations and stray hints that I leave lying about."

Papa did think well of him but was nonetheless certain that son Amos was the one destined to support the Wilder family, "especially hopeless Thornton."

5
Yale and the War

A YALIE WAS KNOWN to be a clear-eyed, clean-cut, high-minded, upright, downright, forthright Christian young man who went to hops and tea dances and parted his hair in the middle.* The popular impression was roughly accurate, in Thornton's estimation. An undergraduate's day began with prayer in chapel, the proctors noting empty seats and the back rows half-filled with kneeling, muffled figures in white ties and tails who'd been partying in New York and had just got off the milk train. Classroom attendance was mandatory, as were weekly examinations. Because of a less than brilliant academic record at Oberlin (grades had come second to writing), Thornton was admitted as a sophomore, not a junior, and selected English as his major, Latin as his minor. From the French Revolution he went to biology 1; from the history of philosophy to Elizabethan literature; from Chauncey B. Tinker's Age of Johnson to Tennyson and Browning taught by William Lyon Phelps. Students aspired variously to edit publications, captain teams, get elected to fraternities and societies, sing in the glee club or the Whiffenpoofs, or act in plays supervised by Monty Woolley. In all this scurry for place and distinction, Thornton came close to being left out but was shoehorned into Alpha Delta Phi, thanks to Harry Luce and Bob Hutchins. One night a week, the brothers ate at the fraternity house and after dinner adjourned to a windowless chapter room for hocus-pocus. Conviviality, persiflage and wit were the esteemed qualities.

* Isabel was invited to one of the Yale tea dances, but Papa put his foot down. "Do you realize," Thornton wrote his brother in 1959, "that Father broke up every attention to his daughters? Taboo, taboo!"

Sex? By and large the college didn't worry about the chastity of its charges; a high moral tone was prescribed by the students themselves. In the center of the campus stood Dwight Hall, which sponsored elevating discussions, social-service programs and prayer meetings, and from Dwight Hall came most of the campus leaders — "ponderous, humorless, unctuous" in Thornton's opinion. These were the Big Men who in a big-brotherly way rebuked any who fell short of expected behavior. The voice from Dwight Hall ruled that certain things were to be talked about rarely, and then in terms of evasive solemnity. "To us," Thornton said, "living in a forcibly delayed maturity, sex was fascinating, of course, but also discomforting and a little frightening. But that is what it had been to most of the citizens in the United States for over a century."

Skull and Bones had been Papa's most cherished undergraduate affiliation; Thornton's was the Elizabethan Club, whose members gathered in a white colonial house across the street from the music building, had tea and conversed on high literary topics. It was the circle he aspired to make his own, and in a letter of October 4, 1917, to Professor Wager, signed "Thorneybush," he drew a touching picture of how this Yale literary coterie first appeared to an impressionable newcomer from Oberlin:

> This evening, the young [Stephen Vincent] Benét asked me over so that he could read some of my stuff as potential for the *Yale Lit* of which he is the whole power, although not printed as even on the staff. He is a perfectly unromantic looking person, although not commonplace. His hair is short and light and curly. His face is round and quizzical and snubbed and his eyes are mole's eyes. He rocks his shoulder from side to side while talking. He was somewhat late for our appointment, so I went into his room and made myself at home. Everything was in an awful disorder. Clothes and books covered the floor. I found out later that four boys used this room as their library. There were hundreds of titles: an awful lot of Zola, Samain and Maupassant. *Sinister Street* and Lord Dunsany galore, Synge and Fiona, Lionel Johnson, Francis Thompson, *Alice In Wonderland* — the eternal affectation of the so-

phisticated — and so on. A fair-haired, good-looking boy in
R.O.T.C. khaki came in. In a most beautiful southern accent
he asked me if I was waiting for Steve. Then he asked my
pardon for changing his clothes, which he did, talking casually
the while. Did I read in French? Oh, I was the boy who read
those things to Steve the other evening? "He said they were
very good, which is more than he ever said of mine." Damn,
where are my socks; no, not those, I want the blue ones. . . .
He was in a fearful hurry but he couldn't wear white ones
— no, nor those garters — I'll have to borrow (and he dashed
across the hallway). I had grasped by this time that I was talking
to the most perfect of southern aristocrats. But soon another
came in — a dark one this time with tortoise-shell glasses and
a proud subdued air. He introduced himself, but had to give
his attention almost immediately to the sock-and-garter hunt
across the hall. When he came back he said that he was on
the staff of the *Lit* and would I mind letting him read the
things until Steve came. He had a remote and wandering graciousness that quite equaled in distinction the other boy's gold-
en casualness. Soon Steve came in and devoted himself to
my papers [and] while my smudgy typewritten sheets were
passed silently between them, I again was left to my thoughts.
They were wealthy boys; all the books I have named were
bought at our little deluxe Brick-Row Bookshop where you
ask for Yeats and he takes it for granted that you want the
autographed copy on Japanese paper. But this Olympian indifference and interchanging of clothes was the real earmark.
They had been reading [my] *Angel on the Ship* and *Solvs inter
Deos Potens* and when Benét finished he got up and said some
very nice things and showed me out all the way down the
hall. Poor Lost Socks had not got off to his urgent engagement
yet, and he shouted out of the door a vast good-bye, and
the dark one bowed and backed into the wall in a particularly
distinguished manner. I myself was obsequious and Uriah
Heepish the while, but you doubt not that I shall assert myself
in time. But what a glimpse I got of what I thought I would
have to go to Oxford for. And I don't suppose they ever let
it occur to them that they are so perfect. It takes one from

the jaded middle class, one too used to pinching and window shopping and chatting with grocers' sons, to really appraise the amenities, and timbres, of such a group.

With the closing of Berkeley Oval to save coal that winter, Thornton transferred to a room over the dean's office, which his mother helped decorate with yellow hangings and pillows. He considered inviting friends in, so that he might read them his unfinished comedy, *Vecy-Segal,* but he hesitated, for while he had edged himself nearer the *Lit* crowd, he was not yet at ease in their company. His classwork was mediocre, a fact that did not prevent his stealing away for weekends in New York, roaming reverently around Washington Square, buying the cheapest tickets to theater or a concert by Galli-Curci. In his room or at the Elizabethan Club, he wrote play after play, most of which were torn up. There was no one at Yale to whom he felt artistically or intellectually accountable, and Papa, who insisted that he attend business school in New Haven three nights a week, had not given up trying to press him into the mold of the practical, diligent American boy, which he didn't fit.

In great excitement, Thornton wrote Professor Wager of meeting a Welsh actor, Gareth Hughes. "Sheer genius and poetry. And when his glasses are off the divinest thing to look upon that I have ever seen." They had talked until the early morning hours. "He didn't want me to go even then and assured me it was the nightingale and not the lark I heard." The next evening, he took Hughes to Mount Carmel to be introduced to his mother. The friendship ended several years later when Hughes disappeared into the West, having abandoned the stage for work with the Paiute Indians.

Thornton was becoming bolder, more self-willed, even speaking up in class. "Thank heaven," a professor complimented him, "there is someone who can illustrate the points as a cultivated gentleman should." On Sundays, he was invited to Benét & Company's *conversaziones,* where he recited his dubious poetry:

Oh, Rose that brakes upon the night sky we wait for thee.
Voices and paradisal chants, we may elate for thee;

Our egos are quick for harps, our eyes for blue, where Mary's mantle-folds shade Heaven's dew.

His one-acts were beginning to appear in the *Lit* and be reviewed — original and interesting, according to Professor John Chester Adams. "But I must postpone discussing his work as art," he added, "until he learns spelling and grammar." Professor John Berdan prayed that someone would advise young Thornton Wilder not to waste his unquestioned talent in concocting pale fantasies.

January 1918 was one of the few months Thornton kept a daily diary, in which he listed dramas of the season, music heard, calls on classmates Harry Luce, "Ish" Prentice and Bill Whitney. He cautioned himself to drink less coffee, mentioned smoking a cigarette (thus forfeiting the gold coin Papa had promised if he would abstain until he was twenty-one), noted that he was going bald, that he had written his third letter to Gareth Hughes, had begun a classical comedy about Queen Elizabeth I and was rewriting a scene from another play. Each submission for publication was meticulously recorded — date sent, date returned, and why rejected by the Yale University Press, the *Little Review,* the *Dial,* the *Atlantic Monthly,* the *New Republic.* He audited a senior seminar on the plays of Aeschylus, read John Masefield's sonnets, played hymns on a harmonium at the city prison's Sunday services, listened to Bach suites and D'Indy's Second Symphony, swam with Benét and confessed to tearing a photograph of Rupert Brooke out of a bookseller's catalog at the library ("Bob Coates took the one on the cover"). In the first three months of 1918 he saw twenty-six plays, including Arthur Hopkins's production of *A Doll's House* with Nazimova, David Belasco's *Tiger Rose* with Lenore Ulrich, J. M. Barrie's *The New Word,* David Warfield in *The Music Master,* Ethel Barrymore in A. A. Milne's *Belinda,* Billie Burke at the Henry Miller Theatre in *A Marriage of Convenience.* Exams came and went, scarcely noticed.

Six days before his twenty-first birthday Thornton informed Isabel in confidence that his faculty advisers had said his marks were so low he might be put out of college. She was not to tell Papa. Home for a weekend, he seemed to his mother "too excited" and too indifferent to "courses on which his very presence at

Yale depended, relishing his freedom at the expense of his health."
His fantasies were distressing. He told her he had dreamt of being
present at the canonization of Joan of Arc in Rome; the cardinals
suddenly decide to canonize *him.*

But he survived academically, without sacrificing his playwriting.
The first act of *Madison Avenue* (alternate title *Noah's Ark*), finished
before he'd thought about a second or third act, was planned as
a Restoration comedy transplanted to New York and again por-
trayed his make-believe world of the well-to-do. The curtain opens
on bald Mr. Vantover, a retired banker, who is reading the newspaper as the butler pours coffee. The author then had to find some
way of explaining that New York is the Flood, previewing a scene
he would write in *The Skin of Our Teeth.* His friends on the *Lit*
judged *Madison Avenue* dull and it was shelved.

Thornton's single lasting playwriting accomplishment that year
was a four-act drama, *The Trumpet Shall Sound,* which won Yale's
Bradford Brinton Award and was published in the *Lit.* Patterned
after Ben Jonson's *The Alchemist,* it would be the first of his plays
to be professionally staged. It is an obvious allegory, and the idea
of servants taking over their master's (God's) house in his absence
first occurred to Thornton as comedy, then as a Renaissance tragedy
and finally as ironic farce. Profound questions are raised: what is
the just penalty for unfaithfulness, what is the meaning of unrequited passion, what price is paid for despair? The heroine sacrifices
all for love and commits suicide. The master of the house, from
whom we expect perfect justice, has a soul of stone. *The Trumpet*
is ambitious, but the message is cloudy and the dialogue stilted.

War, however, not the scribblings of writers was on the public's
mind that summer of 1918. Who could spare any anguish over
the burning by the U.S. Post Office of James Joyce's *Ulysses,* published in the *Little Review,* or give serious thought to Booth Tarking-
ton's *The Magnificent Ambersons,* which won the Pulitzer Prize?
War came first.

Through some connection of Papa's, Thornton landed a summer
job with Bernard Baruch's War Industries Board in Washington,
D.C., earning thirty-five dollars a month as a clerk typist and boarding at the Chevy Chase School in Maryland, just across the District
of Columbia line. A few weeks earlier he had had a strong fit of

militarism, but Papa reminded him that his aptitudes were not along the lines of Alexander the Great and that for the present, preparation for a quartermastership was advisable. "Oh, I was a little rampaging terror for a few hours, but here I am again, as smug as a Buddha."

Steve Benét was in Washington in the Aviation Reserve, and they met for lunch, dinner and a performance of Arnold Bennett's *Helen of the High Hand.* Sundays, Thornton typed *The Breaking of Exile,* a three-act play intended for producer Arthur Hopkins, who knew nothing of it, and for actor John Barrymore, who was equally innocent of its existence. It is a play about "people in a white heat of intensity," and when he sat down to put this intensity on paper he was in a fever himself; "the terrible thing pours out onto the page." The action occurs in a cheap French hotel on the Yangtze River where a handful of exiles are staying when war breaks out. How his mother would "hate" one of the characters — the Baroness Dorothea von Ulmins, who is recalled to Germany. And how she would "hate" John Barrymore as the English officer who is dismissed from the army for scandalous conduct and marries a poor, deserted fool. Marooned in this French-Chinese Grand Hotel are a Dutch lady manager, two pleasant French officers, a young English lieutenant (a part reserved for Gareth Hughes), an elderly Russian who is a benefactor of the peasants (Tolstoy), a drunken husband, and a Chinese scholar educated at Oxford. The author was sure that everyone in the audience would scream loudly or die of horror. *The Breaking of Exile* was never produced.

The *Atlantic Monthly*'s rejection of an essay, "Our Unknown Phrasemaker," did not daunt Thornton, for the editor wrote politely that had there been "a bit more room at our disposal" they would not willingly have gone without it.

On August 14, having decided that he could no longer avoid military service but still resisting the role of combatant, Thornton applied for induction into the Coast Guard Artillery Corps. Advance clearance had come from Mount Carmel. "If he is put through the physical life and experience of a soldier in a service adapted to him," Papa wrote Amos, "it will be better for him than Washington." Despite his poor vision and the fact that he

fainted during his medical examination, the Coast Guard accepted
him and on September 14 Thornton was inducted as an office
orderly and sent to Fort Adams in Newport, Rhode Island. He
was sick the first week, the noncoms were "vicious, vain and vituperative" and, sleeping in a barracks with thirty men, hearing
their profanity and obscenity, he was oppressed by the "vacancy
of their lives." But when he walked along the Newport shore
in the evenings and heard the swishing of the tide turning, he
thought of Chefoo and the Yellow Sea and knives of joy went
through him. The ladies of the parish church invited him to their
homes to meet their daughters; his response was smiling but elu-
sive.*

Military duties were undemanding, largely typing and drilling.
A play was fermenting in his mind "like sodium in water." He
was also preparing a scene for a musical, reviewing for the *Boston
Transcript* at nine dollars an article, and drafting a character study
for the actress Nazimova. "I wrote a magnificent, fierce love scene
last night," he reported to his mother. "I am almost frightened
at the size of my canvas and the explosive nature of my *dramatis
personae.*" Mother was asked to send a dozen or so playlets that
had been turned down by the Yale University Press to Sergeant
Glenn Hunter, Thornton's latest enthusiasm, who was acting with
the Fort Ontario Players. She would like Hunter, "full of wonderful boyish charm," although he was not a Gareth Hughes, who
at his best was "near to something divine."

Within two months of Thornton's induction the First World
War was over. Eight and a half million had been killed, 21 million
wounded, 7.5 million had been taken prisoner or were missing.
After twelve more weeks of routine service at Fort Adams, he
was released and returned to Yale. He was twenty-two.

Postwar classrooms were graveyards compared to the *Lit* and the
Elizabethan Club. Here were the playing fields for literary energy.
Thornton's contributions to the *Lit* were bringing him a modest
Yale reputation, though not the attention of the great world of
New York. He saved a letter from producer Arthur Hopkins,

* Some of this would find its way into Thornton's 1973 semiautobiographical
novel, *Theophilus North.*

regretting a delay in returning *The Breaking of Exile;* in spite of its "many fine qualities," there was no possibility of its being accepted for production. After the Second World War, Hopkins would beg for a play. "You are much the best informed theatre man I know and I naturally turn to you for advice."

Thornton's 1919 diary has only sporadic entries, none mentioning academic studies, athletic events, precarious Wilder family finances or the state of the world. Instead he records his excitement over a debate on the values of rewriting, with examples from Brahms trios and George Moore's novels, a talk with Harry Luce on qualifications for Elizabethan Club membership (Luce was not admitted), a session with Steve Benét at Mory's, a symphony concert, an evening at the Quincy Porters' (both musicians) at which he read aloud; teas, canoeing parties, four-hand piano recitals, lunch in the basement of Alpha Delta Phi and a midnight supper with Brit Hadden — "wonderful toasted cheese on toast and beer at a joint near the firehouse." Happening on Thornton in the Elizabethan Club, Wilmarth Lewis noticed a distinct change in his Thacher acquaintance; the oddity and insecurity were still there, but this was no freak.

Thornton continued earning pocket money by reviewing, this time for the *Boston Transcript,* and hung around the stage door of the New Haven theater until he finagled an introduction to Helen Hayes and Alfred Lunt. If he wasn't seeing plays or writing he was reading — Lytton Strachey's *Eminent Victorians, Huckleberry Finn,* the fifth discourse of Newman, the second book of *Paradise Lost, The Education of Henry Adams.* In his forties, he would hear Gertrude Stein tell young writers, "Work hard in your twenties or nobody will love you when you are thirty." The advice would have been gratuitous in his case; he was squirreling away at least as many nuts as anyone else in his Yale class. Steve Benét told Papa in 1919 that his second son was "the surest candidate for secure fame of anybody who has ever eaten at Mory's. I don't believe in his artistic ideals, but have a horrible fear that they are right." Papa would not have gone that far, but he conceded that Thornton's writing had in it an "underlying sound *principle.*" On Thornton, too, was the Puritan mark, "less affirmative than in you or me," Papa wrote Amos, "but let each singer choose his own tune." He worried, however, that Thornton "studies not at all, yet is bright enough to 'get by.' " Whatever would the "dear boy" do after college?

Thornton's Yale contemporaries included painter Reginald Marsh, poet Stephen Vincent Benét, publisher John Farrar, playwright Philip Barry, essayist Robert Coates and journalists Luce and Briton Hadden, who would edit *Time* as they had the *Yale Daily News.* Thornton's Yale achievements were at least a match for theirs. By graduation, thirty-two of his short pieces, most of them plays, had been printed. But none earned him any money.

How was he to live? Amos's path was laid out; he would go to a seminary. Charlotte, who had graduated from Mount Holyoke in 1919, was already supporting herself. Thornton was the woolgatherer and could not be expected to chart a career for himself. Something would have to be arranged.

Papa pondered the problem in light of his own past. He had been a working journalist and he would return to newspaper work in 1922 as associate editor of the *New Haven Journal Courier,* without ever achieving financial security. Anyhow, it was plain that Thornton had no taste for journalism. Teaching? His Oberlin and Yale grades would not impress any school. The possibility that he might pay his bills with literature was unthinkable.

Two things came to Thornton's rescue: his mother's familiarity with the *New Republic,* and an old family friend. Reading travel letters from Rome by the magazine's drama critic, Stark Young, Mrs. Wilder learned that the dollar exchange in Italy at that moment was highly favorable to Americans, which led her to consult Yale's preeminent Latin scholar, Professor George Lincoln Hendrickson, whom she knew from Madison days. Hendrickson had been director of the Department of Classical Studies at the American Academy in Rome and thought there might be a place there for young Wilder, though not as a fully enrolled student. Perhaps he could board at the Academy, take selected courses and participate in digs.

Papa considered. He could not know that the principal dividend of a year in Rome would be a first novel, *The Cabala,* but he could see that a year of Latin and archaeology might interest an academic employer. A serious talk was called for. "My dear boy," it began, "I am going to give you $900, in installments. If the money situation over there is as your mother says it is, that will sustain you very well for a year." If possible, some of those dollars were to be brought back; there were Amos's expenses at Yale Divinity School, and the education of Janet and Isabel would be a continuing burden. "So make the most of your advantages in Rome. When you return, I hope you will be prepared to teach Latin in some school somewhere, and as far as money is concerned, let me not hear another word out of you for the rest of our lives."

6
Italy!

LESS EXPERIENCED ocean voyagers, driven below by high seas, might absent themselves from the table; not this Yale graduate who had crossed the Pacific four times. Traveling second class on the SS *Indipendenza,* Thornton chatted happily with young business representatives, students, foreign service officers, Mormon missionaries. He had with him books on Roman archaeology and in the ship's library found an introduction to Italian. Since a language must be spoken, he practiced it by climbing to the top deck and shouting into the spray: *"Cuando parta il treno prossimo per Roma?"* Parts of Dante's *Divine Comedy* were translated and memorized with the help of a young cabin mate of Italian descent. From another fellow passenger he learned that classes at the American Academy were not scheduled to start until October. A bonus of six free weeks.

Italy! Paradise on a low budget. He put up at a former monastery in Sorrento, now a hotel, and in the mornings boarded the small Amalfi boat for Naples and the Museo Nazionale library. Naples was achingly beautiful. Sun, sea, blue skies; the smoking volcano with ruined cities at its base; a region where Virgil, according to ancient tradition, located the entrance into hell. Thornton was surrounded by the songs of larks and nightingales and the smell of aromatic shrubs and orange trees. One of Cicero's villas was nearby; so was Benedetto Croce's summer house. Ibsen had stayed there! Days in the museum were given to studying the shrines of Pompeii or Greek and Etruscan vases, and when the closing bell rang it was as if he had been awakened from a dream. Pure joy. He would come to know men and women who devoted years to researching Watteau or Shakespeare or Diderot without conveying "one vibration of a gold-digger's excitement of imaginative participation in the genius of their chosen subject." Alas for them. The raptures of research were like victories of Olympic champions, accorded only to amateurs.

On days when he remained in Sorrento, Thornton was up at half past seven, had breakfast, studied Italian grammar, ambled down the hill for a *gelato* and conversation or took a boat ride with a young eighteen-year-old Italian whose "aristocratic little head and earnest eyes added to his sad story." Drifting in the shadow of the cliffs and on the rushing tides in and out of caverns seemed to him truly *Italian,* "in the sense that Shakespeare and Goethe yearned over the word." A romantic play was taking form in his mind, a sweet story of a rich, beautiful American girl who goes to Capri to die.

He had expected to be assigned a room in the main Academy building in Rome but discovered when he showed up on October 14 that only holders of fellowships had that privilege. After some delay he was lodged with three other young men in the nearby Villa Ballacci, a tiny house with a garden and a great grille gate. He could hardly wait to rush to the Piazza di Spagna, and when his eyes fell on the house where Keats had died, he cried and recited lines he had memorized under the olive trees of Sorrento:

> When I have fears that I may cease to be
> Before my pen has gleaned my teeming brain. . . .

He was enraptured by every grass-tufted church, by the underground chambers of the Palatine, the Forum, the Colosseum, the vegetable stalls under the arches of the Theater of Marcellus. From the Villa Ballacci it was only a few minutes' walk up the Janiculum to the large doors of the Academy. One nodded at the *portiere* and proceeded into a spacious open court, past a huge fountain, up wide stairs and through long cool corridors to a billiard room, then on into a high dining hall where students and staff took their meals. Next to one at table might be a teacher on sabbatical or a graduate student writing her thesis on stucco bas-relief.

Founded in 1894 and chartered by Congress in 1905 to aid the fine arts, the American Academy had two classes of students

— *Prix de Rome* winners selected for their artistic promise and classicists pursuing advanced studies in archaeology, Roman history or Latin literature. Thornton belonged to neither group. Indeed, it was unclear what his status was or how he would spend his time. As it turned out, he did pretty much as he pleased. He wandered along side streets, occasionally pausing to unfold a three-foot-square map to pinpoint his location; attended lectures in the Forum on the topography of early Rome, on numismatics, on ancient inscriptions; accompanied an archaeological party to a newly discovered tomb and peered by candlelight at faded paintings of a first-century Roman family. On Saturdays he made excursions to Frascati, Palestrina or Viterbo, sometimes with another young student, Leon Keach, whose photograph he kept in his scrapbook. Hours were given to Raphael's *Stanzae,* the Sistine Chapel and to Santa Maria Maggiore ("my heart in a perfect jelly of delight"), inspecting the gilded ceiling, the green and violet marbles, the bronze and golden doors, and thinking of the councils that had agitated themselves in that vast basilica over definitions of dogma. The laughing young seminarians in the churches seemed to him the only people in Rome who were happier than he.

Thornton was given numerous opportunities in Rome to exhibit his skills as a tour guide. Any audience was an incitement to share knowledge. There, he would exclaim, beneath a rushing street lay the first century! He would gaze at the ruins, "clutching at the past to recover the loves and pieties and habits of the Aurelius family," reminding his awed listeners that the Rome of 1920 would be as great an effort to recover in another two thousand years, and as humanizing an effort.

His spirit flagged only when he contemplated his rejection slips. A play begun in Sorrento was about to be mailed to Mount Carmel for mother's opinion and dispatch to a theatrical producer, but was it worth it? All he could do, he supposed, was "go on writing slightly peculiar plays until I have eight or ten unpublished un-played affairs on a shelf to read from time to time." On the following day, after a walk along the Tiber, he wrote his mother to persist in submitting manuscripts until she could no longer afford postage. "The excitement of waiting will keep us young." A narrative sketch written in Rome illustrates how far he had advanced beyond the baroque Oberlin style:

I encountered a number of people who for one reason or another were unable to sleep between midnight and dawn, and when I tossed sleepless, or when I returned late to my rooms through the deserted streets — at an hour when the parricide feels a cat purring about its feet in the darkness — I pictured to myself old Baldassare in the Borgo, former Bishop of Shantung and Apostolic Visitor to the Far East, rising at 2:00 to study with streaming eyes the Fathers and the Councils, marveling, he said, at the continuous blooming of the rose-tree of Doctrine.

A prudent deference to Papa's sensibilities kept Thornton from relaying more sportive sides of Roman life. Several nights a week he strolled down the Janiculum with a few other "geniuses" to the taverns of Trastevere. In wineshops the conversations grew louder as the hour grew later, and when a number of the geniuses had fallen asleep or off their chairs, the exhausted procession moved into the street to catch the last trolley up the hill, stopping to vomit in the gutter. Drinking parties in the dormitories ended with half-dressed students slapping each other with wet towels and with revelers staggering perilously up the deep stairwell of the Academy and tossing paper bags of water from second-story windows.

Notwithstanding the favorable dollar exchange and diligent economies, by December Thornton was broke and fretting over a delayed remittance from his father that forced him to ask the secretary of the Academy for an advance of 150 lire. Degrading! Was it intended that he stay in Italy as long as he could on $900, or stay for a year under as pinched conditions as possible? A more generous amount from home could "make quite a little agitation on the Roman scene that recognized extraordinary eccentric sharp young men, as it did when Emperors adopted them!" On a somewhat lesser increase, he could do credit to the Wilder name and "gain entrance to regions incomputably valuable to a young writer who misses nothing, as far as observation goes." With a still smaller additional subsidy, he could meet Americans at hotels and study without worry. Even an extra $25 would let him hold up his head in the halls. He immediately regretted having written this to his father and would have given the world to recall it.

On Thanksgiving Day at the American embassy, Thornton was introduced to a group of girls from the fashionable Miss Risser's School and to several American women married to Italians. The next morning he left his card at the homes of the latter, hoping for an invitation to tea, if not a dinner party. Miss Risser's girls did ask him to tea, giving him a chance to brag. Yes, he said, with as much nonchalance as he could command, he was rather neglecting Caesar at the moment in preference for Tacitus. Yale classmates Harry Luce and Bill Whitney, on vacation from Oxford, showed up at Christmas without hotel reservations and appealed to Thornton. After being turned down by thirty small hotels he found them a large room for twenty-five lire a day. They were both barbarians in a gentle way, he thought, both "reaching vaguely toward an aesthetic eye after years of economics and political theory, but they're so honest and naive that their comments are worth hours of opinionated, hastily-contemptuous judgments of my fellow academicians." Luce was all convictions and opinions; "new information finds its way into the orderly chambers of his mind with decorum and dignity. I never knew when I liked him better, not even in China." Inadvertently, Thornton provided another service to Luce. He brought him to a New Year's Eve party at the Academy and introduced him to one of Miss Risser's young ladies, twenty-year-old Lila Ross Hotz of Chicago, whom Luce married in 1923.

The affinity between Thornton and elderly ladies won him the favor of the American novelist Marie Van Vorst, who lived in a palace and fed him small pastries and chitchat about the theater, or what some Italian prince said to his servants. From Marie Van Vorst's, he would make his way to the salon of a Mrs. McCormick of Dayton, Ohio, or to the Princess Youssoupoff's, or the home of the Italian poet Adolfo De Bosis.* He met the family of a prominent man of letters whose daughter was studying Aramaic and whose delicately mustachioed son, "only 19 but conversant, even *passioné,* over higher philosophies," urged Thornton to join

---

* De Bosis's son, Lauro, would share with Edward Sheldon the dedication of Wilder's *The Ides of March:* "Roman poet, who lost his life marshalling a resistance against the absolute power of Mussolini; his aircraft pursued by those of the Duce plunged into the Tyrrhenian Sea."

a small group reading Plato in Greek. There was so much to
read — Stendhal's *Promenades en Rome,* Florio's tra..islation of Mon-
taigne and, most exciting, Pirandello's plays. A chance encounter
in a bookshop sent him delving again into modern German expres-
sionist drama produced in Berlin between 1917 and 1920 by Max
Reinhardt and rekindled his interest in a play he had put away,
"Villa Rhabini," which he finished and read to "lots of ladies."
Its heroine is an American millionairess who falls into the toils
of an Italian adventurer, and in case its import might be missed
he describes it as a "long hymn of love; profane love, of course,
most pagan," but brightened at moments by "some of the most
explicit and tender conversations."

What had happened to the choirboy from Berkeley, the fidgety
Oberlin student with the stamp of the Puritan on him? He was
in danger, he acknowledged, of becoming "a confirmed little
brother of the rich" and must therefore try to wean himself from
elderly hostesses with their five-o'clock compliments. True, he
"never paid a more than languid attention" to the young girls,
although half his invitations came in the form of "oh, Mr. Wilder,
I have some charming American girls staying with me next week,
won't you . . . ?" He teasingly blamed his mother for not making
him "more susceptible to the illusions cast by maidens, very few
of whom divert me for long (thank God)." It was the old women
with their malicious stories, their wise disillusioned comments and
their bemused pseudo-motherly conversion to his ingenuousness
who intrigued him — and against whom he resolved to protect
himself, a resolve strengthened by a "strange little sentimental
experience" proving that Continental women, "however impersonal, comradely and full of good sense" they may seem, "cannot
understand friendship that is without romantic concomitants, cannot, cannot. Queer!" Well, at least the tea parties and dinners
were costing him nothing, not even a new necktie, for "the old
birds rather liked the fact that the awfully attentive, tirelessly flattering Mr. Wilder wasn't (like their own sons) so perfect and shiny
and elegante."

As his time in Rome neared its close, the claims of middle-
class, Congregational America reasserted themselves and Italy suddenly appeared a crumbling fresco. The tales of woe, broken en-

gagements, insult and injury he'd listened to from *grande dame*
to servant girl "would freeze your spine," he wrote Isabel.
"There's something in the air over here; everyone is unhappily
in love every minute of their lives." He was overcome by nostalgia,
he wrote Papa: "A snowy walk in Mt. Carmel, Mother sewing,
and you with your pipe hold for me now all I hold of order
and peace. Your queer 'aesthetic,' over-cerebral son may yet turn
out to be your most fundamental New Englander."*

But the eight months had sunk deep. "For one who with pick
and axe has laid bare a 2,000-year-old highway," he wrote, "the
world is never the same again." He could imagine an archaeologist
of the next millennium saying of Times Square and Piccadilly
Circus, "There seems to have once been considerable activity
here." And something more personal, about which he was very
guarded, had affected him profoundly in Rome. He had, he confided to a friend, "loved with all the exaggeration one can imagine." The loved one was never identified, but Thornton was "not
only not loved so in return," he was laughed at. "The cleverest
humiliations were set for me. And for a long time I'm going to
be the most cautious, most distrustful (of myself) man in the
world." It was time to leave Italy.

---

* Amos believed that no foreign experience alienated his brother from the "poig-
nancies and ordeals of the commonplace or the deeper root-systems of our American way."

7

Schoolmaster

IN MOUNT CARMEL a familiar story was about to be repeated. The Wilder family physician advised Papa that for her health Mrs. Wilder must change her surroundings. Mother, Isabel and Janet would spend the summer in England, first in Oxford, where Amos was studying at Mansfield College, then in London with Aunt Charlotte, helping her supervise a YWCA-sponsored hostel.

Alone in New Haven at his desk at the *Journal-Courier,* Papa had plenty of time to think about his second son, who might do things if he could be saved from "the drama-huckster Jews of the great city." But what? There was a possible opening for a Latin teacher at the Blairstown School and a French teacher at the Lawrenceville School in New Jersey. But was his son qualified for either? Before leaving Rome, Thornton sent a strong hint that if he was to teach it would be useful to polish his French in Paris. Unexpectedly, Papa saw merit in the idea.

Thus, at half past ten the morning of June 6, 1921, a jubilant prospective language instructor stepped off the train at the Gare de Lyon in Paris and raced off to ten different banks, hunting for the agent of Brown Brothers, who, he had been told, was holding money for him. Twenty-four hours later the agent had not been located and Thornton was stranded with just enough in his pocket for a few nights in a cheap hotel on the rue des Saints-Pères, bedbugs *compris.* When the delayed remittance reached him, he changed to a pension at 269 rue Saint-Jacques, still lacking sufficient funds and desperate.

Armed with an introduction from Steve Benét, he was interviewed by a Mr. Leland of the *Telegram,* the only English-language evening newspaper in Paris, who suggested that he submit an article on the theater. Several were submitted, none printed and he was paid nothing.

After six weeks Thornton outlined his misfortunes to his father. "By August the 26th I will be looking for someone to rescue me. In other words, I offer you the chance to ship me home. The awful depth of things has arrived, the unextenuated circumstances you so often prophesied in your letters have come to pass." He would continue looking for work, but half a dozen good opportunities had been missed. He had little hope of getting anything. He had "ruined" himself and must be "sorrowfully lifted home." He hoped Papa would treat the Blairstown job prospect cautiously, regardless of salary, for he might not suit, "and to be well paid but unsatisfactory is horrible. I must dress properly before growing boys. I have gone twenty years now in strange, wild, cheap ballooning clothes. I keep living on here on ninety cents a day, wondering what is to become of me."

From half past ten until half past eleven each evening his wondering was done at the Café Deux Magots on the boulevard Saint-Germain, and ruined though he may have been, Thornton was taking French lessons, hunting up Edna St. Vincent Millay and Sylvia Beach, attending plays at the Vieux Colombier, an organ recital at Saint-Sulpice and a Palestrina mass at Sainte-Chapelle.

Blairstown was not interested in Thornton; Lawrenceville was. Its headmaster, Mather Abbott, had been looking for a French teacher at fifteen hundred dollars a year, and Yale professors Tinker and Berdan had said there was no doubt Thornton could fill the post. If a definite offer was made and accepted, Papa wrote, Thornton should carry on a bit longer in Paris, then "come home the same dear, noble-minded boy. Pray to be guided and keep the vision." This was followed by a cable on August 15: "Have accepted Lawrenceville French for you. Remain and perfect language." "Yes," Thornton replied. A letter from New Haven gave details: "To finance you, especially this new extension in order that you may be ready to teach French, is hard on me when I thought your calls had ceased. Yet I *can* get the money and want to stand back of my children where it means creditably getting on their feet." Thornton must "fairly eat" French, so that he could fit boys for examinations. Furthermore, he must be on hand before the start of term, for Abbott was "not a man who will stand for a moment any laxity like a new teacher turning up tardily with some weak excuses." His son must put in twelve hours a day studying, for Papa had often "heard mother say your French is not very good."

The offer to teach was not taken lightly by Thornton. Lawrenceville, he wrote his mother from Paris, was "the smart prep school for Princeton and entertains only big husky team material. I better grow a mustache for maturity. Well, well, I am as excited as a decapitated goose."

He returned sufficiently early to enroll in the Berlitz School in New York for several weeks of language training. Thirty-four years later, he acknowledged that for all his exposure he couldn't speak one foreign language worth a bean. "Imagine my shame when Frenchmen ask me what I taught!"

Dr. Mather Almon Abbott, "the Bott," was an imposing figure in his mid-forties, born in Halifax, educated at Oxford and a master at Groton before being called to Lawrenceville, seven miles from Princeton. He did not seem disconcerted by his first sight of the new French master. Before him stood a courteous, rather slight twenty-four-year-old with a receding hairline, a dab of a mustache and cockleshell glasses, properly dressed in a button-down shirt and suit with vest (just purchased from the proper Yale tailor, A. N. Rosenberg) and wearing shoes of proper brown saddle leather. He assigned Thornton to Davis House, of which Edwin Clyde ("Tubby") Foresman was resident Master. Foresman taught ancient history and football; his wife, Grace, a Cornell graduate, had taught Latin and geology. Their only child, Emily, was two.

Thirty-two lower-form boys slept, ate and studied in Davis House, about a mile from the central circle of Lawrenceville buildings, most of them constructed in the 1880s. The daily routine began with breakfast, over by 7:20, giving the five hundred or so boys and the masters time to get to chapel service at 8:10. The new French teacher was placed several pews behind the headmaster and served as a spotter of anyone who failed to be in his assigned seat. Boys returned to their respective houses for lunch at noon. There were afternoon classes except on Wednesdays and Saturdays. Dinner was preceded by grace. A buzzer sounded at 7:00, summoning all students to a discussion of house business. No cigarette smoking was permitted in Davis, although pipes and cigars were tolerated among older boys who had parental consent and who confined their smoking to an outside room on the ground floor. Mr. Wilder never entered that room, thereby avoiding any embarrassment to boys with nonconsenting parents. He himself was addicted to cigarettes. "You certainly smoke a lot," one boy remarked. "Oh yes," Thornton replied, "an unbroken chain since 1918."

In reality there were two assistant housemasters of Davis, identical in appearance, both named Thornton Wilder. One taught, examined, monitored, took part in the academic, administrative and social life of the school from early morning until ten at night. After ten, on weekends and during vacation periods, the other Wilder emerged. This was the Wilder who was writing *Memoirs of a Roman Student.* The light in his office-bedroom at the top of the second-floor stairs in Davis was usually on until two or three in the morning, and at first no boy knew that by that light he was putting together a novel. His fellow teacher, Leslie Glenn, knew, for Thornton was reading him parts of the story.* By November 1922, a good deal of the *Memoirs* had been written and almost the whole projected.

There were times when it was tedious to correct papers, interview indifferent boys and fight a seemingly losing struggle against disorder, yet Thornton liked Lawrenceville and the school liked him; he seemed born to teach. Four evenings a week he sat in his study from seven until ten while the boys in their rooms prepared for the next day's lessons or dropped in to ask about a difficult phrase in Caesar, some French, a trigonometry problem. Or to have a little chat: "Please, sir, what does mendacity mean?" "Would you like some fudge my sister made, sir?" Every now and then at the sound of scuffling on one of three floors, the

---

* It was a lifelong friendship. Glenn, who had aspired to an acting career, ended as an Episcopal clergyman, canon of the Washington Cathedral and a familiar figure in the Georgetown social set.

assistant housemaster descended the stairs, "dispensing awe and order like fragrance." Finally, fifteen minutes' freedom before lights-out, sudden activity, four Victrolas playing, a rush for the bathroom. Then the last bell and lowered lights. "An expansive benevolent peace invests us," he wrote Professor Wager.

> My heavy reconnoitering footsteps flower into symbolic signifi-cance as I lock the back door and try the windows. Follows about ten minutes of furtive whisperings from bed to bed, and they fall off to sleep — most of them having sustained the incessant impacts of football practice throughout the hours of the afternoon. People said to me *never teach school! You will be so unhappy. It will deaden you.* But what happy surprises you find here; the relations of teacher and interested class; casual encounters with retiring boys on the campus, and at lights-out the strange, big, protective shielding, locking the doors against dark principalities, and the great lamp-eyed whales that walk ashore in New Jersey.

The boys were entertained by his rapid walk and talk and grateful for his cheerful tolerance of their nonsense. He was *different.* "Mr. Wilder seemed to find us endlessly intriguing and disturbing," one of the boys, Marshall Sprague, recalled,[*] "though we knew that his interest was that of a spectator at the zoo watching the monkeys, charming and repulsive by turns, happy to be noticed, especially when he erupted like a volcano at some misconduct of ours and threw blackboard erasers and chalk at us." They retali-ated by dropping a trunk down the stairs from the third floor, so that it would knock the door off his room and end up inside.

Despite the damp, inhospitable New Jersey winter and chronic head colds, Thornton was fit, taking his relaxation in cross-country runs, long walks and, in the spring, tennis with the registrar, Lans-ing Tostevin, or with the senior master in mathematics, Ira Wil-liams, who ran a camp at Blodgett's Landing on Lake Sunapee in New Hampshire, where Thornton would tutor several summers. He tried without conspicuous results to introduce French into

---

[*] *New York Times,* January 27, 1974.

everyday conversation. For the enlightenment of one lad who was having trouble with irregular verbs, in this instance the present tense of *venir,* he leapt over the back of a couch, flapping his arms and shouting "On wings of gauze they come! they come! ILS VIENNENT!" Crash. If afternoon class on a warm day was sluggish, he called out to a boy in the back of the room: "Open the windows! Class now stand! Inhale with a deep breath! Exhale slowly!" He was at the piano for half an hour after dinner, leading hymn singing. "At the ivories will be that well-known virtuoso of holy music, Thornton Wilder," he announced.* First-year boys were directed in scenes from a popular Broadway show, *Nelly Kelley,* taught to sing "Don't Send Me Roses When It's Shoes That I Need" and how to form a chorus line. Halfway through study period, Mr. Wilder visited all rooms to observe work habits, decisively solving such problems as a snake crawling between sheets. At bed-check, he rushed to a window and shouted: "No, madam! You can't come in. This is a boy's room!" Yes, Mr. Wilder was *different.*

He took no part in the organized athletics so esteemed at Lawrenceville, but at proms Thornton obligingly sat with the less popular ladies and, without seeming to chaperone, delighted the young dancers by joining them. He was sought after as an accompanist of local or visiting sopranos, for whom he played "The Rose That to the Bluebird Said," and he quickly became a favorite Sunday guest (chicken and ice cream) at the dinner table of one master or another, attributing this popularity to having learned the art of appearing enchanted; while his mind was miles away, his glance continued to imply admiration. He was protective of the slow learner, forever encouraging good reading. Any hint of literary talent stimulated a rush of advice. He became adviser to the Lawrenceville literary magazine and was a founding faculty member of the bookish Pipe and Quill Society, which concluded one meeting with Mr. Wilder, coat collar pulled up around his neck, hands

---

* On lecture tour years after, he began a talk on the pleasures of reading by saying: "We want something whose syllables have been familiar to us from childhood, like 'I know not where his islands lift / Their fronded palms in air / I only know I cannot drift / Beyond his love and care.'" Whenever he used that line from a hymn, he said, "you could hear a pin drop."

in pockets, reciting "The Shooting of Dan McGrew." When he told a circus story in French, he imitated the lion wagging its tail or the kangaroo leaping. He could provoke interest in anything, a former student said, "the crunch of footsteps on a gravel path, a cough in the corridor, a blank piece of paper, a pencil sharpener."*

The modest Lawrenceville salary, supplemented by income from a catalog he prepared for an amateur play publisher, tutoring, and reading Italian with another master seemed wealth to Thornton. At last he had enough shirts and underwear so that there were always some coming from and going to the laundry. "Tonight I am so happy," he wrote his father:

I love each class (and I meet five of them tomorrow) and each curious lifted pair of eyes. Each one thinks himself the most important little prince that ever lived and comes after class with troubles and arguments and jokes and wheedlings. I flunked dozens of them this last bi-weekly period, only to find that they like you all the better for your remorselessness. Today half a dozen boys came asking if they can transfer from other masters into my French sections; of course most of it is based on wild boys' notions that such and such a master has a prejudice against them, and a suspicion that a new master like me is "easier" and that any change is better. But part of it is due to the fact that my pleasure shines in my face and that classes are still delightful to me. The problem of class discipline that had some surprises and unexplained variations my first months is now almost gone. It is 11:12 — even the stealthy creaks of nocturnal visitors on the floor above have ceased and the gentle wheeze of thirty semi-adenoidal adolescents is heard in the land. Outside, a mistaken rooster on the horizon salutes a dawn infinitely far-off; the lovely whinny of one of Dr. Prentice's fancy Arabian horses in the barn across the road; the muted cataract of a water closet in the neighboring house and the gentle groans of the earth as it turns on its side in its fall through space, like a Pullman taking a curve.

* Clark Andrews, "To Us He Was Always 'T. W.,' " *Yankee*, September 1978, p. 122.

The reason I can be happy here is because there is no longer any sense of incompleteness or strangeness about any pleasure I may get out of America. I do not struggle to find grandiose interpretations in daily life; I have found my proportion in things. Nothing I ever did has entitled me to the pleasure I extract from Lawrenceville; it comes to me undeserved and may be whisked away from me tomorrow.

The first morning of the ten-day spring recess in March, the assistant housemaster inspected the bathroom for forgotten toothbrushes, shirts, washrags (all carefully initialed), dented pieces of soap, dirty towels used to clean a bicycle, canvas shoes. It was a world of adolescent borrowing, one comb and brush doing for an entire floor when the others (monogrammed Christmas gifts) had been mislaid or thrown out of the window at a passing cat.Then he boarded a train for New York and theater and supper at the Algonquin Hotel as the guest of two elderly Lawrenceville masters who regarded him as "an amusing little tike." He called on Grandmother Niven and on Aunt Charlotte, who was visiting from England, saw two operas and took a Lawrenceville footballer to Molnár's *Liliom*. They had "as much in common as the empress of Labrador and the ghost of Rudolf Euken" but got on famously and talked until one, when it was time for the boy to climb into his purple roadster and invade New York cabarets. "If for a moment one ceases to have the impression that it's a queer world," Thornton remarked, "on that very hour one ceases to live."

At term's end that summer Thornton returned to New Haven, rented a room for writing in the Yale Divinity School, which he soon gave up, and had breakfast each morning with his father at the Graduate Club. Wandering about the house in Mount Carmel, he came across two unfamiliar photographs of his mother taken when she was twenty. "If you had not been pretty," he told her, "the whole map of your mind and the whole map of my mind would have been different. You never developed the inhibitions and hesitancies of the women who are afraid they're plain." For the first time he was flush enough to give his family money and say, "Tell me when you need more."

But Mount Carmel could not keep him long: not enough privacy, too many demands. He headed for the Newport, Rhode Island YMCA to work on his fictional memoir of his eight months in Rome, lately stimulated by reading Marcel Proust in French. Here was an author who opened a whole new continent in psychology, though Thornton dared believe that if he really sat down to it, he could write even better than Proust. He was also reading Walter de la Mare, more Henry James, four volumes of Walpole's letters, Racine's *Britannicus*, two novelettes of Meredith and *Mansfield Park*. He would have reread *The Divine Comedy*, but the Newport library had no Dante save in translation.

In the top-floor dormitory of the "Y" (four dollars a week), he typed book one of the *Memoirs*, having gone over it with a blue pencil for the sixth time.

An ad was placed in Newport newspapers: "Instructor in one of the foremost preparatory schools and recent Yale graduate is willing to serve as tutor in French, English and Latin."* It brought him two offers, one to teach Cicero, for which Thornton said he had to relearn the whole Latin language; the second to tutor the daughters of a family whose address seemed so grand that he determined to charge $3.00 an hour, a bit above his usual rate. When he came up to the clapboard house and saw the placard in front — "H. J. Green: Furs" — he lowered his price to $2.50.

In late August 1922, he took the night boat to New York for more theater and lunch with his Niven grandmother, and then returned to New Haven to take over some of Papa's newspaper chores, so that his father could have two weeks' vacation in Maine. At the Yale library he picked up Flaubert's letters, Sherwood Anderson's recently published *The Triumph of the Egg*, Paul Valéry's edition of La Fontaine's *Adonis*, several numbers of *La Revue de France* and — best of all — the letters of Madame de Sévigné, on whom he would model one of the main characters in *The Bridge of San Luis Rey*.

Word reached him in September that a short section of his *Memoirs* had been accepted by the *Double Dealer*, an obscure little magazine published in New Orleans. He was elated; it was "the first thing of mine to get into a national monthly!" After reading ten

* He would tell of this in *Theophilus North*, published half a century later.

thousand words, the most distinguished of the literary magazines, the *Dial,* considered taking another part of the *Memoirs* and encouraged him to send the complete manuscript. He had to explain that he hadn't yet begun book two. But as he reviewed eleven pages written a week earlier, he was sure there was a "great book" somewhere there, only it had to be "long brooded."

Then, too, his thoughts kept drifting back to plays. He had come upon a life of the Spanish dramatist Lope de Vega and concluded that theater pieces must be visualized and written quickly; therefore, he must "never write one again without having a scenario first, as melodramatic as possible." Putting aside the *Memoirs,* he composed a strange three-minute playlet, *And the Sea Shall Give Up Its Dead,* in which the spirits of the drowned rise through the water and speak. And he completed a three-act play, *Geraldine de Gray,* in which the melodramatic was allowed full sway.

The time is 1872; the four characters are a young governess (Geraldine de Gray), Royal Percefaunt, his wife, Jessonda, and Bertha, the servant. The governess loves the husband, the wife kills herself, and the second-act curtain falls on:

> *Geraldine.* We have killed, I have killed her.
> *Royal.* Yes, we have killed her. We must pay for it, but let us enjoy what we can. At least what we can. (*With horror, they embrace.*)

It should be remembered that all this was being written during off-duty hours when Thornton was not instructing, monitoring or entertaining his boys in Davis House. Before he took up teaching, he had been warned that he must earn his wage, that these preparatory schools were "out for business." Thornton never doubted that teaching had priority, though if he were free of it he thought he could write "four stunners a year." He learned to follow the fortunes of the Lawrenceville football team "without palpitations." He got along well with Clyde Foresman — "a little stout man, blunt ideas, jovial manner" — and with Mrs. Foresman, "so much superior intellectually" and with whom he played four-hand piano. When he stole away to a play and the Alpha Delta Phi Club in New York, the weekend was shadowed by a morbid conscientiousness about not letting other things rob his Davis duties by "so much as a trifle." A boy's temperature had to be taken, attendance records kept current, papers and tests corrected, grade averages computed, reports prepared for department heads.

Christmas recess, however, belonged to the other Wilder, who could roam about town without scruples. In New York the schoolmaster receded into the background and the young artist stepped forward. "Armed to the teeth, then courageous as a lion," he wrote his mother, "I exhumed all my dead friendships" — the actress Lola Fisher, the *New Republic*'s Stark Young, *Theatre Arts* editor Edith Isaacs, John Farrar, now in publishing and "insufferably famous and disliked," and Steve Benét. He would spend many hours over the years with Benét in New Haven, Paris and New York, but the friendship never warmed. "We have never gotten on well," Thornton said. "His self-criticism is all so muddled through hasty and intentionally bad writing; he's smearing the magazines with treacle and making it all the harder for good authors to be heard."

The most talked-of drama on Broadway that 1922–1923 season was Pirandello's *Six Characters in Search of an Author* which Thornton had seen in Italy. He wrote its producer, Brock Pemberton, describing the play's stormy opening night in Rome and Pemberton invited him to lunch at the Algonquin round-table — a well-publicized gathering of quotable authors, critics and columnists, all brilliant but to Thornton unimpressive. "I still put most stock in the shy, groping producer who had brought me there." He and Pemberton talked of European theater and Thornton felt as though he were a consulting member of the producing firm. "You can imagine how valuable this relation (at present purely social) may someday be to me — when my own manuscripts are properly dressed up."

He dined at the home of Mrs. Isaacs, a friendship he owed to Stark Young, and there met the remote, legendary hermit of Brooklyn, poet Edwin Arlington Robinson. By a combination of impudence, allusive learning and veneration, Thornton achieved what worship and abasement had not been able to do for others — "broke up the devastating reserve that speaks for his [Robinson's] fifteen years of dreadful penury and drink and austere thinking." With Mrs. Isaacs, Thornton discussed possible play reviews

for *Theatre Arts* and lent her what he had of his *Memoirs*. She
was sure that if he could sustain it as begun, there was no doubt
of its publishability, "nor of the sensation it can arouse." He realized with pleasurable shock that no one had complimented him
for months.

A week in New Haven took the edge off his exhilaration. Papa
thought he had "gone to the dogs" and dreaded accounting to
Saint Peter for him. For what reason? Thornton asked. "My bank
account creeps up, though slowly; my morals are demonstrable,
and even my social sharpness, though inherent, is less to the fore."
How was a son to keep his self-respect under this battering? Thank
God for Mother. "No one in all my roaming has been so bright,
so individual, so stimulating as you," he told her. "Aren't I a
lot like you? Claim it!" *She* had character, and character was something that should be held concealed until some crisis evokes it,
"not a thing to brandish from breakfast to curfew, as father advocates."

Why were he and his father so at odds when there was so much
good in Papa? However hard-pressed, he had always found the
money a child needed. He had sent his son to farms not as punishment but to provide lessons in the value of the dollar and in
health building. His strictures were not motivated by selfish concerns, certainly not by dislike. Whatever the frustrations of his
married life, he held that "the drama of the home is a great mystery," a mystery Thornton would celebrate in his plays, and that
nowhere else do all manner of men "grow tender and have long-
ings to be good: hugging their children and walking about in
the dark hours safeguarding their dependents." Moreover, Papa's
conviction that literature would not pay was commonplace for
his generation. Recounting his boyhood and the attitudes toward
literature at the turn of the century, Henry Seidel Canby would
observe that "even the artist warned young men away from writing
because it was difficult then to make money by it. . . . Creative
wildness, that longing to shape and invent, to make life richer
or better balanced, more vivid, less perfunctory, was regarded
as eccentricty or weakness."* Papa even had the humility to say

---

* *The Age of Confidence* (New York: Farrar and Rinehart, 1934), pp. 234–43.

that he did not want his observations on Thornton's development to perturb him. "There is much I don't know, you are a good boy." At times he showed a sympathetic interest in Thornton's ambitions, advising him to send "some prose and poetry offerings to the magazines to get acquaintance and confidence." Nor was the religious atmosphere of the Wilder home run-of-the-mill, Bible-belt piety or narrow Calvinist orthodoxy. Papa's most heavily anno-tated books were Boswell's *Life of Johnson,* a four-volume life of William Lloyd Garrison and the works of John Bunyan, George Fox and Thoreau. If Thornton and the other children gave signs of becoming eggheads, Papa could accept it, but, said Amos, he was determined that they should have a "basic substratum of shirt-sleeve experience and the kind of sympathies which earned William Jennings Bryan the title of The Great Commoner."

Thornton's efforts to reach some understanding nevertheless seemed fated to fail.* He disapproved of Papa's publishing in his newspaper Amos's letters from England: "You've got a blind spot in your instinct for what is fitting." He was annoyed by accusa-tions of worldliness: "You hark back to your supposition that my tour through the decaying nations of Europe could have done me nothing but harm; well, Lauro De Bosis is a most advanced, sophisticated young man and yet as sunny and idealistic as any New Englander you can show me. Your generalizations make me despair of you." If the young Wilders exchanged letters among themselves with the postscript "DO NOT SHOW FATHER," it was not because they didn't love him, but as Thornton explained, because "you have always substituted vague idealities for facts; you have never been able to deny yourself the pleasure of making clucking noises of disapprobation. We have irresistibly assumed, then, that you don't care to hear what we are doing."

When Papa pressed his son to save more money, Thornton asked how he was supposed to start a savings account, considering his dental visits, his gifts of money to Mother, Isabel and Amos, and his need for new clothing. When, under renewed pressure, he sent a first installment of $78.44 to the bank, his father wrote him once a week urging him "to think of nothing else but enlarging

---

* "Happy is the man who over and beyond the age of 21 has in his father his best friend," Thornton would remark in an address in Germany in 1957.

it." "Prepare for further disappointments," Thornton burst out. "You are always on the point of washing your hands of me. I guess I'm hopeless." When Papa questioned a $50 check he received from Thornton, he had to be reminded of "a Big Scene in June, after which I promised you that I would contribute $50 a month toward mother's expense. I wrote you on July 21: 'I'm all steeled to forward you $50 a month, beginning October 1st.' Accordingly, on October 1, I sent you $50, which, lost in other indignations, you sent back to me. On November 1st I sent you another, and you wonder what it's for, and make it an occasion for homily. Sure I need it. If you don't want to renew our $50 agreement which comforted you so little that you forgot it, send me back my wandering bucks. If you do want to renew it, keep them with my best wishes, but don't scold me for improvidence." Enclosed was a letter Thornton had received from Stark Young, "to indicate the fact that I am not repulsive to people's taste."

No, he was not "hopeless"; he was preparing himself for "emergence 15 years hence with a work that has its source in the real traditions that lie in the history of literature, and that will stand out strongly from the thin cleverness and scrappy cultures and emotional poverty of my feted friends."

It did not take fifteen years.

8

Roman Memoirs

MEMOIRS OF A ROMAN STUDENT, long sections of which had been written by March 1923, was contemplated as a farewell to the romance and medievalism that barely survived the war, brightened by "archaisms, remnants of ridiculous learning, quaint dead heresies of the third century." To equip himself, Thornton was reading Labriolle's *Histoire de la littérature latine chrétienne.* He was also keeping up with the current stage that spring, and, spying Max Reinhardt at a Moscow Art Theater performance of *The Cherry Orchard* in New York, he had himself introduced during intermission — a "most valuable connection when I get back to playwriting." Mindful of his meager savings account, he took on a summer counseling job at Camp Sagawatha on Bantam Lake in Connecticut, thrashing about with three boys in a tepid lake ("swimming in tea") and taking them canoeing through lily ponds. It was two hundred dollars in the bank.

In the few weeks remaining before fall classes at Lawrenceville, he luxuriated in more New York theater, good and bad, then stayed up until dawn writing. From a rehearsal of Zona Gale's *Mr. Pitt,* to which he had been brought by Brock Pemberton, he hurried downtown for lunch at the *New Republic* with Stark Young, editor Herbert Croly and Langdon Mitchell, author of *Becky Sharp.* How sweet to find oneself among such brilliant talkers, and to be respected as one of them. Sweet but unbankable. He had saved twelve hundred dollars and no longer dressed in hand-me-downs; his learning and conversational dexterity were admired. But he had no security, no literary following and no intimate friends. If he knew any girls as girls are known to their lovers, he did not mention it, and if he did not mention it, he probably did not know them. Well, he consoled himself, "one quarter of my acquaintances are no longer capable of anything but red-eyed pashun"; "sexpression" was overrated.

Fairly certain that the *Memoirs* were "vital, rich, crowded," he was momentarily tempted to quit teaching, finish the novel and peddle it. He compromised in late spring 1924 by requesting a two-year leave of absence from Lawrenceville, a decision reinforced by residence that summer at the MacDowell Colony in Peterborough, New Hampshire. Mrs. Edward MacDowell, benefactress and impresario of the colony, at once singled him out as a young man of "exceptional talent" and praised what he had written. He was a popular resident, an attentive listener who looked straight at one, smiling shyly, but "as if he had always liked us," a fellow colonist, Mabel Daniels, said. He "gave you the feeling that he enjoyed doing things for people, which I think was the case." Elinor Wylie, poet in residence, was ambivalent; he was "either a genius or a fool."

Lodged with four other bachelors in a men's dormitory, Thornton took his turn lighting the bath boiler in the cellar and stoking it. He was the servants' favorite — on time for meals and prompt about laundry, cleaning his room, stacking wood. By the end of his residence, he had polished ten of his three-minute plays, written a "snappy" first act to a never-to-be-finished comedy — *Three Fables and Tirades* — and completed five of the *Memoirs* portraits.

Having no firm idea where he would live after he took leave of Lawrenceville that fall, Thornton didn't answer directly when Isabel, who was working in New York, suggested they share an apartment in the city. He would say only that once he had broken with Lawrenceville he could capitalize on friendships he had made in the theater world or, at worst, teach in one of the boys' schools in New York.

On the brink of this leap into the unknown, he pulled back and applied for admission in 1925 to the graduate school at Princeton as a candidate for a master of arts degree in Romance languages. It was a precautionary step, and Isabel was not to conclude that their move to New York was off forever. At the "least sign of Business from Theater Arts, Brock Pemberton, etc.," he assured her, "I leave Princeton flat." An M.A. was just something to fall back on.

A fragment of the *Memoirs* had been submitted the end of 1924 to Albert and Charles Boni, adventurous New York publishers of modern fiction, but had elicited no response, pro or con. From Princeton Thornton wrote Lewis Baer, secretary and treasurer of the company, who had been with him at Yale, that he assumed "by this time [February 14] the Powers found my *Memoirs* unsuitable (or whatever the euphemism is this year) and that you are too tender-hearted to announce it to me at once. Let fire, nevertheless, especially as I am impatient to have the text back again, for repairs." Baer waited two weeks, then replied, "Albert Boni feels so strongly about your style that he is very anxious to see more. I knew this would be the result of our reading, because I remember so distinctly how impressed I was at your stories in college. I do hope we will be able to get together a book which can mean the start of your career as an author, in print I mean. No one would be happier than I." There was no advance, no mention of a contract, but it was encouragement enough for Thornton. He hurriedly completed another fragment, and additional sections were mailed April 21. "The captivity's over, life's begun." His thought, he wrote Baer, would be to call the book "Marcantonio." There were, he admitted, some hastily written pages that he wanted to work over, "if your firm seriously becomes interested in its publication." The whole second part needed more craziness, more high preposterous impudence, perhaps even some freaks of pagination and some grotesque interruptions. "The thing is not to be mistaken for an Edith Wharton."

The Bonis *were* seriously interested; they liked the pearls he had sent, but there were too few of them and they were strung on too short a strand. "I drag myself to write more," Thornton said in May; he was "frantic to finish this five-year thing and get back to my plays."

A contract was at last signed in November 1925, giving the Bonis the right to publish the novel, now titled *The Cabala,* in the United States, Great Britain, Canada and in foreign translations, an option on Thornton's next three works and authority to dispose of motion picture and serial rights, of which Thornton would be entitled to 50 percent. The author would receive 10 percent of retail sales on the first five thousand books, 12½ percent on the next five thousand, and 15 percent thereafter. The deal proved lucrative for Albert and Charles Boni, and had they known that their young novelist would have let them publish *The Cabala* for nothing, they might have struck an even more advantageous bargain. "My emergence is long delayed but irresistible," Thornton commented.

Tutoring at the Lake Sunapee camp in New Hampshire had taken up most of the 1925 summer, an interval deserving notice because it brought him in touch with Amy Weil Wertheimer, a tall, good-looking matron from Cedarhurst, Long Island who was vacationing nearby with her stockbroker husband and two daughters. From the deck of the Wertheimer summer home, Amy could talk across the water with the young camp tutor. "Can you help me?" he wrote her shortly after leaving Lake Sunapee.

> I am looking for a wise, intelligent and fairly tranquil friend. I should like it to be a lady, somewhat older than myself who will understand me so well (both humorously and with a touch of superiority) that I can write her conceitedly and she will understand that that's only my way; trivially, and she will understand that that's my vocation; tragically, and that that's my nerves. Do you know anyone who would like to receive letters from me? Infrequent ones, but long and frank? About my life and work. Such letters as (constituted as I am) I could only write to a wise impersonal friend who knew even better than I what was best for me. Make sure that the candidate for this role has suffered at some time or other and has come through. Tell her it ought to constitute a bond, for enthusiastic carefree Thornton had an awful experience in Europe that left him so marred with woe that it is unimaginable that he will ever love again. Do you suppose he wrote his plays out of a carefree life?

How could she not help so bright, amusing and chivalrous a twenty-eight-year-old, one so confiding and grateful, so respectful of a woman's mind? It was the beginning of a tangled relationship.

He wasn't seeking an intellectual sparring partner, but a wise, warm-hearted woman who would be sufficiently stable to accept his instabilities in a sympathetic but detached spirit. The fact that Amy was five years older than he, and married, may have emboldened Thornton to open his heart to her, and she was unquestionably receptive to whatever of his innermost feelings he was prepared to express.

At Princeton, Thornton shared a study and small bedroom overlooking the river with a pale, pleasant roommate. Downstairs, the library with its large fireplace offered a cornucopia of books, magazines and newspapers amid which he was free to browse. He dined in a vast hall ("such food, such comfort") lit by stained-glass windows. After dinner, black-gowned students walked along the terrace in a twilight sun that fell on great stretches of golf links surrounding the graduate college. A third master teacher entered his life at Princeton (the other two were Wager at Oberlin and Tinker at Yale) — Professor Louis Cons. Never before, Thornton said, had he had "that highest privilege, a great teacher in the classics."

There were nine hours of class work a week — historical grammar, advanced composition and style, French texts — and a variety of pressing outside assignments. *The Cabala* had been promised the Bonis by December; he was supplying Mrs. Isaacs's *Theatre Arts* with surveys of the New York stage at twenty-five dollars a review; and there was that omnipresent, never-to-be-neglected correspondence, fashioned on walks or before he fell asleep or during class, then handwritten later. Some paragraphs were never put on paper; they were "what scales are for a pianist, practice, eternal practice in the flow of sentences and the technique of persuasion."

As the imposed or self-imposed demands mounted, Thornton panicked and felt he was "in the middle of a sort of nervous breakdown." He was full of plays that couldn't get written, he couldn't sleep, he was "hateful," he wrote Amy Wertheimer. He didn't know how to live with his "poor, spoiled, impaired willpower that cannot be harnessed to my studies." He wasn't "meant for human society" and was "getting pretty tired" of his own. He was now writing her once a week (she'd asked that his letters arrive on Thursdays), telling her of his self-doubts, of how he constructed new plays from the germs of old playlets, of his straying to the library and turning over drawings of Italian masters, of running every morning for three miles, renouncing cigarettes (an intermittent renunciation) and "avoiding artistic people, speaking slowly, refraining from frowns and trying to be good." He sent her a diagram of German repertory — what was being played, on what stage, by whom — and begged her to allow him to put off his next letter by one day and assign him a penance for the delay. And she was not to worry about his "breakdown." He was over it, helped by Professor Cons's tributes to master writers: "When a great author is praised for some transformation he has made of the troubles of his life into the gold of his art I can be discovered crying in the corner. It has nothing to do with grief or regret. It is weak and unmanly to weep because things are sad, and that I do not do; but who forbids us to [weep] when things are beautiful?"

The following week he confided to Amy that he was about to make a mistake. "I told you this summer that I was corresponding with a pretty subdeb named Rosemary Ames who wanted to go on the stage and who kept writing me for advice; and how I first met her at a Lawrenceville prom? Now, she has asked me to a dinner dance a friend of hers is giving at the Hotel Vanderbilt Saturday night. She must have forgotten in the vivacity of my letter that one whole generalization lies between us. [Did he mean "generation"? He was not yet thirty.] Yet that carefree dancing atmosphere sounds awfully attractive to me; I missed it in my time; perhaps it's the very thing my work needs for a change. So I'm going. Just the same I ought to keep within my genre."

At lunch in New York he complimented Amy on her clothes and wide interests, said shyly that since she offered it, he could use a pillow for a couch in his study — with her initials sewn into the pillowcase. Was he blind to the likely consequences of these gallantries and shared confidences, these beckoning and probably misleading signals to a lady who was attracted to "culture" and eager to reach beyond her suburban women's-club life?

On New Year's Day 1926, Thornton was again depressed, and when classes resumed he didn't see a grain of value in them; Princeton seemed a cheap pretense, but Princeton was not to blame. Something humiliating had occurred during Christmas recess. He had been "slapped sharply," he told Amy, for venturing outside "goodness and art." Whatever the incident, and he gave no details, it resembled his earlier experience in Italy and was sufficiently "awful" to provoke a resolution "to do of my own free will what circumstances would presently force me to do anyway. And *I killed myself.* I am no longer a person. I am a heart and a pen. I have no brain. I have no pride (oh, what an amputation was there!). I have no fear. (I wish that were true!) There is something of all this in the epilogue to *The Cabala.*" (He was referring to the lines: "Only a broken will can enter the Kingdom of Heaven. Finally tired out with the cult of themselves they give in. They go over. They renounce themselves.") He thought of running away to Florida or New Mexico.

Mrs. Wertheimer, alarmed, responded effusively, perhaps too effusively, touching a live-wire barrier sensible to him but not to her. His rejection of her advance was swift. It was "naughty" of her to get so excited over "mere phrasing." *To kill oneself* was "a sort of religious idiom for shaking off one's old laziness and trying again." There was no affection in the world that he would be stupid enough to refuse; "all life is made possible by it," he wrote her, but the only kind he was ready for was "a clear, serene, understanding affection" and he must draw back from anything else. The emotional pain he suffered in Italy was still with him; there were hints of it in *The Cabala,* "most indirectly stated." If he were to underline every passage that somehow alluded to his most secret life, he would have to sharpen the pencil several times. "That's why I write fiction and plays instead of essays and poems: The things I have to say are so intimate that I would be ashamed to publish them under *I.*" She must give up any idea of visiting him on a trip "which by the very implication of its secrecy has in it the power to pain other people." Above all, she must discard her illusions about him: "It wouldn't be a very sweet task for me to take each of your idealizations of me in turn and smash it. If I were in a more energetic mood I would paint you no mean picture of the groups that stare at me with almost pitying contempt. Or with repugnance." He wanted to be her friend for thirty or forty years to come but could not if he was not "a

friend of the group — liked and understood by Mr. Wertheimer
and the children and the neighbors." And if this caused her to
suffer? Well, "Only the trivial magazines pretend that life is
happy."

He distracted himself by copying music for a Princeton graduate
school chorus — Elizabethan madrigals, contrapuntal chants, motets of Vittoria or Palestrina — but the discontent persisted. He
was increasingly put off by the insincerity of "nice" people. Society
was "a pitiful grimace." He contemplated selling all he had (not
much) and saying "a long farewell to civilization." Nothing was
going right. The Bonis had had fourteen of his one-act plays for
a year, planning to issue them after *The Cabala*. Now he doubted
whether they would do anything with them: "Through mere familiarity, they may have chilled toward them." Proofs of his novel
had been read and revised, but now they seemed a "monument
of sloppy writing." He told Amy he was "sort of sick," chagrined
at the "duplicity and indirection" of his life, his "inertia and childishness." Belatedly, Thornton struggled to catch up on his neglected Princeton studies, fearing it was too late. He plunged
into Danish and Frankish linquistic influences, differences between
Latin and vulgar Latin, between vulgar Latin and Gallo-Roman,
between Gallo-Roman and Francien, and did well enough to receive his degree.

Not until April 1926, when *The Cabala* appeared, did the skies
clear. It was not a "monument of sloppy writing" after all and
was a far more unified and polished work than one would have
anticipated from correspondence between author and publisher.

Two hundred and thirty pages long, *The Cabala* covers one year
in the lives of a handful of ultraconservatives influential in clerical
and political Rome. The time is the early twenties. On the train
to the Eternal City, the young, learned but puritanical American
narrator (Wilder) falls into conversation with a Harvard archaeologist, James Blair. In Rome, after first taking the narrator to the
apartment of the dying poet Keats (past and present are jumbled;
Rome is pagan deities and the modern Vatican), Blair introduces
him to the wealthy, fretful, intriguing Miss Grier, an American
who lives to "ridicule and insult the fools and innocents of

her social circle." Through her, he meets the principal characters of his story, each of whom enlists him in some service that is doomed to fail. They call him Samuele, that Old-Testament link between dying monarchies and the kingdom of David; or, later, Mercury — the messenger who escorts the dead to Hades.

The four key characters are Marcantonio, a sensuous, scandalous sixteen-year-old son of the Duchess d'Aquilanera, who begs the narrator to "save" him; Alix d'Espoli, who falls in love with Blair; Marie-Astrée-Luce de Morfontaine, who schemes to restore the Catholic monarchy in France; and the worldly Cardinal Vaini, former missionary to China. It is the Cardinal who says, "Who can understand love unless he has loved without response?"

Marcantonio, after a moralistic hectoring by the narrator, is driven to suicide by remorse. Alix d'Espoli is spurned by Blair. Marie-Astrée, having had her faith undermined by the Cardinal's sophisticated questioning, tries to kill him. The Cardinal, hoping to recover the faith of his youth, sets out for China but never gets there. Samuele turns his back on Rome and the cabala's bondage to the past and returns to America. On board ship, he has an imaginary conversation with the poet Virgil ("greatest spirit of the ancient world and prophet of the new"), who tells him that Rome is dying and to "seek out some city that is young. The secret is to make a city, not to rest in it. When you have found one, drink in the illusion that she too is eternal."

"The debut of a new American stylist . . . magnificent literary event," said the *New York Times*. *Time* thought it "one of the most delectable myths that ever issued from the seven hills of Rome." "What a rich and finished book it is," wrote one critic, "and what a collection of extraordinary people."

The novel begins:

The train that first carried me into Rome was late, overcrowded and cold. There had been several unexpected waits in an open field, and midnight found us still moving slowly across the Campagna toward the faintly-colored clouds that hung over Rome. At intervals we stopped at platforms where flaring lamps lit up for a moment some splendid weather-moulded head. Darkness surrounded these platforms, save for glimpses of a road and the dim outlines of a mountain ridge. It was Virgil's country and there was a wind that seemed to rise from the fields and descend upon us in a long Virgilian sigh, for the land that has inspired sentiment in the poet ultimately receives its sentiment from him.

The Cabala portrays the lives of privileged Romans, but Thornton claimed that during his months in Rome he had met few members of the aristocracy, and that the novel's sources were Proust, La Bruyère, the memoirs of the Duke of Saint-Simon, Thomas Mann and Lytton Strachey. If we take the author's word that the novel was "almost entirely imagined," what is the significance of a cryptic letter from England he received years later and bothered to copy out in his journal? Signed "Alix" (the Princess d'Espoli in *The Cabala*) and dated 1951, the letter implies that the story is more autobiographical than Thornton admitted. "Imagine my surprise," the letter read,

> walking the sidestreets with a young friend, to find — your book, an old copy — *The Cabala*. Why had I never seen it? Then or now. What changes.
>
> Palestrina still is heard, but in Albert Hall! And I? Oh, my friend — such colossal egocentricity was mine — and how beautifully you bore with it. And how beautifully you bore with the burden of Marcantonio.*
>
> Why did we not let him be? To find his own way. With our prayers — for they are stronger than persuasion — he might have been at the end a true saint — finding somewhere in the cesspool of his living, solid grounds from which to spring into the blaze of the light.

* If there was a real Marcantonio and Thornton bore with him "beautifully" the story in *The Cabala* is imaginary, for there the author-narrator destroys him: "Heaven only knows what New England divines lent me their remorseless counsels. I became possessed with the wine of the Puritans and alternating the vocabulary of the Pentateuch with that of psychiatry I showed him where his mind was already slipping . . . how everything he thought and did — humor, sports, ambition — presented themselves to him as symbols of lust. My tirade was effective beyond all expectation. In the first place, it had the energy and sincerity which the Puritan can always draw upon to censure those activities he cannot permit himself — not a Latin demonstration of gestures and tears, but a cold hate that staggers the Mediterranean soul."

Blair! How stupid he seems now. It was you — you — who held my hand the long terrible night through. The old imperial egocentricity went out that night, I think, and a new soul was born. Will I ever cease to be grateful? No. No.

And you, child of an old world, and a new. How do you fare now.

      Ever faithfully yours,
      Alix
      Oh, how young you were! — And I was not so old.

Early versions of *The Cabala* that survived Thornton's habit of destroying drafts illustrate how he sharpened his prose in revision. For instance, a reference to the Cardinal in a discarded version reads:

The next thing I heard was that he had received the mission to return to China. . . . He sailed soon after. Being taken with a fever a few days out from Aden, he made the Captain and ship's doctor promise to bury him in the ocean if he died. He told them they would have to face the fury of the Church for such a procedure, but extracted their promise. He dreaded the thought of a marble tomb and the inevitable *ornatissimus,* the *insignis pietate.* These he did not utterly escape; his monument has been lately raised in his titular church and anyone could understand how infinitely preferable it is to be where [he] is now, swinging in the tides of the Bengal Sea, perhaps nosed by a passing shark.

As published:

He received permission to return to China, and sailed within a few weeks. Several days after leaving Aden he fell ill of a fever and knew that he was to die. He called the Captain and the ship's doctor to him and told them that if they buried him at sea they would have to face the indignation of the Church, but that they would be fulfilling his dearest wish. He took what measures he could to shift upon himself the blame for such an irregularity. Better, better to be tossing in the tides of the Bengal Sea and to be nosed by a passing shark, than to lie, a sinner of sinners, under a marble tomb with the inevitable *insignis pietate,* the inescapable *ornatissimus.*

In the end, the ironic tone of *The Cabala*'s earlier pages gives way to high seriousness as the young American Puritan bids farewell to the Old World: "The shimmering ghost [of Virgil] faded before the stars, and the engines beneath me pounded eagerly toward the new world and the last and greatest of all cities."

Variations on themes in *The Cabala* will be heard again and again. The praise of life at the point of death, expressed during the narrator's visit to the dying Keats will be echoed in Emily's hymn to life in the third act of *Our Town.* Her cry, "Take me back [to the grave]" has its counterpart in *The Cabala*'s "My heart is almost started beating again — what horror! Oh, what misery to a man, hurry and die!" Astrée-Luce in *The Cabala* personifies "the futility of goodness without intelligence." So does George Brush in Thornton's later novel, *Heaven's My Destination. The Cabala* and nearly everything else of his are works of a fabulist, a teller of tales that are meant to enforce a useful moral lesson. The lesson is that those who live amid illusions fail, not comprehending that they must "never try to do anything against the bend of nature."

"Not a single whack" from the critics, Thornton wrote Isabel, "yet how uneven the book is." Though he had proofread the galleys, twenty-eight errors had to be corrected in the next edition.

Of all the compliments, Professor Wager's meant most. *The Cabala* was "the real thing," he wrote his prized student, revealing "a sense for situation that you did not even promise to have in Oberlin." Thornton replied that as he kept adding bits to the book at Lawrenceville, he had had the sinking feeling that no publisher would read it, and that, pleased as he was by praise of his style, he would have liked some recognition for the human quality of the book. Had he not "cried and cried at midnight over all these wretched Cabalists"? His aim had not been stylistic virtuosity but the "notation of the heart."

Three months after publication, critical approval notwithstanding, the Bonis were inexplicably unwilling to advance Thornton

$250 on a second novel, a theological fantasy laid in seventeenth-
or eighteenth-century Spanish Peru and tentatively titled *The Bridge
of San Luis Rey,* which would prove to be one of the most profitable
novels on the Boni list.

Thornton was in Mount Carmel for Easter, answering letters
on the family dining room table, helping clean up after meals,
passing judgment on his sisters' dresses and dodging his father's
questions by skipping off to some engagement at the Yale Drama
School, where Isabel was studying stage production. Between interviews, signing copies of his book (often with a quotation from
page 65: "Why read me at all . . ."), and mail that had swelled
tenfold he had little time for *The Bridge.* There was a Mr. Livingston
who asked if the author was related to the Nivens of Orange
County and could Wilder tell him about the deed for a cemetery
plot granted in 1861. A grandmother from Philadelphia questioned
his use of a noun. A San Diego lady sent him life histories of
dozens of mutual acquaintances, all of whom he had forgotten.
Answering them, he felt "a glib and graceful hypocrisy" creeping
into his system.

He had gone home, he said, because he needed to be "cured,"
and Mother was "the only thing I can count on in this tiresome
world." Cured of what? He had been more amused than annoyed
by the "loony" suggestion from the Boni office that he waive
$1,250 in anticipated royalties, which they would match and use
to "plaster the country with advertisements, to try and ram [*The
Cabala*] down the public neck as one of the six best sellers of
the Spring."

He needed to be cured of loneliness; he had not yet learned
to live contentedly without the enfolding embrace of one person
or place. He felt that he had no "sturdy last resource against the
occasional conviction 'I don't belong.'"

Or did the source of his discontent lie elsewhere? At the Mac-
Dowell Colony in New Hampshire that July 1926, he chose to
believe that it did. He was out of sorts simply because he hadn't
been writing. Now that he was hard at work on the new novel
he was more cheerful. *The Bridge* would "fairly stagger even those
who like the first."

From nine until three the only intruders were the boy bringing lunch and Mrs. MacDowell, who would drive up to his cottage in a horse-drawn trap to regale him with tales of her student days. Never a man to keep unpublished pages to himself, Thornton read aloud paragraphs of *The Bridge* in the evenings to his fellow colonists. "Every morning," he wrote Amy, "it flows off my pen for an hour, almost without effort"; it was going to be "desperately sad."

With *The Cabala* in its third printing and the English edition enjoying a respectable sale,* Thornton felt "oh so lucky in everything" except money; he still hadn't received any royalty checks. Were the Bonis letting the dividends collect until he asked for them? Checking his contract he saw that a first payment was not due until February 15, 1927, a discovery that sent him in August back to the camp at Lake Sunapee, tutoring in the mornings, swimming or walking with the boys in the afternoons, supervising study hall in the evenings or taking boys to the movies.

He was at Sunapee in mid-September when it was proposed that he chaperone a twenty-year-old he'd never met, Andrew Townson, to Europe. Townson's guardians had concluded that the young man was unfit for college and needed someone like Thornton to keep an eye on him. It was a chance to travel and be paid for it; the stipend would see him through until Christmas.

But from their first hours together aboard the Cunard's RMS *Lancastria,* Thornton grasped that Andy Townson was going to be a rope around his neck. Andy didn't want to see Europe, didn't want to do much of anything but drink and play poker. He wasn't grouchy, he was inert. Since they were going to be tied to each other for two and a half months, Thornton made up his mind to be hard-boiled, live well on Townson's money and go about his own business. "If he is run over by a taxi some dawn or stakes his $5,000 letter of credit, I can be reproached, but I can't be imprisoned." Fifty years later, Townson affirmed the incompatibility. "Wilder preferred to study and I preferred to play. He was a great walker; that's why I have flat feet. We walked through Italy. Walked! Walked! Cathedrals! I never want to see another

* Longmans, Green would sell more than fourteen thousand copies of *The Cabala* over the next thirty years.

cathedral; after you've seen six or seven a day, you've had it!"

With Townson in tow, Thornton called in London on Aunt Charlotte and on the British publishers of *The Cabala,* who said they could sell quite a few more than the first one thousand they had printed. In Cambridge, he walked through the college grounds and had a good cry over "all that beauty and my lost youth." A fragment for *The Bridge* was inspired by an epitaph he read there on the left wall of Christ Church Cathedral.

There was a fortuitous rendezvous in Oxford with a Rhodes scholar from Harvard, William Nichols, whom Thornton had met five years before when he'd noticed him reading Keats in a New York restaurant. Thornton felt that their second meeting was a "solemn and almost mystical experience," and not accidental. Afterward he wrote Nichols that "all my reading in cynical authors has not robbed me of the sensation of being a disobedient and foolish actor in a play whose author (in spite of me) gives me beautiful scenes and permits me to confront some rare and noble *dramatis personae.*"

Andy was bored to death at the Grand Hotel de Russie in Rome; his chaperone was not. Revisiting the American Academy, Thornton was told that *The Cabala* had been read with scandalous delight. "Even old Romans take it as the hot stuff from the secret circles." His poet friend, Lauro De Bosis, with whom he lunched, was more perceptive, saying the book was preposterous when regarded as realism.

Annoyed with himself for having come to Europe so shackled, Thornton had a sharp attack of guilt. He was eating too magnificently on the Townson largesse, the beds were too grand, the bows of waiters and deference of chambermaids embarrassing. Wherever he went his imaginary Peruvians presented themselves — on trains, in churches and picture galleries. Anecdotes, characterizations, sometimes a single adjective floated across dining rooms. From Florence he wrote his clerical friend, Les Glenn, that it would be "such a beautiful and religious and tender book that you can steal perorations from it."

Berlin, the next stop on the Grand Tour, had as little interest for Townson as the other cities they visited. Until noon he read the news of American football or French train accidents. They lunched at expensive restaurants and took tea at five at a highly polished café with a jazz band and clientele of war profiteers' sons, South American gilded rich and demimondaines. After more sightseeing in Munich — with an exasperated Thornton feeling that he was doing everything except what he was dying to do, work — the farce ended with Andy's departure for America December 2.

Thornton had warned Lewis Baer not to set up pages of *The Bridge* that he had mailed to New York, for they were to be reworked, and bits of local color that he had picked up from a German children's book about Peru were to be added. Now he reminded Baer that Andy's departure would mean the loss of the Townson subsidy, and it would be reassuring if the Bonis sent him $150. A journal note in November, written at Capri, shows how little financial return he expected from his fiction. Writing would have to be combined with some kind of college job, perhaps a special lectureship at Yale or Harvard, if he could first establish his scholarly credentials with a book of literary criticism.

In Paris at Sylvia Beach's bookstore, Shakespeare and Company, Thornton was introduced to Ernest Hemingway, whose *The Sun Also Rises* had been published that week. He and "Hem" solemnly agreed that their immediate predecessors were quite inadequate — Sherwood Anderson, James Branch Cabell, Sinclair Lewis, Willa Cather, Edith Wharton!* Rid of Townson and with two hundred dollars in his pocket, Thornton considered proposing that he and Hemingway share a Paris studio but soon thought better of it: "He eats around with the enormous and flamboyant Rotonde crowd, and his wife is about to divorce him and his new wife is about to arrive from America; so I think I better not try." Still, Hem was "the hot sketch of all times."

Instead, Thornton rented a room in the Closerie des Lilas in Montparnasse. In the mornings he worked on *The Bridge,* and after a late one-dollar lunch he would drift in and out of churches and galleries and read Berlin papers for their drama news. When he was "extra blue," he dropped by Sylvia Beach's bookshop.

* Hemingway's opinion of Wilder was that he "represents the library" (*Selected Letters,* edited by Carlos Baker [New York: Charles Scribner's Sons, 1981], p. 30).

Relations with Amy Wertheimer had attained a certain impersonal serenity, or so he thought until fervent letters reached him
in Paris, prompting a further reminder that he could be only her
friend, "but in the most valuable sense of that word." If, as she
confided to him, she was contemplating divorce she must understand that honor would require him to see less of her. He would
not be "a careless pilferer in other people's happiness." On the
contrary, he looked forward to an "honorable, steady-minded life
[as] a sort of public character in New York's silly life — prominent
in good works for the poor, a friend of its best citizens and an
enemy of the Village and the Shuberts, and the Vanity Fair set
and the divorcees." Shades of Papa! Thornton's letter ended with
best wishes to Amy's children, "if you are still seeing them." After
one of her letters he became so dejected he couldn't work and
wandered about looking in shop windows, angry that she should
have made a matter of suffering what should have been a matter
of delight.

Paris in December was dismal, the pension on the rue Saint-
Jacques to which he had transferred was uncomfortable, the French
had no soul and he was so homesick, he wrote his mother, "that
very likely by the time you receive this letter I shall have telegraphed that I am coming and will be on my way. . . . I'm beginning to understand the conditions under which I can work, and
residence under foreign skies among few or casual friends is not
among them." A remarkable statement, given that those were
precisely the conditions under which much of his best work would
be done. It was not, he explained, that he had no acquaintances
in Paris; he had no will to see them. "They are all more or less
incomplete artists and therefore exaggeratedly interested in themselves. In Paris-American café life the sound of *MOI* is loud in
the land." His real enthusiasm was Hemingway, but Hem's private
life was so exciting that "I only go and interrupt it once in a
while." Thornton just hoped Mother was not too ashamed of him,
and if she didn't love him, he would throw himself into a river
or an ocean or a fire. "I am not married and you're all I've got.
I'm lonesome. That's all. I shall either drink and drink and drink;
or come home. Which will you have?"

He neither got drunk nor went home. Instead, he took the

train to the Riviera for a Christmas holiday at the Pension Saraman-
tel in Juan-les-Pins with Coleman Walker, ex-Lawrenceville, Yale
footballer and Rhodes scholar, and a group of other American
Oxonians, including Bill Nichols.

"Sweeter, simpler, sturdier urchins were never known," he
wrote. Nichols, who had been tutoring in Italy, showed up after
the others in the Oxford reading party and left early, but he and
Thornton hiked to Grasse, the Gorges du Loup, the Phare d'An-
tibes and to Cannes for a Debussy concert. Lodging was cheap,
wine plentiful. In Villefranche he tracked down a young Wisconsin
novelist, Glenway Wescott, whose *The Apple of the Eye* he had
liked. "Thornton started right out teaching me," Wescott recalled.
"I didn't know how to live, I didn't understand the American
people and didn't know how to handle my career. 'You must
get on the front page, a paragraph on the front page.' I must
'think it over' and do something to attract attention."

After the Rhodes scholars had gone, Thornton made the acquaintance of another American from Oxford, Robert R. R. Brooks,
later dean of Williams College, with whom he drank beer, waded
in the surf in the moonlight and discussed the mysteries of Joyce's
Ulysses. Homesick or not, you couldn't beat sun, palms, food, drink
and talk for two dollars a day.

But now what? "Whither? Why? Whence? Wherefore?" he
wrote Nichols. On the last day of January 1927 he sailed for
New York on the RMS *Asconia.*

9

The Bridge and the Champ

THORNTON'S YALE PLAY, *The Trumpet Shall Sound,* had been offered the previous year to a director of the American Laboratory Theatre in New York, Richard Boleslavsky, probably at the suggestion of their mutual friend Edith Isaacs. The play was accepted, opened off Broadway on December 10, 1926, and remained in the repertory several months. But the wordy elucidation of a master-servant relationship aroused as little enthusiasm in the audience as it did in its author, who refused any royalties, a refusal that caused consternation at home. "Mother and sister burst into tears. Father just sick of me for other reasons, i.e., because I don't get a fixed job."

The Wilders were now living on Mansfield Street in New Haven, but in order to complete the first installment of *The Bridge* out of earshot of his womenfolks' "eternal telephone conversations" Thornton rented a room in town. He feared that his whole talent would slip away unless he sat tight, concentrated, and planned ahead instead of muddling through. On Mrs. Isaacs's recommendation he applied for a Guggenheim fellowship and was turned down. Come back to Europe, Hemingway wrote from the Austrian mountains, where you can work, be warm, well-fed and ski — "skiing is a sensation like something between tearing silk and. . . ."

Thornton was about to mail Lewis Baer a chapter of *The Bridge* (which ought to "knock them cold") when his vagabond life took a new twist. Professor William Lyon Phelps, Yale's popular literary lecturer and a friend of Thornton's mother from Dobbs Ferry days, asked him to tutor a Groton dropout in Briarcliff, New York for six weeks. The promised four hundred dollars would pay for typing, publicity photographs and a pair of skates, though it meant a further delay in the novel. When the tutoring ended in mid-April Thornton was at loose ends.

Amy Wertheimer telegraphed suggesting they see *The Trumpet* together — it was still playing three nights a week in New York despite razzing by the critics — but Thornton shied away from meeting her. "You refuse a strong helpful friendship," he replied. "I cannot give you anything else. You must accept the conditions of life as things are: (1) I have never implied that I could love you, (2) You have a rare home and set of friends to whom you can serve as a great wonderful woman." It was time, he jested to Nichols, for Amy to decide whether she was going to shoot herself or him or her husband "and get it over with."

Nichols brought out this flip side of Thornton. Letters to "good old Bill" have a locker-room flavor, as if the writer were still a Thacher "freak" who had managed to strike up an acquaintance with the team captain. How "ripping" it would be if one could choose his own company; a new typewriter was "trick"; he was "dating up for dances and things"; Bill was the "best of geezers"; Thornton was swimming with "an awful nice crowd that never heard of Chekhov"; he had had a "swell bat" in New York. When he sent Nichols "lots of affection," it had to be made plain that it was "as one hearty to another." But when the regular-fella pose was dropped, Thornton's words rang true:

> Dear Bill, Your depressed letter found me in a similar condi-
> tion. How real they are while they last, and how false the
> next morning. They are made up as follows: three parts chemi-
> cal (digestion, or metabolism, or the ductless glands, probably
> the pituitary body); three parts celibacy; three parts religion
> (or whatever it will be called in the next century; Whitehead
> calls religion "what a man does with his solitariness"); three
> parts mere apprehension about the future, the whole mystery
> of tomorrow, physical, financial, social, etc.; and three parts
> homesickness. The respective appeasements are exercise, mar-
> riage, good deeds, hard work, and a return to America. But
> depressions are so valuable and so important to personality

that I trust you won't appease all of them; only keep one eye on the last.

Thornton's own depressions rose and receded like the tides. As he greeted well-wishers in his rented New Haven room on his thirtieth birthday, he seemed cheerful, but his subconscious was grieving and his nervous system didn't allow him to remain elevated for more than a few days. He accused himself of instability. A New York weekend left him "blue and lonesome." He kept losing what was left of his faith like a sixteen-year-old and wondered if the religious emotion was like dyphtheria, "where one may be a carrier, even when one no longer has it." Someday, he noted in his journal, someone would discover "that one of the principal ideas behind my work is the fear of catastrophe (especially illness and pain), and a preoccupation with the claim of a religion to meet the situation."

Meanwhile, the Bonis were getting impatient. When would the last part of *The Bridge* be delivered? Earlier chapters submitted to Edward Weeks of the *Atlantic* had been rejected by the magazine's editor, Ellery Sedgwick.

At this critical moment, July 1927, Clyde Foresman, master of Davis House, died and the Lawrenceville post was offered to Thornton. With it came four thousand dollars a year and a home. His first impulse was to say no; then he reconsidered and told Dr. Abbott that he would come in the fall and stay until the following summer, a decision influenced by the rueful thought that "although *The Bridge* is a much better book than *The Cabala,* it is a much less gaudy one and will make fewer friends among the subscribers to [the *American*] *Mercury;* that it is undeniably sad, and that I'd better not count on too many dividends." The important thing was to *get it done, now.* Within two weeks of his having accepted Lawrenceville's offer, the final manuscript was finished.

Complications. The publisher thought it wasn't long enough to justify a price of $2.50 and proposed adding six to eight illustrations. A difference of opinion arose over foreign royalties. Having no literary agent, Thornton had to fight for himself. "If your firm were in serious difficulties at the edge of bankruptcy," he wrote Baer in July,

I should be patient, but I cannot believe it is. I have always been very grateful and loyal to you for having discovered me. This loyalty is a very real thing to me and I should never dream of leaving your firm merely for bigger terms elsewhere. But my loyalty is being thrown away if you cannot be normally considerate of me these early difficult years. You have not yet caught up to the January statement, you promised me some of the spring royalties; and surely some of the advance on a book of which four-fifths is set up. I shall stay with Boni's not only for the three stipulated books, but for a whole shelfful if Boni shows some interest in me above and beyond the mere literary machine. My new job in Lawrenceville requires my furnishing a house and sends me on a number of trips this summer, so please send me my $500, Louie, and let us keep the association cordial.

He needed the money to ease the way of Clyde Foresman's widow and to "give toward my family and certain 'good works.'" Then he wanted to be floated quietly by a publisher who had faith in him. "The firm that subsidizes me must take the risk that the ultimate book may be even strange and mystical, or even obscure. Is there such a firm?"

With *The Bridge* in the printer's hands, Thornton had six weeks of liberty before starting the Lawrenceville 1927 fall term, and just to say "howdy" he dropped by the Lake Sunapee camp. He stayed all of August. Feeling bold and roaring with health after twelve-mile walks and mile-long swims, he called on "resigned and wistful" Amy Wertheimer, who proffered a piano bench and a bureau for Davis House. "Wouldn't it freeze ya'?" he wrote Isabel. Any contribution was welcome. The seven-room master's residence needed furnishings, and it needed supervision that this unhandy bachelor with no talent for housekeeping felt helpless to supply. Now, if Mother would live with him . . . look after the kitchen, the linen, the plants. Mother thought it over and agreed to come at the opening of term, but only long enough to see the new master established.

The timing was fortunate. When she arrived Thornton was in the infirmary with appendicitis. The attack was mild, and she left after two weeks, but Thornton was back in the hospital for surgery before the month was out. When *The Bridge of San Luis Rey* reached the bookstores he was convalescing in New Haven and itching to get on with his teaching — "otherwise, what will become of my SALARY."

Dedicated to his mother, *The Bridge* is a 235-page speculation on the meaning of a catastrophe. "On Friday noon, July the twentieth, 1714," it begins, "the finest bridge in all Peru broke and precipitated five travellers into the gulf below."* The collapse is witnessed by a Franciscan, Brother Juniper, who resolves to find out why *those* five perished. He concludes that the wicked had been visited by destruction and the good called early to heaven. He is not absolutely sure of this, however, and for his diligent inquiries Brother Juniper is burned, along with his findings.

The author is wary of answering the question whether the collapse is accidental or designed: "Some say that to the gods we are like the flies that the boys kill on a summer day, and some say, on the contrary, that the very sparrows do not lose a feather that has not been brushed away by the finger of God."

The doomed travelers include an eccentric, ugly, drunken Marquesa de Montemayor, consumed by unrequited love for her daughter. The daughter escapes her mother's smothering passion by going to Spain, only to be followed by eloquent, demanding letters that "had to take the place of all the affection that could not be lived." The Marquesa plunges to her death along with her maid, Pepita, a devout girl whom the Abbess Doña Maria of Peru had thought of making her successor. The third casualty is a foundling, Esteban, who, after the death from infection of his twin brother, Manuel, tries to hang himself, feeling shut out from love. Then comes Uncle Pio, a devotee of beautiful women and Spanish literature and the protector, instructor and worshiper of an actress, Camila, who herself despairs after losing her beauty. She rejects Uncle Pio's offer to care for her but allows him to take her young son away to be educated. The boy is the fifth victim of the collapse.

* An earlier version ran: "On Friday noon April 17 [Thornton's birthday], 1781 the suspension bridge made by the Incas over the Rivelerro, the grandest gorge in Peru, broke [and] carried five souls to their death."

Because the English edition had been published prior to the American, English reviews were the first to arrive. The schoolmaster was stunned. E. V. Lucas had "come upon nothing lately so original and striking." Cyril Connolly in the *New Statesman* thought the "subtle idea" had been admirably worked out "and leaves a vivid impression of society in the golden age of the most aristocratic capital of Latin America"; Vita Sackville-West (the *Observer* of November 20, 1927) called it "an extremely competent piece of work." Arnold Bennett (the *Evening Standard*) had never heard of Mr. Wilder but *The Bridge* was "an absolutely first-rate work, it dazzled me by its accomplishment." R. A. Taylor (the *Spectator*) described it as a "well-sung motet, while the intricate beauty of the style is like a white orchid." It quickly entered the London *Observer*'s best-seller list.

The American reception was no less flattering. Supreme Court Justice Benjamin N. Cardozo wrote that it was "very wonderful. . . . I learned [some of the sentences] almost automatically, by heart."* It was a better book than *The Cabala,* said the *New York Times,* with a "style which is learning to conceal its art." To Clifton P. Fadiman in the *Nation* (December 14, 1927), this "very beautiful book" was proof "that an American, if he be willing to exercise rigorous selection, understatement and a measured observance of the prose styles of the masters, can create a novel instinct with a pure grace." "Not for months have I enjoyed a story so," wrote Harry Hansen in the *World.* Isabel Paterson of the *New York Tribune* called it a "little masterpiece." John Farrar guessed it wouldn't win the Pulitzer Prize (he was wrong), "but by cracky, it should." Among serious reviewers, only Edmund Wilson in the *New Republic* of August 8, 1928, belatedly expressed reservations; the author had not written the book Wilson wanted: "Thornton Wilder's feeling for national temperaments . . . had already appeared in *The Cabala* as one of his most striking gifts. But I wish . . . that he would study the diverse elements that go to make the United States, and give us *their* national portraits."

Almost overnight, a bonfire of acclaim spread across the land. Burton Rascoe telegraphed for something to print in his *Bookman.*

* Letter to Aline Goldstone, in George S. Hellman's biography, *Benjamin N. Cardozo* (New York, McGraw-Hill, 1940), p. 283.

Long-distance calls, cables, telegrams every twenty minutes, letters, invitations poured in. Someone wanted to adapt *The Bridge* as a play. "As for Thornton," Mother wrote William Lyon Phelps, "I always knew him for a gifted and altogether a choice spirit. But I confess to you that I feared that his very fastidiousness might separate him from the common lot. I mean make him superior and highbrow. Now I know the humanity in him is strong enough to balance the other. So I am not so much 'proud' as thankful and content."

By December 1927, the Bonis knew they had struck oil. Within two months, *The Bridge* had become the most popular book in public libraries and had earned Thornton $20,000 in royalties. He redeemed $8,000 in insurance against which his father had borrowed and put his mother on an allowance. He was being pressured by his publishers to pump the publicity as hard as he could; he advised them to "keep cool like Coolidge," avoid excessive statements and recognize that "every good paragraph is an almost. There is some little flaw in judgment or vowel sounds or speed. I haven't a copy here or I would take you by the lapel and lead you remorselessly through the 'purple passages.' Spare us the more obvious canvassing." And spare the author. He was half dead, buying Lawrenceville boys their railway tickets to Wisconsin or Denver for Christmas holidays, correcting exams; he hadn't a moment to get "anything more than intermittent thrills out of the reviews." He wanted to escape to sun and quiet, which would cost a lot, but "you can only pretend to be young once. I definitely know that I shall be old next year." Could the Bonis send him $350?

There are novels that bloom brilliantly for a season and wither; *The Bridge* was a sturdy perennial. *Time* of March 3, 1958, would report that more than two million copies had been sold to date and that it had been translated into some two dozen languages. By November of 1981, Pocket Book sales alone would reach 1,189,764.

Nothing this sensational had ever hit Lawrenceville. The boys had been vaguely aware that the master of Davis was an author, but when long after publication, the news broke that *The Bridge* had won a 1928 Pulitzer Prize, he was ten feet tall. Would he refuse the prize, a student asked, as Sinclair Lewis had done? Would his Yale friend Steve Benét refuse the Pulitzer *he* had won that year for *John Brown's Body,* Thornton asked? No, "the refusal of praise is the desire to be praised twice again." Reaction at the school was not unmixed with jealousy. "Many of the congratulations were, I thought, mechanical, overly polite, frankly envious," said one student. "One or two were even on the borderline of rudeness."* But New York publishers practically camped in tents on Lawrenceville lawns, pushing for Thornton's signature on a contract. The phone kept ringing; every day's mail brought requests for interviews, autographs, inscribed copies. It was hard to keep one's mind on French verbs. You write a book, Thornton said, and it "raises such a gas screen that you are never able to write another."

He had written that the bridge connecting us to one another, and to death, is love, and love is "a sort of cruel malady through which the elect are required to pass in their late youth and from which they emerge, pale and wrung, but ready for the business of living." But the bridge (love) collapses, and people no worse than the rest of us die. There is no logic or justice in their deaths, yet the collapse seems poetically appropriate. Thornton doubted whether many critics understood that ambiguity; they were "stimulating without being instructive." In *The Cabala* he had begun to think that love was enough to reconcile one to the difficulty of living and dying; in *The Bridge* he was only a little surer. "Perhaps someday I can write a book announcing that love is sufficient."

Copies sent for his signature were stacked on the desk at Lawrenceville. He had no wrapping paper, no cord, no stamps, no interest, no time. Tired out by trying to be a diligent housekeeper, teacher, correspondent and famous novelist, he took off for an uneventful 1927 Christmas holiday in Miami.

Uneventful except for a new friend. But as the hymn says, "Oh, what a friend!" He was the world heavyweight champion boxer, the man who beat Jack Dempsey, Gene Tunney, to whom Thornton had written asking for an hour's talk, saying that he carried a message from Ernest Hemingway. Tunney phoned back at once

* Clark Andrews, "To Us He Was Always 'T. W.,' " *Yankee,* September 1978, p. 123.

from Florida with an invitation to dinner. A copy of *The Cabala* was on his table when the guest arrived. Tunney said he meant to read it as soon as he finished Willa Cather's *Death Comes for the Archbishop*. Here was no barroom brawler. Because it was a match of opposites, both were nourished and flattered. The ex-Marine, high-school dropout boxer was rubbing shoulders with erudition; the schoolmaster–novelist was identified with an international symbol of manly prowess.

The only other encounter of note that Christmas occurred on the train north to New York. Thornton fell into conversation with producer Jed Harris, *wunderkind* of Broadway, and they came to an understanding that Harris would have first refusal on Thornton's next play.

He was still "dog tired" when he returned to Davis House from his holiday but was committed to carry on until the summer break, when he would be free to resume his deferred leave of absence. Even then he suspected that the "leave" would mark his permanent separation from Lawrenceville. Classroom and administrative duties on top of the hullabaloo of celebrity status left no time for literature.

Nevertheless he found time for a weekend in a house outside Wilmington, Delaware, that had been rented by another new friend, F. Scott Fitzgerald. "All is prepared for February 25," Fitzgerald had informed Edmund Wilson. "The stomach pumps are polished and set out in rows, stale old enthusiasms are being burnished. . . . There will be a small but select company, coals, blankets, 'something for the inner man.' " Wilson had not known Thornton and was surprised to find him a man of positive, even peppery opinions. At dinner the first evening, Wilson wrote, "We were floating divinely on good wine and gay conversation, in which I noted, however, that Wilder, though extremely responsive, remained sharply and firmly non-soluble."*

After dinner and a number of drinks, Fitzgerald, who was not nonsoluble, said he had something to show Thornton and invited him upstairs to the attic. When they got there, Fitzgerald stumbled on a gun, picked it up and waved it around; it accidentally went

---

* *The Shores of Light* (New York: Farrar, Strauss and Young, 1952), p. 379.

off, the bullet lodging in the wall and narrowly missing Thornton. When the incident was recalled to Fitzgerald the next morning, he was appalled; he had blanked it out. Thornton never forgot it.

Their ensuing correspondence was a candybox of compliments. Fitzgerald wrote that *The Cabala* was the very best thing that had come out since Hemingway and that he was grateful for Thornton's friendship, "for it is that, and for being such a hell of a nice person as well as a fine workman. . . . The hit you made with other members of this family simply can't be told." Thornton drafted three replies, tore them up, and in the fourth, which he sent, wrote that he had filled his eyes "with more than they can digest for a long while and my affections with more than they can ever consent to lose. For instance, I met the beautiful and wonderful Zelda and feel as if I had been no-end-awkward and inadequate beside her. Anyway, I know that she understands that in my fashion I was happy and excitedly interested in everything. And now I am more than ever eager to live near you someday on some European beach with long lazy days for talking and just mooning about." It was wonderful to have been liked and told so, "for the self-confidence that I have exhibited toward my work I have never been able to extend to my person." As requested, he sent some French books to Zelda, who found them "divine and very depressing" and hoped he would meet them in Paris, "and we could all go and write novels on the Arc de Triomphe."

Thornton was a fan of *The Great Gatsby* and had written Fitzgerald from Lawrenceville that they ought to have long talks on "what writing is all about"; he would be "awfully proud" if Fitzgerald "arrived in my guest room sometime." When the Fitzgeralds again invited him to Delaware in March, Thornton replied that he would love to come; it depended on the boys' grades in the spring term. The Davis House scholarship was one of the lowest in school and he couldn't let the headmaster start roaring, "No wonder it's low, Wilder is never there. He is always off in New York or Wilmington or somewhere."

Thornton was counting on summer residence at the MacDowell Colony in 1928 to get him well launched on his third novel, *The Woman of Andros,* one that would be "full of inner hopes and dejections . . . finally a religious book, I can do no other," he told his onetime fellow instructor at Lawrenceville, Les Glenn. The plan was abandoned when parents of three Lawrenceville students — Henry Noy, Clark Andrews and Duff McCullough — would not permit their boys to travel abroad unless accompanied by an older person, and the chaperone they had in mind was the master of Davis House. Thornton was agreeable, persuading himself that he could work in some little house in England within call of his charges. Mother, Isabel and Janet would go along.

Apart from this European trip, Thornton was projecting two other moves — building a house outside New Haven for his parents, sisters and himself, and quitting the Bonis for Harper & Brothers.

Eventual extrication from Boni was probably inevitable. Cass Canfield of Harper's had shown keen interest in the young novelist, especially after his Pulitzer Prize, but no switch in publisher was then possible. Thornton was under contractual obligation for his first three books and felt a personal debt to Lewis Baer for having helped rescue him from obscurity. Moreover, royalties were now mounting. "Let it accumulate, I suppose," he told Baer, though he might need another "five grand (hard-boiled idiom picked up from Tunney) on sailing. Anyway, I am not sore at you — in fact you are a swell publisher." The first indication of the impending break appeared in a letter to his mother, marked "Secret." He would abide by his contract and give two more books to Boni, but in June 1928 Harper's would start giving him five thousand dollars a year for three years. Thereafter, all his books would be Harper's, except for playlets published by Coward-McCann.

Why not relax at my Adirondack camp after the Lawrenceville commencement and before sailing, Tunney wrote Thornton, and see how a champion trains for a big fight? "You could keep in good shape by doing some of my exercises with me!!" Don't publicize it, Thornton implored Baer. "I don't want the cordial relations touched by mutual compliments in public. Eventually (God knows) there will be publicity enough from it." He was right, and he was partly responsible for the ensuing hoopla. Interviewed by the *New York Times* on June 13, Thornton announced that he hoped to rent Henry James's house at Rye in the south of England, that Tunney would join him there briefly, that they would then hike in Switzerland, after which Thornton would adjourn to a Greek island to get away from the literary racket, "just as Gene hopes to get away from the prize-fight racketeers." A house for the Wilders was rented in Surrey, but it was not Henry James's.

Questioned by a reporter from the *Bulletin* of Glasgow, Thornton said that it was "quite true that Gene is a great student of literature, and even when training for a fight he spends a lot of time reading. Not long ago I was in a canoe with him on a lake in the Adirondacks and our craft overturned. Tunney had a copy of Hazlitt's essays. It went down with him, but when he came up again that book was between his teeth! When we go on our walking tour we shall make for unfrequented places unknown to the tourist, where there will be opportunities for quiet conversation and literary talks."

The hiking expedition with Tunney had been Thornton's idea. Tunney wrote in January 1928 of his wish "to go abroad this fall but have had only vague notions of what I would do when there. Your outline of the proposed trip with you is just exquisite. I love the idea. That, to me, would be the most perfect way of doing Europe." In early March, Tunney repeated "in no unmistakable terms" that he would join Thornton either in England, France or the Greek islands, but would prefer London in August, "or about the time your 'charges' return to the United States. The late summer and fall will be mine with which to do as I please, and nothing could possibly please me more than spending it with you in the manner you propose. I am watching your rise from the side-lines, and I hope all this lionizing will not affect your well-balanced head. Gosh! I wish I could see you in the privacy of my room here or in New York and talk without interruption. You are a 'kindred-spirit' and our 'kinship' started aeons and aeons ago on some spiritual plain of eternity."

Lawrenceville student Clark Andrews's recollection of the week in Surrey was of the Wilder women forever running upstairs and downstairs, "setting things right." Mrs. Wilder quietly insisted on her maternal prerogatives: a request for a glass of water, for Thornton to have the lawn mowed, or for him to drive to the village inn for some special kind of cake. And she was always after him to buy a new suit, Andrews noted. "Something else besides gray, please. And Thornton, do you always have to wear that dismal little sweater underneath?" Her mild asperity was balanced by Isabel's compliant devotion: "She followed him around like a puppydog, catering to his every wish." Younger sister Janet, eighteen, uninterested in the arts, pored over books on farm management and animal husbandry.

The boys walked with their teacher to the village, Thornton picking wildflowers for his mother, chatting with passing neighbors, giving a short lecture on Thomas Hardy and admonishing the trio to make every day extraordinary. On the train from Southampton to London he had prodded them to *look* at the countryside: "There's history in every speck of dirt. The Romans were right *here* — centuries ago. Think of that! Come now, don't go to sleep. Take deep breaths. You've only got 70 years. Keep turning your head in all directions. Don't blink."*

In Paris with his mother, Thornton ran into Hemingway, who commanded them to come right then to meet his wife, Hadley, and baby, "Mr. Bumby," for lunch. "You've got to, I won't take no for an answer." They shouldn't intrude, Thornton demurred. No, said Hemingway, you walk around the block and I'll break the news, "but mind you, you're going to get potluck." The Wilders gave in, Hadley seemed pleased, the baby was bouncy, and they sat down to paté and French bread. When Hemingway saw paté on the table he screamed at his wife, "I promised them potluck, you've gone and spoiled everything, you've shown off, you've made me a fool." Hadley retreated in tears and the Wilders soon left.

As expected, newspapers were playing up the story that Wilder and Tunney were going to hike in the Swiss Alps. "All the racket," Thornton wrote Bill Nichols, "and the literary introductions leave a bad taste in my mouth. And I wish the noble Gene weren't so famous. I'm gnawing a curious discontent. I hate all the by-products of literature except the money." Tunney was "awfully nice," but at bottom "a little bewildered and pathetic."

The travelogue of the Pulitzer Prize novelist and the heavy-

* Clark Andrews, "To Us He Was Always 'T. W.,' " pp. 152–54. "His bubbling, nervous enthusiasm was constantly urging us on. He was always at the ready, always on the go."

weight champ who, it was said, read *King Lear* while shaving, was to be among the most publicized mini-events of the twenties. The *New York Times* headlined their plan "to ramble about France and Germany for culture" after Tunney's fight with Tom Heeney on July 26. (He knocked Heeney out in the twelfth round.) A photographer caught them in business suits, standing upright on the ice on Mont Blanc. It was the most strenuous climb of the trip. Most of their "walk" was ridden in a sports car given Tunney by Raymond Graham of the Graham-Paige automobile company.

From Chamonix in late September they drove to Avignon. "We've been under cover for a week and a half (except for some local items)," Thornton reported, "and I hope to keep it up. Today Arles and Les-Baux. We did some fine long walks to many of the heights around Aix and Chamonix." But to Isabel the next day, he wrote: "We do everything in an auto! I long for walking and resting and staying somewhere. But at least we saw some of the splendid mountain roads."

Wedding arrangements nearly wrecked their trip. Tunney wasn't in Europe just for hikes; he was there to marry Polly Lauder, and cables from the Lauders left in doubt whether the ceremony would be held in Rome, Marseilles or Trieste. Church dispensations and a birth certificate had to be obtained. "We called on American consuls everywhere, trying to get the law in these matters. Gene is a prince, but I paid an awful price in public kidding for those few weeks of comradeliness."

Thornton had been asked to stand up as best man and declined, and the refusal or some other misunderstanding ruffled the Champ, who admitted he had been "a bit peeved for a moment yesterday after you had for the third time during the day refused to do one thing or other that I suggested. I asked you to lunch, drive and dinner and you refused every suggestion. I may have said something after the third refusal, for I was mad enough to. If I did please forgive me." As to who owed whom and what for the expenses of the trip, Tunney suggested they were at a standoff: "I borrowed 1,000 [francs] from you which leaves you in the red ink for 1462 francs. Surely your layout was twice that or 2924 francs. If not you can give me what balance is due me. P.S.: You paid for my alcohol (rubbing), cotton and adhesive tape. I probably owe you."

Despite the rift, Tunney remembered the trip warmly. "It was all so much fun," he wrote Wilder forty-three years later, "the world a much pleasanter one, it seemed. Or was it just because we were so much younger. I think of you always with affection."

Having seen Tunney off on his honeymoon, Thornton revisited the pension in Juan-les-Pins, where he had had such joyous days with the Oxford reading party. Three chapters and notes for *The Woman of Andros* were meditated during walks to Cannes, Grasse, Vence, Cagnes. In Villefranche he again called on Glenway Wescott, whose second novel, *The Grandmothers,* had come out in 1927. They discussed *The Cabala.* "It can't have fooled you, least of all you," Thornton said smoothly, "penetratingly intelligent as you are, with the added advantage of expatriation. You must have recognized my little derivations, my transparencies; seen right through them!" At times, he made Wescott think of a boy climbing a tree, "carefully placing his feet on limb above limb, finally peering into a bird's nest containing eggs or little birds, and holding his breath."*

Mother had returned to New Haven and in November Isabel joined her brother in Munich. He was to become her life's work, a career she embraced gladly, for she respected him and was proud of his confidence in her. At twenty-eight, small, brisk, bright, emotional, she was happy to be with him, happy to serve him as companion, booster, audience, critic, record keeper, errand girl. They had a round of theatergoing. Thornton's German came back by leaps and bounds. The first chapter of *The Woman of Andros,* which he described as a lyrical invocation of paganism with premonitions of Christianity, was read to an elite circle in Vienna. News from home was heartening. *The Bridge* was a runaway best-seller. His book of playlets, *The Angel That Troubled the Waters,* had sold over ten thousand copies, and two three-minute playlets, *The Message* and *Jehanne,* had been printed in *Theatre Arts.* Thornton and his country in late 1928 were riding the crest of the wave. Prosperity wasn't around the corner, it was here, and America was singing "Makin' Whoopee."

The only dark cloud was a lecture contract Thornton had signed before leaving for Europe. The added income would be welcome

---

* *Images of Truth* (New York: Harper & Row, 1962), pp. 247–48.

and platform appearances would promote book sales, but he disliked blatant self-advertisement, whatever he may have said to Glenway Wescott, and now wished he had a clever lawyer who could find a loophole and get him out of the contract.

The speaking tour set up by the Lee Keedick Agency was bruising — 144 one-night stands — and yet the lecturer's repeated regrets at having undertaken it were not the whole truth. Thornton enjoyed being on stage. Three days after his ship docked in New York, February 29, 1929, he was on the train, and between March 2 and March 28 touched down in Wellesley, New Haven, Montreal, Saratoga Springs, Poughkeepsie, Toronto, South Hadley, Northampton, Methuen, Boston, Providence, Upper Montclair, Philadelphia, Washington, D.C. and Pittsburgh. The following month he did his stint in Cleveland, Terre Haute, Indianapolis, Dayton, Cincinnati, Columbus, Detroit, Chicago, St. Louis, Kansas City, Dallas, New Orleans, Nashville and Iowa City.

The day in Iowa City, April 30, was typical. Eight o'clock breakfast with a professor at the state university, interview at eleven, lunch with the English faculty at twelve, lecture at three, a roundtable conference at four, dinner in company. Somewhere between Wellesley and Iowa City, he wrote an introduction to Philip Sassoon's *The Third Route,* in which he expressed confidence that life would be beautiful two or three hundred years hence, however different. Deploring the future was "a subtle gratification of self-pity."

In hotel rooms at night he read scores of letters about *The Bridge* that Isabel had forwarded — pessimists charging that it was a demonstration of disorder, frustration and cruelty; optimists claiming it was a fable of sweetness and light and scolding him for not having had the courage to affirm triumphantly that all is apple pie in the spiritual realm. To each he answered that he had taken no sides but had tried to hang in midair, "suspended over all that valley of maladjustments — of loves misplaced — of good impulses wasted." Love had so many forms. Had it been cynical to say of the actress Camila that love like hers, "though it expends itself in generosity and thoughtfulness, though it give birth to visions and to poetry, remains among the sharpest expressions of self-interest"?

He discoursed in one lecture, always with a great deal of athletic to-ing and fro-ing, on the story in *The Bridge* of the twins Esteban and Manuel:

I was myself a twin brother, though only for a few hours. The realization has remained with me merely in the realm of amused and affectionate speculation as to what it would be like to have an identical self going about the world with one, writing perhaps, collaborating perhaps. But before I knew it, these tranquil speculations turned out in the book to be more and more serious. But for me the real thing I was interested in throughout that chapter was the sufferings of inarticulate people. People who just endure. I was a schoolmaster in a boy's preparatory school, and my daily life has been anything but literary. The boys in my house were between 15 and 20 and you may well believe that in this world of apparently cheerful, healthy athletes and reluctant learners, there is many a sudden vista of bewilderment or despair or just the vague ache of growing up, of what's-the-world-about. When therefore I say the *inarticulate* I don't mean the *stupid.* Or else I mean *stupid* in the sense that even the wisest human beings are stupid in the face of the combinations of circumstance and the infinitely difficult game of trying to be useful to one's friends and one's community. So at the end of the Book about Manuel and Esteban I put in thoughts from five really happy years at Lawrenceville School. They have come out in that story in an apparently unhappy form, but I hope there is a strain there that is not wholly dejected, made up of a tremendous admiration for the so-called inarticulate with their endurance and their loyalty.

With another audience, he shared his enthusiasm for Madame de Sévigné and told how her letters to her daughter, although they found no specific counterpart in his life or the lives of the people he knew best, could offer a symbol of isolation and loneliness:

So I lifted it out of history. I transferred it to Peru, and with a kind of cruelty, I made the factors much harsher. I made

Madame de Sévigné (as it were) older and uglier and slightly unbalanced. Then I clinched the matter by putting beside her that little girl, Pepita, who personified just the opposite traits — self dependence, self control, courage. Perhaps I shouldn't say I put them there — for in the earlier stages of writing, these things are done in excitement and not by calculation. The climaxes and the contrasts, the plot, are arranged by the very concentration with which one broods over the situation.

Between lectures in Massachusetts he had several hours with Bill Nichols, now an assistant dean at Harvard, and when they met again in June, Thornton allowed that he was "sunk in laziness, aimlessness, procrastination, footlessness and indifference." The only remedy for these corroding blues was work. But when you're down you wonder why you should work. "Why not just sit forever in the stacks of the library casually turning divers pages, or sit talking forever in the Elizabethan Club with any passerby, and sit at home by the piano and drive one's mother and sisters insane with one's moods and dissonances? WHY NOT?" He didn't know. At that moment he was "turning slowly in my vitals the dagger of self reproach." If only life in America were like that in the South Seas (as unfamiliar to him as Peru), "with oceans of time for talk and silence together, for an almost vegetable comradeliness, instead of torn moments and vexed hours."

On the other hand, he told Nichols brightly, he had fashioned a "nice little patch of *Andros* the other night." And the night before that he had been in seventh heaven at a rehearsal of the Yale madrigal choir. And it probably didn't matter that his lecture in Providence hadn't gone well or that he couldn't find anything worthwhile to read or that in Boston he had inadvertently worn a coat and trousers that didn't match.

He lost his voice in Providence and had to rest in New Haven for a week, to the delight of his family. They were enchanted when he fell sick, "first because it will teach me a lesson not to go about 'that way,' and second because they can *hover* about and get things settled," such things as their future residence.

Property for the family home on Deepwood Drive in Hamden, Connecticut had been bought in March 1929 and its construction costs were a worry to the breadwinner, despite an $8,000 advance in 1928 on *The Woman of Andros* and $44,000 in royalties, largely from *The Bridge.* He would earn $73,375 in 1929, but a substantial portion of it would go to the house, his parents, his brother and sisters, Clyde Foresman's widow and a needy Yale classmate. He therefore asked for a further advance. The Bonis gave him $2,500.

He did not mention to his publisher another of his concerns, the rapid decline of Papa. Amos, who was doing graduate work at Yale on the history of religion, had come upon him in New Haven sitting on a block of stone, dizzy, overcome by heat, needing to be led home. Shortly thereafter Amos received a letter from the *Journal-Courier* editor, wanting to talk about the condition of Mr. Wilder, who perhaps did not realize that it "wasn't wise for him to keep up doing what he was doing." It was suggested that he think about retiring. It was all handled tactfully. Papa resigned, took a room several blocks from home where he could nap and be out of the way, and over the next five years went from one sanitorium or health farm to another.

From 1929 on, Thornton was the main support of his parents and Isabel and, beginning in the mid-thirties, of Charlotte as well. His elder brother and youngest sister made their own ways. The Reverend Amos was destined to become a distinguished biblical scholar and teacher, professor at the University of Chicago and at Harvard. "Baby" Janet, at home in the world of landscapes, plants and animals, won a scholarship in graduate school, a Ph.D. and had a brief spell of teaching zoology before her marriage. Her interest in a scientific career had had a skeptical response from Papa, who wanted his girls to become "good Christian women." "Now, Janet," he would say, "never deny a good man's love." Throughout, Mother was Thornton's exemplar. If the counsels of this Scottish clergyman's daughter were prompted by moral and religious principles, she never voiced them, relying, said Thornton, on the only resources mothers have invoked for some time: "a practical sense and her own example." He deferred to her and teased her by singing some risqué ditty at the top of his lungs while she cooked in the kitchen.

Isabel's role had been foretold in a letter of Mother's to Amos in 1917: "Isabel is getting her clothes ready to go away to a physical culture summer course at the Battle Creek sanitarium in Michigan. It is her father's latest and least unhappy scheme (to my thinking), and besides what shall I do without her. Janet and I depend on her for errands, services of all sorts at home, companionship and, in fact, everything." Isabel, then twenty, had been to thirteen different schools but somehow managed to be the only Wilder child without a college degree — something she would always regret. Her day-to-day work for Thornton began in 1929, when he was off lecturing and she dealt with some of his mail. From then on, whatever her own ambitions or accomplishments, and they included three novels and backstage experience at the Yale Drama School, Thornton's well-being was her principal object. Unmarried, lively, strong-willed, and with a good mind and a love of literature and drama, she became his hostess, his stand-in at ceremonies, interpreter to hundreds of inquiring writers of theses and the handler of contract details in which he had little interest. She championed him when he chose not to defend himself, offered discerning but supportive comments on his work; in brief, she carried whatever of his burdens she could.

The interdependence benefited them both. Isabel had a home in Hamden ("The House *The Bridge* Built"), a challenging occupation, access to celebrated and often interesting people, courtesies due the sister of a well-known author, opportunities to travel and financial security, though the security was late in coming. It took a while for Thornton to appreciate that she needed a regular allowance. He was like the merchant who keeps his accounts on the back of envelopes, forgetting to send bills, giving away goods when touched by distress, enjoying the customers' company more than their cash. He needed a storekeeper and got one in Isabel. That their collaboration over half a century generated as little friction as it did can be credited to mutual need, affection and respect for each other's intelligence and privacy.

With six lectures to go in 1929, Thornton had to admit that despite the social entanglements, bad hotels, monotonous train rides and moments when he thought he would "break into a thousand pieces," the crisscrossing of America had given him an idea for a picaresque novel that he would write in the thirties about a traveling textbook salesman. And there had been diverting letters from strangers along the way, such as one from Mabel Dodge Luhan. Of course he had heard of her. She had lived in Italy, had been a friend of Bernard Berenson, of Leo and Gertrude Stein, of John Reed, Emma Goldman, Walter Lippmann, "Big Bill" Haywood. She knew everyone on the frontiers of modern art and bohemian politics. At her avant-garde "evenings" on Fifth Avenue in the early twenties, wrote Daniel Aaron in his *Writers on the Left*, "young men and women of the middle class could consort with notorious radicals who were happily subverting the social order by word and deed." She had ended up in New Mexico, married an Indian, her fourth husband, and taken up the Indian cause. Now she wanted Thornton to "do something" about it: "I don't know a thing about you — what you are like or anything," she wrote.

> Whether you are shy and simply couldn't face coming to stay with a stranger after a mere letter like this, and I don't know who you know who knows me who might reassure you or, in fact, almost anyone I suggested might do just the opposite if you asked them. It's very difficult. Anyway, I must just take a chance and send you this invitation and ask you to come and stay with us here [in Taos] and take a peek at it all and after all if you don't like it you could just spit it out, couldn't you? . . . Anyway — I throw this letter out to you and leave it at *that* — and if it rings a bell in you, you come. Somebody *must.*

Thornton did go to Taos, but not in 1929, and not to write about Indians.

Hers was one of ten to fifteen letters a day that got handwritten replies. He could no more leave letters unanswered, or answered perfunctorily, then he could give up smoking. In the years ahead, he corresponded with girls casually encountered on ships, scholars who shared his passion for James Joyce, wartime buddies, boys he had taught, high school students playing in *Our Town*, alcoholic writers, actors needing an introduction to a producer, hostesses with whom he had dined — joking, airy, counseling, admonishing letters, opening with a gay salutation, giving a short account of where he'd been, where he was going, what he'd been doing and planning and how he felt about it, followed by a whispered confidence ("didja know?" "hadja heard?"), an illuminating quotation, and ending with a bugle call to courage, confidence, joy.

One letter in 1929, from Robert Maynard Hutchins, opened a door Thornton thought he had closed when he quit Lawrenceville. Recently appointed head of the University of Chicago, Hutchins urged Thornton to come and teach there in 1930. The salary was attractive $666.66 a month. More attractive was the prospect of "a congenial daily routine to occupy me while the dim notions for books shape themselves." The invitation was hastily snapped up.

Before leaving for a month at the MacDowell Colony in June 1929, Thornton bought his first automobile, a runabout with a rumble seat that he called his meditation chamber. When Isabel drove, he sat in the back and thought. When she stopped, he joined her in the front seat and told her what he had been thinking. Every ride was an adventure, especially when he took over. He somehow survived his ineptness at the wheel, but, as in *The Bridge*, no one ever knew whether it was by design or accident. The only certainty was dented fenders.

Mornings at the colony were devoted to drafts of *The Woman of Andros*, afternoons and evenings to reading, Bach cantatas, correspondence and journal notes. Journal entries that June and the following month at Lake Sunapee abound in aphorisms, many finding their way into the new novel. Having in mind the "so-called Christers at Yale," he jotted down: "Of all the forms of genius goodness has the longest awkward age," a line he used in both *The Woman of Andros* and his later novel, *Heaven's My Destination*. Or, "Gossip is the art of retelling someone else's tragedy as though it reflected credit on one's self." Or, "The extravagances we commit under passion seem to have little effect on the life of the soul, but the remorse that follows them is its very food."

By now it must be evident that any flight plan of Thornton's was as variable as a butterfly's. He had expected, after a month at MacDowell, to spend the rest of the summer at Lake Sunapee

but instead drove to Maine to be with his ailing father. Months
went by without any of the things he meant to do getting done.
He hadn't taught himself Greek or reread the classics he had to
lecture on in Chicago the following spring. He hadn't read the
eight thousand pages of Goethe he had assigned himself, "nor
carried out any of those projected self improvements that visit
me at midnight." Although he completed two chapters of *The
Woman of Andros* at the colony and blocked out a novel that would
come after it, he said he would much rather have settled down
to a series of six plays. But settling down didn't mean staying
put. In early September, he and Mother were crossing the Atlantic,
bound for Bruges, Ghent, Antwerp and England; thence to Paris
for tea with the Gene Tunneys, lunch with the Louis Bromfields,
dinner with the Hemingways. After a week of music in Munich,
they were back in London for theater and partying with Thornton's
"treasured friend" and London's literary-political hostess, Sibyl
Colefax.

On the return voyage the latter part of October, he applied
himself to *The Woman of Andros,* for which a first printing of fifty-
two thousand copies had been announced, considerably more than
the first edition of *The Cabala* but fewer than *The Bridge.* Reading
over what had been written, he had qualms:

> Is it drenched I ask myself with the wrong kind of pity? The
> perpetual harping on the supposition that people suffer within.
> Am I sufficiently realist? In *The Bridge* the pathetic could lie
> suspended in its irony with less danger of going wrong. By
> irony I mean not the savage forms (Dante, Swift) but the charm-
> ing forms associated with Renan. Charm-irony is the comple-
> ment and sister of pathos, but it is the enemy of deeper feelings
> and in this book it plays little part. Without charm-irony there-
> fore this book must run the greater danger, in committing
> itself to anguish and to the profoundest inner life, and if it
> fails artistically it will be all the more instructive to me, not
> only as a writer, but as a person.

He made so many changes and insertions he had to recopy the
manuscript in its entirety before handing it over to the Bonis in

New York October 29. He saw friends that day and wrote fifteen letters, none mentioning the stock market collapse on "Black Thursday" five days before.

What was left of 1929 slipped by. Concerts, a get-together at the home of a Yale dean, a reception for Yale's president, a "Lawrenceville Bang" at Mory's, a Princeton football game, supper with Amos in Boston, a talk to the Lawrenceville women's club, Thanksgiving at home. In December he saw the Tunneys, editor Maxwell Perkins, and attended a meeting of the Admissions Committee of the Century Club. Christmas Day he was on a train west for more lectures. Classroom duties in Chicago would not occupy him until spring. The well-known teacher-author-lecturer had every reason to be pleased with himself. Yet on his way to California he wrote Les Glenn that he was "a weak vessel, rubbishy, shifting, meaningless, unstable. Every day I resolve to improve and get nowhere. Is it the price I must pay for the artistic temperament and is everyone as tinny as I am?"

Los Angeles seemed to him a wide-eyed twelve-year-old, San Francisco adult to the square inch. He rode the ferry to Berkeley and revisited childhood homes on Dwight Way and Prospect Street, surprised at how little the neighborhood had altered. Following a talk at the Thacher School, "about one hundred times more beautiful than I had remembered it," he fretted that he hadn't been fascinating enough ("I go frantic unless I think I am at least reasonably interesting everybody"). After Seattle came Banff, Chicago for preliminary talks with Hutchins, Detroit, Grand Rapids, Washington, D.C. and New York for public debates on literary matters with the English author Hugh Walpole. Thornton said he counted his days on tour like a prisoner marking off the time of his sentence.

10

Happiest Years

CHICAGO IN 1930 was a fighter's, jazzman's, writer's town; "Big Bill" Thompson's town ("Fellow hoodlums!" the mayor greeted his fellow citizens); a town of tough cops, bootlegging, rackets; of scarface Al Capone, whose pal, police reporter Jack Lingle, had just been gunned down on his way to the racetrack. It was a depression town of workers without work, evicted tenants, race riots. But it boasted a wide handsome boulevard along Lake Michigan from the Blackstone to the Drake hotels, and it was the home of a bustling university on the South Side that was being shaken up by a youthful former dean of the Yale Law School — Robert Hutchins. Thornton came to Chicago because of Hutchins; he stayed because his years there, 1930 to 1936, were the happiest of his life.

Since he had been brought in by the back door and had no previous university teaching experience, some faculty were reluctant to embrace him as a qualified colleague (where was his Ph.D.?), but doubts were soon dissipated; Hutchins's "outsider" was patently a man of letters. And he could teach! Thornton said of himself that he was a teacher rather than a writer, by which he meant that he was a teaching writer. And yet his first ten-week term, which began in April, nearly convinced him that he had waded in beyond his depth. Between preparing four weekly lectures in "classics through translation" and reading themes in "English composition, advanced," he barely stayed afloat. The first class of 160 students met at nine in the morning, the second, 26 students, at ten. After morning classes, he would go downtown to lunch at the railway station or stray Italian joints where an eavesdropper could learn a lot. He was usually in bed by half past eleven, having spent his evening in the library poring over commentaries on the classics. In the middle of the night he would wake in a sweat, wondering if he had enough notes to get through fifty minutes the next morning.

At thirty-three, he had changed little in appearance since his own graduate days. The hair was a bit thinner, the forehead higher, the eyebrows bushier, the spectacles heavier. Motionless, caught in a snapshot, he was recognizable as the schoolmaster — upright, almost prim. In motion, he was a one-man band, and if he were listening to himself, he said, he wouldn't approve of "this mixture of facts out of the Encyclopedia, of humor easily put over by reason of a little platform practice, and of faintly synthetic idealism and elevation." He pranced, scampered, raised his forefinger, gesticulated, took off his glasses, licked them clean, shoved them over his nose or into his pocket, stared into space and resumed his rapid delivery. He seemed to pay no attention to whether his jacket went with his trousers or tie with shirt. At times he looked unshaven because he had grabbed whatever bar of soap was handy that morning. On the platform as in his plays, he was an enemy of the proscenium arch. Down with the wall separating performer and audience! Draw the listener into the action by infusing the classics with such vitality that they are *here*. Charge each thought with such energy and immediacy that it cannot gather dust on a memory shelf. In the middle of a lecture, he would interrupt himself and say, "No, that's a lie; authors are liars," or, "Oh, that's just my Victrola record, I'll turn it off now." This is his fanciful description of a class in Cobb Hall, February 10:

> It is ten minutes of nine. Some of the class has arrived and sits thinking profoundly. One student laughs and is stared down by three tragedy queens and two Hamlets.
>
> Outside the door two girls are saying anguished goodbyes to their beaux. They burst into tears and cling to the men's necks. Finally they drag them into the room and the men consent to become visitors.
>
> 9:20: Mr. Wilder comes airily down the hall, in spite of the fact that he is carrying five brief cases, the Encyclopedia

Britannica and the kitchen stove. He is very cheerful. Outside the door the students of the University of Chicago make a line for him. He distributes smiles, bouquets, chocolate creams and $5 bills. He opens every door in the hall and shouts good morning, my friends.

Arriving at his own classroom, he flings down his burdens and looks about uneasily, sniffing "something's the matter here." With the speed of light he leaps to the ceiling and re-calcimines it; he repapers the walls and sandpapers the floor.

At last he is ready to begin. He takes up a MS and looks at it: "I make a point, class, of never mentioning spelling, punctuation, salability, literature, writing or books in this class. What is it we do mention? Well? Volunteers?"

Silence.

At last a tall gentleman reposing on his shoulder blade suggests:

"Arthritis."

Mr. Wilder beams. "Good! that's right. But that's not what I meant right now — Class?"

Volunteer. *Soul.*

Almost.

Volunteer. *Diaries.*

"Yes — Diaries. Everybody keep a diary. All the slyest, most intimate thoughts of your life and consequently intended for publication.

Or a story — for instance. . . ."

Katie felt tired. The hot wind blew over the cornfield into the kitchen window. Katie was ironing. She thought of her future. Would it always lie among these corn fields? She was expecting her thirteenth child any day now. Would life be one long succession of babies and ironing? What would become of her youth and beauty? She had a beautiful voice and friends had told her she should sing in opera.

Paris, that was her spiritual home. She would sell the new harvester-reaper and go to Paris. She would live. Joy.

She slipped into the bedroom to get her hat. Her eyes fell on little Alfred, Little Georgiana, little Herman and little Ingeborg, little Edweena, little Rupert, little Aspasia, and little

Thomasina, and little Peter, and little Clara, and little Simeon, and Dorusilla, and little Marie Antoinette.

And she went back to her ironing.

A tear blopped onto the flatiron and hissed.

Because he knew that authentic talents educate themselves, he had few illusions about how influential a teacher can be, but he had known three great teachers himself and was always on the alert for vitality and intellectual curiosity. A student's *wanting* to create was enough; he was there to agitate the works.

To some he seemed a Niagara of knowledge, but in fact he had to study at least as hard as his students to prepare for class. He had read and written far more than they, but he was an amateur scholar, running to keep a step ahead of his audience. So that he could have more time for research and for reading manuscripts, papers and musical scores, he vowed not to go out in the evenings. But the longer his stay in Chicago the weaker the resolve to restrict his socializing. It was easier to avoid unwanted, after-class company when he changed residence from a student dormitory to a high, sunny apartment at 6020 Drexel, where he did some of his own cooking, thereby escaping dinner-table chatter at the Quadrangle Club or moping alone in restaurants.

If the Chicago years in the early thirties were Thornton's happiest, it was principally because he was accepted as a member of a gang, most of them ten years or so younger than he, not all of them students but all fond of him, and to be liked is precious compensation to the unattached. Though bright, these easygoing companions were not intellectuals (what a relief!). They were a four-part-harmony, sit-on-the-floor-and-have-a-beer gang, and he, the veteran loner, joined in their joking, singing, talking. "Not only do I love them, but they love me," he told his friend Alexander Woollcott, jester, gossip and influential book and theater critic for the *New Yorker.* "I tremble as I write this. They love me humanly and I love them inhumanly. There they'll sit, those ten, those eleven, eating scrambled eggs and talking to one another, and that awful fact will be right there in the room. And there I will be, pressing more anchovies on them, but dead, tearless and in bliss."

The chief characters in this high-jinks crowd were Charles Newton, who Thornton said wrote the best short story ever handed into his class, and his brother, Joe; Frank Harding, John Pratt, Gladys Campbell, Gertrude Abercrombie, Elder Olson, Inez Cunningham and Lloyd Stow. Inez Cunningham was the eldest, in her late thirties, an art critic for the local Hearst newspaper, something of a collector and a member of the fashionable Arts Club in Chicago. It was she who took over furnishing Thornton's apartment on Drexel Avenue, contributing a Bonnard etching that Thornton later gave Charles Newton. Gladys Campbell taught English at University High School, Pratt and Gertrude Abercrombie were artists, Olson a poet. Stow would become chairman of the Department of Classical Languages at Vanderbilt University, Harding a rancher.

The gang got together most Saturday nights at the Newtons' three-story, rusticated brownstone on Goethe Street or at Inez Cunningham's plushier apartment on Lake Shore Drive. Thornton wanted to know the details of everyone's daily life, but the tables were not to be turned. Personal questions about himself were brushed off and he bristled at any hint of inquisitiveness about his private affairs. On one occasion, when Pratt and Newton dropped by Inez Cunningham's and found Thornton sitting on a sofa with actress Ruth Gordon and started to kid him about their relationship, he came as close to being angry as they would ever see him. The nimble, pint-sized Miss Gordon, who had first appeared on the stage in *Peter Pan* with Maude Adams and who was a year older than Thornton, was a close pal; that was all. Pratt and Newton shut up.

Liquor was plentiful and after the repeal of Prohibition Thornton made a point of contributing a bottle of Teacher's Highland Cream to the parties; as a professor, he thought the brand appropriate. Hours were passed in saloons, the direct inheritors of speakeasies — Agostino's, Vic's, Quigley's, Ballantine's, or the Shoreland Hotel, where the gang drank malt wine on winter evenings and Thornton conversed in German with Adolph the bartender. The raucous nightclub hostess, Texas Guinan, became a friend and he spent an evening in her establishment with three famous Chicago gangsters; "very agreeable young men of a beautiful candor that shames the rest of us." At five in the morning, Tex introduced him from the floor: "All right, even all of you that can't read give the boy a big hand." She later telephoned asking him to certify that she took good care of her nightclub girls. "So I wrote a letter," Thornton said, "and made an honest woman of Tex."

There was one famous cocktail party at the Shoreland, given by Thornton for Woollcott, which began in the bar downstairs and adjourned to rooms he'd rented for the evening. Charles Lederer, a nephew of movie star Marion Davies, sang Irish songs on the elevator and down the hall. Frank Harding sat in a corner, a typewriter on his lap, pounding out a stream-of-consciousness account. Thornton and Woollcott, neither of whom could be long silent, entertained each other with theater talk. A barbershop quartet started up and someone suggested a telephone serenade to playwright Ben Hecht, who was somewhere in South Carolina. "The guy on the left is flat," Hecht said when they reached him.

Thornton's Princeton mania for handball having revived, he and Harding played on the courts under Stagg Field. If they finished late and the guard had locked up, they turned off the lights, dropped out of a window some feet above the ground and, during Prohibition, proceeded to a flat on Ellis Street that dispensed a superior brand of home brew. Or they strolled through ethnic neighborhoods near the university, stopping off at Strulevitz's on Twelfth Street, where red wine was served in white china cups.

Thornton was interested in John Pratt, who later married dancer Katherine Dunham, and in 1935 the two of them collaborated on a student production of Handel's *Xerxes,* Wilder directing, Pratt designing the sets. The collaboration went so well they decided to put together an illustrated "manuscript book" patterned on the English Chatterbox Christmas reader, combining Wilder essays, stories, short plays, scraps of absurd facts, even a piano duet he proposed to write — all to be lavishly illustrated by Pratt. The book was to be dedicated to at least five thousand people, all of whom would have enough money to buy it. Having heard of the project, the *Chicago Tribune*'s critic reviewed it prematurely and was huffy when it didn't appear on schedule. It never appeared.

Among Thornton's young Chicago friends whose literary promise would be fulfilled were short story writer Katinka Loeser;

George Dillon, who translated the plays of Racine, wrote *Boy in the Wind* and won a Pulitzer Prize; Henry T. Moore, the biographer of D. H. Lawrence; Robert Ardrey, whose first play Thornton sent Jed Harris and who later wrote *African Genesis* and *The Territorial Imperative;* and John Vincent Healy, a young poet who had been stone deaf since childhood.

Gladys Campbell had a special niche. Author of a volume of poetry, *The Momentary Beach,* and head of the Poetry Club when Thornton arrived in Chicago, she became his unofficial local hostess. Both were products of a tradition that frowned on a lady's making the advances, and although she would have responded to a more positive show of affection on his part, there was never more than a light kiss and a quick embrace at parting. Picking her up one evening for a dance at the Ambassador-East Hotel, he said that he had had too much Scotch to drive and handed her the keys to the car. After a few minutes on the hotel dance floor, she found herself alone; he was whirling away by himself at the furthest end of the room. But he gave her first name to fictional characters in *Heaven's My Destination* and *The Skin of Our Teeth.*

There were two others in whom Thornton had more than a passing interest. The first, Martha Dodd, was referred to in a letter of June 26, 1933, to his family: "The girl I call 'my girl' — never fear — has just left; her father [William Dodd, professor of history] is the new ambassador to Berlin." Miss Dodd had no scruples about taking the initiative. She was a free thinker and, it was rumored, a devotee of free love. In 1933 and 1934 she bombarded Thornton with letters from Berlin, mixing rumors of intrigue in high German circles with endearments. He was "dear child," "Angel," "Thornton me darlin.' " He *must* come to Germany so that she could seduce him under an azalea bush or in the library of the embassy residence. She was not going to marry anyone else, she could swear it. He must keep tucked away in a satinwood box with a pine cone for scenting her most precious of all kisses, and when she returned she wouldn't settle for kissing the end of his nose and getting in return a warm handshake and a vote of confidence: "I wonder what it is in you that makes your life without rest, without wide skies, without tremendous storms. . . .

Don't be angry with me, I'm being petty and sad and cruel. I do love you, and I know more about the reasons of you than you think."

Those were sentiments that could lead to nothing but withdrawal on Thornton's side. There is no record of their seeing each other after she left Chicago.

The other particular friend was a philosophy major at the university, Robert Davis, whom Thornton took to Europe in 1935. Often and publicly Thornton maintained that Davis, with his "Platonic brow," was a profound philosopher, "perhaps the best of them all; grave and noble at twenty-one." No one else believed it. John Pratt's impression was that being "taken up" was embarrassing to Davis, who could have posed for an Arrow collar ad and was having a romance with artist Gertrude Abercrombie.* Later, he married a model, worked for an advertising agency and as a bit actor in California and was lost to view. In the end Thornton concluded that his soul had gone murky, "like his English style, clouds of smoke." But in the thirties, Davis seemed a paragon — silent, turbulent. Thornton arranged for his psychoanalysis, paid for his sister's dancing lessons and gave an "A" to his class paper, "A Comparison of the System of Plotinus and the Doctrines of Freud." On the SS *Ascania* in June of 1935, Thornton accepted Davis's tutelage in philosophy and from Paris wrote Gertrude Stein (they had met the previous year in Chicago) that he hoped she would receive them both in her summer home in Bilignin. "Custodian Wilder," he told her, had been showing Davis Paris, "including a night among the joints of Montmartre. I almost lost him to a *poule* at the Bal Tabarin; my loud and high-minded *No* must still be echoing among those fly-specked mirrors. I get a shy and grateful thanks the next morning."

Thornton was not aware that his paragon was writing to and receiving letters from Gertrude Abercrombie in which there was a strong suggestion that she was pregnant and that Davis was responsible. Davis did not intend to sneak out of a situation that he alone had created, but "no matter what happens," he pleaded, "do not tell Thornton. This may sound selfish and stated wholly

---

* Abercrombie's oil portrait of Thornton hangs in the Beinecke Library at Yale.

with self interest, but I assure you and with all humility say that it is not for my sake but for Thornton's." She wrote Davis off, noting in her diary that he had paid her five of eighteen dollars he owed her and that he was "a shitheel of the first water."

Thornton's infatuation with Davis was unmistakable, but there is no evidence of any intimacy beyond what he had permitted Martha Dodd or Gladys Campbell.

Thornton's two social circles — students on the South Side and Lake Forest matrons on the North Side — were kept more or less separate. Inez Cunningham was the bridge. She was one of Chicago's "Catholic swells" who had gone to Vienna, been analyzed by Alfred Adler, was a friend of Harriet Monroe of *Poetry* magazine, wrote verse herself, traveled widely, married a well-to-do advertising executive and then a New York columnist with a taste for Victorian antiques. She rode in a custom-made chauffeured limousine, helped liberal causes, was a gourmet cook and hostess to many Goethe Street gang parties. She was also one of the elegant ladies of the Art Club and Art Institute, keeping company with Alice Rouillier, "Bobsy" (Mrs. Charles) Goodspeed, Kate Brewster, and Claire Dux (Mrs. Harold Swift) who sang German lieder so beautifully.

It was a dizzy whirl, and we get a sense of its dizziness by sampling some of Thornton's extracurricular engagements in Chicago, New York and New Haven from February 4 to April 19, 1933. He lunched with Mrs. Murray Crane of *the* Cranes, Alexander Woollcott, Jed Harris, Noel Coward and with Edward Levi, a student of his and future president of the University of Chicago; dined with Sibyl Colefax visiting from London, the blind and paralyzed playwright Edward Sheldon, Marc Connelly, Robert Frost, the Goodspeeds and the Hutchinses (for Henry Luce); had evenings at the theater (*Dinner at Eight, Design for Living, Take a Chance, The Alien Corn*); attended play rehearsals and a Vladimir Horowitz recital; visited hospitalized Dorothy Parker; drank with Willa Cather, Woollcott and Clarence Day; lectured at Yale, the Academy of Music in Brooklyn and the Chicago Art Institute on Dante; heard T. S. Eliot read his poetry; showed up at an exhibit of Georgia O'Keeffe's paintings; saw Lady Colefax embark for England, and had a reunion with Bill Nichols.

During one week in Chicago he went to three tea parties, had cocktails with the Hutchinses and separate lunches with Inez Cunningham, *Chicago Tribune* book reviewer Fanny Butcher and John Pratt, spoke at the Art Institute, dined with the Edward Ryersons, Florence Lowden Miller and the Ralph Lillies (followed by a four-hand piano performance). Everyone wanted to meet the engaging Pulitzer Prize winner. "Yesterday," he wrote home, "Mrs. [Potter] Palmer called up and asked when she could see me, so I wedged her in between lunch with the Brewsters and a quick call on Helen Harvey." It was a heady life for one who a decade earlier had worked for nickels and dimes. At Mrs. Robert McCormick's, the table was laid with a service Napoleon had given Josephine. Dazzling. But it was not something *he* wanted to own. "Things don't speak to me. People give me presents! Imagine! What does one do with a present?" He lived in two suitcases and a briefcase and in summer had two suits, one for wear and one for the wash. When he later put on weight, Isabel let out his pants at the seams so they would last another five years. It was a positive duty to get rid of objects — books, manuscripts, the Pulitzer Prize certificate awarded for *The Bridge of San Luis Rey.*

As his income increased, so did his charities. A check went to Janet with a note, "Sew this into your corset-cover. Travelers — especially girls — should always have *lots* of extra dough concealed on their person. Things happen. Sudden downpours. No taxis. Airplanes are boarded by pirates and directed to Cuba. Purses are snatched. If no 'call' is made on this money, do *anything* with it, except mention it to me." He called this "mad money," spend-it-on-anything money. He brought food and drink to Goethe Street gatherings, sent flowers to hostesses, a $500 "valentine" to a young actor, money to a Negro baritone from Hamden High School, to Yale University. Leftover travelers' checks were handed to impecunious students. A thousand dollars went to the American Civil Liberties Union, $250 to a struggling painter (any picture would do in return; he didn't keep it), $100 to someone in Texas who had written him a despairing letter (Thornton told him he "despaired easily"). There would be gifts to hospitalized veterans, the Thacher School, a Brooklyn church, German refugees, a godson for travel ($2,000), a preservation society, the Red Cross,

CARE ($1,000), Recordings for the Blind, Berea College, and of course to the Wilders. In 1930, Thornton spent $23,853.22, of which $6,855.00 was for the family, $3,037.20 for charitable contributions, $2,355.94 for the new home in Hamden and $3,360.90 for federal income tax. He never wanted to think about or to be reminded of what he earned. It gave him pleasure to give pleasure and he devised ingenious ways of doing it. When his New Haven friend Catherine Coffin took one of her grand-daughters to Europe, they found on arrival at their hotel in Cannes flowers and a dinner invitation from Thornton, who picked them up in a chauffeured car, drove them to the casino, then to a three-star restaurant. It was all laid on to brighten the eye of a seventeen-year-old.

Thornton enjoyed the "bustle after 5:00," and the older he got the more he drank — martinis, whiskey, wine, and at least two nightcaps before retiring. Infrequently, he was seen the worse for wear; no one saw him drunk. His engagement calendar noted the names of bartenders, so that he could address them familiarly. On one trip to the Mediterranean, when a blind passenger to whom he took a liking asked for his autograph, he said, "My dear, why ask me? Ask the barman. He gets an autograph every ten minutes." Meeting a friend at the Algonquin Hotel one morn-ing, he proposed they have a drink. "But Thornton, it's only 11!" "Well, the bar's open." Any time would do. Bars were windows on the world, and Thornton reflected "with grateful awe" on those generations of Maine farmers and Hebridean fishermen — or were they dominies on the Isle of Skye? — who bequeathed to him a tough physical structure. "Never have I shown the faintest signs of gliding toward that death-gulf which is dependence on strong spirits. I can take my twelfth drink without collapse and without subsequent self loathing (I can't explain this)." However many drinks, however late the hour, he was up early. He had a theory that if an author drank when he wrote, the alcohol's imprint was visible, and he didn't drink while working on novels or plays, though pages of his letters and journal bear the mark of a wet glass.

He also relished food — heavy soups, German sausages, pasta, kippers, finnan haddie. Hold the salads! Gertrude Stein's companion, Alice B. Toklas, would say that his taste was too rich and indiscriminate, but then she was a perfectionist in the kitchen, as he would find out.

Gertrude Stein had come to Chicago from France in late autumn 1934 to talk on "What is English literature?" It was her first visit to her native land in thirty-one years. Unacquainted with her writing, Thornton thought she gave the best lecture he'd ever heard on any platform, and the friendship formed then became central to them both. Her intellectual passion was the exact description of inner and outer reality, the unfolding of the continuous present and knowing the "bottom nature" of everyone. She dressed, talked, laughed, thought *her* way, an originality that was not contrived to impress or shock. To the Oberlin motto "Clear your mind of cant," she added, clear your mind of audience. "Never read what they write about you," she told him. She pushed to its extreme the position that, at the moment of writing, one should rigorously exclude from the mind all thought of praise and blame, of persuasion or conciliation. Her *Three Lives* had been published when Thornton was ten.

She had always wanted to be a lion, Miss Stein announced when she arrived in America, and Thornton was the perfect lionizer — obliging, always understanding and worshipful. It was at his urging that Miss Stein returned to the University of Chicago in the winter of 1935 for a series of lectures to a small group of students personally selected by him.* He turned over his apartment to her and Alice B. Toklas while he camped out in the visiting preacher's suite in Hitchcock Hall. "I called up Gertrude yesterday," he wrote his family. "She had just got in from the plane five minutes before; said that already she had played the piano and Alice had made her a cup of hot water and that already she had had for the first time in many months the sensations of home."

"Oh, kinder," he burst forth after she had gone, "I can't tell you how some of those Ideas have been fermenting in me. Wherever I turn my eyes I see illustrations: audience, human nature, human mind . . . listening . . . about *listening!* Oh that's incorpo-

* Stein's lectures were printed by the University of Chicago Press in 1935 under the title *Narration*.

rated in my Inner Language forever"; she had "left a holy perfume" on his life. He had a delirious dream that he, Stein and Toklas would take a house together in Washington Square in New York. "I can see you up in your [Alice's] sewing room surveying the Park while I solemnly walk Basket [Miss Stein's white poodle] around for his constitutional. I'm quite serious about it all and have been cudgeling my brains about how to get rich. I'd come home every evening at 11:30, dizzy with applause, and we'd all have oysters and champagne until my excitement abated."

He sent her proofs of his introduction to her Chicago lectures, "simpler than I first planned" and "no intellectual treat," but "redolent of happy admiration and persuasive tact." Anticipating a visit with her in Bilignin in the Haute Savoie the summer of 1935, he assured her that if having him as a houseguest was inconvenient, he and Bob Davis would go to a hotel in nearby Belley: "You never have to be concerned about such matters as housing with me. I don't notice places as *having any relation to me*. I want to look at you both often and hear you talk to me; I want to be with you, and that can be arranged in a great many ways." After leaving Bilignin, he wrote her excitedly that he had discovered he was "crazy about America, and you did that to me . . . my country 'tis of thee. I always knew I loved it, but I never knew I loved it like this. Every Childs' restaurant, every shoe-blacking parlor. I don't feel as though I ever had to leave it again. I was born into the best country in the world. Gertrude told me so."

Working on an introduction to a second Stein book, he cast himself into the "open seas of friendship" and hoped to be supported and understood, for there were long stretches of her *Four in America* that mystified him. Anyway, it was no news to her that he was a slow plodder, "still stuck in the literal 19th Century, but very proud every time I feel I've made more progress and have been given more and more flashes of insight into the endlessly fascinating individual expression which is Gertrude's style." In response, she sent him her manuscript of *The Geographical History of America* and the suggestion that he write an introduction to that also. "What a book," he told her, "I mean what a book! I've been living for a month with ever increasing intensity on the conceptions of Human Nature and the Human Mind and on the relations of Masterpieces to their apparent subject-matter. It's all absorbing and fascinating and intoxicatingly gay, even when it's terribly in earnest. Here's riches. Here's fun. It's fine." However, "Don't be mad at me if I say again there are stretches I don't understand. This time it doesn't seem important that I don't understand, because there is so much that I do understand and love and laugh at and feed on. Gertrude, Alice, what a grand book. What an airplane ride. What a quilting-party, what a spelling-bee." Yes, he would prepare an introduction and greet her the end of October and "see the rue de Fleurus at last and my friends in it. And the pictures around them." He would have five days in Paris, "and every day I'm going to pay a call on two of my most loved Americans in the world."

Chicago had brought Stein into his life and he was grateful, as he was for other friendships made there. But those "happiest years" exacted an exhausting price. He took on too much — instructing, reading, writing, partying — and the remainder of his five-year lecture contract had still to be fulfilled, engagements from North Carolina to Utah, Texas, California, Hawaii. He had reckoned on managing his life sensibly, not "leading a hodge-podge one of teaching in Chicago, living in New Haven, and barely doing either because of the flurry of lectures, translations, novels, laziness and daydreams." But there were few signs of orderliness. In the spring of 1935 he fainted twice in a Greek restaurant and for days found himself trembling after any conversation or interview that lasted more than an hour. He recognized that he "overworked like mad" during the fall and winter; the result, "a little, and finally unimportant, nervous breakdown." It was "Nature's Warning." He had taught eight university classes a week the first three months of 1935, lectured elsewhere, conferred with incipient authors, enjoyed fun and games with the South Side gang and the North Side matrons, directed *Xerxes,* presided over Miss Stein's residence on campus — and in the intervals reminded himself that he had books and plays to write. He tried to steer clear of his fifteenth class reunion at Yale but was put on the reception committee in charge of preparing and helping manage the class headquarters. That same month, his brother's marriage to Catharine Kerlin required his presence.

He needed peace and quiet. Hutchins was understanding. The university granted him a year's leave of absence and he went to Europe.

In Vienna he was taken to supper by novelist Franz Werfel and assorted Rothschilds, dined with Max Reinhardt in his castle in Salzburg and was pressed to accept the directorship of Reinhardt's dreamt-of drama school in southern California, one offer that he did, after some deliberation, refuse. He felt all the better for his little shakeup in health and built up his strength walking in the mountains. At the Salzburg Festival he feasted on music, then spent two days in Zurich, almost persuading himself that it would be his future home town, just the right shade of dullness and enough rain to encourage him to stay indoors and write.

Thornton often acknowledged his indebtedness to Freud, whom he met at the seventy-nine-year-old's villa on the outskirts of Vienna that fall of 1935. They were together an hour and a half, and Freud spoke of many things that Thornton recorded in his journal. "I don't do anything anymore — loss of interest — satiety — impotence," Freud said. His work had not required any particular intellectual gifts; many could have done it. "The quality I had was courage. I was alone, and every discovery I made required courage. Yes, the courage to publish it, but first the courage to think it, to think along that line." He'd read *Heaven's My Destination;* no "seeker after God," he'd thrown it across the room. "I come of an unbroken line of infidel Jews. My father was a Voltairian. My mother was pious, and until eight I was pious, but one day my father took me out for a walk in the Prater, I can remember it perfectly, and explained to me that there was no way that we could know there was a God; that it didn't do any good to trouble one's head about such; but to live and do one's duty among one's fellow men." While Freud talked, Thornton took note of cases around the room filled with images of dieties — Greek, Chinese, African, Egyptian. Only in the past several weeks, Freud said, had he found a *Formulierung* for religion: "Hitherto I have said that religion is an illusion; now I say it has a truth — it has an historical truth. Religion is the recapitulation and the solution of the problems of one's first four years that have been covered over by an amnesia.* They parted with Freud expressing regret that his daughter, Anna, had not been present. "She is older than you, you do not have to be afraid. She is a sensible, reasonable girl. You are not afraid of women? She is sensible, no nonsense about her. Are you married, may I ask?"

"The two greatest living human beings are Jews," Thornton wrote Isabel. Stein was the second.

During their talk, Thornton had said: "Professor, I've always been surprised that the insights of psychoanalysis only appeared on the planet at the beginning of the twentieth century. I think that Shakespeare, who was so fascinated by dreaming, would have been delighted, surprised to learn that the interpretation of dreams was now approaching an exact science." Here Freud looked down his nose and breathed: "Ja, vielleicht, das ist neu." "Really, a beautiful old man," Thornton said. Henceforth he would call himself a Freudian. He was never analyzed and thought that although psychoanalysis could "further an adjustment," it "cannot create an ethics." "All we Wilders are crazy as coots," he wrote Amos, "and no wonder we are. It's Father who is neurotic, not Ma. Mind you, neurotic in general is no word of reproach. . . . We all come up out of the great well which is the Oedipus-Complex. Freud is not only a clinician; he's a great metaphysician and philosopher. I'm not unskillful myself. And many a burst of tears has taken place from the callers on my hearth rug. Remember that the thing that seems too trivial or embarrassing to tell may well be the big clue."

The breather in Europe strengthened Thornton's determination to make the coming year at the University of Chicago his last. He would see it through the summer of 1936 and resign in September, despite Hutchins's strenuous effort to dissuade him:

---

* When Thornton and Freud met in London long afterward, Freud said: "You aren't angry with me because of what I told you in Vienna?" Freud had criticized Wilder's *Heaven's My Destination* for making religion a theme for amusement. "Why should you treat of an American fanatic; that cannot be treated poetically." In 1938, he would ask Thornton to take an interest in his nephew, who hoped to come to America: "Need I tell you . . . the sympathy a refugee and newcomer is in need of?"

How can you bear to leave me? Here's the University of Chicago just at the point when something might be made of it. Here is your old friend Hutchins at the crossroads. You told me you had to leave because you couldn't work and teach at the same time. Well, if you stop teaching you've got to work. And I don't mean Hollywood. I had at least consoled myself with the thought that you would be roosting on the top floor of the Midway Drexel apartment composing that immortal work that brought undying fame to the South Side. How can you talk so glibly of California? You might as well run a hot (or cold) iron through my heart.

Hutchins had been told of a telegram from Metro-Goldwyn-Mayer offering Thornton at least six weeks' work, and that his visiting professor had agreed to go to Hollywood in December 1936. Thornton granted that he would "never be as happy as this again," but he was temporarily revolted by being asked wasn't Katharine Cornell wonderful last night in *Saint Joan* or what he thought of thisa-and-thata, of inquiring after the health of absent relatives, of hearing people say that Bob Hutchins had good ideas but was tactless, of agreeing that things looked bad in Europe. He loved his friends, his students — "Damn it, I love my thoughts; apparently nothing can cast me down, [but] I'm not going to teach anymore." Maybe it was because he was almost forty, and "that's my natural age," he wrote Stein and Toklas. Anyway, he was going to California, and in April or May "some small Cunarder or *The American Banker* will deposit me at Le Havre, wild with anticipation to look into your beautiful faces and to see hurled upon the carpet the tumultuous store of all that we have to say to one another."

11

Attack and Counterattack

WHAT, OTHER THAN lectures and introductions, had he been writing? Two novels were produced in the thirties — *The Woman of Andros* and *Heaven's My Destination*, the first published in late February 1930, six weeks before his Chicago classes began. That so slender and serene a book, set on an imaginary island in the Aegean two centuries before the birth of Christ, could have provoked such polemical debate is astonishing.

Derived from the *Andria* of Terence, a first-century B.C. Roman writer of comedy, the legend had been used in the early eighteenth century by Sir Richard Steele as the basis for *The Conscious Lovers.* In Thornton's reconstruction there is little visual detail, so few notations that the reader's imagination is forced to build up the background. *The Woman of Andros* traces the passion, disappointment and death of a cultivated courtesan, hopelessly in love with a young man. "I have known the worst that the world can do to me," the *hetaira* Chrysis says; "nevertheless I praise the world and all living." It is a more compressed novel than *The Bridge,* but the question it raises is common to all Thornton's work: when a situation is more than a human soul can be expected to bear, what then? *The Cabala* was a series of three such extremities, *The Bridge* implied that at the heart of love there lies an intuition that offers sufficient strength for crises. *The Woman of Andros* asks whether paganism has any answer for the inquiring sufferer and, by anticipation, whether the maxims that entered the world with the message of Christianity are an adequate guide.*

The opening paragraph is one of his most graceful:

* A paraphrase of Wilder's summation, reported by Norman Fitts in the *Atlantic Monthly,* March 1930.

The earth sighed as it turned in its course; the shadow of night crept gradually along the Mediterranean, and Asia was left in darkness. The great cliff that was one day to be called Gibraltar held for a long time a gleam of red and orange, while across from it the mountains of Atlas showed deep blue pockets in their shining sides. The caves that surround the Neapolitan gulf fell into a profounder shade, each giving forth from the darkness its chiming or its booming sound. Triumph had passed from Greece and wisdom from Egypt, but with the coming on of night they seemed to regain their lost honors, and the land that was soon to be called Holy prepared in the dark its wonderful burden. The sea was large enough to hold a varied weather: a storm played about Sicily and its smoking mountains, but at the mouth of the Nile the water lay like a wet pavement. A fair tripping breeze ruffled the Aegean and all the islands of Greece felt a new freshness at the close of day.

We are meant to glimpse the cyclical character of experience, day following night, death following life, civilization succeeding civilization, the singularity of each person, place and time, and their insignificance against the backdrop of Always, the awareness of each moment heightened by knowledge that creation is continuous. As in *Our Town* eight years later, in *The Woman of Andros* a character is allowed to return to earth and relive one day of his youth, as participant and onlooker. As in *The Cabala* and *The Bridge*, we witness the pain and humiliations of passion. A note from *The Bridge* is reechoed: "He stood for a time, quiet as the stones about him, asking himself whether the associations in life are based upon an accidental encounter or upon a profound and inner necessity." A sentence from *The Woman of Andros* would be spoken by Caesar in a later novel, *The Ides of March*: "Where there is an unknowable there is a promise." Thornton is not preaching stoic resignation but a nobility arising from the purification of passion, its liberation from self-centeredness. It is this emancipation that allows Chrysis to die without despair.

Though nowhere matching the sale of *The Bridge*, *The Woman of Andros* was a best-seller and reviews were generally favorable.

The bomb burst eight months after its publication, in a *New Republic* article by the proletarian writer Michael Gold, whose slashing attack gave *The Woman of Andros* an unjustified notoriety. The idea of inviting Gold to review the book had been Malcolm Cowley's, acting in the absence of the *New Republic*'s literary editor, Edmund Wilson. Cowley thought it would be "amusing," not anticipating the vituperative essay he got and which he hesitated to print. It was held several weeks, printed without alteration on Wilson's return, and triggered a cannonade of letters. "Scurrilous," wrote one of Thornton's defenders. "I have been taught, erroneously no doubt," wrote another, "that the final test of any piece of writing is the manner in which the material is presented, not the material itself."

Essentially, Gold was accusing Thornton of not having written a working-class novel, and in an unsigned *New Republic* editorial a month later Wilson appeared to echo that condemnation: "In Wilder the pathos and beauty derived from exotic lands of the imagination may be, as Michael Gold suggests, a sedative for sick Americans." Entitled "Wilder: Prophet of the Genteel Christ," the Gold review blasted the author for concerning himself with "an historic junk shop" and worrying over "little lavender tragedies." The book's "religion" was that of "Jesus Christ, the First British Gentleman;" it was a pastiche, dilettante religion without blood and fire, "a daydream of homosexual figures in graceful gowns moving archaically among the lilies." It was Anglo-Catholicism, "that last refuge of the American literary snob." Where, Gold demanded, were the modern streets of New York, Chicago and New Orleans? Where were the unemployed, the cotton mills, the child slaves of the beet fields, the stockbroker suicides, the labor racketeers or the "passion and death of the coal miners"? Where was Wilder in the class struggle?

After the controversy in the *New Republic* fizzled out, Wilson concluded that there had been a class issue involved in the dispute, but that Gold had been insufficiently respectful of literary craftsmanship. At any rate, Wilson and Cowley thought the review served its purpose by turning Thornton's attention to his own country, as shown in two new one-act plays, *Pullman Car Hiawatha* and *The Happy Journey to Camden and Trenton,* and in his next novel, *Heaven's My Destination,* which relates the adventures of an innocent, Bible-reading textbook salesman, George Brush. Wilson said flatly that the novel was "partly in answer to this challenge to write about his own time and country." Thornton admitted no such causal relation. "No," he told Professor Daniel Aaron of Harvard in a letter written thirty years later, Gold's criticism "didn't have that effect. I had been teaching *Don Quixote* at the University of Chicago, and had been writing of the American scene in those one-acts (*Happy Journey,* etc.). I was not interested in Communism as such — never read Marx; but I had much interest in what was called civil rights, social justice, etc. and had joined a number of organizations that were later blacklisted. Primarily, however, I was interested in my writing and teaching and felt no need to exert myself in meetings, committees, platforms."

What had had an effect on Thornton was his cross-country lecture tours in the early thirties — the train rides, the glimpses of boardinghouses and shady hotels, salesmen on the road, waitresses, small-town businessmen, housewives and their children.

By July 1932, between teaching terms, he had written fifteen thousand words of *Heaven's My Destination* and remarked to Les Glenn that it was "our old friend, the Arkansas-Texas *picaresque.* From Baptist fundamentalism to *gross-stadt* tolerance in three years; or How Rollo learned to be a Babbitt. Only my ending is not to sophistication, but to troubled wisdom. You'll see, all about the Depression. Funny, vulgar, heartbreaking — and a bit sociohistorical document. The best thing I have ever done." Elsewhere, he described it as "that heavenly book whose subject is our idiotic daydream that tomorrow we will do a big generous thing, that tomorrow we will [be] heroic, magnanimous, and wise [and] tomorrow night shows us we have been interfering, pompous and more than usually stupid — the inconquerable idealism and the inevitable inadequacy of us all."

Heaven's My Destination had its genesis at the MacDowell Colony the summer of 1932 under the title *The Ideas and Adventures of Jethro Bentley* and is the funniest book Thornton ever wrote. It is a sympathetic picture of middle-class Midwestern America in the twenties (and perhaps the eighties), a *Pilgrim's Progress* burlesque of awkward virtue and a commentary on fundamentalist pieties. From one angle, it is the tale of the traveling salesman and the farmer's daughter, but there is nothing villainous in soul-saving George Brush, whose good intentions lead him into one predicament after another.

The novel was the first of Thornton's to be put out by Harper's, and he was somewhat defensive about the switch. Sensitive to the allegation of ingratitude, he justified it by claiming that the Bonis were so disappointed with *Heaven's My Destination* that he "was permitted to take it to Harper's who published it, thus terminating my contract with the Boni Brothers." More to the point, as we have seen, Cass Canfield of Harper's had been angling for Wilder since 1928, when Thornton showed up in Canfield's office, asked some questions about a forthcoming Harper's prize contest and suggested that if Canfield was ever in the neighborhood of the Lawrenceville School he should drop in. "Of course I dropped in very quickly indeed!" Canfield recalled. At their Lawrenceville meeting, Thornton had been quite agitated. White-faced, he handed Canfield a piece of paper on which he had written: "Dear Mr. Canfield, I've decided and wish to have all my work published by Harper's at 15 percent royalties," whereupon Canfield replied, "Oh, Mr. Wilder, the best thing to do is to tear that up, because you might write plays or movies and 15 percent is nothing like what you ought to get for them." Through the intervention of Glenway Wescott, whose sister, Beulah Hagen, was one of Canfield's assistants, Thornton was invited to New York for further talks with Harper's, an invitation he then declined, meanwhile hoping he could "repay your kindness someday."

The Bonis must have heard rumors and been nervous. What were his intentions? In February 1930, having submitted *The Woman of Andros,* Thornton told Lewis Baer that he never thought the words "I may still be your author six or seven years from now" would cause any confusion. "It means that I may write plays for years now, teach, travel — anything except write books, so that the books we still have together [under contract] may not be written for a long while yet. As for the other firm [Harper's] I scarcely know them, a polite friendly remote acquaintance with some of them, but though I feel strongly that *in time* I shall be with them, all I know is there is no idea in anybody's mind as to when or what their first book will be." The letter ended by assuring Baer that he did not reproach Boni for the hurried completion of *The Woman of Andros.* "My writing inertia is so strange that a book would lie partially written for ages unless I said to myself: I must finish it by January 6th when I start out on my lecture tour. That's all I meant. If there is any hurrying the fault is only mine probably, and probably with more time the book would have ended in much the same way anyway."

The misunderstandings, reservations and reassurances went back as early 1928, when Thornton had telegraphed Baer apologizing for having "injured you" and promising that the next book would be Boni's. The following day, he wired Baer that he was "deeply grateful for your goodness in trying to understand me. Try and make good old Albert and Charles [Boni] forgive me. We have perhaps many years' association still before us." But sometime after publication of *The Woman of Andros,* on a painful walk in Lawrenceville, probably with Baer, he "got rid of the Boni brothers," because "they had shown themselves (a) doubtful of an audience for *The Bridge of San Luis Rey,* (b) deeply disappointed by *The Woman of Andros* and (c) downright indignant about the first chapters of *Heaven's My Destination.* I went to Harper's and have never given a thought to any other publisher since."

There is no doubt that prestigious Harper's had more to offer than the smaller Boni house. *Heaven's My Destination* had a first printing in 1935, of 11,750 in hardcover, 103,219 in Avon paperback. Over the next thirty years, 55,470 hardback copies and 131,847 paperbacks were sold, and it was translated into Norwegian, Swedish, Danish, Dutch, Portuguese, French, Punjabi and Arabic. He had an advance from Harper's of $4,147 and an additional $3,500 from the Book-of-the-Month Club.

Edmund Wilson was gratified; Wilder had come home. "I do not see any reason," he wrote in the *New Republic,* "that the radical reviewers who have been nagging at Thornton Wilder to write about his native country should not find *Heaven's My Destination* acceptable." George Brush was "a more complete and living person than any in his other books. His sentimentality is nowhere in evidence. The tone is always comic or matter-of-fact with the result that Mr. Wilder's vision of an imperfect and suffering humanity comes through a good deal more tellingly than in any of his earlier novels. He has handled his Sinclair Lewis material with his characteristic elegance of form and felicity of detail, his Mozartian combination of lightness and grace with seriousness."

Although he couldn't say exactly what the author was up to, Burton Rascoe in the *New York Herald Tribune* conceded that the novel was "unusual and entertaining." Critic Henry Seidel Canby thought it was what Voltaire would have written "if he had been sent to Hollywood and going by bus through Illinois and Kansas, had tried his hand at *Candide* rewritten in terms of the farmbelt, the Bible, a closed mind and a well-intentioned heart." "No, George Brush is not a boob," the February 20, 1935, *Christian Century* pronounced: "There is too much consistency and sincerity in him for that. There is a core of sanity and spiritual health under the absurdities that lie on the surface."

Nothing of Thornton's, not even *The Bridge*, prompted so many interpretations of what he had set out to say. He was to tell Malcolm Cowley that the novel was an effort to come to terms with the pious didacticism of his upbringing, but his beloved Charles Wager of Oberlin thought Thornton must be pulling the public's leg and asked whether he really preferred this sort of "devilishly clever" book to one that was "a joy, humanly speaking, forever." How shameful, Thornton wrote Amos, to have written something "which everyone misunderstands." A southern lady adored the book but "hated the protagonist, George Brush." Thornton replied: "Thank you, but the book is autobiographical." In letter after letter he felt impelled to convince readers that he meant no satire, that the novel was about "all of us when young; you're not supposed to notice the humor — you're supposed to look through it at a fella who not only had the impulse to think out an ethic and plan a life — but actually *does* it." There were no second meanings, he assured Emily Foresman, daughter of his former Davis House headmaster, "beyond the fact that George Brush is a sort of Short History of the American Mind raised by exaggeration into humor: Idealistic, but unclear; really religious, but badly educated in religion. A subtitle also might be: 'How instinctive goodness learns to express itself in a contrary world.'"

Afterward, he told Amos's daughter that the depression in the thirties had "killed" his kind of novel (*The Woman of Andros*): "I went on my second lecture tour, what I saw 'fed' *Heaven's My Destination* which is in every paragraph a Depression novel." Finally, he gave up explaining; he was simply "fond of that book. I never before liked any of my books. They embarrassed me."

He amended that judgment later and rated *Heaven's My Destination* a relative failure. "I was thoroughly book-taught in politics from Aristotle down, and I took a lively interest in Presidential elections that turned on our hopes that a wise government would repair the appalling condition into which the country had [sunk]." Without knowing it, he had written a political novel he was unequipped to write: "My ignorance consisted in an inability to relate the general ideas which are called politics with the relations of the individual citizen to the agencies of government that shape his life." Ignorance there may have been, but Edmund Wilson was right when he told John Dos Passos that *Heaven's My Destination* was Wilder's best book so far.

Meanwhile, playwriting had not been slighted. By summer's end at the MacDowell Colony in 1930, Thornton had six one-act plays ready for publication by Yale University Press and Coward-McCann the following year. Three of them, as Professor Malcolm Goldstein pointed out, marked Thornton's emergence as a serious dramatist — *The Long Christmas Dinner, The Happy Journey to Camden and Trenton,* and *Pullman Car Hiawatha.**

The Long Christmas Dinner opens on a family dining room where the table is handsomely spread. The action covers ninety years. Inconspicuously dressed actors carry wigs of white hair, which they adjust upon their heads to indicate aging. They eat imaginary food with imaginary knives and forks. There is no curtain.

Both *The Long Christmas Dinner* and *The Happy Journey* have autobiographical overtones. In the former we are made to feel the tension between father and son in every generation:

* "Nothing in any of the plays," Goldstein wrote in reference to *Happy Journey,* "surpasses the girl's question to her father: 'Are you glad I'm still alive, Pa?' Into this line, composed of some of the homeliest words in the language, Wilder packs three of man's basic feelings: a desire for love, the fear of rejection, and the fear of death"; *The Art of Thornton Wilder* (Lincoln: University of Nebraska Press, 1965), p. 82.

Roderick.   What did I do? What did I do that was wrong?

Charles [*Father*].   You were drunk and you were rude to the daughters of my best friends.

Roderick.   Great God, you gotta get drunk in this town to forget how dull it is. Time passes so slowly here that it stands still, that's what's the trouble.

Charles.   Well, young man, we can employ your time. You will leave the university and you will come into the Bayard factory on January 2nd.

Roderick.   (*At the door into the hall*) I have better things to do than go into your old factory. I'm going somewhere where time passes, my God!

Mother is the sun around which *The Happy Journey* revolves. That play, too, requires no scenery. As in *Our Town*, the curtain rises on a Stage Manager leaning lazily against the proscenium pillar and smoking. The dialogue is out of Madison and Berkeley:

Arthur [a teenager].   (*Solemnly*) Hm! Ma's always taught me about God. I guess she got a letter from him this morning.

Ma.   (*Rises, outraged*) Elmer, stop that automobile this minute. I don't go another step with anybody that says things like that. Arthur, you get out of this car. Elmer, you give him another dollar bill. He can go back to Newark by himself. I don't want him.

Arthur.   What did I say? There wasn't anything terrible about that.

Ma.   God has done a lot of things for me and I won't have him made fun of by anybody. Go away. Go away from me.

Caroline.   Aw, Ma, don't spoil the ride.

Ma.   (*Slowly conceding*) Alright, if you say so, Elmer. But I won't sit beside him. Caroline, you come and sit by me.

Arthur.   (*Frightened*) Aw, Ma, that wasn't so terrible.

Ma.   I don't want to talk about it. I hope your father washes your mouth out with soap and water. Where'd we all be if I started talking about God like that, I'd like to know! We'd be in the speakeasies and nightclubs and places like that, that's where we'd be.

And after another five miles:

Arthur.   Ma, I'm sorry. I'm sorry for what I said. (*He bursts into tears and puts his forehead against her elbow.*)

Ma.   There. There. We all say wicked things at times. I know you didn't mean it like it sounded. (*He weeps still more violently than before.*)

Ma.   Why, now, now! I forgive you, Arthur, and tonight before you go to bed you . . . (*She whispers*) You're a good boy at heart, Arthur, and we all know it. (*Caroline starts to cry too. Ma is suddenly joyously alive and happy.*) Sakes alive, it's too nice a day for us all to be cryin'. Come now, get in. You go up in front with your father, Caroline. Ma wants to sit with her beau. I never saw such children. Your hotdogs are all getting wet. Now chew them fine, everybody. Alright, Elmer, forward march. (*A dreamy silence descends upon them. Caroline sits closer to her father. Ma puts her arm around Arthur.*)

Alexander Woollcott, one of Thornton's noisiest boosters, called *The Happy Journey* "an amazing piece — so deeply touching, so full to the brim of loving kindness. Women like this mother are the justification of this world and the glory thereof."

The two one-acts were produced by the University of Chicago Dramatic Association in December 1931, having been premiered a week earlier at the Yale University Theater. Both were influenced by what Thornton had read of Michel Saint-Denis's staging of plays by André Obey, especially Saint-Denis's having a character prowl through a house by merely walking between posts set up on the stage, and the presence on the stage of two commentators.

Produced off Broadway thirty-five years later along with his *Queens of France, The Happy Journey* and *Christmas Dinner* would be commended by critic Richard Watts, Jr., as "quiet, modest and simple, but they also happen to possess the quality of warm-hearted enchantment. No one could mistake them for negligible triviality." The *New York Times's* Dan Sullavan picked *The Happy Journey* as "the winner." "People being nice to each other! It is a sensational idea for a play. Ma combines the best qualities of a marshmallow and of a rock."

In the less effective *Queens of France,* three New Orleans women come separately to a lawyer's office in 1869, each having been led to believe that she is the long-lost heir to the French throne. As the third "queen" leaves, a boy enters pushing in a wheelchair a woman some hundred years of age, wrapped like a mummy and wearing a scarf about her head and green spectacles. The mummy extends a hand, which the lawyer kisses, murmuring "Your Royal Highness." The curtain falls.

Two other one-acts of the thirties are of minor interest. *Love and How to Cure It,* sketched out at the MacDowell Colony in 1930 and finished the following year in Salzburg, is acted out on the stage of a music hall in London in 1895. Linda, dressed in a white ballet costume, is a beautiful, hardhearted girl of sixteen, Joey a stout comedian, Rowena a mature soubrette. The fourth member of the cast is Arthur, who is in love with Linda:

> Linda. (*Suddenly*) Oh, I hate him, I 'ate 'im! Why can't he let me be?

Rowena.   Yes, yes. That's love.

   Linda.   (*On the verge of hysterics*) Auntie, can't it be cured? Can't you make him just forget me?

Rowena.   Well, dovie, they say there are some ways . . . but I say there's only one way to cure that kind of love when it's feverish and all upset. Only love can cure love.

Such Things Only Happen in Books offers ironic, but uninteresting comment on a writer who plays at life as if it were a game. *Pullman Car Hiawatha*, first performed in November 1931, is, on the other hand, an imaginative and convincing enactment of happenings on a railway car traveling from New York to Chicago and foreshadows techniques and themes Thornton would develop in *Our Town* and *The Skin of Our Teeth*. Again, there's a Stage Manager, no scenery, few props. A berth is two chairs facing each other. The one-act ought to have confounded anyone who thought Wilder too remote from common folk. His dialogue is on pitch in every line. A young woman accompanied by her husband dies on the train and is led away by archangels Gabriel and Michael, dressed in blue serge suits. First she protests: "I belong here. I shall be perfectly happy to roam about my house. . . . You know I wouldn't be happy there." They whisper to her, and she says, "I see now, I see now. I understand everything now." As she leans her forehead against an archangel's shoulder, she laughs softly and delivers her farewell: "Goodbye, 1312 Ridgewood Avenue, Oaksbury, Illinois. I hope I remember all its steps and doors and wallpapers forever. Goodbye, Emerson Grammar School [which Thornton attended] on the corner of Forebush Avenue and Wherry Street. Goodbye, Miss Walker and Miss Cramer who taught me English and Miss Mathewson who taught me biology. Goodbye, First Congregational Church on the corner of Meyerson Avenue and Sixth Street and Dr. McReady and Mrs. McReady and Julia. Goodbye, Papa and Mama. . . ." She is the forerunner of *Our Town's* Emily.

Thornton, who was himself so often on the move, saw the human journey as an endless movement through space and time. *The Cabala* and *Heaven's My Destination* begin on a train, as would his later novel, *The Eighth Day*. His last novel, *Theophilus North*, starts off with an automobile ride. Toward the end of *Pullman Car*, as in *The Skin of Our Teeth*, a moment in the journey is placed in its cosmic setting: "So much for the inside of the car," the Stage Manager says, "that'll be enough of that for the present. Now for its position geographically, meteorologically, astronomically, theologically considered." Figures appear on a balcony outside the train windows. One speaks for a field in which there are "51 gophers, 206 field mice, 6 snakes and millions of bugs, insects, ants and spiders. All in their winter sleep." The figure representing Parkersburg, Ohio (1,604 souls) announces that it has seen "all the dreadful havoc that alcohol has done and I hope no one here will ever touch a drop of the curse of this beautiful country"; she then beats a measure and they all sing unsteadily: "Throw out the lifeline! Throw out the lifeline! Someone is sinking today-ay." The ghost of a German workman speaks for a trestle over which the railway car is passing; a watchman in a tower observes that the signals are operating all right; a mechanic gives the weather report. Time takes the stage: the minutes are gossips, the hours philosophers, the years theologians. The planets come forward, each with a sound of its own. Then we return to earth and listen to the "thinking" of the passengers.

Millions came before you, millions will come after you, the playwright is saying; the universe is vast, time is indifferent to pride and ambition, do the best that you can in this short span, that's all you can do, God knows why — or perhaps God doesn't know. As the Pullman approaches Chicago, the Stage Manager announces: "South Chicago. See the University's towers over there! The best of them."

In the spring of 1932, at the request of producer Gilbert Miller, Thornton undertook an adaptation of *The Bridge of Toruzko* by the Hungarian playwright Otto Indig, but it wasn't used and some-one else's version closed on Broadway after twelve performances. That same spring he also translated from the French André Obey's *The Rape of Lucrèce* for Katharine Cornell, produced by Guthrie McClintic and starring "La Cornell," Brian Aherne and Blanche Yurka. He had not met Obey (he did later, at Obey's home outside Paris) but had read whatever he could about him and admired

Obey's biblical play *Noah,* in which actors mime animal roles. The translation of *Lucrèce* closely followed the original, but Thornton had to agree soon after it opened at the Belasco Theatre on November 29, 1932, that it was a failure and that its short run was deserved. One critic called it "dull, for the most part uncomfortably dull" and "no more than a polite commencement study." Thornton took only 2 percent of gross receipts; the main share went to Obey. As Miss Cornell's assistant, Gertrude Macy, remarked: "Wilder was a pushover on contracts."

12

Goldwyn to Stein

WILLIAM JAMES thought that life is a series of interruptions;
perhaps he meant self-interruptions. Whichever, Thornton seemed
bent on proving it. August and September of 1933 were to have
been spent in Taos with Mabel Dodge Luhan, but movieland had
intervened, dangling a salary that provoked yells of derisive laughter from the Wilders; *no* one was worth that much! They might
not understand money, but they understood the fantastic. The
deity responsible was Samuel Goldwyn ("Jupiter"), whose impulse
it was to have Thornton add words to a former silent picture of
Ronald Colman's *Dark Angel.* Mr. Goldwyn had a reputation for
paying for the best, and he put the author of *The Bridge of San
Luis Rey* in that class. The words were added, and the following
spring, 1934, Thornton again went to Hollywood, this time in
response to a telegram from his film agent, Rosalie Stewart. RKO
would pay him $1,500 plus transportation from New Haven to
Los Angeles and Los Angeles to Chicago for two weeks of conferences with producer Pandro Berman and director George Cukor
on a treatment of *Joan of Arc.* Since Cukor was leaving for England
in ten days, Thornton must come immediately! He could write a
thirty- or forty-page synopsis when he returned to his teaching
duties in Chicago and then, when he was free in July, they would
engage him to do a screenplay for $15,000, minus the $1,500.
"Little Chefoo's boy very excited at big new adventure in his
life," Thornton wrote Woollcott from the Twentieth Century Limited. "I enjoy this town," he wrote his family from the Chateau
Elysée, above Hollywood Boulevard,

though it's sometimes hard to catch one's breath from laffing. I enjoy going to my STUDIO and looking about into corners at scenery; and eating in the lunchrooms among actors all made up as Cleopatra's court. There is so much to tell you I don't know where to begin. Rosalie Stewart takes me to all the other studios and has me shake hands with the officials so that they'll know me and call me into work someday. She is under the impression that I am on the make and am planning to wrench bigger and bigger money out of this town. I've already gone beyond my assignment and written a splendid, sublimeopening for *Joan* and several big passages later in the work. Tonight I go to dinner with George Cukor and Zoë Akins and presumably read my stuff aloud. They leave me so much to myself and yet are so respectful and interested that I think I'll be allowed to go ahead and have my work treated with very little dismemberment by the gag-men. It seems to be settled in everybody's mind that I am to return here for at least six weeks this summer to take part in the final preparation and the shooting of the picture. It is planned that Katharine Hepburn return here by June 1st to do a modern picture before she goes into *Joan*. No earthquakes. Yet. Beautiful sunlight; faintly misty before noon. Went swimming my first Sunday here, pretty cold. Story department at RKO is astonished AT ALL I KNOW. They are going crazy hunting for material for [Charles] Lederer and Hepburn and I run off ten suggestions (from European sources mostly) as quick as artillery fire, and they grow dizzy taking them down. The eccentricity and extravagance of this town have to be seen to be believed. Just a walk down Hollywood Boulevard at 11:00 in the morning or 5:00 in the afternoon is like nothing else in the world. *Joan* is going to be the biggest picture of the year.

Cukor got to England, Wilder to Chicago in time to deliver his first lecture of the term, and the synopsis was finished and mailed in May. Rosalie Stewart's partner wired: "Just wanted to tell you this office all terribly enthusiastic about your magnificent job in the treatment of *Joan of Arc*. Following up with RKO." The synopsis had been put together between classes, student interviews, four evenings at the Russian Ballet, a YMCA banquet, several concerts, dinners with the Hutchinses, Ryersons, Goodspeeds, Harveys, Lillies, a speech to the YWCA, another (on Shakespeare) in the Blackstone's Crystal Ballroom, a fitting at Marshall Field, a housewarming at Chuck Newton's, lunch at the Arts Club and an evening tour of Chicago slums with his friend in the social science department, Herb Blumer, during which they ate at a one-cent restaurant, went to Communist debating clubs, saw a midnight burlesque show and finished up at a black-and-tan dance hall.

Hepburn did not do *Joan of Arc* and never knew that anyone had her in mind for it. The film was made long afterward with Ingrid Bergman, and not from Thornton's script.

Hollywood changed radically after the Second World War, but in the mid-thirties it was a baronial empire of powerful fiefdoms, highly paid and pampered stars, a Legion of Decency to protect the morals of the American family, as well as committees to save Spain from Franco or elect Upton Sinclair governor on an EPIC (End Poverty in California) platform. On Thornton's return to Hollywood in July, Eddie Cantor had him to dinner in a studio dining room reserved for Their Eminences. Helen Hayes and he chatted on the set of *What Every Woman Knows*. He met Marlene Dietrich, who was impressed by his knowledge of German theater. He was charmed by the Charles Laughtons, to whom he wrote that he was about to turn in "a whole SCRIPT of an intermittently interesting movie to Jupiter Goldwyn."

The movie was *We Live Again* (Tolstoy's *Resurrection*), starring Anna Sten and Fredric March. Not satisfied with it, Goldwyn had summoned "the best" to advise what was wrong. The ending is suddenly, cheaply, unpreparedly happy, he was told. "Gentlemen," Mr. Goldwyn said, "I throw myself on your mercy. I want you each [Thornton, Paul Green and the author of the original script] to write a big closing scene. We have only one day to shoot it — Friday — because Fredric March is going to Tahiti and can only give us one day's work." The final scene was almost entirely Thornton's. Goldwyn said it topped everything that preceded it, and Thornton's $3,000 two-week option was taken up.

He could have pitched his tent in lotus land, rented a house in Malibu or an apartment alongside other famous writers in the

Garden of Allah and gone on drawing fat paychecks. But movies were "time out." Not even the chance of doing a script for Greta Garbo tempted him to make Hollywood home.

There were other offers, too. Mary Pickford's heart was set on a stage role. Now if he could write something especially for her and Lillian Gish, something Chinese. She was disappointed that a Chinese story did not take root in his mind but she understood: "Naturally, in order to do convincing work, one has to be in complete sympathy with the subject and to thoroughly know the characters." Perhaps he could think up something else for her. Then, William Randolph Hearst telephoned that his friend Marion Davies, who stuttered and was partial to booze, was filled with a passion to star in *Twelfth Night.* Would Wilder prepare the script and additional dialogue? "Of course I will," he wrote Mabel Dodge Luhan, who had become one of his regular correspondents. "I'm an adventurer; that means that all the values of life fluctuate. One minute honor and decorum seem to be a worthy price to pay; the next minute impulse seems superior to society's respect. The fact that such a curious nexus as an ex-follies girl and a newspaper millionaire who pathetically adores her and William Shakespeare and myself should appear, is more interesting than all the dignity and artistic honor in the world. Since in the twentieth century the sublime has departed the earth, let us at least cherish the beautiful image of the ridiculous."

He couldn't join Hearst and Miss Davies at Hearst's San Simeon castle in California for Christmas but didn't refuse a collaborator Hearst dispatched to Chicago to help him fashion a film about a girl who dresses as a boy. So, for four hours a day in the fall of 1934, Thornton strode up and down a sitting room in a suite at the Shoreland Hotel, talking script with Hearst's writer: "You see, Essex was . . . How about if Rosaleen gets in a duel . . . Well, if we have a scene showing Shakespeare planting pear-trees at New Place . . ." By then Miss Davies's passion for Shakespeare had spent itself.

Absurd, of course. Could anyone tell him, he asked, when "sheer curiosity, adventuring, 'trying everything once,' and putting oneself objectively to test — when all that finally defeats itself and proves meaningless and harmful?"

With all their interruptions, the Chicago years were neither meaningless nor harmful. Before they were over in 1936, Thornton had written *Heaven's My Destination,* three enduring one-acts, splashed about in the Hollywood pool, learned and taught a great deal and earned a creditable income.

What next? "You can write like a fool," stage designer Norman Bel Geddes challenged him, "and the theater is more lacking in writing talent today than anything else. You love the theater. Why don't you write a play?"

When word came in the spring of 1935 that his father was failing, Thornton felt "like a cad" not to have been standing by and attending the "protracted exasperating unloveable death" of Papa. He did get to New Haven, briefly, showed up at the hospital on tiptoe at the allowed times, then returned to Chicago. Depressed and enfeebled, Papa was operated on toward the end of the year for an intestinal blockage, wrongly diagnosed as cancer, lingered on for seven months and died on July 2, 1936, at the age of seventy-four. Thornton came East for the funeral.

"Did I tell you that my revered Papa died?" he wrote Gertrude Stein. "Yes . . . Yes . . . All of us five children were back. (Space Here Reserved For Thoughts.) Mother is simply fine. I am so happy about that. She looks well, she sleeps solidly at night, she's full of interest and energy. She bought in my absence several new dresses and a lovely new hat. Can it be? See what I mean? The house of mourning."*

The death coincided with what Thornton assumed was his last quarter at the university. He said his goodbyes to friends, to teaching, to externals. *He was going to be a WRITER.* But first he had

---

* Isabel wrote Amos that she had come to see her father as a "highly gifted, extraordinary man of great charm, wit and abilities but shackled in many cruel ways. His suffering was enormous on several levels. He was never able to harness and use his rare talents. Mother with her unusual array of abilities and personal endowments could never reach her fulfillment either, but she had rare good looks and personal charm [and] her unique courage and intellectual abilities and attainments and her wonderful high spirits and natural bent for finding good joy in music, art, poetry supported her." Father had "seemed to admire WOMAN but it was one kind — a 'noble woman' — made in the image of his mother and the girl [his early love, Edith] who was the same comfortable build and dominating personality that his mother was."

to visit Woollcott and his companion-manager Joe Hennessey on Woollcott's private island, Neshobe, in Lake Bomoseen, Vermont, where the literati played croquet, "cops and robbers" and "murder." Then he was due in New York for lunch with Cass Canfield and Carl Van Doren, a Theatre Guild play, drinks and dinner with Ned Sheldon, a quick tour of the Frick Gallery and a performance of *Dead End*. Finally, on October 9, 1936, he broke loose and boarded the SS *Nerissa* bound for the Virgin Islands, Antigua, Montserrat, Guadeloupe, Martinique and Saint Lucia.

The hot, empty days were conducive to thinking, "and thinking makes me write." He had had nothing published in two years; now he was at work on four things simultaneously, a sign that the Real Right One hadn't taken hold. It might have helped concentrate his mind had he cut back on social engagements, but he didn't. After the Caribbean cruise he had dates in New York with Lady Colefax, lunch at Voisin's with Woollcott and Rebecca West and a party at Ned Sheldon's with Gertrude Lawrence.

Edward (Ned) Sheldon had had considerable success as a dramatist but for years had been bedridden, a victim of osteoarthritis. A few, like poet Conrad Aiken, thought that the atmosphere of reverence as friends approached Sheldon's bed or couch was so thick you could cut it. The illness had blinded him, his face was covered by a black satin mask, but he could listen and talk. In early 1937, Thornton read him a rough draft of *Our Town* and was told that he "broke every rule, . . . but every seven minutes — no, every five minutes — you supplied one thing — some novelty — in the proceedings which is at once a pleasure in the experience, and, at the same time, a contribution to the content of the play."* "With Ned," Thornton said, "you shared a thing in a state of growth." The man was a legend and his bedside the center of a wide literary and theater network.

Almost two dozen lectures still had to be got out of the way, taking Thornton from Florida to California. To deliver two talks he traveled 2,214 miles, four nights on a train. And for what? His receipts from the entire 1936 tour had been $2,665.12; but by the spring of 1937 the contract had been fulfilled and he was

* Quoted in *The Man Who Lived Twice*, a biography of Edward Sheldon by Eric Wollencott Barnes (New York, Charles Scribner's, 1956), p. 220.

looking forward to Europe and to seeing Stein, who was expecting "dear, dear Thornton." They would compare plays, she wrote. She had two to show him. "We will talk when you get here and you will get here and that will be nice."

It would have been nice, if Jed Harris, whom Thornton had been seeing off and on, had not sent an S.O.S. in April "commanding" him to revise an acting version of Ibsen's *A Doll's House* for Ruth Gordon. Rehearsals were already scheduled.

Thornton might have been able to say no to Jed, but not to Miss Gordon. He worked like a laborer under the lash, preparing a wholly new translation from the German and English versions only to have the production postponed, which freed him for the MacDowell Colony in June. In the first three weeks there, he completed the opening act of *Our Town*, made considerable progress on the second and third, and, if it hadn't been for the Carnegie Foundation, might have stayed in Peterborough through July and finished the play that would put him in the front rank of American dramatists.

Carnegie had offered $322 to underwrite a round trip to Paris in July so that Thornton could serve as the first American delegate to the annual meeting of the Eighth Institute for Intellectual Cooperation, sponsored by the League of Nations to discuss "The Immediate Future of Letters." The immediate future of *Our Town* was more on Thornton's mind, but a summons to duty was not to be ignored, nor was free passage to France.

On the SS *DeGrasse,* he fell in with two brainy, good-looking young ladies, Therese Lewis and Elizabeth Duval, friends of Woollcott's friend Joe Hennessey, who had told them Thornton would be aboard. In Paris he put on his best tour-guide act, showing them where Joan of Arc had stood and escorting them on the eve of Bastille Day to watch the street-dancing. "I got a free education and a lot of gorgeous wine," said Terry Lewis, who wrote for the *New Yorker.* They in turn introduced him to tiny, volatile Marie Louise Bousquet, later Paris editor of *Harper's Bazaar,* "the Lady Colefax of Paris," Thornton called her, a friend of Proust and Anatole France who knew everybody or wanted to.

Conclaves of intellectuals are tests of forbearance, for each delegate feels obliged to talk at length. Thornton's main contribution, in English, was an unchauvinistic defense of American ways and language. He also made a plea, in French, for the independence of the writer from material and political constraints, to the displeasure of delegates from Mussolini's Italy. Gilbert Murray and E. M. Forster complimented him. There were the customary French receptions ("I'm a boy that likes champagne").

Most evenings around seven, when not otherwise occupied, Thornton turned up at Harry's Bar on the rue Danou, sat alone in the corner downstairs over two or three martinis and later mixed with visiting film celebrities — Preston Sturges, Orson Welles — and resident or roving American journalists. Schiaparelli and Madame Chanel had him to dinner. He was invited by the Duke and Duchess of Windsor to accompany Lady Colefax to their Austrian hideaway in Käruten and would have been delighted to accept, but Sibyl declined on his behalf: "They don't speak our language, dears though they are." She went by herself.

Stein was expecting him and urged him to "make the pretty and timid girls [Lewis and Duval] come to see us, that's the way we like them." So from Aix-les-Bains, he and "the girls" journeyed to Bilignin for several days. Miss Lewis found Stein rather forbidding, "a Mount Rushmore type."

Like all summer guests, Thornton was put to work hoeing in Alice Toklas's vegetable garden, a task for which he had been well trained. His hostess had a more important task for him, however, to which he had already been alerted. "I have loved the word collaborate," Stein had written him, "and I always wanted to and now will you oh Thornton will you will you collaborate on *Ida* the Novel, we must do it together. A really truly novel is too much for me all alone we must do it together, how we will talk about it and talk about it, oh dear it will be wonderful to collaborate at last, you would not say no Thornton and worse still you would not do no just think how we could do *Ida* a novel together and what a theme."

What *was* the theme? The more they talked the greater his confusion. She seemed to have in mind a novel about Wallis Simpson, Charles Lindbergh and Abraham Lincoln, but Thornton was in it, too. Stein was serious. She had been impatiently awaiting his arrival: "You are coming near and any day almost any day here we will be collaborating, oh happy day." He would do anything for Gertrude, if he only knew what to do. Everything was dandy, he wrote Terry Lewis after she left Bilignin, "the only cloud being this collaboration. We have long talks about the subject of the novel which is occasionally glimpsed by me as very fine indeed, but for the most part I still don't understand it. I'm afraid that in a day or two I'll have to put my cards on the table and cry off."

Alice Toklas's cooking was perfection, the walks with Stein through the countryside mind-shaking, but the spinster rhythm began to irritate him: starting to go somewhere and not going, the cult of the large white poodle and the small Mexican chihuahua, endless stories about the neighbors, hour-and-a-half waits for the bathroom (there was only one, and Stein had a leisurely soak in the tub every morning). The future of Stein's papers was brought up; the Yale University Library was eager for them and she was agreeable but wondered whether she would be giving them or depositing them. "If I should get poor later on and need to sell them can I or do I. You see. I speak as one not able to earn but who likes to spend money to one [Thornton] being able to earn and who does not like to spend money." Her remark was a half-truth; Thornton didn't like to spend money on himself. He reassured her, and the papers were subsequently placed in Yale's Collection of American Literature; none had to be sold.

Stein drove him in her Ford to Belley, where he took the train for Salzburg and two weeks of Toscanini, Furtwängler and Bruno Walter. There was news from Ruth Gordon; the Toronto audience had been silly drunk on the opening night of his adaptation of *A Doll's House* but it had had twelve curtain calls. Jed Harris cabled that Toronto was hailing Thornton "critically and editorially as [the] greatest adapter of classics."

Sibyl Colefax was in Salzburg. So were Mrs. Murray Crane of Chicago and a countess friend who begged him to have a holiday with them on the French Riviera. He put them off politely and said privately that he had no interest in the "slatternly evil-tongued riff-raff that lives on that glorious coast." Anyway, he was going into seclusion in Switzerland to finish *Our Town*.

13

Men and Women

WORKING HIS WAY north from Salzburg through the Engadine valley in early September, Thornton took lodgings in Ruschlikon, about four miles outside Zurich on a slope overlooking the lake. It rained and rained. He spoke to scarcely anyone but waitresses, in German they understood. Nothing would be allowed to get in the way of *Our Town;* the second act would be "radiant," the third "awesome." Ruschlikon was ideal for writing, "clean as a whistle and quiet as a snow-bound village."

The quiet was broken by a young American who had been visiting Stein. Thornton wrote her on September 9 that when he received her letter about Samuel Steward he had "joyously left a note for him at the American Express telling him where he could find me."

Steward was a slightly built, heavy-drinking, twenty-nine-year-old instructor at a Catholic college in Illinois, which he would quit after having, according to his Chicago friend Wendell Wilcox, "done as much as I can to undermine the faith of the students." He had a campus novel to his credit, *Angels on the Bough,* and aspired to familiarity with literary luminaries. In later years he would make his home in the San Francisco area, take up tattooing professionally, write sexually explicit novels under the pseudonym Phil Andros, narratives of his libidinous adventures, and act as consultant to Dr. Alfred Kinsey in his studies of sexual behavior. In a letter to his "dear girls" in Hamden, Thornton referred to him as "Professor Sam Steward of Loyola University (a Gertrude Stein scholar)."

By Steward's account, Thornton was exploding with enthusiasm in Zurich. "He never stopped talking; neither did I." They had drinks, more drinks, dinner. Hoping to make an impression, the younger man launched into an attack on the Catholic church, whereupon Thornton slapped the table and said sharply, "Don't talk like that; just suppose it might be the right answer." He questioned Steward about his unsettled personal life and prescribed a four-point program: learn how to teach as easily as possible without draining yourself too much; write some essays; dredge up all the unpleasant and disgusting things from your past life about sex or anything else and face them squarely and they will gradually go away; study the lives of the great homosexuals from Leonardo to Michelangelo to Whitman and beyond.

"And after that wordy preparation," according to Steward, "we jumped into bed." It was the first of numerous such meetings — in Paris at the Hotel d'Alsace and in Chicago at the Hotel Stevens.

If one accepts the essentials of Steward's story (supported by testimony of another whom Thornton knew in America and Europe and whose experience was like Steward's), the sexual act was so hurried and reticent, so barren of embrace, tenderness or passion that it might never have happened. Steward felt that for Thornton the act was literally "unspeakable."

During Steward's three days in Zurich, Thornton kept to his schedule of writing in the morning, but in the late afternoon and evening they walked in a drizzle to bars, getting wetter and wetter, to the Café Odeon, where Tristan Tzara started Dadaism, and the house where Nietzsche wrote some of *Thus Spake Zarathustra.* The only remark of Thornton's to Steward that approached the confessional was that in his male friendships, there was "always a touch of Eros."

After Steward had gone, Thornton told Stein that he was "a fine fella and it was a pleasure." To Steward he wrote:

> Lord's sakes, you arrived in my solitude and we had some very happy times and you left me to my solitude and I've missed you. I think of you often and wonder how it's all going. I lectured you so much over here that I'm not going to put a single didactic in this letter, but you know all that's between the lines. Except, allow me one: I forgot it before. Don't read

modern novels. Nothing since *War and Peace* — Natasha is one of the greatest creations in all literature. Not even Proust. There is no danger of your thereby unmodernizing yourself. We're all modern enough. I write and moon about all morning; late afternoons I usually walk into town for my mail and sometimes a concert or a play. I can see your letters have elegance — in that wonderful Roman sense. You can't help it, so this won't make you self conscious. I look for more. And thanks a thousand times for your dropping-from-Heaven, unexpected and felicitous.

Wendell Wilcox, who knew them both in Chicago, was of the opinion that Thornton could have had any of a number of permanent attachments. "Why he didn't choose to have them I don't know." What we know from another of Thornton's intimate companions is that any physical encounter was brief, awkward, left Thornton slightly discomfited and probably remorseful. In each instance, practical counsel was offered: "There was always something of the preacher about him." This particular companion felt that he had been "in communication with some very wise man who was interested in helping. He made a glowing impression." Glenway Wescott, who bragged of his reputation as dean of the homosexuals, said that Thornton was forever hoping Wescott would repudiate that reputation: "He was so shockable it was intimidating, and you wondered how he dared write fiction. All *that* was so sordid, not sordid but so bothering. Colette shocked him. He protested my adoration of Colette. He said she knew nothing about love, she knew only about lust."

It is undeniable that Thornton avoided scenes that might be thought scandalous. For instance, in the fifties after a dinner in New York, when a friend suggested they visit a "gay" playwright at his apartment, Thornton refused; he didn't want to be "drawn into that group." In New Haven, when Gore Vidal teased him about his hike with Gene Tunney, he told Vidal that "a writer ought not to commit himself to a homosexual situation of the domestic sort," that one's career was stunted by such a liaison. He had long understood that he was disqualified from any situation of the domestic sort. All that power of affection had to be channeled into arms-length friendships that fell short of intimacy or furtive, inhibited, infrequent physical encounters — and into words on paper.

He had, of course, a reputation to protect, which dictated steering close to accepted decorum. Equally constraining was devotion to family — his own and the idea of family. Any advertised act repugnant to the conventional sexual code would have been insufferable. One might be led into such acts by the necessities of one's makeup, but they had to be concealed. If he had been born thirty years later his story might have been different. Whether it would have been happier or more productive is unanswerable.

Furthermore, Thornton's adoration of woman, Goethe's *"Das Ewig-Weibliche zieht uns hinan"* — "eternal Woman draws us upward" — was genuine. He flattered, respected, amused and instructed women; above all, he appreciated their roles. If a lady was unmarried or widowed and had enough money and wit, she should have a salon, for men always talk their best when there is a woman in the room. But the lady must never fall in love with any of the men; that ruined everything. When any man or woman for whom he had special affection married, Thornton deliberately distanced himself. He told one of them that he would step out of his life for two years, so that the newlywed's life would not be complicated by Wilderisms. Though Thornton never said so, it was alleged that he proposed marriage to Ruth Gordon and to actress Judith Anderson. If true, it is doubtful that he expected an affirmative response. "Single ones," he said, "miss much, but let us clutch what we have; a different valuation of what is close, occupying and important."

The idea that Thornton's attraction to men had a strong erotic component was challenged by many who knew him well. Bill Nichols regarded him as asexual, even antisexual. He recalled Thornton's telling him that since creativity is a rationed commodity, if one expended one's energies sexually there was that much less to be used artistically. "And he said this with a kind of priest-like conviction." His traveling companion in France, Terry Lewis, never detected "any interest in guys, and there were lots of them around." Jerome Kilty, who would direct a stage production of Thornton's *The Ides of March,* spent days and nights with him in

Atlantic City during the planning of the play: "I would have heard rumors and I heard none; he was a most fastidious man." Actor William Roerick, who saw him often, never thought of him "that way." Charles Newton and Frank Harding were contemptuous of any insinuation that Wilder was "gay." A bit shy with girls, Harding thought, which made him "basically a neuter — it was easier."

Nowhere in his writings, private or public, is there any outright declaration about his sexual nature. The nearest he came to self-revelation, and one must strain for the parallel, may be in his last novel, the semiautobiographical *Theophilus North,* which catalogs the narrator's "nine ambitions," one of which is to be a lover. But what kind of lover? "An omnivorous lover like Casanova? No. A lover of all that is lofty and sublime in women."

"Years later," he wrote in *Theophilus North,*

I found in very knowledgeable company a description of the type to which I belonged. Dr. Sigmund Freud spent his summers in a suburb of Vienna called Grinzing. . . . Without any overtures on my part I was invited to call at his Villa on Sunday afternoons for what he called *Plaudereien* — desultory conversations. At one of these delightful occasions the conversation turned on the distinction between "loving" and "falling in love."

"Herr Doktor," [Freud] asked, "do you know an old English comedy — I forget its name — in which the hero suffers from a certain impediment [*Hemmung*]? In the presence of ladies and of genteel well-brought-up girls he is shy and tongue tied, he is scarcely able to raise his eyes from the ground; but in the presence of servant girls and bar maids and what they are calling emancipated women he is all boldness and impudence. Do you know the name of that comedy?"

"Yes, *Herr Professor.* That is *She Stoops to Conquer.*"

"And who is its author?"

"Oliver Goldsmith."

"Thank you. We doctors have found that Oliver Goldsmith has made an exemplary picture of a problem that we frequently discover among our patients. *Ach, die Dichter haben alles gekannt!"* (The poet-natures have always known everything.)

He then went on to point out to me the relation of the problem to the Oedipus-Complex and to the incest-taboo under which "respectable" women are associated with a man's mother and sisters — "out of bounds."

"Do you remember the name of that young man?"

"Charles Marlow."

He repeated the name with smiling satisfaction. I leaned forward and said *"Herr Professor,* can we call that situation the 'Charles Marlow Complex?' "

"Yes, that would do very well. I have long looked for an appropriate name for it."

Theophilus suffered, as they say (though there was no suffering about it), from that *Hemmung.* Well, let other fellas court and coax, month after month, the stately Swan and the self-engrossed Lily, let them leave to Theophilus the pert magpie and the nodding daisy.*

"The crown of love," Thornton wrote a young lady friend, "and its glorious contribution to our consciousness is that it gives us a sensation of endlessness. All the rest is barnyard."

In notes for lectures he would give at Harvard in 1950–1951, referring to "Whitman and the Breakdown of Love," he remarked that it is fashionable to say that the neurotics' woes all have to do with an inability to make harmonious sexual adjustments. Thornton suspected their troubles had to do more deeply with love. "One can talk all one wants about the libido-element in parental and sibling love — yes, but one falls into the danger of overlooking the sheer emotional devotion which is a qualitative difference, and must be continually recognized as such." The neu-

---

* The relevant dialogue from *She Stoops to Conquer: Charles Marlow:* "Where could I have learned that assurance you talk of? My life has been chiefly spent in a college and in seclusion from that lovely part of the creation that chiefly teaches men confidence. I don't know that I was ever familiarly acquainted with a single modest woman — except my mother. . . . They freeze, they petrify me. . . . " *Hastings:* "At this rate, man, how can you ever expect to marry!" *Marlow:* "Never, unless as among kings and princes, my bride were to be courted by proxy. . . . I'm doomed to adore the sex, and yet to converse with the only part of it I despise."

rotic, "starved of the environment of love," may forever after exhibit so greedy and omnivorous an expectation of love that no affection received is adequate. What is worse, the affection for others in this instance is not truly love "but a demand and command to be loved." He speculated on the effect of good looks on men, how the pleased playful attention accorded them when they are growing up is mistaken by them as a tribute to their capacities of will, intelligence and talent. "This indulgent bath of appreciation exempts them from effort"; they pass their lives in

> bewildered resentment that their successes as charmers are not translated into successes as businessmen, citizens and husbands. Many of them drift into the theater; all of them should, for by the time they are twenty-five they have been conditioned to expect rewards from mere appearances. It is very fortunate *for them* that they generally marry exceptionally fine women. Nature is helping; the fine women are urged to produce fine-looking children; and these good-lookers have something un-completed and dependent about them which calls forth the creative part of the woman (*she* has character for two).

In his journal he took up the case of a married acquaintance who was an alcoholic, a man of occasional five-day bouts of appalling proportions. "I was to learn much later that he was a homosexual, and it may be laid down as a law that in America 80 percent of all married homosexuals are frantic alcoholics." All honor to the wives of such men for the undiscourageable effort they make to "keep their heads above water in the pathless morass of American middle class life and its middle class marriage." He saluted the "sheer force of the will-to-make-out in them." As he thought of them he was reminded ("may my comments be interpreted charitably") of the insects of Fabre whose nests are destroyed and limbs cut off, whose offspring are removed, but who continue performing "all that they know to do for their *genus.*"

A great writer, Thornton was convinced, can handle the confusions of sexual identity. "Someone once told me," he wrote Professor Harry Levin of Harvard, "I was an idiot for not having seen that in the *Golden Bowl* we should read Charles for Charlotte.

. . . A sharper intelligence than ours has preceded us and has seen to it that Charlotte is Charlotte in every passage that is relevant to her being Charlotte; just as Albertine is Albertine when Proust so orders it. When there is an ambiguity it is a controlled ambiguity; not a confusion and not a cheating."

He deemed "highly regrettable" a book on Emily Dickinson that gave currency to allegations of sexual irregularities, "not because it shocks you or me," he told Edward Weeks, but because it will "whip up a prurient oh-ah! in millions of people; it will be hotly contested by many professors — for reasons not connected with research — and all this without at least the dignity of a finality, or a Proven."

Again and again, he hunted for explanations of breakdowns he saw around him. "Can I say that in our time the faculty of loving is being replaced by the craving for being loved? Moreover can I say that in a patriarchal age, one *loves;* and in a matriarchal age one waits to be loved? All I dare say at present is that there are four in my immediate acquaintance who are in shipwreck or approaching shipwreck from an omnivorous demand for love, in whom there is scarcely visible the faintest evidence of a power to love — who repel love by the self-centeredness of their demand." They were spoiled children who "want in perpetuity the being-loved condition of infancy, and the being-loved situation in which American Protestantism presented the Cosmos": God is love, God is father.

When he came to consider Herman Melville's *Billy Budd, Foretopman,* so "filled with a sort of vibration of homosexual feeling and intimation," he identified the off-center sexuality, the strain and tension, not with a serene "rising above" sexual love, but with a fear-latent repudiation of it — "a shrinking from it which inevitably constitutes a fretting relation to it." Melville, through his infatuation with Billy, "almost murdered his story."

The *idea* of love, usually unrequited love, is a recurrent note in *The Trumpet Shall Sound, Love and How to Cure It, The Woman of Andros, The Cabala, The Bridge.* When love descends from the heights of disinterestedness, when spirit becomes body, all is changed. When Manuel in *The Bridge* falls in love with the actress, he loses "that privilege of simple nature, the disassociation of love and pleasure." In a fragment of a story never completed, "The Life of Thomas Everage, American," Thornton compared the sentimental erotic life to "some battlefield at night — bonfires suddenly extinguished, collisions, joyous forays, abrupt isolations, and wounds, ever more wounds bleeding into the sand." Would-be lovers "resolutely shut out from their minds all hope of finding their way in that confused and confusing darkness," turning their attention "to matters that held no possibility of reawakening those rejected vibrations. They were not exempt from the sufferings of love, but they were released from the effort to understand it, to be adequate. They knew that for them it was a fogbank; for them that way madness lay."

Love was not to be confused with the courtesies Thornton showed women. When it was confused, there was trouble, as evidenced by his relationships with Amy Wertheimer and Martha Dodd. One lady wrote him that "the very sound of your voice numbs me with excitement — and I look upon your every word as 'law' and do exactly as you suggest." It depressed him. He couldn't bring himself to answer all this "silly, platsch-platsch mail." It's "terrible," he wrote Isabel, "the amount of mad love letters I'm getting from dames." A lady of thirty, a schoolteacher, audited one of his classes in Chicago and fell in love with him: "That first meeting just did it. I just thought he was it." She made the mistake of telling him. He replied with gratitude for her "concern and regards," but since he was "not able to respond to the further terms you employ I think our correspondence had better come to a close." Another wanted to adopt him: "Angel Child, I grieve sorely that thou hast been ill." "What is there about me that makes women want to mother me?" he asked.

Such idiocies did not diminish the homage he paid women or his pleasure in their company. It is true that the "conversation" was often one-sided. Upon first meeting one woman, he talked animatedly for forty-five minutes without her getting a word in and afterward remarked that she was "the most intelligent woman in New Haven." She could have listened for another forty-five minutes, but it never entered her head that he had any interest in her as a *woman*. If a man was interested, Terry Lewis said, "a gate went up"; with Thornton "the gate never went up."

Kierkegaard wrote that "he who cannot reveal himself cannot love, and he who cannot love is the most unhappy man of all." Reading Kierkegaard led Thornton to reconsider something he had written in *The Woman of Andros*. In that book he had rather prided himself on the observation that the state of civilization of any country can be judged by whether young men first fall in love with women older or younger than themselves. If they wasted their youthful imagination on thin, unnourishing young girls, they were forever impoverished. Now, he thought *une femme mure* could civilize, but she could not "irradiate, could not provoke a man to invest her with that overwhelming ideality which, in turn, both renders him creative and endows him with *la conscience de l'immortal-iste*. (Or perhaps she can only do this for him if his love is not gratified physically, which Søren Kierkegaard implies, and perhaps Goethe illustrates)."

He returned time after time to the ideality of selfless love. Of the young girl of whom Kierkegaard was enamored but who married another, he wrote that she had no

> faint understanding of the thunders and lightnings she has released in her lover; she takes it all to herself as food for her vanity. Even though she is exceptionally intelligent she will appear to be a *goose* viewed against the cloudscapes of ideality which she releases in a man. But consider her state ten years later, she who had dimly felt herself to have been Empress and sorceress; at that time she did not know how she came by such powers but they seemed natural to her; now she does not know how she has lost them. She assumes that it was simply sex and youth — and so it was, but in categories she cannot understand. She has been "spoiled" in the current sense of the word. In America — which makes an anti-ideal glorification of that young-girl-ideality — the women over twenty-four are in a rage to recover those magics of which they feel themselves to have been *despoiled*.

The sense of female ideality, he was persuaded, can rarely if ever be sustained by an actress; it was no accident that since the beginning of the theater the actress had been regarded as a courtesan. Ideality lives in our minds under two aspects, he wrote in his journal: "the untouchable, the revered, surrounded by taboos (and a taboo is a provocation-plus-veto), and as accessible, even — in spite of the masque of decorum and dignity — *inviting.*" To maintain the first of these two roles all the buttresses of society are necessary: the marriage institution, the prestige of virtue, law and custom.

> A woman on the stage is bereft of these safeguards. The exhibition of her bare face in mixed society, for money, under repetition, speaking words not her own, are sufficient. But far more powerfully is she delivered into the hands, into the thought-impulse life of the audience, by the fact that she is on the stage — the realm of accumulated fictions — as Woman, as bird of prey, hence attacker, and as willing victim, that is, *piège.* Under those bright lights, on that endless platform, all the modesty of demeanor in the world cannot convince us that this is not our hereditary ghost, the haunter of our nervous system, the friend-enemy of our dreams and appetites, the eternal courtesan.*

Offstage, they "walk in a narcissist daydream and can barely distinguish truth from falsehood."

Let women be like Shakespeare's girls: Rosalinds bringing order out of emotional chaos; Lady Macbeths, never infirm of purpose; Sylvias with their constancy; high-spirited and audacious Katharinas; powerful and decisive intellects like Portia; true and loving Desdemonas, loyal and humble but with wills of their own.

He wanted wider recognition of women's strengths, outside as well as inside the home. He wrote Les Glenn in 1972 that "Women's Lib is 3,000 years overdue," and when Hutchins announced that he was stepping down as head of the Center for Democratic Studies, Thornton was sorry he had not advanced the suggestion that the position be filled by a woman. "Men are entangled with their exhausted preeminence and exhausted postures. My instinct tells me (you can't go higher or lower than that) that

---

* These lines, he notes, were "written while mildly drunk on a quart of Bordeaux."

the pendulum has been swinging rapidly from the patriarchy (under which you and I were brought up, and how!) to the matriarchy, and that the matriarchy after passing through a confused, insecure and comical phase is entering a mature self-reliance. Men distrust men as men; not a sincere, generous note for decades. We are in an age when men will rally round an experienced and authoritative woman." "Don't overdo the notion," he wrote unmarried Isabel in 1937, "that a woman has nothing to say or be or give unless she's wife-mother-and-home-decorator. We're all people before we're anything else. People even before we're artists. The role of being a person is sufficient to have lived and died for. Don't insult 10 million women by saying a woman is null and void as a spinster."

He believed in coeducation and spoofed women's colleges as hothouse nunneries, repositories of vestigial monasticism. When they objected and said their campuses were crawling with men every weekend, he countered: "Yes and that's what's wrong. A Date is an object you parade before the eye of your fellow-students — not primarily a friend you are having congenial hours with."

The feminine ideal was his mother, managing on her own during the absence or illness of a husband whose temperament and tastes were not hers, who made do without self-pity, who moved from stove to piano, from sewing and scrubbing to gardening, exchanging thoughts on the spiritual life with her son Amos, writing and translating poetry, taking part in civic affairs, gathering with like-minded ladies to converse in German and Italian, reading the stories of her excitable younger son, whose every message left for a laundress was "simply wonderful." She is in *The Long Christmas Dinner, The Happy Journey to Camden and Trenton* and in Thornton's most popular play, to which we now turn, *Our Town.*

I4
Our Town

"I AM WRITING the most beautiful little play you can imagine,"
Thornton informed Stein in October 1937. "Every morning brings
an hour's increment to it and that's all. But I've finished two acts
already. It's a little play with all the big subjects in it; and it's a
big play with all the little things of life lovingly impressed into
it." *Our Town* would "re-open the theaters." In it, he would dramatize the daily life of Grover's Corners, its living and dead, its
birth and death statistics and how Mrs. Gibbs ironed Dr. Gibbs's
shirts, "all in one great curve: *Quod Erat Demonstrandum.*" (*Quod
Erat Demonstrandum* was Stein's first novel, published after her
death under the title *Things As They Are.*)

Sam Steward had departed, and Thornton was at the Hotel Bel-
voir, an hour-and-a-half walk to Zurich. He was up at eight, wrote
or copied all morning, lunched on the balcony or at his window
and was "so happy that I'm not even afraid of being happy."
He bought himself a greenish, rough-felt Tyrolean hat and summed
up his life at forty as "work and the loaf-to-prepare-the-work."

Nearly ten years earlier, on the train from Florida to New York,
Thornton had promised producer-director Jed Harris a first look
at his next full-length play. Giving a play to Jed was like giving
money to J. P. Morgan to invest; you couldn't lose. In the late
twenties Harris had had four concurrent hits on Broadway. Several
scenes from *Our Town* were mailed to Harris, then in London,
who cabled Thornton in Switzerland: "I am most anxious to see
you or speak to you on the telephone. Can you come to Paris a
few days. What is your phone number and address. Please wire
me immediately Savoy. Much love." Six days later: "Am very

anxious to get on with *Our Town* and if I could have the script Monday morning I would have it typed in Paris before going back to America."

Sibyl Colefax cautioned Thornton that Jed was a bully, and with a bully one had to be firm; Jed was *never, never, never* to be trusted unless one had the upper hand. She was not alone in that judgment. Actress Lynn Fontanne wondered "furiously" why Thornton gave Harris first crack at his plays. "Is it all your plays, for God's sake. Everybody prophesies some dire débacle always with Jed."

Jed was difficult, but he knew his business. Anyway, Thornton had given his word. He went to Paris, turned over the finished play and reported that Harris was "very enthusiastic and hurried home to America to put it on for the Christmas season. So he says. I follow soon for rehearsals."

Paying a farewell call on Stein at 27 rue de Fleurus, Thornton took charge of two trunkfuls of her manuscripts and notes bound for Yale. She and he rarely talked politics and rarely agreed when they did. She, believing that "the Republicans are the natural rulers of America," distrusted Franklin D. Roosevelt. He did not. She was positive there would be no second world war. He was not. Now he told her that in his opinion fascism was a greater insult to the human mind than communism, "though communism is no picnic." His father, he said, had been "an unconscious fascist — he wanted to be wise for other people, willy-nilly; so my political notions flow from that."

The following day he was in London, strolling through Hyde Park, having tea with Lady Ottoline Morrell and poet Walter de la Mare and dinner with Lady Colefax.

What was he doing in London? Harris cabled. "Please if you possibly can do sail this week as I need you very badly for about two weeks work before we go into rehearsal. Casting provisionally under way." *Our Town* was to try out in Princeton, and since no scenery was required it could be taken out of town as much as Harris wanted, with Jed "lightly thumbing his nose at the Unions," Thornton wrote Terry Lewis. "How you will weep during Act 3. Nothing cures a cold like a good cry."

Harris was waiting at the pier in New York and whisked his playwright off to Long Island for last-minute revisions in the script.

Thornton called it "being imprisoned," but the "prison" was a red-barn, gentleman's country cottage in Old Brookville, a gunshot from Oyster Bay, adorned with chintz, cocktail shakers, butler and an expensive gramophone: "the gilded cage; sing birdie sing." Christmas week, Thornton's adaptation of *A Doll's House* finally reached Broadway, and *Our Town* was ready for rehearsal.

The play opens on the Stage Manager casually puffing on his pipe, looking at his watch and deprecating latecomers. He then describes Grover's Corners and takes us to the adjoining houses of Doc Gibbs and his wife and children, George and Rebecca; and editor Webb and his wife and children, Emily and Wally. The year is 1901; the plot is as bare as the set. Emily marries young George Gibbs, then dies in childbirth in the second act. At her cemetery burial in the third act, we see and hear the townspeople, living and dead. Emily pleads to return to life, is given one day to relive, then willingly goes back to the realm of the dead.

The last revisions of which we have record, made during Thornton's "imprisonment" on Long Island, are minor and confined to the third act:

> *First Dead Man.* Those northeast [instead of "southwest"] winds always do the same thing, don't they?"

And:

> *Mr. Webb.* Yes, well it's colder than that [instead of "twenty below"] at Hamilton College.

And:

> *Stage Manager.* (*He winds his watch*) [instead of "the clock striking"] Um . . . 11:00 o'clock in Grover's Corners.

And Thornton added here a concluding line to the audience: "You get a good rest too. Goodnight."

In his preface to the published play, Thornton said that *Our Town* was not offered as speculation about the conditions of life

after death ("that element I merely took from Dante's *Purgatory*").
It was an attempt "to find a value above all price for the smallest
events of our daily life. Our claim, our hope, our despair are in
the minds — not in things, not in 'scenery.' " Like several of the
one-acts of the early thirties, *Our Town* reflected his dissatisfaction
with the current theater: "The response we make when we 'believe'
a work of the imagination is that of saying 'this is the way things
are, I have always known it without being fully aware that I knew
it.' It is this form of knowledge which Plato called 'recollection.'
Of all the arts, the theater is best endowed to awaken this recollection within us — to believe is to say 'yes'; but in the theater of
my time I didn't feel myself prompted to any such grateful and
self-forgetting acquiescence." Plays had been shut up in a "museum
showcase" and the "box-set stifles the life in drama." With its
bare stage, *Our Town* was out to capture "not verisimilitude but
reality."

"My Dear Thornton," Charles Wager wrote his star pupil:

> I have read the play twice — it came yesterday — and it moved
> me the second time even more than the first. What it would
> do to me at a third reading I can only guess for I do not
> intend, at present, to try the experiment. You remember Jou-
> bert's remark, repeated by Matthew Arnold, that in literature,
> we weep not at what is sad, but at what is beautiful, and the
> tears that your play has made me shed were caused by its
> terrible beauty. Your "Aeschylean silences" — "They are si-
> lent," "Mrs. Gibbs does not answer," "Pause" — what must
> they be like on the stage when they move me so deeply in
> the book? The effect of the Stage Manager's speeches in the
> third act, like the effect of the play as a whole, is beyond
> any words of mine. "And they went and died about it!" You
> haven't read your Greeks for nothing. I know Grover's Cor-
> ners, the feel, the sound, the very smell of it, and I know
> the "windy hilltop," too. There is one at Hamilton, New York.
> But words fail. You have done the greatest piece of work
> you've ever done, and I don't use the adjective "great" lightly.

Over the next thirty-five years Samuel French would sell 290,000
copies of *Our Town,* at least 100,000 more than any other play

Three-year-old Thornton in Madison, Wisconsin with brother
Amos (standing) and sisters Isabel and Charlotte to his left.

Thornton's mother, Isabella Niven Wilder, Berkeley, California, 1907. A "loving, serving, vivid life."

Outside the Wilder house on Dwight Way, Berkeley, 1911. Janet in her mother's lap, and, left to right, Isabel, Amos, Thornton, Charlotte.

Amos Parker Wilder and his sons, Amos
and Thornton, New Haven, 1915.

Thornton at Oberlin, September 1916.

Lawrenceville School, spring 1924. The boys of Davis House with assistant house-master Wilder (seated at right) and housemaster Clyde Foresman (second from left, front row). (*Courtesy Mrs. Elizabeth Miller*)

Holiday in Surrey, England, 1928. Left to right, Isabel, Thornton, Mother, Janet.

Hikers: Gene Tunney and Thornton in Switzerland, September 1928.

Chaperone Wilder aboard ship with his Lawrenceville School charges — Clark
Andrews, Henry Noe, Duff McCullough, 1928.
(*Courtesy Clark Andrews*)

"The best of geezers." Bill Nichols in 1924,
shortly before he met Thornton.
(*Courtesy William Nichols*)

Samuel Steward, 1935. (*Courtesy Samuel Steward*)

Charles and Joe Newton, two of the "Goethe Street gang," 1934. (*Courtesy Charles Newton*)

An evening of song with Southside Chicago pals in the summer of 1936.
(*Courtesy Charles Newton*)

Chicago in the mid-thirties. From left, Robert Maynard Hutchins, Mrs. Harold Swift, Thornton, and Maude Hutchins.

Fun in France with Terry Lewis, 1937. (*Courtesy Therese Lewis Robinson*)

"The Happiest Years." Professor Wilder arm in arm with Katinka Loeser (left) and Betty Ito at the University of Chicago. (*Courtesy Katinka Loeser De Vries*)

Old friends in England, 1939. Max Beerbohm, Alexander Woollcott and Thornton.

"Collaborators." Thornton and Gertrude Stein at Bilignin, 1937. (*Collection of American Literature, Beinecke Rare Book and Manuscript Library, Yale University. W. G. Rogers photo*)

Partying with Mabel Dodge Luhan in the thirties. (*Collection of American Literature, Beinecke Rare Book and Manuscript Library, Yale University*)

Making an opera of *The Alcestiad*.
Composer Louise Talma at the piano at
50 Deepwood Drive, September 1956.
(*Matthew Wysocki*)

With Lillian Gish in Berlin, September 1957. (*Courtesy Eleanor Lansing Dulles*)

Thornton and director Max Reinhardt going over the script of *The Merchant of Yonkers*, New York, 1938.

The playwright in the role of Mr. Antrobus in *The Skin of Our Teeth*.

The original 1942 cast of *The Skin of Our Teeth*. Left to right,
Tallulah Bankhead, Florence Eldridge, Fredric March, Frances
Heflin, Montgomery Clift.

The Boy Wonder of Broadway, producer Jed Harris (left) with actor Frank Craven
and Thornton, shortly before the New York opening of *Our Town*, 1938.
(*Culver Pictures, Inc.*)

Rendezvous in Paris, 1950, with Sylvia Beach (left) and Alice B. Toklas. (*Collection of the author*)

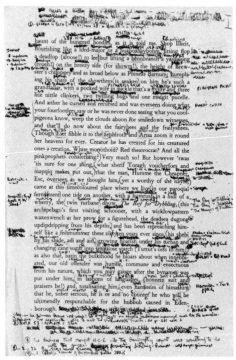

A page from Wilder's annotated copy of James Joyce's *Finnegans Wake*.

Pen pal Amy Wertheimer, 1955.
(*Courtesy Nancy W. Kleinbord*)

Thornton and Isabel on his fifty-second
birthday, April 17, 1949.

With friends Ruth Gordon and Garson Kanin, 1959. (*William Tague*, Berkshire
Eagle)

The author at his desk in Hamden, Connecticut several years before his death. (*Photograph* © *1983 by Jill Krementz*)

on their list. It would bring its author more attention and income
— $400,000 by 1964 — than anything else he would write. Its
lines would be memorized in dozens of languages, thousands of
American high schools would perform it, but few who played it
or saw it knew of the labor pains that accompanied its birth.

It opened at the McCarter Theatre in Princeton January 22,
1938, to a tepid reception. *Variety* thought that "as theater, it is
not only disappointing but hopelessly slow. Jed Harris has endowed
it with a superlative cast, headed by Frank Craven, and it will
probably go down as the season's most extravagant waste of fine
talent. It is hard to imagine what the worthwhile wonder boy of
Broadway saw in this disjointed, bitter-sweet affair of small town
New Hampshire life."

William Roerick, one of the baseball players in the original
cast, recalled that when they arrived in Princeton for dress rehearsal, a piano was being moved into the theater for a recital
that night and Harris had a tantrum. The cast was told to go to
bed and come back at midnight. They rehearsed from midnight
until eight the next morning. Spaghetti was brought in for breakfast
from the only restaurant that was open. In Boston the following
week everyone associated with the play, but particularly Harris,
was hit by a thunderbolt — the suicide of the wealthy and beautiful
Rosamond Pinchot, with whom Harris had been living and who
had been helping backstage.

On opening night business was bad. E. Martin Browne, a British
theatrical director who had met Thornton at the MacDowell Colony in 1929, said he "applauded like mad, but no one else seemed
to care; the notices were disappointing or condescending. I
dropped a note at the Stage Door to suggest to Thornton that if
this was how Boston received his wonderful play he should put
it on our liner which was still in harbor and try London." Glenway
Wescott came upon the author backstage, wearing an old trench
coat and looking "as though he had walked for miles in haste. I
took his arm and noticed that he was trembling slightly, all the
way up from his knees." *

On the first day of the Princeton tryout, Thornton, disturbed

* Glenway Wescott, *Images of Truth* (New York: Harper & Row, 1962), p.
303.

by what he had observed in rehearsals, had written and sealed a memorandum on elements in the production "likely to harm and perhaps shipwreck its effectiveness." The first act and in large measure the play was in danger of "falling into trivial episodes, through failure to build up the two great idea-pillars of the Stage Manager's interruptions." One speech had been reduced to "pleasant fooling, instead of being made forceful and informative, as I have often requested; the passage on the future has been watered down, and the actor has not been vigorously directed." The element of the "Concrete Localization of the town," his memo continued, "has been neglected; in fact, the director [Harris] has an astonishingly weak sense of visual reconstruction. Characters talk to one another from Mrs. Webb's back door to Main Street; and from one end of Main Street to another in the same tone of voice they use when they're in the same 'room.' They stroll practically in and out of Main Street when they are in a house; Emily's grave is one minute here and soon after there." Despite promises to remove them, "a series of interpolations in the first act remain: each one of these has the character of amiable dribbling, robbing the text of its nervous compression from which alone can spring the sense of significance in the trivial acts of life which is the subject of the play." In addition, "The recent alteration to the closing words of Mrs. Gibbs and Emily in Act Three are soft, and pathetic." There seemed "every likelihood that a pseudo-artistic inclination to dim lights will further devitalize the Stage Manager's long speeches in the last act. The eternal principal that the ear does not choose to hear if the eye is not completely satisfied particularly applies in this play."

Harris considered withdrawing it. Woollcott recommended closing it down in Boston and coming directly to New York, but poor reviews persuaded the Shuberts to deny it a theater. Bring it to New York anyway, Woollcott told Harris, and the first night will show that he could have any theater in the city. *New York Times* drama critic Brooks Atkinson came to a matinee but left early, saying he wanted to review it afresh in New York and with the exuberance of an amateur. Playwright Marc Connelly, summoned to Boston to judge whether *Our Town* had a future, said it *had* to be taken to New York.

Harris gave in and brought it to Braodway a week ahead of schedule, putting it into the temporarily vacant Henry Miller Theatre for ten days to see what would happen.*

"It's been one long fight," Thornton wrote Stein February 1, "to preserve my text from the interpolations of Jed Harris and I've only won fifty percent of the time. The play no longer moves or even interests me; now all I want out of it is money. Money so that I can feel justified in going off to Arizona and write some more — reconstruct the mode of life I had in Zurich. The play may be a failure. The whole blame of my state rests at Jed Harris' door." But as Woollcott predicted, when *Our Town* opened at the Henry Miller on February 4 it was cheered.

The cheers did little to lower tensions between author and producer. Harris was nervous. He had some of his own money in the production and had worried that if he kept it going for a second week in Boston he would lose fourteen thousand dollars. Moreover, he made no secret of his conviction that the play was "terribly overwritten" and said that he had pruned it mercilessly. When Thornton asked, "What happened to my beautiful prose?" Harris shot back, "Prose doesn't play."

For all his seductive charm and theatrical competence, Harris, Yale class of 1917, was very tough. According to his biographer, when the business manager of Local One said that two property men had to be added to the *Our Town* crew, Harris agreed to the hiring but forbade them to touch any chair on the set. A few minutes before the curtain was to rise, each of the "grips" was nevertheless holding a chair in his hand. Harris ordered one of them to put the chair down.

"Got orders to move the chair," the stagehand said.

"I give the orders around here, you unwashed bindlestiff, and I said *put that chair down.*"

"I can't do that, Mr. Harris, accordin' to the book. No actor is suppose to touch a prop."

"Why, you slimy, contemptible oaf, you ignorant pediculous loafer, you untalented, worthless, parasitical bloodsucker, I'll give you one more chance to put the chair down." The curtain began

* In his autobiography, *Watchman, What of the Night?* (1963), pp. 79–81, Harris wrote that *Our Town* had been booked in New York for only one night.

to rise, the stagehand lifted the chair, Harris's fist caught him squarely on the chin, he went down. Then Harris collared the second man and "choked him into insensibility." * Thereafter, actors moved chairs without union interference.

Our Town won Thornton his second Pulitzer Prize and added to Harris's already lustrous reputation, but the bickering went on. Jed said that he hated and despised Thornton, that he was a phony, a man without talent or character. They were constantly at odds, Thornton trying to reclaim the play from attempts to make it more "entertaining." "Jed and I wrote the play together," he said bitterly. "Such *fun* working with him. He's so considerate and self-effacing and has such impeccable taste in the choice of *words!*" Ten days before the Princeton opening, Thornton had written Stein that "as long as [Jed's] suggestions for alterations are on the structure they are often very good; but once they apply to the words, they are always bad and sometimes atrocious. There have been some quite-hot flaring fights. At present we are in a lull of reconcilement. Even with Jed's sentences in it — which I hope gradually to *abrade* away — it is a very good play. The cast is fine."

There was a new row when Harris tried to sell *Our Town* to Hollywood, with the condition that the author write the screenplay. Thornton refused, the deal fell through and Harris threatened to sue Thornton for the loss. Recalling the acrimony, motion picture producer Sol Lesser was of the opinion that Harris got a sexual satisfaction out of being a sadist. "A cold man, a very unappreciative man. He imposed himself on me and hung around the house until I had to throw him out." When relations were at their most strained, Isabel advised Thornton to "send some overtures of regard"; that Jed didn't know how bad he was. "I think he knows," Thornton answered, "and I'm longing to ask him to give [Max] Reinhardt the West Coast rights of *Our Town.*"

Less than three months after the Broadway opening, another ugly incident surfaced. Thornton was informed that a check for $450 made out to him personally had been endorsed "Thornton Wilder, For Deposit, Jed Harris" and deposited in the Irving Trust

* Recounted by Maurice Zolotow, *No People Like Show People* (New York: Random House, 1951), pp. 224–25.

Company in New York. On the face of it, Harris or one of his managers had forged Wilder's name and stolen the money due him for three weeks' royalties on *A Doll's House*. Harris explained that the endorsement had been an error by one of his subordinates, whom he fired. Thornton let the matter drop, "for former friendship's sake," but he was angry. Jed is the "father of lies," he told Isabel. "You say he is lonely; well, let him retain old friends instead of setting out on new journeys perpetually to captivate and to spoil new ones. If you have the theory that man is purely a conditioned animal and that his sins are merely the result of unhappy early environment or hereditary distortion, then all men become innocent victims and are to be pitied and spared the consequences of their acts; but man is the master of choice and a possessor of inborn standards and however tangled the background must be held responsible."

By October 1938, Thornton was saying that he and Jed were "all washed up, and Ruthie [Gordon]'s silence [Jed was the father of her son] — in spite of divers phone calls and notes from me — implies that [Jed's] painted me out as black-hearted and she's off me too. Ishkabibble. I'll take to Ina Claire." When Harris threatened to close the road show of *Our Town* because he claimed it was losing money, Thornton accused him of "ugly cheap shrill blackmailing methods." Blackmail or not, the threat worked. Jed had asked for a 50 percent reduction in the author's royalties, and Thornton's New Haven attorney, J. Dwight Dana, advised that a compromise be accepted: if the gross receipts were less than $7,500 a week, a 50 percent cut, but only 25 percent if the gross was more than $7,500 and less than $8,000. The reduction, effective for nine weeks through September 3, 1939, would give Harris "all the relief he fairly needs," Dana felt. "Okay," Thornton wired.

What is incongruous about these contretemps is that Thornton had enormous respect for Harris as "the new theatrical wizard of Broadway." Yet a friendly letter of Thornton's (they were both in New York City) had this reply: "I received your latest communication and like all others I ever get from you it is a characteristic blend of fatuousness, vanity and superb unconscious buffoonery." After a pleasant meeting in Hollywood, Harris telegraphed: "It is simply this, I would prefer that we do not communicate with each other about anything whatever. I am sure you understand." At the bottom of the telegram, Thornton penned: "A real Jedism. A sudden snap and bite after a completely congenial evening!" A letter from Jed followed: "Tell me, where in what is left of this world is there any place for such animosities as ours?" "Get a load of this," Thornton wrote Isabel. "I answered amicably."

In 1972, after an estrangement of many years, someone told Thornton that Harris was staying at the Hotel Royalton in New York and Thornton invited him for a drink. "Why would you want to see *me?!*" Harris asked. Nevertheless, they shared two bottles of wine and talked for hours. "I'm reconciling with my enemies," Thornton said.

Thornton went to great pains to make sure that the printed text of *Our Town* was cleansed of some of Harris's alterations. In a memorandum prepared for control of the text as presented in all subsequent productions, he stated that "in spite of the fact that I left in the Jed Harris offices three copies of the specifically marked Definitive Copies of the text of the play, I found during the final rehearsals of the play a number of unauthorized readings were still being used. I called Harris' attention to them; he made notations of the readings, and assured me they would be corrected." Thornton nonetheless entered his own notations on the Samuel French acting edition.

He did not see *Our Town* as sad and sentimental but as a celebration of daily life in the knowledge of death's inevitability. It was a "very autobiographical work," bringing together memories of New England and "many lights from a Wisconsin household." (*Dr. Gibbs:* "I tell ya Julia, there's nothing so terrifying in the world as a son. The relation of father and son is the damndest, awkwardest. . . .") The bare stage had not been influenced, as some suspected, by the theater of China and Japan but by the theater of Elizabeth I and Phillip II and III. It owed something also to Pirandello's *Six Characters in Search of an Author,* which had so appealed to Thornton by its liberation from the box set and the use of theater aisles and lobbies as settings.

One word in the printed text, left unchanged, caused him distress, particularly after he himself played the role of Stage Manager.

As he wrote critic Malcolm Cowley: "At the close of act two the clergyman thinks aloud and ends up, 'once in a thousand times [marriage] is interesting.' How did I happen to give such a chilling and cynical impression? Because I had incorporated into myself Gertrude Stein's use of the word [interesting], and failed to realize that the rest of the world didn't use it in the same sense. One of the reasons I like to play that role is that I can attempt to 'save' that moment; I do the first half of the speech dreamy and grave and then suddenly break out into a smile at that word!"

Grover's Corners was no particular town. "For several summers," he told Cowley, "I taught at a tutoring camp on Lake Sunapee. I did a great deal of walking in those days — New London (New Hampshire) is not far away. That went into it. Lots of observations in Peterborough which has no cemetery on a hill (that I saw once in Vermont) and has no 'Polish Town' across the tracks — I forget now where I picked that up — maybe Keene or one of those mill towns on the way to Keene." In a note to an edition of *Our Town* printed for members of the Limited Editions Club in 1974, he said that

> the recurrent words (few have noticed it) are "hundreds," "thousands," and "millions." Emily's joys and griefs, her algebra lessons and her birthday presents — what are they when we consider all the billions of girls who have lived, who are living, and who will live? Each individual's assertion to an absolute reality can only be inner, very inner. And here the method of staging finds its justification — in the first two acts there are at least a few chairs and tables; but once she visits the earth and the kitchen to which she descended on her twelfth birthday, the very chairs and table are gone. . . . Molière said that for the theater all he needed was a platform and a passion or two. The climax of this play needs only five square feet of boarding and the passion to know what life means to us.

There was no doubt about *Our Town*'s human appeal. (Too human for Russian authorities, who closed it down in Berlin shortly after the Second World War.) Willa Cather wrote Thornton that it was "the loveliest thing that has been produced in this country in a long, long time — and the truest. Exiled Americans, living abroad, to whom I have sent the book of the play, write me that it has made them weep with homesickness. I love everything you have ever written, but you have done nothing so fine as this." Critic John Mason Brown called it "one of the sagest, warmest, and most deeply human scripts to have come out of our theater." To Lillian Gish, it was "the greatest play of our century."

When *Our Town* was revived in the fifties, one New York critic was very severe on its author, but Thornton was unabashed, believing that anyone who entered attentively into it would find "few of the comforts generally furnished by sentimentality." His confidence was not misplaced. Raves outnumbered slams — "one of the most important theatrical experiences of this generation" (*Chicago Tribune*); "any season could count itself proud to bring forth *Our Town*" (Robert Benchley, the *New Yorker*). Raymond Massey, who played the Stage Manager in seventy USO performances in Europe in 1945, shortly after the fighting stopped, never forgot "those faces [of the GIs] — the tense, rapt, even desperate looks. Some were wiping tears from their eyes." *

All that came later. *Our Town* having been successfully launched, Thornton turned his back on Broadway and its bickering and the accolades, hid himself in Arizona, and by late spring of 1938 was caught up in a four-act, rapid-fire farce, full of twists and turns and with a happy ending for lovers.

---

* *One Hundred Different Lives* (Boston: Little, Brown, 1979), p. 302.

15
Reinhardt and
The Merchant

PARKED TEMPORARILY in Tucson's Santa Rita Hotel, Thornton hunted for a twenty-five-dollar-a-month furnished apartment and found one with a Murphy bed that came down halfway at night ("I slept almost standing up"). Apart from an occasional meal in town, he ate whatever came out of cans, along with zwieback and peanut butter and boiled eggs laced with salt, pepper, paprika and whiskey. Mornings he wrote. Afternoons he walked, the only person in Tucson, he said, who used his legs. "Everybody else drives dusty cars or stands against storefronts with half-closed eyes." Secluding himself for eight weeks, he finished the first two acts of *The Merchant of Yonkers*, first titled *Luck and Pluck*, and sent them to Max Reinhardt in Hollywood. Reinhardt wired that he awaited the rest with "the greatest suspense and eagerly wish to put it on the stage. I particularly hold Mrs. Levi to be a *hostleiche* [precious] addition to the play. I would further wish to discuss with you whether songs and music as in the original would be appropriate and desirable."

"The original" was a comedy by Viennese playwright Johann Nestroy, *Einen Jux will er sich machen,* written in 1842 and itself based on John Oxenford's earlier play, *A Day Well Spent.* Dolly Levi, the central character in Thornton's play, set in the 1880s, does not appear in Nestroy, and she — the matchmaker who snares the rich elderly Yonkers merchant — is the heart of his one-hundred-percent American farce.

Thornton's two ambitions for *The Merchant* were at odds. He wanted it to be directed by his boyhood idol, Reinhardt; he also wanted Ruth Gordon, his favorite actress, to play Mrs. Levi. Reinhardt was willing to have her, Miss Gordon was not willing to have him; it had to be directed by Jed Harris. But Harris was out of the question as far as Thornton was concerned; "Jed gypped me on the cosmic overtones [in *Our Town*]." The leading role eventually went to an actress of first rank, but no one's first choice, Jane Cowl.

"The fourth act's developed fine," the playwright wrote his family. "I who never could finish a novel correctly seem to have the knack of last acts. But the third act has been terrifying me. Ever since I got here I've been in a cold sweat about it. It wouldn't come right. I have thought of laying the play aside and telling Reinhardt that maybe I'd be a year or two at it. And then last night I got the key — the direction. All my plots came to a head at the right moment, with Mrs. Levi ruling the roost. Rejoice with me. Now it'll go very fast."

He had just written a passage on merchant Geyermacher's fifty-year-old "apprentice," very little of which was retained but which bespeaks Thornton's flair for the comic:

Cabman. Who's your friend?

Melchior. Friend? That's not a friend; that's an employer [Geyermacher] I'm trying out for a few days.

Cabman. You won't like him.

Melchior. I can see that you're in business for yourself, because you talk about liking employers. No one's ever liked an employer since business began.

Cabman. Aw — !

Melchior. No, sir. I suppose you think *your horse* likes you.

Cabman. Hortence? She'd give her right feet for me.

Melchior. That's what all employers think. You imagine it. The streets of New York are full of cabhorses winking at one another. I've had about fifty employers in my life but this is the most employer of them all. He talks to everybody as though he were paying them.

Cabman. I had an employer once. He watched me from 8:00 in the morning until 6:00 at night — just sat and watched me. Even my mother didn't think I was as interesting as that.

Melchior. Yes, being employed is like being loved; you know

that somebody's thinking about you the whole time.
Come on. You know, I had an employee once. And
like all employers, I thought he liked me. (*Shrugs
his shoulders*) No . . . finally I got a dog. You can
always imagine a dog likes you.

Not a word of that passage is from Nestroy, yet it has the flavor
of Nestroy — sardonic, good-humored, sliding between general
ideas and specific illustrations.

On his forty-first birthday, April 17, 1938, Thornton was far
enough along to read *The Merchant of Yonkers* to guests at a cattle
ranch, but instead of taking the play to Reinhardt in California,
he decided to hold on to the third act for another month and to
return East, where he had a long-standing spring engagement.

Thornton had promised journalist Vincent (Jimmy) Sheean and
his wife Dinah that he would show them around New York on
Sheean's first trip to America since the publication of his brilliant
travel memoir, *Personal History*. Sheean was not only a colorful
reporter on the international scene but also, like Thornton, loved
and spoke glowingly about great music. Dinah had known Thornton since the twenties, when they met in England at the home
of her father, Shakespearean actor Sir Johnston Forbes-Robertson.
The guided tour of the city was conducted as if Thornton were
Toscanini leading the Philharmonic. The three of them rode about
in a chauffeured limousine, Thornton waving his arms and pointing
out the landmarks: "If you could see it [the day was foggy], *that*
would be the George Washington bridge." No mention was made
of *Our Town,* the most popular play in New York. It was a day
for Dinah and Jimmy and he didn't want to draw attention to
himself.

Several weeks later, from Woollcott's Vermont island play-
ground, Thornton mailed Reinhardt the third act of *The Merchant,*
over the protest of some of Woollcott's guests who thought it
wasn't right for the Old Man. But "loyalty, fascination and homage
to a great career, and fulfillment of boyhood dreams," Thornton
answered, "all combine to make me lay that play entirely at his
feet." In mid-June he was on the Chief for Los Angeles, to help
Reinhardt any way he could — "Yes, sew cheesecloth for him,
if he needs it."

Having in his youth kept a record of Reinhardt companies in Berlin and Vienna, Thornton remembered the names of the actors and, when he met them long afterward, could tell them what part they had played and in what theater. Moreover, during the fall and winter of 1928–1929, he had been present at nearly sixty stage performances in Europe, many of them Reinhardt's, and while teaching at Lawrenceville he had seen The Master's production of *The Miracle* in New York and, later, *The Eternal Road*. Reinhardt, now sixty-five and with five years to live, was the towering theatrical figure of his generation. He had put on his dramas in circuses, open-air theaters, ballrooms and on cathedral steps and had come to Hollywood not only to produce plays, but also to establish a school that would instruct actors and directors in concepts of production and design calculated to involve the audience intimately in the make-believe.

"Well well," Thornton wrote the folks in Hamden from the Beverly Wilshire Hotel on June 22:

> Monday night I went to dinner with the Reinhardts way up on top of the mountain. Helene Thiming [Reinhardt's wife] driving the car called for me. Wonderful, beautiful, sad woman. Troubles troubles. They live frugally and obstacles and troubles on every hand. The Chamber of Commerce subsidizing the [Reinhardt] festival has cancelled *The Blue Bird* in the [Hollywood] Bowl and is trying to veto *Faust*. Apparently the Pilgrimage Theater [an open-air theater in which *Faust* was finally performed] only holds 1,300 people and even if they filled it every night for four weeks it would only just meet the budget. Maybe my play [*The Merchant of Yonkers*] will be the only one done. He had me read it aloud to him. He made a few gentle suggestions. They both love Mrs. Levi's monologue which is not yet in the typed copy. I came home with his suggestions and I've already written some delicious new stuff. It's growing into one of the most enchanting plays ever written. About it all hangs the muted doubt about money.

Reinhardt's business manager told Thornton that *The Merchant* would open in Los Angeles, go to San Francisco, then gradually work its way east.

Inevitably, there were more dates than could be entered in

Thornton's small engagement book — Robert Ardrey, the Otto Premingers, Jerome Kern. He attended Helen Hayes's performance of *The Merchant of Venice,* lunched with Janet Gaynor, had a Sunday evening at Douglas Fairbanks, Jr.'s beach house and drove with Terry Lewis, who was on a Hollywood writing assignment, up the Pacific Palisades highway toward Ventura, stopping at a restaurant that featured an outdoor swimming pool for seals. Hollywood informality — polo shirt, slacks, loafers — was not for Thornton. Dressed as an eastern schoolmaster — hat, coat, vest, tie, white shirt with collar that curled up at the ends — he stood by the tank and tossed fish to the seals. "The most fun of any man I've ever known," Miss Lewis said. "I'd double up in laughter."

Five thousand dollars a week to work on a script of Clifford Odets's *Golden Boy* was refused; Thornton was in California for Reinhardt. Unfortunately, The Master at that moment could give little attention to *The Merchant of Yonkers,* and there Thornton was, he confided to Woollcott, "in the only part of the U.S.A. that I cannot love, with a month's time to kill. If I'd been alone I'd have gone to Monterey and Berkeley." But Isabel had joined him and had to have "more companionship than that"; so they decided to visit Mabel Dodge Luhan in New Mexico.

Mabel greeted them at the station in Taos with the news that one of her guests, Mrs. Robinson Jeffers, had just tried to kill herself by slashing her wrists. That set the tone for nine days with the Luhans and Jefferses. Thornton didn't take to Jeffers; all he saw was "Carmel's self-indulgent little Prometheus shaking his fist in incurably minor poetic stance." And Mabel? Well, now . . . "in the long run all she wants to know is all about her friends' sex lives."

Thornton came down with psychogenic laryngitis, which gave him a plausible excuse for returning to Hollywood, where nothing had changed. "Yes, madam," he wrote Terry Lewis, who had gone back to New York,

> everything's just like when you left. I'm still waiting; the professor is mildly making plans; the sun still beats down, only much hotter; and I still hate the town like everything. For weeks I attended all rehearsals of *Faust.* Nine P.M.–two A.M., daily.

It's not a good example of Reinhardt, and it's no pleasure to discuss it. . . . I'm deep in the German-Austrian-Jewish colony. Albert Einstein wrote me an inebriating fan-letter. The First Congregational Church of Los Angeles wants me to preach at their evening service next Sunday. If *you* were here, I'd do it, just to show you, but since you're not here, I refused.

Another diversion came in September, while Reinhardt was casting *The Merchant of Yonkers*. Harris somehow persuaded Thornton to leave Hollywood and take over Frank Craven's role as Stage Manager in *Our Town* for two weeks in New York. Thornton's only caveat was that he rehearse with Ed Goodnow, the play's actual stage manager, without Harris present. "I cannot *begin* rehearsals with Jed — things would stick in my throat. I'm going to ask $300 a week and give it to the Actors' Fund."

It was his first Broadway acting experience and he had trouble memorizing his own lines, got the shakes and was sure that he'd disgrace everybody. Once on stage, however, he lost his fright. Frank Craven congratulated him ("Thank God for me you didn't play the part first"). Ina Claire came backstage and hugged him. But the critics had reservations about his staccato performance; he was "no ball of fire," said the *New York Times*.

Reinhardt, meantime, had announced that *The Merchant of Yonkers* would make its debut not on the West Coast as planned, but in New York about November 1. In the end, it opened in Boston December 12 with Woollcott present, holding the author's hand and helping him get tight in the Copley Plaza Hotel. Something had gone wrong. Thornton's old-style comedy had been rendered bland by a humorless production, and it closed after four weeks at the Theatre Guild in New York, just before Christmas.

Variety said *The Merchant* was overacted; others thought the director's touches were too obvious. The play itself was probably not at fault, for after minor revision and a new cast and title, *The Matchmaker*, it would have a long run in 1955. Before the Boston opening, Reinhardt had proposed twenty-one changes, leaving the author with dwindling hope that the play would ever be his ("Where is our modest little farce?"). But Thornton stoutly defended Reinhardt and said he had done "a wonderful job."

He wrote Reinhardt's son Gottfried that the obstacles had been those of timid management and noncooperative actors in the leading roles.

However disappointing the result, Thornton's debt to The Master had been paid and he was at liberty to think about his next play — not a farce this time, but a drama appropriate to the rush to the abyss that was visible throughout the world in January 1939. Shanghai was occupied by the Japanese; Austria was in Hitler's grip; the Spanish Republicans were about to be overwhelmed by the Fascists. It was the hour for a war play, one that would address the universal question: When a human being is made to bear more than a human being can bear, what then?

Thornton had touched on that question in the closing lines of *The Happy Journey:* "It was awful, Mama," Beulah wept. "It was awful. She [Beulah's baby] didn't even live a few minutes, Mama. It was awful." And Ma had answered: "God thought best, dear. God thought best. We don't understand why. We just go on, honey, doin' our business." Now Thornton wanted to declare more explicitly and resoundingly that whatever the cataclysms — ice age, flood, wars — mankind would "go on." That was to be his message in *The Skin of Our Teeth.*

In less sophisticated form, the message would be popularized a decade or so later as the power of positive thinking. Thornton's conditional optimism derived from deeper insights. He knew that self-hypnosis wouldn't make the world go right, and that the testing moment often finds us unready. Nevertheless, he held that there are always second chances, and that acceptance of the "irresistibly given" does not preclude the power of will to invent new means for survival. In *The Skin of Our Teeth,* he wanted to chart mankind's wrong turnings, dead ends, pain, treachery, brutality, absurdities while simultaneously underlining the fact of human endurance. "Maybe your upbringing misinformed you about the structure of human nature," Thornton wrote his godson, Julian LeGrand. "Neither rottenness nor the quasi-angelic position are true. For me this 'evil nightmare' is a new journey into self-knowledge with possibilities of great fruitfulness."

Here, perhaps, is where Thornton differed from many of his American literary contemporaries. He could write of suicide, mur-

der, betrayal, of affection rejected, noble intentions ridiculed, innocence punished. He could grant that "there is no courage without
fear, no faith without doubt, and no love without abandon." But
then he added: "Let us be willing to pass through fear, doubt
and abandon *in order to be* stronger in courage, faith and love."
Our lives were not to be summed up in shattered dreams, spiritual
exhaustion, victimization or self-destruction. It is that attitude that
helps explain why some critics dismissed him as out-of-date. To
be taken seriously as a modern, a writer presumably had to locate
the rock bottom of existence in impoverishment, deprivation, disil-
lusion, hypocrisy, violence, greed, lust. The heroes of such critics
were Sinclair Lewis, Hemingway, Fitzgerald, Faulkner, Dos Passos
and, later, Norman Mailer, J. D. Salinger, Tennessee Williams,
Saul Bellow and William Styron. When Wilder was praised, it
was for style.

Yet he was as sensitive as they to the underside of life, to the
emptiness of obsession with money, power, sex. But the suffering
in his novels and plays is not purposeless, dragging one down to
defeat. "Intermittently," he remarked to Mabel Dodge Luhan,

> most of us have a positive life. Here a great marriage (the
> older I grow the more I love to see and affirm that mystery);
> or an ever-renewed intellectual passion; or a warm friendship-
> generosity; and then there are a few artists who do not torment
> themselves with ideational probing into what they do, but sim-
> ply sing their gift. So often, Mabel, I remember with an affec-
> tionate smile, your smiting the table and saying: "Now, now,
> now, lets not talk negative." I've taken that over from you.
> Not from evasion of the tragic background of life, nor evasion
> of the sad fact that 20th Century man has lost an idea-system
> in which he has justification and dignity. But from a conviction
> that the Positive still lies about us in sufficient fragments to
> live by.

The Skin of Our Teeth was intended to dramatize that conviction.

Mexico bound on the SS *Siboney* the third week of January 1939,
Thornton lunched in his cabin on thick soup, a club sandwich

and a half bottle of wine, worked on his war play and looked forward to tramping about alone in Mexico City's back alleys. Mexico was "wonderful," he wrote Woollcott when he got there, but he was "leaving it at once." He couldn't work, couldn't sleep, was constipated. He had to get north.

He was in Hamden in March for duty work, including a letter to Orson Welles on behalf of an unemployed actress. Turnabout was fair play; the little-known Welles had been recommended by Thornton in 1933 to Woollcott and producer Guthrie McClintic, and Welles had written Thornton gratefully, "You have given me a whole ring of keys to this city, and I've been busy all this week excitedly fitting them into their locks and opening important doors. If I don't cover myself with glory now you've opened up this New York to me, why then there's nothing to cover. No one has been a greater benefactor, no one has ever been so plunged in debt as the subject of your charities."

An invitation to teach at Princeton lay on Thornton's desk in Hamden, and for a day or two he was inclined to accept it. "I was at the point of being untrue to you," he wrote Hutchins. "A University in New Jersey, in the person of its universally admired dean, had asked me to join its staff for a year. No classes. Interviews with twenty-five recommended freshmen, and vague parish work with whatever writing upperclassmen might call at my office hour, the whole to be genially subsidized by the Carnegie Foundation." On reflection, he decided he was a fool to have been tempted: "I have to have a few years yet of none-too-happy alternations between solitude and gregariousness. I shall be here until the middle of May and then I shall go over to the forest of Fontainebleau."

It looked for a time as if the departure for Fontainebleau would be delayed by a conflict with Jed Harris over the sale of movie rights to *Our Town,* for Thornton was determined to uphold the position that no author should sell his work to Hollywood without some assurance of respect for the text, and Harris, according to Thornton, was frantic for money and "willing to hurl *Our Town* indiscriminately to a certain bidder without the faintest guaranty of fidelity." Columnist Walter Winchell picked up the story: "Thornton Wilder, author of *Our Town,* and Jed Harris, the producer of it, are cutting each other dead." Jed backed down, the threat of a lawsuit faded and Thornton sailed for Europe on schedule in May.

Before unpacking his bags in the Hotel Buckingham in Paris, he called on Stein and Toklas, who presented him with a social schedule for his visit. So did Mme. Bousquet. He retreated to London, where a third indomitable hostess, Lady Colefax, handed him her list of command appearances. Thornton said he was being "torn limb from limb." In fact, he enjoyed it.

Shuttling back and forth between England and France, he dined in Paris with Jean Cocteau, had tea with painter Marie Laurencin, and took Mme. Bousquet to a Nijinsky benefit. After a few days in Bilignin and Fontainebleau, he was back in London for dinner at the Savoy Grill with Sibyl, Clare Boothe Luce and Ruth Draper.

While in Paris, he had written his former Chicago student George Dillon, now associated with *Poetry,* suggesting that the magazine publish parts of Stein's *Stanzas in Meditation* and offering to bring the manuscript to America. "I think you'll like them, but at least you'll be the first to look at them." Thornton wanted Stein to be read, yet his responsibility as caretaker of her largely unknown writings was never clearly defined. He had arranged for deposit of her papers at Yale University Library, spent considerable time sorting and listing them, and in her *Everybody's Autobiography* Stein stated that he was her literary executor. But the "appointment" was never put in legal form and was canceled by mutual agreement. "Obviously," commented Donald Gallup, former curator of Yale's Collection of American Literature and Thornton's literary executor, "Gertrude Stein came to realize that Thornton Wilder would be far too involved in his own work to cope with the knotty problem of the publication of all of her unpublished manuscripts; whereas Carl Van Vechten, having 'given up' writing, would be pleased and honored to be assigned the task — as indeed proved to be the case."

The travels didn't end with Thornton's return from Europe. He was up and down and across New England, playing the Stage Manager in *Our Town* and running from beseeching local hostesses. In Stockbridge he lunched with the play's producer and his family and after lunch asked their six-year-old daughter, Mouse, to spend the afternoon with him. They inspected the Indian burial ground, after which he invited her to Benjamin's Drug Store, the center of Stockbridge's juvenile social life. "When you finish your soda, Mousie, why not pick out some magazines from that rack." Returning her home with her windfall of magazines and with chocolate syrup on her sweater, Thornton reported that he had had a most pleasant afternoon, and as he went out the door he said to the six-year-old, "Keep me green, Mousie, keep me green."

16

"Dear Sol . . ."

THE WRANGLE with Jed over who would film *Our Town* had ended with Sol Lesser's purchase of motion picture rights in 1939 for $35,000, 60 percent to Thornton, 40 percent to Harris. Lesser had been captivated by the play in New York, and after the sale he attended a Bucks County performance at which Thornton played the Stage Manager. To the consternation of the audience, a bat had flown in through an open door, but Thornton had deftly incorporated it into his narrative, assuring everyone that the invader would fly out, attracted by light. As if on cue, the bat vanished. *That,* Lesser said, was a showman. He proposed that Thornton write the screenplay and was turned down. However, they did confer on the script in Lesser's suite at the Sherry-Netherland in New York, and when their six-day conference was over, Lesser — who associated writers, particularly eminent writers, with expense — asked Thornton what he owed him. Not a cent, he was told, "I got more out of this than you did." It was a novel experience for a Hollywood producer and he couldn't leave it at that. On Christmas Day a Chrysler convertible wrapped in cellophane and a red bow was delivered to 50 Deepwood Drive in Hamden, compliments of Sol Lesser.

Their association was remarkable in several ways, not least of which was Thornton's refusal to accept money, though he would share screen credit with two others who were paid — Frank Craven and Harry Chanlee.

Lesser was an astute businessman — he owned a number of theaters — but he had not heretofore been identified with motion pictures of distinction; this was by far the most serious creative project he had undertaken. But he was attracted by *Our Town*'s humanity; he wanted to make a film that was wholesome and soul-stirring, as well as profitable.

For six months following the Sherry-Netherland meetings, he and Thornton engaged by telegram and letter in a unique, long-distance collaboration. They agreed on the veteran Sam Wood as director and on Martha Scott as Emily, the role she had played on Broadway. Thereafter, the minutest details of text and screen technique were dealt with. Thus, in a letter to Lesser on October 7, 1939, Thornton commented on the Stage Manager's appearing at the door of his drugstore as the film opens and saying: "Well, folks, we're in Grover's Corners, New Hampshire. . . . " That opening was "far less persuasive," Thornton wrote, than an overall shot of Grover's Corners: "There should be constantly maintained by the camera a view of the whole town — our feeling that *there* is choir rehearsal; *there* are the children at work; *there* is Dr. Gibbs reading; these episodes are very slight to be received in succession; but all gain when they are given with an air of being simultaneous. At present the camera directions don't pick up the whole town until page 49."

Thornton worried that if it was realistically photographed, the wedding of Emily and George would reduce many of the surrounding scenes to ordinariness. He pointed out that on the stage, novelty had been supplied by the absence of scenery, by the Stage Manager's playing the minister, by thinking-aloud passages, by the oddity of hearing someone gabble during the ceremony, and by the young people's moments of alarm. "You have none of these." "Now, Sol," he wrote diplomatically,

> it's just you I'm thinking about; will you have as *interesting* a picture as you hoped? This treatment seems to be in danger of dwindling to the conventional. And for a story that's so generalized that's a great danger. The play interested because every few minutes there was a new bold effect in presentation-methods. For the movie it may be an audience-risk to be bold (thinking of the forty millions) but I think with this story it's a still greater risk to be conventional. I know you'll realize I don't mean boldness or oddity for their own sakes, but merely

as the almost indispensable reenforcement and refreshment of a play that was never intended to be interesting for its story alone, or even for its background.

Hating to seem like a "vain author [who] thinks every word sacred," Thornton nonetheless insisted that cuts in the death-and-immortality speech harmed it; "in its present shape it reads like a sweetness-and-light Aimee McPherson spiel." And the wedding scene was still not fresh enough: "I don't think that realistic boys in a realistic village would hoot and guy a friend on his way to his wedding. That's Dead-End-Kids city life."

In November he was telling Lesser that criticisms seemed to make the producer unhappy, "and God knows I don't mean that"; still, he hoped to dissuade Lesser from having Emily regret that she had been "an unwise wife." That made the heroine into a superior schoolmarm kind of person, and the play, reposing between vast stretches of time and suggestions of generalized multitudes of people, required that the fathers and mothers and especially George and Emily be pretty near the norm of everybody. "If this is made into ineffectual-but-goodhearted-husband and superior-interfering wife, the balance is broken."

When Lesser again suggested that Thornton come to California, he replied that he would be "very unhappy and helpless and would communicate some of that to you, just when you should be feeling most constructive." However, he volunteered a few additional alterations; for example, on the stage the simultaneous presentation of two houses gave a lively kick to the two mothers' calling their children to breakfast. It was a laugh. "Now that the houses are in different shots, however closely they follow one another, I imagine the laugh has gone. Will you talk over with Sam [Wood] the possibility of some process shots here — a Polish mother calling in Polish; a colored maid at the Cartwrights knocking at a door, '7:00 o'clock.' " And incidentally, "The best man and his ring business seems to me to be dipping into the Old Jokes, the expected gags. It's as though we included a shot of a farmhand eating peas on his knife, or, a hulking oafish schoolboy who winks at his friends and gives teacher a big red apple; and so on. Maybe I'm just carping about this; so don't mind me!"

On New Year's Eve 1939, Lesser received a "few notes" (a four-page letter) about little Wally's asking whether Emily's little boy will be a good baseball player. "Seems mere bathos to me. Wally's always been effective through his silent presence. Open his mouth and the force is gone." And please, "no black-plumed horses at the funeral. That's city and that's Roman Catholic and that's Masonic. A real little horse-and-buggy funeral. The horses don't even go in 'slow cadence.' Farmers drive to a funeral. New Hampshire wouldn't even go solemn-slow. They just go."

Thornton did not object, however, to a major change from the stage version — Emily's survival.

> Emily should live. I've always thought so. In a movie you see the people *so close to* that a distant relation is established. In the theater they are halfway abstractions in an allegory; in the movie they are very concrete. So insofar as the play is a generalized allegory she dies — we die — they die; insofar as it's a Concrete Happening it's not important that she die; it's even disproportionately cruel that she die. Let her live — the idea will have been imparted anyway. But if she lives, I agree with you that after all that graveyard material the survival may seem too arbitrary and abrupt and out of relation to the Stage Manager presiding over the experience. Hence: Your first suggestion is fine. Sick-in-bed we hear her say faintly, "I want to live! I want to live." Then the whole graveyard sequence and the return to the birthday and back to the sick bed; and a louder "I want to live." This may give the impression that all the intervening material was a dream or hallucination that took place in a second of time — that is: between her second and third cries of "I want to live" — which is the right idea.

On the train from New York to New Haven for Isabel's birthday in January 1940, Thornton read the latest *Our Town* script and was dissatisfied with additional business that might get a laugh but would establish the wrong tone: "A few more stealing-donuts, dish-towel errors, four spoonfuls-of-sugar, drinking-coffee-out-of-saucers, mothers-looking-behind-sons'-ears — and the audience would be justified in believing this is one of those pictures of Quaint Hayseed Family Life."

Over the next six weeks, Thornton tossed out congratulations and more suggestions for Lesser. How about that cat arching its back at the presence of dead Emily? Wouldn't it distract the audience's mind to introduce the notion of ghosts and of animals being aware of ghosts? Also, he had discussed the Civil War veterans' grave markings with everybody he'd met, and he drew for Lesser two possible forms of decoration. "However, I have sent a special delivery letter to a woman in Peterborough who would know and I expect an answer from her any minute and will forward it at once." It was all free advice.

A request for a publicity statement from the author prompted the reply, "Wild horses could not persuade me to add into my account the commendatory adjectives that are I suppose indispensable to such outlines." Musical background? He appreciated Lesser's hesitation about Aaron Copland, since Copland was associated with modern dissonant work, and the same held true for George Antheil. But on the whole, "the non-sentimental tartness they inject would be on the safer side. . . . I should think the choice might be, in this order, [Virgil] Thomson, Antheil, Copland, unless you think of someone who might be still simpler. It's the simplicity of the musical background that will make the old hymn stand out, and those hymns have always played a large part in the audience's reaction." He sketched on an enclosed sheet the tune best known for each hymn. When Copland was selected, he and Wilder had a long talk in New Haven. "As usual," Thornton wrote Lesser, "I was shy of expressing much suggestion — believing always that such distinguished artists must have the rope to do things their own way. However, before we got through we had agreed on many things. He's a very likeable fella."

The film, which was to prove as popular and enduring as the stage version, had a triumphant premiere in Boston on May 22, 1940, with Isabel and an incredulous Thornton present. The governors of Massachusetts and New Hampshire were there to applaud; so was the Mayor of Boston. Lesser had spared no expense; it was a glittering Hollywood gala, "disproportionate under any circumstances," said Thornton, "but in the light of war . . . !"

Within weeks, British forces were to evacuate Dunkerque, the Dutch army would surrender, Belgium capitulate, and the Germans would invade Norway and Denmark and enter Paris.

The previous October, when the cameras had been turning in Hollywood and Europe was frozen in the "phony war," Thornton, had hidden away in Atlantic City, sitting at his window for hours, looking at the waves, meditating on his war play, bereft of inspiration. Why, at that moment, he chose to set himself up in a New York apartment is a mystery, but he did. He might as well have remained in Atlantic City; it would have given him more seclusion at less expense. From 81 Irving Place, he wrote Amy Wertheimer in November that the state of the war and the world and his work had made him so boorish and unsociable that whole days went by when he talked to no one; he was "tired of human talk" and had refused every kind of invitation.

Within four months he had given up the New York apartment, gone back to Hamden, and, after a few driving lessons in Lesser's Chrysler convertible, at Isabel's insistence ("she's trying to keep up the fiction that I'm an incompetent"), he had started south, visiting Aunt Charlotte in Winter Park, Florida, then driving to Saint Augustine, where he was confronted by an oppressive accumulation of forwarded mail. An Austrian refugee had a play she wanted staged; another, about to lose his job as Thomas Mann's secretary, asked for advice; the son of novelist Arthur Schnitzler was seeking work and needed a recommendation. A former pupil sent a short story for criticism; an editor solicited an introduction to a volume of plays for a Catholic group; an Iowan submitted a thesis titled "A Study of Act Divisions in the Classical Drama"; someone yearned to translate *Our Town* into German; a lady in Columbus said she would like to have his views on Shakespeare's heroines; an art designer was interested in *The Merchant of Yonkers;* a director had in mind a radio production of *A Doll's House;* an actress hinted that she would be an ideal Mrs. Gibbs; university women in Rochester proposed dramatizing *The Bridge;* an unknown admirer invited him to the Adirondacks — she'd heard that he was bald but didn't mind.

As he drove back to New York, Thornton followed with anguish the war news on his car radio. The German army had reached the English Channel; May 22, 1940, seemed to him the most fateful day in history, "the moment for a miracle." A presidential campaign was under way. To Thornton, Franklin D. Roosevelt was "the only man to carry the country through these times." A pro–Wendell Willkie editorial by Henry Luce struck him as "the silliest drivel ever offered by a public man," and to an old Lawrenceville friend, Waldo Greene, he exclaimed, "Willkie! You can read those speeches without nausea? You can deny that FDR has done a wonderful job with an immense and desperate country? You will hand over this country to an ignorant adolescent butter-and-egg man!" It amused Thornton when people thought of him as a "lapdog Republican."

In the Edwin Arlington Robinson studio and bedroom at the MacDowell Colony the next month, he worked on his war play and considered calling it *The Ends of the Worlds*, but during the latter part of July and all of August he returned to acting in summer stock performances of *Our Town* — Cohasset, Woods Hole, Stockbridge, "all frightfully unimportant."

He needed at least two months of solitude if the play was to be finished, and hoped to find it in Canada. But there were prior commitments: a speech October 5 at the centennial anniversary of the First Congregational Church of Madison, Wisconsin ("Papa'd be pleased") and a lecture at the University of Chicago on "True and False Realism in the Theater," followed by a supper for sixty friends given by Hutchins, who pressed him to give the University of Chicago one more teaching term, next summer. Summer seemed very far off and Thornton agreed. In late October, he registered at the Chateau Frontenac in Quebec.

Like Zurich, Quebec was a fine work town, and for some of the same reasons: vast bodies of water, distant mountains, foreignness and "the unattractiveness of its people." But if one lived alone, one had to change scenery "or go nuts." He was in Montreal the first week of November, downcast by the omnipresent war and by remorse over his recent Chicago visit,

a remorse which is not a penitence — a remorse not of acts nor of temperament, but what I can only describe as a morti-

fied condemnation of the quality of my mind, particularly in
its expression in social life and public life. Hence my loathing
for my lectures; hence my eagerness to be gone from any
place I have been staying, my carefully concealed delight at
goodbyes. I have no particular sense of shortcoming in regard
to my visits to Gladys Campbell, Inez [Cunningham] or the
Hutchins'. It is deeper than that; it is as though I were haunted
by the idea that the spoken word should be as precise as the
written, and that the encounters of friends should have the
character of a work of art, — hence, my care that the close
of a conversation should allude to the matter that opened it
and should contain some statement of the elements that seemed
during the time to have unfolded or progressed. I cannot say
that this repudiation applies to what I have written, though
my refusal to re-read it is certainly a reflection of it, my refusal
even to think about it, and my violent refusal to read letters
I have written in the past (I cannot bring myself to consider
looking at my letters to Dr. Wager which have been returned
to me) is an extreme example. In writing these lines I see
(and should have stated at once, for the point is not new to
me) that the matter is far deeper than one of the spoken or
the written word; it is simply that I regard myself as unfailingly
inept at the social relation. It is not only the *gaffes* that I make
— and which worry me far less than they used to; even when
things are going well, when a congeniality or friendship is
as well established as that with Alec [Woollcott] or Bob Hutchins I am never free of a sense of inadequacy; I feel that I am
forever dry when warmth is called for, and warm when judi-
cious impersonality is called for, and this inadequacy is primarily represented in the spoken word. Hence the luxury of silence, that is: absence. One of the elements of the happiness
of this residence has been the learning this — I should say
the learning this *all over again* — and the excitement of planning the mode of life for the future. Another is the beauty
of the place. I seem to be seeing landscape for the first time;
perhaps the silence is a therapeutic element bringing me to
this present state of unprecedented well being in which the
eye particularly profits. Another is my reading. I am reading

nothing particularly remarkable (Alain's *Les dieux* and *Propos sur le bonheur,* Thibaudet's *Histoire de la littérature française*) but with a liveliness of attention that makes for such vitality in distinguishing the good from the bad that the reading becomes something more than receptivity. Even the reading of the newspapers three times a day has grown out of that deplorable practice (of which I was so ashamed but could not escape from) of seeing the war — and the [presidential] election — as a game in which one is emotionally immersed, wishing, deploring, pushing, despairing. I should like to think, finally, that one of the elements is *the play* and that even during these last three days when it seemed to me that what I had written was all wrong, that there would be for me no "right," even then my subconscious knew that the play would come out all right. All I can say about that is that through it all my "happiness" has been unshaken, my gratitude for the effects of morning and evening light on the river and its shores no less spontaneous, my mental health no less *Béat,* and that the work done on the play today has been more encouraging.

"Jed is to do it, hélas," he confided to Cass Canfield. "The best (and only) director in the U.S.A.; but I hope to arrange it so that I don't even attend rehearsals."

Thornton was asking for punishment and knew it; but he also knew that Harris had a sure instinct for stagecraft. Hadn't Brooks Atkinson said that Harris's name on a production was "the hallmark of the most clairvoyant mind in the theatre"?

Jed had telephoned him in Quebec, "very chipper." When would he get a manuscript of *The Skin of Our Teeth?* Not yet, Thornton answered, but the back of the third act would be broken by mid-November and maybe the whole play finished before he left Canada.

It wasn't. Nor was it finished by Christmas, which Thornton spent in Hamden, helping celebrate the engagement of Janet to Winthrop Saltonstall Dakin. "A very nice fellow," Thornton wrote. "When we saw the diamond and the string of pearls she got, all the gypsy-Wilders gave slow veiled smiles, purring in our dreams of anticipated parasitism." The play was coming along, he told the assembled family; one more month's retirement and it would be done.

Again, he was overly optimistic. *The Skin of Our Teeth* was about to be laid aside, for at the request of the State Department Thornton had agreed to go to South America — Colombia in March 1941, Ecuador in April, Peru in May. It would be his first sight of the country of *The Bridge of San Luis Rey*.

17

The Skin of Our Teeth

AS THE FURY of war mounted in Europe and Asia, isolationism in America had fallen to the ground, and with it the isolation of the artist. Increasingly, beginning in 1941, Thornton would be drawn into nonliterary public activities. He would aid refugees fleeing Nazi Germany and Austria, providing affidavits of support enabling them to obtain American visas, welcoming them at the dock in New York, handing them five hundred dollars, arranging hotel accommodations, taking them to dinner and sending them theater tickets. He would accept the presidency of a committee raising funds for Albert Schweitzer's hospital in Africa; serve on the American delegation to a UNESCO conference in Venice; join a national committee supporting the election of Senator John F. Kennedy for president; sign a petition to Congress demanding that American troops be brought home from Vietnam; protest the practice of racial discrimination in theaters and auditoriums in Washington, D.C.; write a get-out-the-vote appeal for the American Veterans Committee; prepare a script for the National Conference of Christians and Jews honoring America's religious and racial diversity.

But he was of divided mind about his goodwill mission to South America in the spring of 1941. A very small expense account had been provided by the State Department, and Thornton expected that his attorney in New Haven would "shake his head sadly as my letter of credit flows out in dinners for the writers, professors and students and flowers for their wives." He would have to be "damned gregarious" in Bogotá, Quito and Lima — and in Spanish, he told Stein. "But! Voyages and Duty are the two most meretricious temptations that can haunt the human mind from its only justifiable activity, and this mission combines both." At least he felt reasonably well prepared, having read the works of many of the writers he would encounter, been checked out by the dentist and bought a new suit at Brooks Brothers.

Sherwood Anderson and his wife were fellow passengers on the Grace liner *Santa Lucia* that sailed February 28. Thornton did not know the sixty-four-year-old Anderson well, but they both admired Stein, and in Paris in the twenties he had taken his Oxford friends to tea with the author of *Winesburg, Ohio.* The first week at sea, Anderson was stricken, carried off the boat at Colón, Panama and died there of an intestinal obstruction and peritonitis. The *Santa Lucia* reached Colombia March 6.

Within twenty-four hours, Thornton was swept up in a whirl of appointments that would keep him spinning for three months. The telephone at the Hotel Granada in Bogotá began ringing before breakfast: the rector of the university, a professor from Berlin, the editor of a local newspaper, a young poet. "Tea" went on from five until nine. He was besieged by callers with books for him to read. "Everybody's impulsive, enthusiastic, and child-like, and so am I and we all like one another," Thornton wrote home. If he wasn't meeting journalists, students, professors, writers or diplomats, he was boning up on his Spanish: "Last night I was with an editor and poet from 8:00 to 12:00 without a word of English and we certainly told each other plenty." He was inter-viewed on the radio, entertained at dinners and toured the old city with a former Yale student, Mario Laserna, whose future career as rector of the university and Colombian ambassador to France Thornton followed with pride. Exhausted, he had only to lean out of his hotel window and be revived by the panorama of moun-tains, tile roofs and graceful church towers. He envied the Colom-bian "that drop of Indian blood that would confer on me a patience as wide as the ocean," he told Woollcott,

> even if at times it would let me fall into a vacancy that's like despair, and a paralysis of will that's like petrifaction. And I envy them that drop of Negro blood that would inure me against discomfort under the heat, and would set my blood

circulating with a God-like well-being, even if it did bring with it a preoccupation with sex so obsessive that any other activity in life would seem like a boring automatism. No, but I'm very Colombian. If anyone shows any sign of liking me I lay my heart in their hand without asking for a receipt. I confide the story of my life to the first person who alludes to a lesser known incident in his own; I am subject to a melancholy that — it's the only kind — does not proceed from any occasion in external life: meaningless melancholy. I have a passion for poetry and tears come into my eyes at the mention of a great poet's name.

Leaving Bogotá April 4, he rode for five and a half hours on a train to Cali, high up and near the Equator, where he dined at the American consul's. All English-speaking colony parties were much alike, he concluded. Two hours of drinks, one hour of buffet supper, two to four hours of more drinks, cards, singing and trivia. "Take it away. Oil men, gold men, General Motors men, cable, refrigerator, Chrysler and adding machine men. Their wives nice little Ohio-village girls with or without spectacles and wearing evening gowns that they don't know anything about. Rootless, bewildered, without the faintest interest in South America. Take it away."

It was the same in Quito, Ecuador — top speed from morning to night. Exchanges of books, interviews, holding hands with aspiring theatrical troupes, reading novels he'd been given ("all of them leftwing, and with justification, all things considered"). The rains washed away half a dozen bridges, he couldn't get to the airport, his Lima flight was delayed a week. He wrote, swam and laundered his white suits and shirts.

Peru was disappointing, primarily because communication with Peruvian writers was blocked by the Anglo-American colony, by official academic bodies and pushing Europe-minded authors who wanted to be noticed. It wasn't the European veneer on the Spanish strain that interested him in these countries, it was the Indian. He was therefore delighted by the Mexican ambassador, an authority on the Indian, which made the ambassador unpopular in Lima, for "as everybody knows," Thornton said, "there have never been any Indians in Peru; just Spanish aristocrats and some llamas and other animals." In Arequipa he met the kind of Peruvians he liked, "and there are some darlings. I wish our lives were two hundred years long and I could devote ten to these three Republics. What new friends and *correspondents* I have acquired." The inn where he stayed in Arequipa, *Quinta Bates,* and the famous woman who ran it were to appear in a novel of Thornton's twenty-five years later.

A letter from Chicago welcomed him home in early June. "The band, the floral tributes, and the latchkey are all out," Hutchins wrote. "Your first class is Tuesday, June 24. Please come a week early and hold my hand." Oh yes, salary. Four thousand dollars for teaching three summer courses — translation, the story, and advanced composition. The pay was "shocking," in Thornton's judgment. Too much.

There was one chore that had to be got out of the way before classes, a report on his South American trip to Secretary of State Hull. In twenty-one hand-written pages Thornton set forth his view that if the United States was to win the cooperation in wartime of the three republics he had visited, it could not secure it by money, in the German manner, or by compliments, deference, reason or logic. "All we can do is prepare in their minds, with all possible speed, as favorable an interpretation as possible of our disinterestedness, our absolute conviction of the democratic form of life and our firmness to defend it, and our cultural maturity." Nor was it useful to export exhibitions of our own contemporary arts. "Their extreme individualism prevents their being able to enter hardily into projects which are not their own creation." In the long run, he wrote, their adherence "must be gained by force. . . . Not only does [the South American] watch Hitler's progress with bedazzled admiration, he secretly enjoys the element of ruthlessness with which it is carried forward, and derives vicarious well-being from the contemplation of cruelty. Such temperaments are always in danger of identifying kindness with weakness. When the momentous hour arrives for requiring the northwestern corner of South America to declare itself between democracy and totalitarianism, their choice must be aided by an expression from the United States of some of that firmness they admire."

When the U.S. ambassador to Bolivia, Spruille Braden, to whom he had sent a copy, objected to Thornton's reference to force, he replied that he had intended to use the phrase "forceful pressure."

The summer quarter teaching assignment in Chicago seemed easier than in the past, and he played it *con brio,* improvising as he went along. The term was over before he knew it, and no sooner was he free than he was off on another mission, this time to England for a PEN (International Association of Poets, Playwrights, Editors, Essayists, and Novelists) conference September 10.

On the plane crossing the Atlantic he and John Dos Passos had long conversations filled with polite consideration for their differing opinions. To Dos Passos' pessimism about the war, Thornton countered that it was "the Utopianists who are least willing to admit a favorable view of the shorter range."

It wasn't the worst he ever made, he said of his PEN speech, but he wished he had had more time to prepare it. The competition was exigent — Rebecca West, H. G. Wells, E. M. Forster. In elections to replace as international president the "now despised Jules Romains," Wells and Wilder refused the presidency but agreed to serve on a presidential committee to which Thomas Mann and Jacques Maritain were added.

London in the blackout was as spine-tingling as Sibyl Colefax had promised. Stepping from the brilliant Savoy lobby through a swinging door and curtain into a dark, mysterious world of tiny white and green lights was almost exalting. He had dinner at the Albany with Edith Evans and a hasty supper with E. M. Forster; an evening with his British publisher; a tour of a bomber headquarters; a speech in Glasgow; another to the English-Speaking Union and over the BBC. Sibyl arranged lunch with the new editor of the *Times* and the Vincent Masseys (high commissioner for Canada), Walter de la Mare, critic Desmond MacCarthy, the Hamish Hamiltons and Cecil Beaton. "Busy — busy — but everything unforgettable."

Why had no one told him that Bristol was so attractive? "Weather-blackened Victorian commercial districts with bits of Gothic and Renaissance churches; in the residence districts some echoes — in a smaller scale — of the crescents of Bath, with something of the Palladian majesty." And now, after the bombing, "whole blocks of ploughed brick and riven iron. Halves of great warehouses from which all the interiors have been burned out and which resemble, with their regular rows of windows, a Roman viaduct, or the baths of Caracalla." St. Mary Radcliffe, which Elizabeth I had called "the goodliest, fairest and most famous parish church in England," had been spared, he was told, "as though by the hand of God." The remark shocked him. "I really think," he wrote Woollcott, "I better go into the ministry where I was always supposed to be. A few more flippancies like that and I become Amos' pupil."

Thornton was with Woollcott on his island the end of November and in December he escorted visiting South Americans around New York. Act three of *The Skin of Our Teeth* had yet to be put right and couldn't be put right unless he locked himself up somewhere. Shortly after the Japanese attack on Pearl Harbor, manuscript in hand, he took off for the Viking Hotel in Newport and copied the play onto new paper, "which is my way of Awaking the Fancy."

In Samuel French's standard library edition, Thornton described *The Skin of Our Teeth* as a comedy about George Antrobus, his wife and two children, Henry and Gladys, and their maid Sabina, all of Excelsior, New Jersey, who survive "fire, pestilence, the seven-year locusts, the ice age, the black pox and the double feature, a dozen wars and as many depressions." Alternately bewitched, befuddled and becalmed, "they are the stuff of which heroes are made — heroes and buffoons." The first act had been written in six weeks in early 1940, but by that fall in Quebec Thornton feared he had lost the play. It was "the most ambitious subject I have ever approached," he had noted in his journal, and he was faced as never consciously before with the question: "Do I mean it? In this case, in what part or level of myself am I actually interested in such a problem (problem for literature, that is; hence, burning problem for the self) as the struggles of the race and its survival?" Had he been "making up" emotion and contriving an earnestness? Is that why his play had bogged down?

He had faced three difficulties:

(1) Simplicity. With what dismay I see some of the passages I wrote this afternoon, passages which under the guise of theatric liveliness uprooted the play from its forward drive. My old dread of being "boring," my reluctance to trust to strong subject matter. (2) Working perseverance. These two years of picking up subjects and dropping them, of desultory reading, of an evasion from writing, of mixed activities — have undermined what little collection-to-work I used to have. I particularly find great difficulty in fixing my mind on the play as a whole, that exercise *sine qua non* of composition. I seem only able to "flog the reluctant and tired horses of my mind" when I am out walking and have walked long and hard. (3) Inspiration without emotion. This is the only phrase I can find to describe the moments when the material is really forwarded. The great danger these days is that when I do get "inspiration" it comes in tides of tears which are not only, as formerly, the legitimate tears of nervous excitement, but which bring with them the distortion of the material into a host of humanitarian, "pathetic," didactic directions which are not fundamentally real to me, but which are self-admiring or substitute-self-pitying interferences. Will these difficulties clear up? I cannot say.

The attempt to construct a play whose protagonist is a 20,000-year-old man and whose heroine is a 20,000-year-old woman and 8,000 years a wife made him see how necessary it was for James Joyce, with a similar self-assignment, "to invent a grotesque tortuous style of his own." But Thornton considered that he had one advantage. By shattering the ossified conventions of the well-made play, the characters in *The Skin of Our Teeth* could emerge as generalized beings. "This advantage would no longer be mine twenty years from now," he predicted, "when the theater will be offering a great many plays against free-er decors; the audience will be accustomed to such liberties and the impact of the method will no longer be so great an aid to its myth-intention."

The subconscious, Thornton believed, digests during the night the daytime demands made upon it, "ceaselessly groping about for the subject's outlets, tapping at all the possibilities, finding

relationship between all the parts to the whole and to one another."
Had he not long been convinced of this, "I would have been
the other night. Turning over the play in feverish insomnia I suddenly saw that there, waiting for me in the structure [of act three]
was a felicity, integral, completely implicit and yet hitherto unfore-
seen."

Two months later he was again bogged down, and frightened.
He had rewritten the opening five minutes several times, changed
his mind about having women's roles played by men, but the
third act was still not right. What could he offer the audience as
explanation of Mr. Antrobus's (man's) endurance? "Hitherto, I
had planned here to say that the existence of his children and
the inventive activity of his mind keep urging him to continued
and better-adjusted survival. In the third act I was planning to
say that the ideas contained in the great books of his predecessors
hang above him in midair, furnishing him adequate direction and
stimulation. (1) Do I believe this? (2) Have I found the correct
theatrical statement for it? (3) Is it sufficient climax for the play?"
And if ideas of great masters *are* motive forces for man's progress,
how were they to be represented on the stage? Treating the hours
as philosophers ran the danger of being a cute fantasy and not a
living striking metaphor, and he couldn't find citations from philosophers' works that succinctly expressed what he needed.

A year passed, and in 1941, in an Atlantic City hotel room
— the same room he'd occupied on previous visits — he ran into
unanticipated obstacles in the second act; it was too realistic and
pathetic. "My God! — An Act that begins with a 6,000th annual
convention of mankind and ends with an Imaginary Kangaroo
carrying a turtle down the central aisle of the theater cannot dare
to be realistic-pathetic for ten minutes." A bigger danger lay in
the seduction scene between Mr. Antrobus and Sabina: "If Sabina
is a beautiful girl the whole scene settles down, slackens, becomes
easy — Farce Situation 89, Musical Comedy convention — satire
easily grasped — and there is no support for the next surprise:
Sabina's announcement to the audience that she refuses to play
the scene. All this is correctable if we return to my first idea.
Sabina is LIVELY — SHRILL and pretty UGLY. Almost the
COMIC VALENTINE, ugly servant-girl. Then the preposterous-

ness of her being a siren and a peril to Mr. Antrobus keeps the high wind of absurdity blowing through the act."

At last, on New Year's Day 1942, he felt satisfied with his "fine American family," who come through every catastrophe with "screaming absurdity and a few shreds of dignity."

The first two acts were sent to Jed Harris. Silence. If he did not hear from Jed promptly, Thornton wrote, he would assume that the hesitation was final rejection. No reply. He telegraphed Harris that he didn't wish to hurry a decision but would like a frank discussion of the problems *The Skin of Our Teeth* might present. Still no response. Then a letter from a Harris associate, E. P. Goodnow, writing from Hollywood on RKO Radio Pictures stationery, informed Thornton that Jed had "twice insisted that there is no answer to your telegram, but I am taking it on myself to acknowledge it just the same — secretly!" Harris's mind was far from the theater. He was working on a story of his own, discussing possible casting, furnishing a new home in Santa Monica and in all probability would be tied up for three or four months. It would be advisable to send act three to Goodnow.

Act three was mailed and Goodnow answered that it had been so long since Jed had read the first and second acts, it was only fair to the play to hold the third until he could reread them. Acts one and two were either in the basement of the Gotham Hotel in New York or the basement of an apartment in Hollywood: "You know Jed."

Old grievances notwithstanding, the play was so audacious in technique that Thornton had not been able to imagine any other director than irascible Jed. Now he considered putting it in other hands. All doubt was removed by Harris's letter of January 27:

Dear Thornton:

I need hardly tell you that I have given a great deal of thought to your play, and for a long time I could not quite make up my mind whether or not I wanted to speak about it with the utmost frankness. Finally I decided that to be less than frank would be not only a disservice to you, but a thorough betrayal of my responsibility toward you as an artist. So here it is.

Your first act is noble, not merely in statement, in conception, in theme, but in sheer comic aptitude. If I could only see you and talk to you I believe I could convince you that your whole play lies in the potential materials of your first act. Your second act seemed to me a comparatively faulty and confused re-statement of theme. And while many of its isolated scenes gleam with the most imaginative humor, coming as it does after the high, brilliant level of the first act, it seemed to me to be rather ineffectual. The third act, after all that had gone before, seemed to me utterly trivial. In the first act I could hear you playing Mozart and Beethoven on the piano. In the third act you began to sound like . . . cute imitations of Hoffmann and Paderewski.

Perhaps it is too much to expect, but I hope from the bottom of my heart that you are neither disappointed nor resentful of these remarks. And I must believe that you know me too well to feel that I am too lightly dismissing so magnificent an effort as *The Skin of Our Teeth.* If I were a religious man I would go to church and pray: Pray that you don't give this play to some foolish producer or director who will be so carried away with it that you will be persuaded to let it go into production. I think that such an event would be at least a minor disaster for you and the play and for me.

Please remember and think again of what I have said about your play lying in the immense and beautiful scope of your first act. If this is something that you would care to take up and explore further with me, I am at your service. I think it's a subject that I can talk about three days and nights running.

I'm getting so old now [he was a few years younger than Thornton] that I find myself preferring my old enemies to new friends. But somehow, you seem to me younger than ever. Of course I say this with the deepest possible envy.

> Ever and ever encourageable,
> Jed

Because Thornton wanted Harris, he put forward possible ways in which the play might be made more acceptable — laying down the Sabina menace-to-the-home much earlier, building up the motif that the world is a conventioneer's riot-and-orgy. Their differences couldn't be ironed out long distance, Harris wrote from Hollywood: "Don't be a fool and come on out here."

At that point, *The Skin of Our Teeth* was given to Michael Myerberg to produce, Thornton having refused it to Max Reinhardt.

It was an odd choice. Myerberg was not a theatrical producer. He was a tall, gawky public-relations representative for conductor Leopold Stokowski. Thornton had come across him at Mabel Dodge Luhan's in Taos and been charmed by his ramblings on music, about which he knew a great deal, and his familiarity with unconventional production design and ways of using light in the theater. Myerberg was interested in puppets and had a theory that one could get across human passions and philosophies with these impersonal figures better than one could with living actors. He had invested in a studio to build large marionettes. In Taos, when he announced that he was going into theatrical production someday and hoped to have a Wilder play, Thornton had replied that he had nothing to give him and that when he did he would probably turn to Jed Harris. Now Myerberg had what he wanted.

Elia Kazan seemed a promising choice to direct *The Skin of Our Teeth* and was offered the job, though the selection came under fire from Ruth Gordon. Kazan, she wrote, did not have the necessary self-discipline or the practicality or the theatrical imagination. And hadn't Thornton himself said that only Jed could direct it? Then there was the matter of the casting. Miss Gordon felt that she was born for the part of Sabina; alas, she was about to sign a contract for something else. She could not stand in the way of another actress, she said, but would never rest easy until she played Sabina.

Thornton anticipated that rehearsals would start in the spring of 1942, but Myerberg postponed them until Fredric March and his wife, Florence Eldridge, were free to assume the leading roles of Mr. and Mrs. Antrobus. Several months passed. Thornton kept his fingers crossed. "Myerberg's learning about art," he wrote Woollcott. "Will it break him? Is he the Diaghilev I'm seeking?"

A more urgent, personal search was also underway. Now that his play had a producer and director, Thornton was bursting to get into the war, and to do it before his forty-fifth birthday in

April 1942. At the Century Club that March, he told Archibald MacLeish that he wanted no writing assignment, he wanted to be *in* it. MacLeish said that "they" were hunting for men like Wilder, "they" being Army Air Intelligence, and that he would get back to him within two weeks. Nothing may come of it, Thornton told himself, but he started clearing his desk, studying technical-aviation Spanish and reviewing types of fighter planes. MacLeish had hinted he might be sent to South America, Switzerland or Australia. Sure enough, he was summoned to Washington in early May, passed the interviews and the physical examination and was accepted for duty by Army Air Intelligence, though he would not be called up for several months. He said he would take "the khaki veil with an explosive cry of relief."

The same week, a thousand-word telegram from Alfred Hitchcock was delivered to 50 Deepwood Drive, urging Thornton to come to California to write a screen treatment for *Shadow of a Doubt,* a film about American small-town life and a big-city murderer. A wire from Thornton's Hollywood agent, Rosalie Stewart, confirmed that a deal was set with Hitchcock-Universal, under which Thornton would receive $15,000 for a first draft, payable $2,000 a week for five weeks, the remaining $5,000 during the fifth week, plus round-trip transportation, a secretary and an office.

Why not? Since the army didn't want him yet, he would "compromise with time, art and money and accept the money," primarily because of his dependents. Sister Charlotte was sick and not getting better, and if *The Skin of Our Teeth* failed, he would be supporting his family from capital. If the war went on for long, he was afraid they would be "living in a Florida cracker's house on a Captain's pay."

After a final physical examination at an army hospital near New Haven May 18, Thornton boarded the train for Hollywood and the Villa Carlotta.

Each morning at ten Hitchcock and he thought up new twists in the diabolical murder plot and looked at one another in conspiratorial silence, as if to say: "Can the audience bear it?" Hitchcock's *Suspicion* was screened for the writer's benefit, the director whispering technical procedures in Thornton's ear. He was left alone in the afternoons, but the days were long and when he got back to

the Villa Carlotta he fell asleep on the sofa, awakening for a som-
nambulist's supper about nine.

Because the locale of *Shadow of a Doubt* was a small town, "the
name of Thornton Wilder, who had written *Our Town,* was the
first to be considered," the ponderous Mr. Hitchcock told an interviewer. Various towns were looked over before Santa Rosa, in
northern California, was selected. "Thornton and I examined one
old big frame house and Thornton said 'it's too big but it would
do.' Without asking anyone, the delighted owner of the house
thereupon had it repainted a beautiful white, and when Thornton
saw it, he said, 'oh my God, look what he's done.'" Hitchcock
ordered it changed back to its earlier dirty self. "You see," he
said, "I engaged Wilder with a great deal of respect. I said, 'Thornton, you do what you think is right, you have a free hand.' And
that was the essential thing. He wasn't treated like a hack movie-
writer. One of the finest people I ever worked with; not arrogant,
just the opposite."

It was a race against time, but the script had been completed
when military orders arrived June 16. Thornton rushed out and
bought a uniform — three shirts, two pairs of pants, tie, belt, socks,
visor, hat, an overseas cap and a trench coat. "I'm supposed to
wear 'em when they're ready, by order of the President," he
wrote his mother, "but I'd feel foolish around here." It was critically important that she understand the conviction behind the oath
he had taken: "It's not just a part of me behind it. It's all of me.
Be sure of that." The third week of June he was eastbound on
the Super Chief, accompanied by Hitchcock so that they could
continue discussing the film.

Captain Thornton Niven Wilder, serial number 0908587, had
been ordered to report in Miami June 26 for six weeks of basic
soldiering, then to proceed to Harrisburg, Pennsylvania for another six weeks' training for Army Air Intelligence. He explained
to Hutchins:

> Only men between 19–24 can pilot the new bombers. But
> the young pilots are emotionally immature. Returning from
> raids, they approach the interrogator's table in an inner turmoil.
> They do not wish to speak to a human being for 24 hours.

They fantasize, or worse develop mutism. The Army has sent out word that there must be a new kind of officer at the interrogator's table. It's not enough to know maps, read photographs, and compute ballistics. There must be a psychologist. He must know with which pilots he must be hard as nails, with which he must be patient and indirect. Yes, all war is ugly, not less so when it tries to be humane. So it was laid before me. Entering the Army in wartime is like getting married: only the insecure feel called upon to give the reasons for their decision. So I won't go into them. But it's a pleasure to describe the relieved rush with which I turn my back on civilian life. The level to which "society" has fallen, the fine arts, the "public speech," the talk one has to exchange. The Army, imagine, is a place where one no longer hears the war "intelligently discussed." The Closing of the Door — that to civilian life — is almost pure joy and the anticipation of what's ahead: being pure instrument, however modestly, in a movement-wave that's so important to me is all joy; but looking backward I have one big regret: that in the last years of intermittent writing and intermittent, ill-organized experiencing I have not made myself to rejoice enough in two friendships — you and Amos. It's only secondary to say, though true, that you are one of the persons I admire the most in my whole life. When Armistice Day comes, I shall walk among the bonfires of celebration, I shall permit myself a luxury of cynicism about mankind and civilization, but I shall be thinking of you and Amos and Gertrude, and saying that the world may wag its way hither and yon, but as for me I shall love my friends and do it much more wisely than "before the war."

18

Plagiarism?

Captain Wilder reporting from room 323, Hotel Wofford, Miami Beach, Florida. "We're on the drill field at 7:00 A.M. and already dripping wet, and I love it. And scarcely a moment to think until 6:00. In quarters absolutely at 8:00; lights out at 10:00. Packs of work and a sense of no time to do it, but I love it." Best of all, close-order drill, "endless to's and fro's under a boiling sun." He had never been hotter or harder-worked; every inch of him was changing. What a relief to have an imposed order; a definition of duty, fitness and rank by which one's hours and associates are regulated.

At Harrisburg his goal was transfer to a combat zone ("I didn't enter the Army to write essays"), but because there was a dearth of instructors he was afraid he would be sentenced to a training school. "Please, Mother, do *not* put both a post office box and AAAIS on envelopes. The post box number is meant to conceal the fact that there is an Intelligence school, in fact everything we do is secret. If it got out in the papers that I'm at Harrisburg Intelligence School I bet I'd get practically reduced to rank."

His whereabouts were not that secret, at least not to Michael Myerberg, who showed up and poured out his misfortunes. *The Skin of Our Teeth* was in trouble, trouble that would follow Thornton from Harrisburg to the headquarters of the 328th Fighter Group at Hamilton Field, California and to Washington, D.C., where he would be on detached service the winter of 1942.

The play had been hard to cast. Tallulah Bankhead was to play Sabina, Helen Hayes having turned down the part; Fredric March, Mr. Antrobus; Florence Eldridge, Mrs. Antrobus; Frances Heflin,

Gladys; Florence Reed, the Fortune Teller; Montgomery Clift, Henry; and they were all at sixes and sevens. Fredric March had insisted that his wife be hired; Bankhead didn't like Mrs. March (the dislike was mutual), nor did she approve of Myerberg. Montgomery Clift repeatedly jumped his lines and overran a speech of March's in the third act. Isabel, Thornton's surrogate, had been carrying messages back and forth and sitting up at night with Tallulah until she fell asleep after two or three pills. The director, Elia Kazan, managed to stay clear of the line of fire most of the time, but Thornton could not. He was harassed by letters and calls and in desperation at the end of August arranged for a pass to New York to find out for himself why they were all in such an uproar. Unfortunately, "Michael wants to give us dinner *and* Tallulah!" he warned Isabel. "How can we upset this plan for Tallulah's sake? I must invent an 8:00 date. So discussions 5:00–7:30. Then you and I disappear and, I hope, Tallulah. Then resume at Sardi's. I want to meet Montgomery Clift and *I want to be in Sardi's.* All of us chewing the rag at Sardi's."

Tempestuous Tallulah, with her drink and pills and entourage of young men dancing attendance, was "unforgivable," Thornton thought. "Fighting everything, nagging everybody. She hates the ramp, the idea of it, the use of it. I think she fears the audience sees too much of her too close — gives her away." Thornton was the one person she didn't nag, behaving in his presence like a little girl, never dropping an off-color remark, calling him "sir," taking care to say nothing that might offend him. She admired his play as a tribute to mankind's indestructibility but had no respect for Myerberg, whom she described as "an erratic, tactless man, lean as Cassius, who had been fiddling around the theater for a dozen years with little success."*

"Darling, precious Thornton," she wrote after he had gone back to duty, "the likes of Alec Woollcott have never gotten me down! I have never been one of his admiring little clique — and

---

* *Tallulah* (New York: Harper & Brothers, 1952), pp. 249–51. Thornton was concerned about certain errors in Miss Bankhead's biography but did not want it to appear that he was delaying its publication. That, he thought, would look "so self important on my part." Instead, he asked for and received assurances from the publisher that the errors would be corrected in a later edition.

vice versa." But really, Woollcott must *not* appear in the play during its first week in New York in the role of the Announcer, insignificant though the part was. "I have tried repeatedly to get you on the phone to discuss this with you. I have in my contract the approval of the cast, in conjunction with the Author. *Please* bear me out in this. I speak for all of us — it isn't only me. Woollcott must be kept out of the play!" (Woollcott's explanation was that Myerberg had asked him to record his voice and that he had agreed so that the producer could "discover his mistake for himself.") Tallulah was unappeasable. "Anything you want me to do I would do, but every day something arises that torments me so that I am almost ready to give up the ghost. The general impression is that I am having a wonderful time in the part, and there is no reason in God's World why I shouldn't, except for that MONSTER, Myerberg — his attitude is that of a Gestapo agent in a conquered country, and his ignorance of everything is dementing. One is *never* told if something that directly concerns me is going to be changed; also he is a pathological liar." She enclosed a copy of a three-page, single-spaced typed letter she had sent Myerberg, which she accurately described as vitriolic. "If she were just as good as she is bright," Thornton said, "what an angel she'd be."

Miss Bankhead's notion of the liberties allowed a man in uniform was amazingly liberal. On October 18 she wired Thornton at Hamilton Field, California that he "must come" to New York; Myerberg was behaving like a madman, while "the two Florences [Eldridge and Reed], Freddy [March], Kazan and I are all in tune, loving each other and the play." If Miss Bankhead and Florence Eldridge were loving each other, it was because they weren't speaking. Mrs. March was bewildered by the contention, and after the play opened told Isabel that Tallulah's performances were "miracles of restraint compared to what had been going on before, until Gadge [Kazan] had a knock-down fight and did eliminate such tasty bits as the Mammoth sticking his snout up her [Tallulah's] dress." From the beginning of rehearsals, "Tallulah had the bit in her teeth."

Perhaps the character of Sabina-the-seducer was itself an invitation to overkill. Indeed, two key female roles in Thornton's plays ran the risk of bathos or burlesque. *Our Town*'s Emily had to be restrained from weeping, Sabina from slapstick; one overreaching for tears, the other for guffaws.

Captain Wilder heard it all. Tallulah wired that the play was on the "razor edge of danger"; frantic appeals arrived from Florence Reed. He soothed them both, telegraphed Myerberg and wrote his sister: "Oh, Isabel, what I do here is tiny, but I can't ask for leave. The Army's not made that way." He was horrified at Myerberg's removing the line "he's only 5,000 years old" and upset at his turning down, probably for financial reasons, the suggestion of live music during the play.

The Skin of Our Teeth, having previewed in New Haven, moved on to Baltimore, where Myerberg charged that Bankhead was "constitutionally unable to fit harmoniously into a group effort" and that the situation had come to a head because of her "open criticism of Gadget during rehearsals and before the entire company, and her whispered directions, audible to everyone, to the Marches, and to everyone else in the cast." The Marches, he reported to Thornton, had revolted — "open conflict between Miss Eldridge and Tallulah and Gadget's effectiveness completely destroyed." Two members of the cast threatened to quit unless Myerberg fired Tallulah; *she* demanded that Kazan be replaced, wept, stormed, promised to be good and then decided that the sets were all wrong. "She immediately got Florence Eldridge and Florence Reed on her side," Myerberg charged, "and the three ladies pulled a mild strike. From that time on, she has conceived the idea of combining the company against me — and I must say that she has accomplished this." To cap it all, he said, the play threatened to impoverish him for the next year, despite favorable reviews.*

Thornton's dramatic agent in New York, Harold Freedman, stepped into the controversy and advised that although Myerberg was having trouble with Tallulah, "who is a tornado," many of the things she was saying were right. He cautioned Thornton against accepting Myerberg's word for what the play needed or

---

* In the fall of 1943, Myerberg asked Thornton to waive his royalties in the amount of $7,553.45, claiming that after two years he had received only $8,000. Not until January 1944 did Myerberg agree to pay past-due author's royalties on *The Skin of Our Teeth.*

the audience's reaction to it: "You can get a great deal more of what is going on from Kazan, who understands perfectly and has done an excellent job." Thornton replied that he hadn't let himself "be pushed around by others' accounts," conceded that Myerberg's "lion tamer's technique" might be necessary in handling Tallulah but hoped "such provocation of her hatred can be gradually transferred to something more paternalistic; that would be the real triumph." But he could hardly believe that after the play had been performed in New Haven and Baltimore, Myerberg had been able to raise only ten thousand dollars. "Oh my God! Does that mean that no one, under any conditions you could accept, came forward with any more money than that!!"

The Marches wrote Thornton "manly" letters; he had "more and more admiration for them as persons." Also, reports from discriminating friends convinced him that Kazan was doing a masterly job. It was Myerberg who had some explaining to do. "Something must be the matter," Thornton wrote him.

> And I don't want to hear the story from other people, but from you. What lines have been removed from the play that I or others would regard as integral? What actors have been removed that would seem to so many people as essential? And why couldn't these things have been done without so much sincere alarm and regret? Remember that no actor or co-worker ever worked with Reinhardt who didn't long to work with him again, and remember that no one (except Ruth) ever worked with Jed without loathing the thought of ever working with him again. The great manager is also the peak of consideration and tact, even when business considerations or decisions as to entertainment values require his doing difficult things. And they deeply value actors and actors' peace of mind and find ways to secure their undistracted concentration on the play.

Myerberg answered silkily. The Marches were completely in accord and happily so, and he was doing many nice little things for them, such as building special dressing rooms, and Tallulah was "now very much in the family again." Woollcott had brought

Brooks Atkinson to a performance and "Atkinson was very much impressed."

Orders transferring Thornton from Hamilton Field to Washington, D.C. came shortly before the New York opening and he was given leave to attend dress rehearsal. What he saw was not encouraging; everyone backstage was apologizing to him. Pay no attention, Woollcott counseled, "no American play has ever come anywhere near it." On Thornton's one evening with the cast, Florence Eldridge had her first chance to question him about Mrs. Antrobus's speech when she throws into the ocean a bottle containing "woman's secret." The line that had been bothering her was: "It [the secret] has never been told to any man and it has never been told to any woman." She didn't know why it *needed* to be told to any woman. Thornton himself was puzzled. Perhaps, he replied, she should just inflate herself with woman's pride "and do it like an aria."

On opening night November 18 at the Plymouth Theater in New York, the scenery, what there was of it, was not in place by curtain time and the performance was held back nearly an hour and a half. Predictably, Woollcott gave *The Skin of Our Teeth* high marks, though he thought Bankhead played the first act "like a female impersonator." Brooks Atkinson said it was "one of the wisest and friskiest comedies"; Howard Barnes of the *Herald Tribune* found it a "rare and electrifying experience . . . daring and exciting." Burton Rascoe in the *World-Telegram* called it "the best play the war is likely to produce" and said it gave Tallulah "the first part she has ever had that has allowed her to be the sardonic wit she is off stage. Mary McCarthy scorned it as repetitious, undramatic, a play for middle-brow conservatives ("it affirms the eternity of capitalism"*). Nor, she wrote, does it express the Christian view ("Christ . . . regarded the family as an obstacle to salvation") but is rather "a bowdlerized version of it, such as might have been imparted to a class of taxpayer's children by a New England Sunday school teacher forty years ago." It was Wilder nostalgia, not for the past "but for an eternal childhood, for the bedrock of middle-class life, for *The old Sunday evenings at home with the*

---

* *Partisan Review,* January–February, 1943, pp. 82–83.

tinkling piano our guide.'' Louis Kronenberger was less contemptuous but said that by the third act it "bogs down in talk."

Commenting more than a decade later, critic John Gassner concluded that the theatricalism in the third act was "not only inappropriate because it is played in the wrong key and is perhaps insufficiently climactic for a dramatic masterpiece, but it is evasive as well. The author has apparently nothing to say that he hasn't already told us twice. So he repeats himself again, quotes the right authors, who give the right schoolbook assurances in a pageant-like procession of the show's backstage personnel; and he reminds us for the third time that *The Skin of Our Teeth* is just a show."* Gassner's judgment paralleled Jed Harris's original criticism. Undoubtedly the first act is the most powerful, closing with the coming of the ice age and Sabina addressing the audience from the footlights: "Pass up your chairs, everybody. Save the human race."

Skin would have many revivals. John Houseman directed it in Los Angeles; it was produced in Dublin, and in Paris in 1955 with Helen Hayes, George Abbott and Mary Martin. It was performed by stock companies with Carol Stone as Sabina and Thornton as Mr. Antrobus, and in Germany in a bombed-out church immediately after the war. Laurence Olivier directed a postwar production in London, starring Vivien Leigh as Sabina. Forty years after its first production, it was presented on January 18, 1983, by the Globe Theater in San Diego over national television, its vitality and relevance intact. It also won Thornton his third Pulitzer Prize, in May 1943 — but not before a teapot-tempest had blown up around it.

In the *Saturday Review* of December 19, 1942, two literary-puzzle addicts, Joseph Campbell and Henry Morton Robinson, charged Wilder with stealing *The Skin of Our Teeth* "in conception and detail" from James Joyce's *Finnegans Wake*. Robinson was senior editor of *Reader's Digest,* Campbell a teacher at Sarah Lawrence College. "What of it? Who cares?" critic Burns Mantle asked. Edmund Wilson took the accusation more seriously but not as an indictment:

* *Directions in Modern Theater and Drama* (New York: Holt, Rinehart and Winston, 1956), p. 143.

The general indebtedness to Joyce . . . is as plain as anything
of the kind can be; it must have been conscious on Wilder's
part. He has written and lectured on *Finnegans Wake;* he is
evidently one of the persons who has most felt its fascination
and most patiently explored its text. This derivation would
not necessarily affect one way or another the merits of Wilder's
play. Joyce is a great quarry, like Flaubert, out of which a
variety of writers have been getting and will continue to get
a variety of different things; and Wilder is a genuine poet
with a form and imagination of his own who may find his
themes where he pleases without incurring the charge of imita-
tion.*

When the *Saturday Review* asked Thornton to comment on the
Campbell-Robinson article, he prepared a temperate reply and
filed it away. In that unpublished statement he explained that in
deciphering Joyce's novel the idea had come to him that one aspect
of it might be expressed in drama: the method of representing
mankind's long journey by superimposing different epochs of time
simultaneously. He had even made sketches employing Joyce's
characters and locale but soon abandoned the project. The slight
element of plot in Joyce's novel was so thinly glimpsed amid the
distortions of nightmare and the polyglot distortions of language
that any possibility of dramatization was "out of the question."
The notion about mankind in *The Skin of Our Teeth* and the viewing
of the Antrobus family through several simultaneous layers of time
did persist, however, and began to surround itself with many inven-
tions of his own. From Joyce, he had

> received the idea of presenting ancient man as an ever-present
> double to modern man. The four fundamental aspects of *Finne-*
> *gans Wake* were not to my purpose and are not present in
> my play. Joyce's novel is primarily a study of Original Sin,
> and the role it plays in the life of the conscience. Its recurrent
> motto is St. Augustine's *O felix culpa.* Nor could I use its second-
> ary subject, the illustration of Vico's theory of the cyclic sea-

* *Classics and Commercials* (New York: Farrar, Straus, 1950), p. 83.

sonal repetitions of human culture. Nor could I find any place
for its primary literary intention, the extraordinary means Joyce
found for representing the thoughts of the mind while asleep,
the famous "night-language." Nor could I employ his secondary literary intention, the technical tour-de-force whereby
through puns and slips of the tongue he was able to represent
several layers of mental activity going on at the same time
and often contradictory to one another. If I had been able
to transfer to the stage several or any one of these four basic
aspects of the book, wherein its greatness lies, I would have
done it and would have gladly published the obligation at
every step of the way.

He had acknowledged his obligation twice before — in *The
Woman of Andros,* though Terence's riotous farce had been changed
into a reflective tragedy, and in *The Merchant of Yonkers,* though
its principal personage did not appear in the Austrian prototype.

In *Finnegans Wake,* a woman looks for a match to warm her
husband's supper; Campbell and Robinson quoted this passage
and said that it resembled Mrs. Antrobus's and Sabina's asking
for fuel to warm the household against the approaching glacier.
Comparably, Thornton wrote, they could have derived *Junior Miss*
from *Lady Chatterley's Lover.* "The ant-like industry of pedants,
collecting isolated fragments, has mistaken the nature of literary
influence since the first critics arose to regard books as a branch
of merchandise instead of an expression of energy."

Thornton had given and would give hundreds of hours to explor-
ing *Finnegans Wake.* It was his intellectual recreation, his detective
story. His copy of Joyce's novel was heavily annotated, comments
on it filling 656 pages of his journal. In Dublin he walked through
Phoenix Park in the early mornings, tracing Joyce's steps. "Think
of all the years I have spent on *Finnegans Wake* when I could
have been doing my own work," he would say to Isabel. "But
think how much you enjoyed it," she retorted. He exchanged
views with Joyce scholars on the meanings of lines and sections
— five long letters to Edmund Wilson, others to Professor William
York Tindall — and went so far as to say that Joyce made almost
all other modern fiction "unreadable."

Farfetched as it was,* the allegation of plagiarism sufficiently intimidated the Critics Circle of New York that in April 1943 they denied *The Skin of Our Teeth* their annual award and gave it to Sidney Kingsley's *The Patriots,* a retelling of the Thomas Jefferson story. The vote had been close, six to six on the first ballot, but George Jean Nathan, always unfriendly to Thornton, carried the day. Some called the Critics Circle the League of Nathans.

When the play was revived in 1955, Henry Morton Robinson again brought forward his accusation and called for a debate. The challenge was ignored. Not until thirteen years after the Campbell-Robinson article did Thornton reply to a query about "the circumstances under which you conceived the double time situation in *The Skin of Our Teeth*" by saying that "the treatment of several simultaneous levels of time was borrowed from Joyce's *Finnegans Wake* and Henry James' *A Sense of the Past* and is even in Mark Twain's *Connecticut Yankee at King Arthur's Court.*" A year before his death, Thornton wrote Amos that although "the narrative mind is working in a field of apparently free association, there is really no such thing as free association. Every story is consciously based upon some story already in existence; it adds little increments or manipulates it — reverses the situation or puts plus signs for minus signs." Once, jokingly, Thornton suggested that every word of Hamlet's soliloquy beginning with "To be or not to be" was a direct translation from a mid-sixteenth-century Italian collection of philosophical essays known as *Consolazione,* which included a passage beginning "Essere o non essere, quest'e il problema."

Trust Goethe! "There is nothing worth thinking, but it has been thought before." Was *Faust* a plagiarization? Goethe told his friend Eckermann that "we are indeed born with faculties; but we owe

---

* In *Thornton Wilder,* University of Minnesota Pamphlet on American Writers no. 341 (Minneapolis: University of Minnesota Press, 1964), Bernard Grebanier dismisses the charge: "It is as intelligent as accusing Sophocles of plagiarizing Aeschylus in his *Electra* and Euripedes of plagiarizing both in his; or Racine of plagiarizing Euripedes in his *Phèdre;* or Shakespeare of plagiarizing North, Holinshed, Riche, Cinthio, Belleforest, Lodge, and many others. . . . Whatever Wilder's indebtedness to Joyce, what he may owe he had made his own, and his hand is evident everywhere in this great play — one of the greatest, I believe, in the history of the American theater" (pp. 33–34).

our development to a thousand influences of the great world, from which we appropriate to ourselves what we can. My Mephistopheles sings a song from Shakespeare, and why should he not? If, too, the prologue to my *Faust* is something like the beginning of Job, that is again quite right, and I am rather to be praised than censored." A writer is not so much a myth maker as a myth restorer, searching for the universal in the particular, the timeless in the moment, the profound in the trivial. Far from apologizing for this, Thornton went out of his way to credit his sources. The third act of *Our Town,* he informed a correspondent, was based on a subject treated in *The Woman of Andros;* the closing first-act speech of *Our Town* could be found in Joyce's *Portrait of the Artist as a Young Man;* the catalogue of Emily's goodbyes was after that of Achilles in the underworld; the character of Mrs. Levi in *The Matchmaker* was borrowed from Molière's *The Miser.* "As the shoplifter said to a judge in Los Angeles: 'I only steal from the best department stores, and they don't miss it.' "

I9

Intelligence Officer

DURING THE HUBBUB over *The Skin of Our Teeth*, Captain Wilder had been learning his new trade — IFF (Identification, Friend or Foe) radio reception, safeguarding military information, military police regulations, drill, defense against chemical attack, proper forms for military letters, administrative training, mess, command and staff procedures, Intelligence, transportation, discipline, dress, military courtesy. Among his duties was the questioning of prisoners, and in one case he served as investigating officer in the court-martial of an eighteen-year-old Mississippi dirt farmer's son who had hitchhiked home to help his father with the harvest. Charge: desertion. Penalty: death. But "the Army just *says* that; he'll get off with some guardhouse and some deduction from pay."

Thornton relished the physical toughening, the acquiring of technical skills, his acceptance by a company of unliterary men, and it was not until the second half of his first year in the army, the months of detached service in Washington, D.C., that he became jittery, sitting at a desk in the Pentagon and fighting off maneuvers by his superiors to use him as a scriptwriter for an Air Force movie or as a speech writer for some general. The discontent could not be accounted for by any absence of amenities. He was billeted in the Hotel Raleigh, socialized with Attorney General and Mrs. Francis Biddle, Buckminster Fuller, old friends from Chicago, his Thacher and Yale classmate Wilmarth Lewis. He was allowed weekends in New York, even a few days in Hamden, but he was wild to get overseas.

At the end of March he thought the Washington job was winding down, but three weeks later, on his forty-sixth birthday, he was still at the Raleigh. "Six months in this *cul-de-sac.*" The worst of it was that his daily routine was exacting enough to prevent using leftover time for anything else, and the comfort of the hotel seemed almost indecent.

The law of the army — hurry and wait — applied equally to raw recruit and the winner of Pulitzer prizes, but signs of imminent departure finally became unmistakable — dental inspection, tetanus, typhus, yellow fever shots — and as of May 21 Thornton's address was Bachelor Officer Quarters, North Atlantic Wing, Air Transport Command, Presque Isle, Maine. "It's 2:30 P.M.," he wrote home.

> I'm in the officers' club writing at a long pine trestle. Officers and trans-Atlantic pilots are playing chess, reading and sleeping all around the big room. My summons may arrive anytime. I am enjoying the ludicrous inconveniences of barracks again. Little rooms with two double decker beds; barely enough room for the luggage, coats, gas masks, etc. of four people. The noise in the building until midnight, the phone at the door, and always paper work. It's called "clearing the post." You collect signatures on documents. I was a minor sensation in the personnel office. Autographs for secretaries and signed dollar bills for members of the Short Snorters Club.

Having dispatched last-minute instructions and pleadings to Myerberg, Tallulah, Harold Freedman and his lawyer, he could turn his attention exclusively to his Italian and to his Harrisburg notes, "bursting with anticipation of what's ahead, though trepidation about meeting the requirements that might abruptly fall on me as Intelligence Officer. However, if I keep my mouth shut for awhile I can 'assemble' the orientation and begin to furnish the work."

The next day Major Wilder (he had been promoted) flew to Scotland and twenty-four hours later landed at Casablanca for two nights. Then a plane eastward, Oran for a day to get his orders, and on to Constantine, Algeria, where he was assigned to the Intelligence section of the Twelfth Air Force, General Carl Spaatz commanding. He was where he wanted to be — A-5, Mediterranean Allied Armed Forces Headquarters — three weeks after Tunis and Bizerte had fallen to the Allies and two weeks after Germany's North African army of 270,000 men had surrendered. He would be working with his British Intelligence counterparts preparing air plans, largely from reconnaissance photographs, for Allied landings in Sicily.

He was deeply engrossed, and not only in technical computations that would help Allied forces pinpoint bombing targets in Europe. He had been antifascist since the Spanish Civil War. He had seen the Hitler menace as an assault on the foundation of his intellectual and spiritual life, on those inspiriting words that to him *were* Western civilization, words as necessary as sight; an assault on a history of humane discourse that could be traced from Homer to Sophocles, from the biblical authors to Aristotle, Virgil, Dante, Shakespeare, Goethe, Tolstoy, Flaubert, Molière. It had taken him a year to get to a theater of operations; now he was doing practical combat tasks, hearing a minimum of that cultivated conversation that so quickly repelled him, enjoying recognition as a celebrity but not so much as to make him self-conscious or separate him from his fellow soldiers. It would be a "good" war to Thornton, unlike the war of cartoonist Bill Mauldin's muddy, unshaven, shot-at Willie and Joe.

In Constantine he was billeted in a Frenchwoman's apartment on the main boulevard, along with two other officers, one a medical doctor, Joseph W. Still, the other a regular air force colonel. To preempt the colonel's domination of dinner conversation — guaranteed boredom — Thornton prepared stories in advance, so that the initiative at the table would be his. Letters home provided no details of his work or location but contained numerous instructions on how he wished his sister to handle publication rights, who should be allowed to put on his plays and casting alternatives.

Shortly before the Allied invasion of Sicily June 10, he was transferred to Algiers and from there made frequent air trips to Tunis, Sousse, Oran, Casablanca, Marrakech. In Algiers, A-5 had commandeered a commodious villa of seven rooms, one of which Thornton shared with three other officers. Dirt and mosquitoes were omnipresent, it was hot, but the Mediterranean was a heav-

enly blue and he would remember one air raid "as the most magnificent display of pyrotechnics that a small boy could imagine. Forty
planes of the enemy did little damage and were driven off with
losses. It was at 4:00 A.M."

Woollcott's death from a heart attack June 23 was bitter news,
but there wasn't time to grieve. The Italian surrender on September
7, 1943, foreshadowed the move of the air plans section of Mediterranean headquarters from North Africa to Caserta, Italy, about
fifteen miles from Naples. Wilder, now a lieutenant colonel, was
billeted in a trailer in the English Gardens that Lady Hamilton
had laid out for the Queen of Naples. There was no hot water
for shaving, but a palace stood nearby and behind it an arboretum,
spacious grounds, tall trees. During off-duty hours Thornton
walked alongside the ancient aquaduct that supplied the city's water, composing in his head material for a postwar novel about
Julius Caesar.

Earlier, a brigadier general in the U.S. Strategic Air Forces European headquarters had tried to snare him for London, one of
several high-level efforts to attach him as decoration to some superi-
or's staff. Determined not to be extricated from a combat zone,
Thornton turned wily. Respectfully informing the brigadier general that the request gave him "great pleasure," he hid behind
the authority of his immediate commanding officer. "Undoubtedly,
Air Commander Pankhurst would have authorized my release if
I had expressed the whole extent of my desire to accept it. I hope,
however, that I am right in thinking that your advice to me at
this juncture would have been to comply, as I did, with the wishes
of my commanding officer, as conveyed to me in an earlier private
conversation." Then he poured syrup over the brigadier's head:
"This mark of your confidence in me recalls an earlier occasion
I shall never forget, how when I first arrived in this theater, you
took the time to explain to me the larger issues of the campaign
and the operations that lay ahead. Your generosity and the ideas
you expressed on the war situation have remained as a stimulus
to me ever since. I am glad that this correspondence has given
me the opportunity of sending you my deep thanks and regard."
Thereupon the brigadier general wrote Air Commander L. T.
Pankhurst that he appreciated "the predicament in which you find

yourself and how heavily you must lean on Wilder. I wish to assure you that I will not make further attempt to have him join my organization. In the event your Planning Section should break up, I should at this time like to go on record as stating that we would be very happy indeed to have Thornton Wilder join our official family in the U.K."

Notwithstanding Italy's surrender, the Allied advance up the peninsula the spring of 1944 was slow and hard fought. The Fifth Army did not reach Rome until June 4. On the sixth, the day of the Allied landings on the Normandy coast, Thornton was up as usual at half past six, following his normal routine: shave, shower, walk to breakfast and the office, buy some oranges to eat at noon, nap for fifteen minutes before going back to work. After dinner at seven he read (Veblen's *Theory of the Leisure Class* — "full of laughs") and turned out the light by quarter past eleven. He slept on one blanket, using the other for a pillow. At three in the morning the pillow became a coverlet. Occasionally, he strolled through relatively undamaged Caserta. "They're singing still, and probably sang under the Germans, too. But I get a lot of the Italian air, sky, clouds and trees, and even in all this heat, I love 'em." It would be no use, he wrote Amos, to ask him what war was like. The few occasions when he saw men from combat, he listened and probed, but "essential war does not traverse my ken."

In September he had a three-day pass to Rome. It had been twenty-four years since he'd first leaned on the balustrade before the Villa Medici and heard the bells of the city disputing the hour. "Rome is invaded again!" he wrote his family. "The uniforms of the Angles and the Gauls and the outlandish Americans are thronging the streets as so many times before, a little awed." Rome had decided that the war was over and he was luxuriously ensconced at the Majestic Hotel. "Sheets, Mama!, but I didn't dare use 'em, it being very warm and with these fading and moistened eyes I saw the ceiling of the Sistine Chapel and the Palatine Hill. And yesterday morning very early, the view from the Pincian Hill." He was reading Italian, talking it to Italian prisoners and assuring his "Dear Chicks" that when the European war folded he would not insist on being transferred to the Pacific: "I shall plead my advanced years and my capabilities of being useful in the domestic scene and return to your hearth as soon as transport and Army orders permit it."

His winter uniform was brought out of the duffel bag the first of October, the third time he had worn wool khaki. Offered a chance for reassignment to the Pentagon, he maneuvered his way out with the excuse that he had a play to direct in Caserta — "that old chestnut, *Our Town*," which was to be staged with an all-military cast in the small, baroque palace theater, a replica in miniature of the San Carlo Opera House in Naples with its tiers of boxes festooned with gold ribbon, cupids, roses. Aides to generals telephoned, asking if director Wilder could get them seats for their masters. If Jed Harris could see him now! The director was busy pleading with commanding officers to release a corporal for rehearsal or to get "Mrs. Gibbs" off a night shift, or phoning Rome to track down a hamper of costumes. A GI present at the performance remarked that the American soldiers were not very good theatergoers, "so the audience was composed primarily of British 'other ranks' who applauded politely but wore an expression of bewilderment as, I suppose, would our troops about local Lancashire or Yorkshire mores." On opening night, Lt. Colonel Wilder stood at the rear of the stalls, as agonized as if he were on Broadway and relieved to the point of tears when the curtain fell.

With the Germans driven back to their last line of defense in northern Italy — the "gothic line" guarding the Po valley — and with Allied armies advancing toward the Rhine and the Russians sweeping toward Berlin in early 1945, Thornton's duties varied from interrogations of Italian partisans to identifying bombing targets in southeast Europe and mapping airfields in Austria. Off-duty, he speculated in his journal about national characteristics and how they expressed themselves in military planning. Weren't Americans masters of the disposition of time, though they appeared to be mastered *by* time? Those who worked in the Allied Combined Command were constantly confronted by this basic difference:

The English and French thought first in terms of place, the Americans in terms of time. The Europeans built vast interlocking plans on the basis of taking and cleaning up and completely possessing a succession of places. With one's feet solidly planted

in one place one can move on to another. The Americans
built vast interlocking plans on what musicians would call a
groundbass of time. Accomplishing this by August, we can
do this in October and crown the operation in December.
Clouds of bewildered and irritated misunderstandings surrounded the planning. Both saw the war as an advance over-
ground. Yes. But to the Americans it appeared so self-evident
that it seldom occurred to them to express it, that when you
plan your advance in terms of time you are in a position to
accelerate (and there is nothing more exhilarating than acceler-
ation), whereas if you plan spatially you are so much more
temperamentally and practically committed to advancing, like
the clock, in a regular and evenly measured continuum.

Where did the Americans derive this time sense? The answer
was to be found, he thought, in the experience of making their
way in the American wilderness, their liberation from established
barriers and systems.

A break in routine came in February when word was passed
along that Marshal Tito, now in effective control of Yugoslavia,
had expressed a desire to have *Our Town* performed in Belgrade.
The city had only recently been liberated by Tito's forces, and
the new government had the bright idea that *Our Town* should
be translated into Serbo-Croatian and produced by Partisan thespi-
ans. It was left to Arthur Macy Cox, liaison officer of the Office
of Strategic Services at Allied Mediterranean headquarters at Caserta, to arrange the details of Thornton's participation.

The prospect of having his play performed by Communists who,
after five years of guerrilla warfare, had boxed up and defeated
almost thirty of Hitler's divisions was intoxicating, and though
Belgrade proved to be gray and grim, there was plenty of drink
and conversation. The play was a "smashing success"; all in all,
a pleasant digression from duties of the past eighteen months.

When Thornton returned to Caserta in late March, he was admitted to the hospital and for the first time in two wars had to be
put to bed. It was nothing worse than a deep-lodged cold, not
improved by the flight from Yugoslavia, and the enforced idleness
gave him a chance to reread Plato and *Moby-Dick,* skim through

some detective stories and turn over in his mind the themes of plays that were waiting to be written. His forty-eighth birthday was spent at a rest camp in Capri. "Bottles of weak Italian champagne and speeches, and many poor but gay jokes."

Six days before the German surrender on May 7, 1945, Thornton received orders to "proceed by military aircraft from this headquarters [Army Air Forces, Mediterranean Theater of Operations] without delay to the United States," presumably to be discharged. What serviceman is ignorant of the meaning of "without delay"? More than four months would go by before Thornton's separation from the army.

He said he "wouldn't have missed it," and he had every right to take satisfaction in the job done. He had helped assemble Intelligence material necessary to the preparation of air plans issued by the Mediterranean Air Headquarters, written the Intelligence paragraphs in the air outline plans for Buttress, Goblet, Barracuda, Avalanche, and Dragoon, as well as for other operations that were discarded. Staff studies made under his direction included "Allied Air Activity in the Event of Romania's Obtaining a Separate Peace"; "Appreciation of the Town and Marshalling Yards of Zagreb as Bombardment Targets"; "Organizing Increased Aid to the Partisans in Yugoslavia"; "Potential Use of Corfu as an Advanced Airbase"; "Allied Air Capabilities in the Event of an Allied Advance to the Pisa-Rimini Line." In addition to such specific studies, it had been his duty "to take note of numerous intelligence publications and call the attention of officers and all planning sections to items that might concern them."

He was in Miami Beach the day the Germans capitulated, writing Tallulah Bankhead from Redistribution Station No. 2 to remind her of the words they had exchanged before he left for the war:

"I'll be thinking of you on Armistice Day, Tallulah, glass in hand."

"I've ordered the ambulance already."

With ninety days of accrued leave, he planned to go directly to New Haven, then return to Washington for his discharge, but a week later he was still in Miami Beach. "Their attitude here is 'what are you so restless about — just enjoy yourself.' "

When he showed up in Hamden May 24, he appeared to Isabel

to be a gray-green, limp image of his former self. "At first it was worrying to see his condition," she wrote Sol Lesser, "but he began to mend slowly and soundly." For the next three and a half months until his discharge, Thornton traveled between New Haven, New York, and Washington. In one city or another, he dined with Ned Sheldon, Jed Harris, Ruth Gordon, Montgomery Clift, the Gerald Murphys. On the day the Japanese surrendered, he had dinner in Washington, D.C. with his sister and brother-in-law, Janet and Toby Dakin. Toby had been serving as chief of the International Law Branch in the judge advocate general's office. "We were having a fine time when the news broke," Thornton wrote his mother and Isabel. "I took them to a nightclub and we had champagne and hotcha." He was ordered to Camp Devers Separation Center September 8. Eleven days later he was a civilian and "all hopped up on that novel about Julius Caesar."

20

A Gypsy Life

HOME SWEET HOME. Study, desk, books, piano, Mozart quintets on the phonograph, old clothes hanging in the closet, Mother, Isabel. Thornton stayed long enough to pay his respects and drove off in his convertible to Florida. "Very homesick, miss you lots," he wrote as he neared Ponte Vedra Beach. Parts of the Caesar novel were in his briefcase, along with sketches for *The Alcestiad,* a play based on the Greek legend of Alcestis and Apollo that he had put aside in 1940 for *The Skin of Our Teeth.* By the time he turned north again, two acts of *The Alcestiad* had been written, but it had been like "hewing granite."

In Hamden for Christmas, Thornton felt caged. He bounced back and forth between New York, Washington, Philadelphia, Atlantic City, Newport, energetic as ever, well enough for a man in his late forties who drank and smoked more than he should. Why then did he feel so restless? Or was that how all war veterans were supposed to feel? And why had he so little will power, perseverance or concentration? "Is it the war, or old age, or just that I'm no good?"

Or was he again trying to do too much? He was swamped by professional and public solicitations — committees, grants, fellowships. Had he a recommendation? Would he serve as a speaker, as chairman? He pleaded incompetence. "My mind wanders during *all* public discussion," he told Van Wyck Brooks; "I make atrocious speeches; I always want to go home when I hear the strains and stresses of vanity, self assertion, and clique-maneuvering around me." Nevertheless he agreed to attend a UNESCO conference in Washington the end of January and a meeting of the Friends of Salzburg Festivals in New York. He showed up at the national office of the American Veterans Committee and thought he might "really work in it — speeches at forums and everything." "Every week he goes off to Washington or New York City for days," his mother wrote her sister, Charlotte. "I was present when he was given the Legion of Merit order two weeks ago at an Army headquarters here. A storm was blowing and falling in half-frozen sleet and no car available, but I felt I *must* be present as Isabel was ill in bed with a cold. Thornton delegates everything to Isabel as he did before. He is departed for a clear month of writing and hiding at Atlantic City. He wants to finish the last act of *The Alcestis* [*sic*] and get on with his novel (Julius Caesar). Got the idea living in Caserta near Naples. What a life!"

The clear month for writing in Atlantic City was cut to three weeks, many hours of which were given to counseling amputees at a nearby army general hospital and to quick trips to New York for lunch with anyone willing to hear about his new enthusiasm, Jean-Paul Sartre.

Thornton had been reading thousands of pages on existentialism. What it amounted to, he wrote his war buddy Joe Still, is that "there is no God; there is the concession of the absurdity of man's reason in a Universe which can never be explained by reason; yet there is the freedom of the will defended for the first time on non-religious grounds, and how." The soul of freedom is choice; the soul of choice is risk; you make up your morality as you go along. Responsibility without father. He had met Sartre, and the Frenchman, mystified by such lively interest from so distinguished an author, had placed the American disposition of his plays in Thornton's hands.

Jed Harris's postwar London production of *Our Town* opened in May to a frosty, *Sunday Times* review. "Though it comes from the land of go-getting, speed and efficiency, it moves at a pace that would send a tortoise to sleep and that would make a snail yawn." The absence of scenery seemed to the reviewer an affectation, "as though Mr. [John] Gielgud would take to traveling around London in a sedan chair, or eating breakfast with his fingers." Jed was miffed. Isabel, who had assisted in the production, thought that exhausted London wasn't in the mood for the simplicities of a homespun play presented on a bare stage; it wanted silk and satin. Thornton airily dismissed the criticisms. *Our Town* was past, the burgeoning Caesar novel was present. He didn't need Rome outside his window; he had the Gideon Putnam Hotel in Saratoga, in which he had taken a room.

An alarming message from Isabel put a stop to Thornton's writing. She and Mother were vacationing on Nantucket and on June 18 Mrs. Wilder had fainted. Two days later she was taken to the hospital. Thornton left at once for Nantucket. She died June 29, 1946, at age seventy-three, with all the children except Charlotte at her bedside. Cancer had been developing for several years; the family had not been able to persuade her to see a doctor. Her death was shattering. All Thornton could think of was her "holding us up in the air, more than we knew," and his "gratitude for her loving, serving, vivid life." An early poem of hers came to mind.

> Level with my table
> While I write,
> Two eyes bright
> Follow every motion.
> Try as I am able,
> Smiles I scarce repress
> At their eagerness
> Of quiet and devotion.
> When the work is over
> And I reach,
> Kissing each
> Little clinging hand
> Of my little lover,
> Then the sober face
> Breaks into a lace
> Of curves and smiles,
> like ripples on sea-sand.
> Clinging hands and little kisses
> Are as sweet as poet blisses.

Sister Charlotte's absence from Nantucket and her mother's funeral had a tragic background, alluded to by Thornton when he repeated

a line of Freud's: "In every large family there is one who pays."
Of the five Wilder children, the one was Charlotte, a year and a
half younger than he. For a short period as an infant she had
been sent away to be cared for; the two boys, Amos, three, and
Thornton, sixteen months, were all that Mother could then handle.
Again, when Thornton entered the Thacher School, Charlotte had
been placed with a family in Claremont. After graduating from
Berkeley High, she had gone to Mount Holyoke, earned a bachelor
of arts, then a master's degree at Radcliffe and taught in the English
departments at Wheaton College and Smith, where she was considered brilliant. A prize-winning volume of her poetry, *Phases of
the Moon,* was published in 1936; a second book of verse, *Mortal
Sequence,* appeared in 1939. She had done editorial work on *Youth's
Companion,* written for the *Atlantic Monthly,* the *Saturday Review,*
the *Nation,* the WPA Writers' Project and edited two books.

In 1934 she resigned her assistant professorship at Smith and
moved to New York, where she became a close friend of the
novelist Evelyn Scott. She had had several crushes on young girls.
A long novel of hers, which Thornton described as a "Proust-
like evocation of her childhood in Berkeley and China," found
no publisher. She was passionately attached to the poor, went to
Gastonia, North Carolina during the depression to help in a strike
and was arrested. Left-handed as a child, she was trained to be
right-handed, became a proficient typist but couldn't abide erasers.
If one comma was out of place, she retyped an entire page.

On February 28, 1941, in New York she broke down. She
had been living on fruit juices, was weak and confused, and while
walking in Greenwich Village with her mother abruptly ran back
to her apartment and locked herself in. Taken to Doctors Hospital
and attended by psychiatrist Carl Binger, she was removed to Payne
Whitney, where she remained several months for observation. At
the Westchester branch of New York Hospital in White Plains,
she was given electric shock treatments and insulin shock therapy.
The beneficial results were short-lived. She was forty-three.

Not long before Thornton entered the army, Charlotte was
placed in the state hospital in Wingdale, New York, where shock
treatment was resumed, but she became more and more depressed.
During visits from her family, she crouched in a corner. Three

years later, she had a prefrontal lobotomy, with no discernible effect for two and a half years, after which she showed marked improvement, began to smile, asked after relatives and was permitted to take outdoor walks. Isabel and Thornton were encouraged to stay away, however; they were among the "haunts" in her attic. She was transferred to the Long Island Home in Amityville, New York and by 1950 seemed better. After a brief vacation in Maine in 1951, she was thought to be well enough to return to New York City and an apartment on Sullivan Street just off Washington Square, the rent paid through Thornton's attorney. A good deal of the money sent for her upkeep was given away. She went without food and sleep. Her apartment was in disorder. To get from the door to her bed, one had to make a path through newspapers stacked nearly to the ceiling. She developed gastric ulcers, was treated surgically and had to leave New York.

After six months, Charlotte came back to Sullivan Street, collapsed in the lobby of her apartment house and on July 18, 1953, was brought to the Long Island Home. Part of her stomach was taken out. She was then placed in an "open house," given freedom to go to the village occasionally and make day trips to New York several times a month. During visits with the family in Hamden on Christmas or Thanksgiving she locked herself in her room. She became immensely fat. At the threat of institutional confinement, she flared up in a blaze of temper. Like all Wilders, she was endowed with great vitality, and when she became uncontrollable she was placed in a disturbed ward. In 1964 she was moved into a larger, locked house and confined to the grounds. By then, Janet had assumed visiting responsibilities. Charlotte refused any cooperation with psychiatrists and never referred to herself as a mental patient.

Her last confinement was in the Brattleboro Retreat, by which time her upkeep, financed by two trusts set up by Thornton, had risen to $130 a day. No one dared mention his name in her presence. On one of Isabel's last visits, Charlotte had screamed: "I know you think every word Thornton writes is perfect; well, I don't and I never have. I'm a better writer than he." She outlived him, dying at eighty-one in Brattleboro on May 26, 1980, and was buried not far from the old Wilder home in Mount Carmel.

"I was my own worst enemy," she said to Janet shortly before her death.

So many whom Thornton had cared about were gone by 1946, or would soon go — Woollcott, Ned Sheldon, Stein. When Thornton heard of Stein's death in Paris, a month after his mother's, he wrote Alice Toklas that in whatever company he had been he had silenced aimless talk in order to "tell them about Gertrude,"

> about the several Gertrudes, the Gertrude who with zest and vitality could make so much out of every moment of the daily life, the Gertrude who listened to each new person with such attention and could make out of her listening such a rich reenforcing friendship, the Gertrude of intellectual combat who couldn't let any nonsense or sentimentality or easy generalization go by unpunished, and finally the greatest Gertrude of all, the inspired giant-Gertrude who *knew,* and who *discovered* and who broke the milestones behind her.
>
> Oh, miserable me, I lost my mother this summer. I haven't a right sense of time. I've lived as though I assumed we'd have these infinitely treasurable people always with us. I never foresee their not being there. It may be that this makes my losses twice as cutting, but I think it has one consolation: While they were alive I had them really as a possession. *I didn't feel them as temporary.* My Gertrude is always there, as she was there before I knew her. Which is to say: Always here. My poignant self reproach at not having written her is acute. It doesn't help that I remember that she taught me how all those audience-activities — articles, letter writing, and conversation itself are impure at the source — but oh! that I had at least sent her signs and signals of my ever-deeper love and indebtedness.

After his mother's funeral, Thornton and Isabel had remained briefly on Nantucket, dealing with messages of condolence, cleaning the house, having meals with friends. In two weeks he was due to play Mr. Antrobus in *The Skin of Our Teeth* and doubted whether he could go through with it. He got laryngitis, the doctors pumped drugs into him and by late July he was rehearsing. There would be "no thinking, no writing, no looking backward or forward." Except for Thanksgiving in Amherst with Janet and Toby Dakin and meetings in New York of the Century Club Centennial Committee, the MacDowell Colony, the American Committee for the Foreign Born, Thornton kept close to Deepwood Drive most of the fall of 1946, helping reorient home around Isabel. "It's not been easy." He had almost given up trying to work on his half-done Caesar novel, *The Ides of March.* He was cranky. Social contacts seemed futile. Gladys Campbell begged him to come to Chicago. "No, dear. I can't come to Chicago in January. I'm still moody and group-shy."

1946 had been a year of readjustment to civilian life, a year of mourning, lassitude, restlessness and of sparse accomplishment. A playlet for the hundredth anniversary of the Century Club had been written, as well as his best essay on Stein, an introduction to her *Four in America* published by the Yale University Press, "probably with intermittent vertigo in their stomach," Thornton said.

On Sunday, January 19, 1947, he broke loose from Hamden and was again on the run.

Following ten days in Mandeville, Louisiana, across the lake from New Orleans, he sailed for Yucatán, intending to remain three months. One was enough. Too hot. He was home May 14, left after three days and returned a month later for the Yale commencement and the award of an honorary doctor of letters degree. Then he had five days in Saratoga Springs, was in New York to meet producer Sol Hurok, be photographed and appear at a Gertrude Stein evening at the Gotham Book Mart. A cold had settled in his ear, leaving him partially deaf. He again resolved to give up cigarettes. At Blanche Knopf's request ("the word is too mild") he wrote a publicity notice for a Sartre novel, justifying this exception to his rule against blurb writing by saying the hand of Pa was on him, "industrious in trivialities, evasive of the essential."

Work on *The Ides of March* seemed to stretch into infinity, and he now made a "wicked" decision. He was not going to bite his fingernails and search any further for certain devices and high utterances, but "get it off and out so as to take up other projects — isn't that awful!!" The final lines were written by October, and Thornton went through "that funny period" when a writer doubts whether his book "adds up to anything."

Thanksgiving and Christmas belonged to the family, and, however brief, these reunions meant a great deal to Thornton. Paradoxically, despite his bachelor gypsy life, he was a family man. *The Happy Journey, The Long Christmas Dinner, Our Town, The Skin of Our Teeth* are family plays. His longest novel, *The Eighth Day,* which he would write in the sixties, is a family saga. He believed that Christianity's ethical injunctions and anguished striving are projected and illustrated for us in terms of family life. To his sisters and brother, he was attached by unbreakable bonds of loyalty and affection. He greatly admired thoughtful, kindly Amos. Toward Isabel he was protective and considerate, and if he was the dominant of the two, it was not an intimidating dominance. She could scold him like a termagant for being unnecessarily friendly to people who were taking advantage of him. Thornton would listen calmly and do exactly as he wished. Having reached his fiftieth year, he claimed its exemptions and prerogatives. When Janet became engaged to lawyer Dakin, he had made it his business to go to Amherst and check out his prospective brother-in-law.* He was as proud of her knowledge of biology and zoology as she was proud of not being one of the literary Wilders.

The Ides of March, whatever Thornton's misgivings about completing it "anyhow," shows no trace of having been rushed. It is a polished study of the mind of Julius Caesar and of power in the last days of the Roman Republic, a fantasia in the form of imaginary letters and documents. Historical fidelity is irrelevant. It is improbable that Caesar contemplated moving his capital to Troy or Alexandria, since he was then rebuilding Rome as an imperial capital. Catullus, as Elmer Davis pointed out in the *Saturday Review* of February 21, 1948, is kept alive in *The Ides* almost ten years after the traditional date of his death. But few readers, Davis included,

---

* In his account to the author of the courtship of Janet, New Englander Dakin said, "I rather took a liking to her; so we pursued matters."

were disturbed by the fact that characters bear the names of historical personalities who in some cases were quite different.

Throughout, the novel reveals the influence of existentialism.
Several examples suffice: "There is no liberty save in responsibility"; "the Romans . . . have become parasites upon that freedom
which I [Caesar] gladly exercise — my willingness to arrive at a
decision and sustain it — and which I am willing to share with
every man who will assume its burden"; "on the Meaningless I
choose to press a meaning and into the wastes of the unknowable
I choose to be known"; "it is by taking a leap into the unknown
that we know we are free." But the existentialist aspect went largely
unnoticed, even by the Kierkegaard scholar Walter Lowrie, who
read the book but didn't recognize a sentence taken from his translation of Kierkegaard's *The Concept of Dread.*

The idea for *The Ides* predated Thornton's study of Kierkegaard
and Sartre, however, and also his Roman visit during the Second
World War. On his first trip to England, in 1929, he had written
the eminent classicist Sir Edward Howard Marsh, regretting not
having seen him, since "I want advice on a conversation-novel I
want to do someday, turning upon the famous profanation of the
Mysteries of the *Bona Dea,* with Clodius, Clodia, Catullus, Caesar,
Cicero." He had given it no further attention until 1945, when
"a funny thing happened." He had been writing *The Alcestiad*
too quickly. He was not a fast writer; "it dictates itself to me in
little spurts of its own choosing, and my pushing and pushing
doesn't do any good." So "just for fun" he began the Caesar-
Clodia-Catullus-Cicero novel in letters. Parts of it were the hardest
writing he'd ever done — the letters between Caesar and "Ned
Sheldon" (on whom he drew for his portrait of Lucius Mamilius
Turrinus), on poetry, love, religion, politics. "Of course, it's dan-
gerous to interrupt *The Alcestiad* with another work," he had written his mother, "It's a thing I've never done before, but for the
present I take the sign of my enjoyment as a sign that all's well.
The letter form is intensely readable. The pages crackle with diversity, dowagers exchanging gossip, frantic love letters, meditative
essays, Cicero being elegant, Caesar's wife being a little goose."
In the early stages of the novel, new letters popped into his mind
"lively as a Mexican jumping bean." A real letter from Cicero

to his brother was inserted so artfully that no one could suspect
it wasn't invented.

Cleopatra had long fascinated him. In one of his earliest journal
entries, 1917, Thornton recalled the moment "when as a little
boy I heard of Cleopatra for the first time and how in the following
days the name seemed to be mentioned in everything I read and
how chance sights and sounds became reminiscent of her and stray
objects would suddenly suggest an association with her."

What would reviewers make of so philosophical a novel fashioned in so unconventional a form? "An intellectually interesting
stunt," wrote Orville Prescott in the *New York Times;* not a work
"that can stir the emotions. It is cold, precise, artful and quite
lacking in the divine fire that glows about a major work of art."
Edmund Wilson remarked that it was not "one of Thornton Wilder's best efforts." When novelist Paul Horgan congratulated the
author and said that "everybody's reading it," Thornton replied,
"Thanks. Tell me, how are they doing with *Black Beauty?*" He
was not offended by critics who thought the book was plain bad,
but by charges that he had run up a cold, calculated work that
had nothing to do with life. "I don't mind being condemned for
being in error as long as the errors are awfully human and involved
in our humanity; but oh! I hate to be described as mechanically
clever or as a sculptor for a wax museum."

The Ides had its partisans. It meant more to Glenway Wescott
than any other novel of his generation. From New Zealand, where
he and Vivien Leigh were on tour, Laurence Olivier sent Thornton
a fourteen-page letter on how "superior" the book was. At least,
the sales were sufficient to "house me and my dear dependents
a little longer," Thornton said. A year later he had practically
forgotten it, retaining only the memory of a Julius Caesar he would
like to have known. On a hint from history, he had made Caesar
"a great weeper — but over the wonder of life, not over life's
much-advertised pathos, and that's what I liked best about him.
Goethe was like Caesar — amazed wonder, not tender sympathy."

Half facetiously, he did his own "review" in the margins of a
copy given to Terrence Catherman, a young American he'd met
in Germany shortly after the war. Alongside one passage Thornton
wrote, "You can imagine what art it required of Caesar to glide

in and out of the beds of these warring Clytemnestras!" (He was thinking of Max Reinhardt.) He noted that the "broadsides of Conspiracy" launched against Caesar and circulated by Caesar's enemies had been inspired by the leaflets dropped on Mussolini's Rome by Lauro De Bosis, on whom the character of Catullus is modeled. As to the graffiti on Roman walls, "It's true that the Roman populus had dirty nicknames for this great aristocratic dame [Clodia] and believed she engaged in incest with both her brothers. The wall-writings, however, are by me, and my father'd turn over in his grave." He identified Clodia with Tallulah Bankhead — "brought up in the lying myths of Southern gentry; every Southern woman a magnolia of purity; every man a perfect knight [and who] discovered in time the appalling TRUTH — and broke loose with a yell." Hutchins was the source for Caesar's statement that "dictators must know the truth, but must never permit themselves to be told it." Referring to Caesar's remark that he found it "difficult to be indulgent to those who despise or condemn themselves," Thornton wrote: "Had I known it at the time, I would have 'stolen' the awe-inspiring sentence of the late Simone Weil: 'Even God finds it difficult to love those who do not love themselves.' "

Does the reader have to know something of ancient Rome to appreciate *The Ides?* "Horsefeathers" was Thornton's answer. "I knew no more than anyone who would happen to read a book about the late Roman republic. I began and *made it all up as I went.* I simply assumed that people have been much the same in all times and places." He viewed the novel as a kind of crossword puzzle: "Many of the events we traverse four times. In this way I get (for my own interest, anyway) a sense of the density of life — its intermixedness, its surprises — its mysteries. The way of telling a story chronologically, from beginning to end, bored me — seemed too slick — not rich and complicated and true enough. In life we often hear much later what really took place."

Twenty-four years after *The Ides* was published, Thornton mentioned it in response to a question on whether the novel form is dead: "Gertrude Stein once said to me, 'One of the things we have to face in the Twentieth Century is the decline of belief in an imagined thing.' I tried to get around this by trickery in *The*

Ides of March — documents, letters pseudo-authentic. We are beginning to see the decline of belief in an externally reported 'life.' The name of the new approach is 'myth' — significant truth presented in a narration form in the light of a universality that does not exclude the innerness of every existing human being."

The fortunes of *The Ides of March* had become a matter of "immense indifference." But no writer is indifferent to sales. "Did you see me climbing up the best-seller lists in today's paper?" he asked Isabel. By March 1948 the book had sold nearly fifty thousand copies, and its author was in Europe.

2 I

Goethe and the Germans

LATE AFTERNOON aboard the *Queen Elizabeth.* January 13, 1948. Tossing sea and gray skies. Two ladies wrapped in blankets recline in deck chairs. A middle-aged man wearing a fedora and an overcoat with the collar turned up around his ears rushes by.

"Who's that?"

"Glasses, bushy eyebrows?"

"Yes."

"Thornton Wilder. You know, *Our Town.*"

"He was in the bar last night. Talking his head off."

"Seems very democratic."

"I never see him in the morning."

"The steward says he stays in his cabin. Writes on a card table."

He was translating Sartre's *Mort sans sépulture* as a language exercise, and when his translation was produced in Greenwich Village that year as *The Victors,* he refused any production royalties.

His room at the Authors' Club in London's Whitehall Court had a sweeping view of the Thames, but he was seldom there. That tireless letter writer, celebrity-collector and interior decorator, Sibyl Colefax, gave him an expensive lunch at the Dorchester with the Michael Redgraves, Peter Ustinov, Pamela Brown (foreign affairs editor of the *Economist*), V. S. Pritchett and the Hamish Hamiltons. The Laurence Oliviers had him to their home, Notley Abbey. He addressed the American Association at Oxford and met the gangling undergraduate head of the Oxford University Dramatic Society, Kenneth Tynan, to whom he expounded the thesis that he, Wilder, had done nothing of importance in the theater, but that *he,* young Tynan, could do wonders.

Every minute of his time was taken up. He dined with Aunt Charlotte, his British publisher, the British secretary of PEN; had tea with T. S. Eliot, an hour or two with the Michael Redgraves, a day with his wartime friends the Roland Le Grands, a morning rehearsal of *The Skin of Our Teeth* directed by Olivier, finally a drink with Sibyl before departing for Paris. And because he was ill at ease when others spent money on him, he picked up the check wherever he could. "Money trickles out of my heels like gunpowder."

The French in 1948 may have been living in a fools' paradise, but Thornton found them less careworn and "more vivaciously interested in whatever they are interested in than those seen on the street across the channel." Actor-producer-director Louis Jouvet, whom he saw twice, gave him a hug. Marie Bousquet led him to the great houses of Paris — "armies of footmen, sumptuous food, liquor in floods, celebrated guests and beautiful women." Should he feel wicked at enjoying such pleasures? "Perhaps, but the French would be the last to reproach me."

It was spring when he sailed for home on the SS *DeGrasse,* uncertain what to do next. No subject was waiting to be shaped into a book. *The Alcestiad* lay dormant. In May he would go with Isabel to Nantucket for a week. Before that? He would serve on the editorial board of a magazine Dorothy Thompson said she was starting but didn't, and there was something to look up in the Princeton library, and then he'd go to Atlantic City and Washington and a MacDowell Colony directors' meeting, and the Charles Laughtons had asked him to drinks at the Algonquin, and he had a date with the English editor John Lehmann. . . .

In mid-June, Thornton rehearsed for *The Skin of Our Teeth* at the Berkshire Playhouse in Stockbridge and in July and August played Mr. Antrobus in Westport, Connecticut and at the Bucks County Playhouse. A New Hope performance was sold out for the week, and there was "no hour of the day at which we do not have private rehearsals and soulful discussions of the play — so I have no time to write letters or to do anything else." But he found the hours to lose himself in research on the Spanish dramatist Lope de Vega — a hobby that was to become as consuming as *Finnegans Wake.*

Lope de Vega, creator of a national theater in Madrid in the sixteenth and seventeenth centuries, was the author of at least 750 plays, many written in twenty-four hours and of which about 450 survive. Thornton's ambition was to date accurately the known plays. In early 1948 he was concentrating on the period 1591–1595, which he'd once thought an "impenetrable thicket"; now the plays were "falling into place, like cordwood." Three years had passed since he had first given thought to the name of Lope, and Thornton refused to appraise the time already spent or the time it would take before anything important could be written on the subject.

> So many of the hours are truly wasted [he recorded in his journal] — wasted in the sense that one has not yet discovered the several additional clues that would light up the texts. I feel certain now that if I lived solely in the Lope plays and Lope biography (prior to 1615) for ten years — I feel certain that I could (a) ascribe to most of the plays a date within a three-year margin of error, (b) from that chronology reveal a host of fascinating allusions between the lines, (c) reconstruct a hitherto unguessed activity of Lope as *entrepreneur,* builder and destroyer of companies, (d) make clear the extent to which his plays were built for, around, and on actors and were influenced by them. One question I cannot put squarely to myself is whether that book would be worth that time. Fear that it is not worth it does not arise from a realization that the Lope studies interfere with or abort other plays and novels I might be writing. I have few enough of those to write anyway; as interim work, the Lope studies on the contrary are excellent. My regret is that the Lope theory interferes with my pursuing other marginal curiosities as interesting as itself, "thinking through" a host of other notions that I might bring to a limited but real expression — observations on the style, the rhetoric, of Mozart and Beethoven; writing the "lost chapter" of a Kafka novel; finishing up the

paper on an aspect of *Finnegans Wake,* or the Seven Sins against Shakespeare; really applying myself to Greek and probing the lost plays of Sophocles; devoting myself seriously to this Journal.

Before he was through, 1,198 pages of his journal would be covered with notes on Lope de Vega.

Other researchers had documented the births, marriages and deaths of actors of the period and occasionally their contracts with managers. Antiquarians of Seville or Cordoba had collected fragmentary reports of the Spanish troupes' visits to their city. Thornton spent days examining these records, "porous with lacunae," in the Yale, Columbia and Harvard libraries, the New York Public Library, the Hispanic Museum and the Duke of Alba's private collection in Madrid. In the end, his studies produced two essays: "New Aids toward Dating the Early Plays of Lope de Vega," published in the Karl Reinhardt *Festchrift,* in Germany, and "Lope, Pinedo, Some Child-Actors, and a Lion," printed in *Romance Philology.* "Reading and rereading all those millions of words of Lope," he wrote Professor Harry Levin, "on the look-out for these kinds of guides, does what reading *Finnegans Wake* does — sharpens the attention in all reading."

Still, what business was this of his?

None. Even if I published it in a learned journal who would be interested? Twenty people. Isn't life too short to devote such time and energy to 5,000 such notations as: *May 27, 1623. Valder threatens to put unnamed actor in prison for debt.* I knew that there were some more of these facts in *Boletin de la Real Academia de Espana,* Volumes I and III, and that Widener was one of the only libraries in the country that had them. So Monday morning I was there and fell in when the doors opened. I forgot everything. No lunch. I even went without smoking. At 4:15 I had exhausted all these veins could yield. Did you ever hear of an escapism so pure? And, of course, it's just a little bit crazy. The apologies of [the] irresponsible are not convincing documents, but I'm only irresponsible *in libraries.*

He need not have apologized. Escapism is an avoidance of reality by absorption of the mind in imaginative situations. But Thornton was a fabulist; imaginative situations *were* his reality, feeding his fiction as surely as an underground stream feeds the deepest roots.

Summer had gone. The only irrevocable engagement on Thornton's calendar that fall of 1948 was a lecture in late October that he had promised Hutchins he would deliver at the University of Chicago Center in Frankfurt am Main.

An earlier departure for Europe than planned was prompted by Isabel's health. She had been suffering from cervical arthritis and the doctors had advised a sea voyage. They sailed for Ireland September 15 and had almost a month in Dublin, sightseeing, mixing with theater groups and the principal men of letters, "when they were and when they were not sober." An evening was given to a performance of Shaw's *The Doctor's Dilemma,* another to Verdi's *Requiem.* Additional passages of *Finnegans Wake* were decoded and notes for a new play, *The Emporium,* jotted down. In mid-October at the Hotel Vendôme in Paris (fourteen dollars a day) Thornton had five meetings with the future director and star of a French performance of *The Skin of Our Teeth.* The day before he took the train for Frankfurt, Alice Toklas cooked him one of her three-hour gourmet lunches.

German audiences made Thornton nervous; they took him so seriously and expected such profundity. In Paris he had drafted his lecture for Frankfurt, but as he went over his remarks on the train, they seemed dredged up from an old, tiresome, sententious self; "bad enough," he remarked, "to serve me as a lesson, if I am capable of learning, not to venture into enterprises where I am so out of touch with my resources, my habits of mind. If I had that forthrightness and simple courage that I so admire in others — particularly in great painters — I would announce that I am ill, that I cannot fulfill the German engagements, and I would then apply myself to what truly concerns me."

The Frankfurt hall was packed. All over Germany, *The Skin of Our Teeth* had been playing in crowded, unheated theaters. Was the character of Henry Antrobus (Cain) meant to represent Germany? he was asked. No, he replied, he hadn't had that in mind;

he'd been thinking of Ur and Chaldea. But at least the Germans recognized that *Skin* was a war play, "a thing which never seemed to have struck the Americans in a year's run." A secretary had to be engaged so that Thornton could answer a portion of the letters that came to the hotel each morning. In December 1948 he was flown to blockaded Berlin and addressed large, respectful student audiences. No doubt about it, he was "catnip" in Germany.

When the tour was over, he confessed that the older he grew, the more he saw to confirm what he could have divined without leaving his chair. But the confirmation was necessary: "One's divination of these things — the evil of man to man; how the Americans would administrate an occupied country; what the Germans are like under such conditions — all these 'knowings' are not hot, live enough in the chair." Travel, immersion, engagement forced one's recessive knowing into a more acute, foreground position. He would never write about the war, nor of his trip to Germany, but he hoped that nothing he wrote would ever fail to reflect those experiences.

Coming on the heels of Berlin's austerity, the amenities of Saint Moritz at Christmas were welcome, but Switzerland was too cold, too cloudy, and a week later he and Isabel were relaxing alongside the sapphire sea of Portofino and Rapallo. It was Thornton's first trip to Italy since the war and he was curious about the state of mind of the Italians. They, too, were curious, about the Wilders. Thornton was tormented by trailing photographers; one climbed to the hotel roof to take pictures of Isabel on her balcony. Feeling like pawns of *turismo* propaganda, a "kind of vulgarity [that] is called Americanism," they left. Several days in Madrid, where the Duke of Alba's archivist brought out treasured Lope de Vega material, were followed by a nostalgic return to Rome and a short stop in Paris. Two weeks later, Thornton was lunching with Hutchins at the Century Club in New York, after which he was off to Washington to see novelist Czeslaw Milosz at the Polish embassy. By then, he was ready, temporarily, to be stationary and silent, to sit behind his desk in Hamden and let Isabel answer the phone and close the door to importuning callers.

The closed door did not, however, apply to Montgomery Clift, who telephoned asking if he could drop by Deepwood Drive.

He and Thornton had first met in Boston in 1945 at a rehearsal of *You Touched Me!* by Tennessee Williams and Donald Windham, in which Clift, then twenty-five, had an important role. He was extraordinarily handsome, talented and something of a lost soul. "Here," Isabel said, "was a person asking, 'what do I do next?' He was beginning to be after parts in the movies and on the stage, and he wasn't old enough to judge himself just what he could do or couldn't do, and there weren't many parts ready for him yet because he was still so young. Well, Thornton was great about that. He knew the theater and parts so well and he could suggest plays and say perhaps you can do this. The teacher–young actor relationship deepened."

Thornton was smitten; they both were. "I have a new friend," Clift wrote, "one T. N. Wilder — novelist-playwright. Such adjectives as he had for me — well — right then and there I was convinced he was the greatest playwright on the continent! This is a real intellectual — I who never went to college can listen to this extraordinary man speak with infinite knowledge and above all Truth about that which most concerns me — the theater and all its allied arts."* At Thornton's recommendation, Monty was selected to play Henry in the first New York production of *The Skin of Our Teeth* and would have a role in Thornton's adaptation of *The Sea Gull* in 1954.

Clift had been with Thornton and Isabel in Saint Moritz that 1948 Christmas, and the older man had attentively listened to confidences about Clift's father, the apronstrings of his mother, his twin sister, his older brother, who aspired to act. Monty was like a puppy that had to be patted. In Paris, Thornton took him to meet Alice Toklas, who was "absolutely charmed." They were to see a good deal of each other in New York and to talk long hours of things in common. Both were twins, roamers, stagestruck. After reading *The Ides of March,* Clift wrote that "most lovely man" that it had been on his mind ever since, and that on seeing Thornton he would throw his arms about him, "which of course means for T. Wilder a gradual avoidance of public places: 'we might run into Monty.' " On a drive to Boston, Isabel at the wheel,

* Quoted by Patricia Bosworth in *Montgomery Clift* (New York: Harcourt Brace Jovanovitch, 1978), pp. 111–13.

Thornton and Monty in the rumble seat, the two of them went over a play Monty had brought along. As they raced up the parkway, pages flew out of the car and they got the giggles. "We had lovely, crazy, family times with him," Isabel said — until the mid-fifties. By then Clift had become a Hollywood superstar, was drinking heavily and taking drugs to pick him up when he was down, and he was often down.

In the summer of 1956 he spoke to Thornton of his eagerness to appear in the forthcoming production of *The Alcestiad* in Edinburgh. "You know," he later wrote, "I wish it were 'my' play." When Thornton said that there was no part in it for him, or only a very small part, Clift insisted that the part could be built up. Thornton said it couldn't. All right, Monty would play it as written. But then he grumbled, demanded that the part be rewritten and made longer, and finally backed out. It was the last straw; Thornton stopped seeing him.

It wasn't just Monty. "It is probably an aspect of my age," Thornton wrote in his journal, "that I have lost the faculty of ardor which I brought to so wide a variety of friendships. . . . I accept this condition within myself without any particular regret — merely, however, with a theoretical concern, for have I not always believed emphatically that all and every derivation of *Eros* is the sole fount of energy? It's all become spread and abstract."

Isabel went the second and third mile with Monty. Invited to his house in New York, she would wait downstairs an hour and a half until Clift could be put on his feet by his attendant. At restaurants, he sent things back to the kitchen, complained of the food, discovered he hadn't brought enough money to pay the bill. When he died at forty-five, in 1966, Isabel asked Thornton if he minded her going to the funeral. "Do you really want to go?" She did. "That's wonderful of you. I can't." It was not in his nature or the nature of his affection to pass judgment on Clift, but prolonged dissipation of talent and energy was unbearable. Thornton saw man as *work*.

A creative writer may be working while he's loafing, but if he slips into a traveling salesman's schedule, as Thornton admitted he had by 1949, work suffers. He was seeing friends, keeping up with the New York theater, socializing in Washington, being photographed by *Life* magazine. New York University and Kenyon College awarded him honorary degrees. He agreed to speak at the Aspen Goethe Festival in June — more time out from the only work that paid. A request for a loan of several thousand dollars prompted a review of his financial obligations. As his lawyer firmly pointed out, he was supporting three separate persons — hospitalized Charlotte, Isabel in Hamden and himself. In productive years the government took a large share of his earnings. The state of his fortune hung on his future output. *The Emporium* was half done; he was "churning the waters of nihilistic despair in order to isolate one gram of affirmation."

Before leaving for Aspen, Thornton roamed from Atlantic City to Washington, from Saratoga Springs to Potsdam, then to New York for an evening at the Gotham Hotel and a talk with Glenway Wescott, a "real talk" on a serious subject and with an agenda of Thornton's devising. The waiter brought two buckets of ice. Two bottles of whiskey were produced and, face to face, the two authors got down to burning questions of métier. "In my mind's eye," Wescott wrote, "he is always springing to his feet. Every time I open my mouth, or almost every time, he would advance upon me and talk me down, using the stiffest forefinger in the world for emphasis, beating time for his ideas."* They parted at half past two the next morning. Thornton walked the streets to cool down.

He might have driven to Colorado just for the enjoyment of motels, beers drunk in prairie taverns, prowls through towns at six in the morning, breakfasts in diners. To all these pleasures was added the prize at the end of the journey, a convocation on his revered Goethe.

In an address to the convocation, titled "World Literature and the Modern Mind," Thornton advanced the thesis that Goethe's God-in-nature is wishing us well — "you and me and all artists and all species of animals and plants; it wishes us to develop into ever more excellent states." But, he reminded his audience, nature is capricious and does not necessarily reward our merits or long-

---

* Glenway Wescott, *Images of Truth*, p. 267.

ings. All we can do is work, wait and hope — and perhaps be passed over, because nature is also playing. "There are these dae-monic forces lurking about its action," yet Goethe had not feared them. "He had long since made his peace with nature. He had found his place among two hundred thousand billion and had accepted his moment in uncountable light-years."

"Maybe I'm a good public speaker after all," Thornton said after the speech.

It wasn't his only contribution to the Aspen Festival. He was called on to translate from German the remarks of Dr. Albert Schweitzer, three sentences at a time, and José Ortega y Gasset's lecture from Spanish. He said he was "the pack mule of the convo-cation," on the platform six times, but he reveled in the late sup-pers, the reminiscences with old colleagues, the conversations with students who had hitchhiked a thousand miles to be there. And the music! That alone would have made up for sharing a bathroom with six others.

The town of Aspen seemed to Thornton full of more people at the edge of dissolution than Capri or Taos, and it was hard not to be embroiled in the intrigues. One had to guard against catching other people's malaises, he said. "Sym-pathy means suffer-with — but not in *my* vocabulary. They must divine that I'm not suffering with them; but they don't seem to like me the less for it, nor does it prevent their revisiting me with their woes." He suspected that the Aspen gentry was embarrassed at his being thick as thieves with waiters, ski bums, barmaids, drunks, derelicts and tourist-camp owners.

Some writers lose their books or plays by talking them out before they are written. When it came to his own work, Thornton talked only what he had put on paper. At the ranch home of Mr. and Mrs. Walter Paepke, about a hundred miles from Aspen, he read aloud the first two acts of the unfinished *Emporium* in the presence of actors Louis Calhern and Spring Byington. Calhern was so ex-cited he rushed to the telephone and called New York, not realiz-ing that it was three in the morning there, woke up producer Gilbert Miller and shouted: "Thornton Wilder has written his greatest play. It's called *The Emporium.* I want to act in it; you must *grab it at once."*

Before boarding the Zephyr for New York, he had a call from Cary Grant, asking him to adapt and write film dialogue for the first two books of *Gulliver's Travels*. He begged off.

In retrospect, the festival had exceeded his expectations. It might have been pedantic, "all these Herr Doktors"; it might have been emptily eulogistic and bleakly edifying, chatty or summer-school informative. Instead, it had been "simple and deep-based as one of those peaks that surround us. We were all borne up and along by Goethe," whose genius was "all sublimation and sublimation always entails a few fumes not only of a 'normal' animality but of the twisted — the price that must be paid for that very offense against nature which is sublimation."

And now? A jaunt to Europe. And then?

Thornton Wilder of Oberlin, Yale and Princeton was to be Charles Eliot Norton Professor at Harvard University, 1950–1951, having been assured that his only duties would be six public lectures and accessibility as a campus personality. The assurance turned out to be pure fiction.

2 2

Harvard

Sunday afternoon, March 26, 1950, Hôtel de l'Angleterre, Saint-Jean-de-Luz, France:

A Look-Around My Situation

I feel as though I were in a canoe in mid-ocean. I left no forwarding address and entering Spain tomorrow shall be unable to telegraph one for five or six days. I was astonished on arriving here to find myself inexplicably fatigued. I slept at all hours; I flagged easily on my long walks. Worse than that, a cold came on so rapidly during dinner last night that my right ear became stopped and I feared being in for a long siege. Yet I welcome this isolation as promise of the new mode of life which I must enter resolutely or abandon all hope of significant experience or work. What I must put behind me is the continual passing from one "false situation" to another. It is not a false situation that I call on Sibyl in London, but it is one that I greet so many at teas where conversation can be nothing but reminiscence or polite expressions of regard; that I go to plays as guest of the star and producer — as one whose opinion is awaited with interest — and furnish these opinions (about texts which leave me totally indifferent) from a field of reference which it is impossible to communicate to my listeners — nor do I mean by this that my opinion is *ipso facto* of an absolute justness. That the life in New Haven is a false position and for many reasons goes without saying.

The false position into which I am most continually and wearyingly thrown is that of accepting the assumption that I

am the author of works of which I am proud — that is, that
I *am* these works, that whatever self confidence I have is a
tacit allusion to having written them. It is a part of my pleasure
in the company of my best friends that this never comes into
play (Alice [Toklas]; Helen [McAfee, managing editor of the
Yale Review]; Monty [Clift]; Joe Still; etc.); with them *me,* for
good or ill, is what I offer and all that I offer.

This removedness from the writings, let it be said in paren-
thesis, does not proceed from modesty nor from any repudiation of them as mine. Though it may come in part from a
mortification that they are not great works and from a fairly
clear realization of why they are not, those facts do not play
the larger role in this removedness. I should like to think
that it proceeds from a valuable basis, namely that a writer
at the moment of writing, nor ever thereafter, may not ask
himself whether this be good writing or bad writing; its reality
for him, its excitement, its fashioning, are his only relation
to it; the operation known as *judgment,* the discovery and application of *standards* — these are social acts, distressingly fallible
and variable and remote, very remote from the practice of
imaginative narration. I like to think that this point of view
so deeply engrained in me is a counterpart of that unworldliness
which my two parents — each in a different way — did instill
into us all, and which thereafter by extraordinary good fortune
I heard so richly illustrated and reasoned and practiced by
Gertrude Stein. It would be difficult to explain to many people
that this total indifference to the judgments cast upon my work
does not inhibit the fashioning of new ones; just as it is difficult
to explain that all discussion of them in my presence makes
for a distressed confusion on my part, one that constitutes
with advancing years one of the chief false situations with which
I have to cope. (Before leaving this subject which makes me
uncomfortable even in this soliloquy, I note the contradiction
at the opening of this paragraph: There I do so far pass judgment on my works as to say that they are not great. All I
can say about that is that there is one operation — perhaps
field — of judgment which a writer must exercise in regard
to his work: He must after a time decide whether it is con-

temptible or not. Where I derive my assurance that my work is not contemptible I do not know; but I think that from that same source comes my conviction that it is not great.)

As I look forward to a new mode of life I may look back on some of the false situations from which the years are gradually freeing me. First come those from which the subsidence of the passions — as promised by Sophocles, if denied by Goethe! The overwhelming idealizations — "crystallizations" — which must be, I think, quite different on the part of the artist from those of the non-artist. A lover burns to share himself and to compass also the life of the beloved; but the artist-lover burns in addition to share his thought-world, his *Schauen*, self evident to him, and communicable not in living-together but only in the finished works. For the artist, love then has always something of the false position; and particularly marriage which I profoundly believe in *for others*, but which I am glad not to have entered into. Of the other passions with their consequent false relations two remain with me, sloth and that form of self-destruction which is the counterpart of my almost uniform kindness and generous respect for the life-in-others. I suspect there is another, of such complexity that I am never ready to probe into it — that curious problem as to whether in many of my associations I am truly fond of people or merely indulging in self-approbation for the interest I take in them, or expressed differently: cloaking in assumed sympathy a very real interest which is fundamentally cold-hearted.

All that inquiry leads further and deeper into terrain which I have variously labored, but now I return to my present situation. Tomorrow I go to San Sebastian for two nights; then two nights on *wagons-lits* to Granada.

This is then a Lope de Vega hunt. Preposterous in many ways — its very absurdity being an indication of how deeply such researches now possess me. Preposterous by reason of the shortness of time now before me to accomplish anything; and by reason of the fact that I come armed with none of the letters of introduction and other aids which I could marshall. All that is a sign of the irrational character of the whole pursuit: I wish to pursue it in my own way; an independence which can tend to defeat itself; an appetite parading itself in the guise of an intellectual discipline.

We must take ourselves as we find ourselves, always hoping for some improvement but accepting the basic cast of the die. As a flight from these interlocking false situations I have fastened on Lope studies (they are impersonal; they are precise; they are mine own; they are related to great literature; they somehow express the collecting instinct; they advance). They not only obstruct my writing; they obstruct my very thinking. They are like a banyan tree in my garden which saps all shoots save its own. Already they have robbed the life of *The Emporium* of whatever energy it possessed. The death this week of Arthur Hopkins [Broadway producer] removes whatever external pressure I had to pursue that. Let me now, then, rub my nose in Lope so thoroughly that I can somehow get it out of my system. Then let me rub my nose in the American Literature problem for Harvard so absorbedly that my "nonfiction" interests will be temporarily drained. Then and only then will it be possible for me to return to the theatre.

One last word: The disarray in my psychic life which was perhaps caused by the uprooting which was the war and which has been so advanced by the even deeper immersion in the "false positions" I have recounted, have one still more harmful result. All these activities have been *flights from seriousness.* I am deep in *dilettantism.* Even my apparent preoccupation with deeply serious matters, e.g., the reading of Kierkegaard, is superficial and doubly superficial because it pretends to be searching. Gradually, gradually I must resume my, my own meditation on the only things that can reawaken any writing I have to do. I must gaze directly at the boundless misery of the human situation, collective and individual.

If the autonomy of the inner man were only absolute. That 1950 journal entry portends a retreat from the insincerities of society, a concentration of energies on creative potential, a "new mode of life." The reality was quite different.

The first eight weeks of 1950 Thornton had been in and around New Haven, Princeton, Middlebury, New York, Washington (a reading for the Institute of Contemporary Art), Poughkeepsie,

Bermuda. He had sailed for Europe February 27, done Amsterdam and The Hague, been overwhelmed by publicity and hospitality and dreamt of being "a moody, solitary stroller." We pick him up in mid-March in London; tea with Lady Colefax and with Lady Rothermere, Beverley Nichols, Osbert Lancaster, choreographer Frederick Ashton; theater and supper with the Oliviers. Lunch in Paris with Toklas. Spain: Valladolid for Holy Week, then San Sebastian. Having vowed that he wouldn't enter Italy, not even to visit "the adorable Beerbohms," he went to Rapallo, where the amusing Max and he laughed "as I haven't laughed in ages." He returned to Paris for more engagements and had three crowded days in London the next week: Sibyl's every afternoon from half past four to seven with, "hold your hat," Noel Coward, Lord Wavell, T. S. Eliot, Barbara Ward, Hamish Hamilton, Lord Birkenhead, Lady Rothermere, Sir John and Lady Anderson and others. Dover for the night; Oxford for lunch at Wadham College; Covent Garden with Sacheverell Sitwell, Lady Violet Bonham Carter and Sir Shane Leslie; a matinee of *Hamlet.*

On May 3 he flew home to be in Ohio on the eighth for an appearance in a student production of *Our Town,* for which he took no payment. There was no need; he had earned $66,675.55 from his writing in the preceding twelve months. Then Chicago, Potsdam, Stockbridge, Boston, Yaddo, Provincetown, Cambridge, Newport, Saratoga Springs — entertaining and being entertained. After a week in New York in June, pub crawling in Greenwich Village with Dylan Thomas, he drove to the Red Lion Inn in Stockbridge, "not because it's any good, but because it is so tranquilly certain that it is — which makes for an endearing drollness." Here he did at last apply himself to *The Emporium,* long stretches of which were finished by early September, when he stole away for two weeks somewhere else to devote himself "solely to my still unfinished play before I take up my work at Harvard on October 1."

Six months had passed since that journal entry in Saint-Jean-de-Luz.

Thornton described his room at Harvard's Dunster House as too small even for his jar of blackstrap molasses. He wondered if every breakfast, lunch and dinner necessitated polite chitchat with educators. If so, he'd take to eating crackers in his room, if he was ever in his room. Before arriving in Cambridge, he had accepted fifty-four speaking invitations.

As a defense against time-wasting, he drew up a plan of work. He would concentrate on four subjects while at Harvard, including but not confined to the Charles Eliot Norton lectures. First, "The Omniscient Narrator as Analyst" ("If you are omniscient why do you stoop to explain? *You know, so it is sufficient that you tell.*"). Second, "Time in Narration." Third, "The American Time-Sense." Fourth, "The Elements Which Dissuade the Reader to Believe a Literary Fiction." The last of these bored him. "Isn't my objection to it that it is so much more a purely literary technical problem while the others, though literary, are also about the operation of Mind, pre-literary and para-literary?" Insofar as diversions permitted, he kept to his plan of work, but he was frequently diverted.

Because he had vaguely nodded acquiescence to a request that he speak on theater at Brandeis University during his first weeks at Harvard, he had to write a four-page outline on a subject he didn't want to talk about. Then a Harvard professor of English died, and who better to fill the vacancy than the visiting Charles Eliot Norton lecturer? So, in addition to six formal lectures, Thornton took on a large class for an entire course and by November was punch-drunk with fatigue. A woman in Providence asked him to meet her in Boston to discuss music she wished to compose for *The Skin of Our Teeth.* No, he couldn't, because he had all he could do to fulfill his duties in Cambridge. In confirmation, he cited his Harvard schedule for one day:

> *10:45 A.M.*   Conference with Dunster House Committee on the House's Christmas play — much of the writing of which has fallen on my shoulders.
>
> *12:15 P.M.*   Received deputation from Cambridge High and Latin School. They have a project called "Writers Living in Cambridge."
>
> *1:00 P.M.*   Weekly Wednesday lunch with Dunster House senior tutors.
>
> *2:30 P.M.*   Try to get a nap but phone rings constantly.

5:00 P.M.   Club which has made me a member and of which
T. S. Eliot was an undergraduate member gives a reception
for Mr. Eliot. He reads aloud *The Dry Salvages,* so I am
late for —

5:50 P.M.   Tea by people interested in the Brattle Street Theatre to interest potential donors in a present, very real crisis.
I have been placed on the Board and must stimulate patron-
age.

6:30 P.M.   Arrive late for dinner at Winthrop House — we
carry our trays down the cafeteria line — invited by Society
of Graduate Students (Law, Medicine, English, etc.); address
them and answer questions for an hour and a half on "The
Dramatist and the Novelist."

10:00 P.M.   Home. Letters. To bed.

The Providence lady was succeeded by another who wished
to send him a "rare blue-cloth binding" first edition of *The Cabala*
for signature, in fact for a "signed presentation inscription with
a few lines regarding its conception." He replied asking if she'd
mind bringing the book to a lecture that he was to give on Emily
Dickinson in January at the Poetry Center of the Young Men's
and Young Women's Hebrew Association in New York. "I am
duly in receipt of your postal of the 21st instant," she answered,
"and, in reply thereto, beg to advise you that I have no interest
whatever in the Y.M.H.A, or anything connected with the race
in other than a fictional or historical relation." Would he send
her a photograph? ("Go fly a kite," he had replied to a similar
request, and sent a photograph of Beethoven.) "The first sentence
of your letter," he wrote her, "made me shudder so that I keep
it by me all the time to remind me of how slowly the world is
learning the lessons by which it must live and pursue happiness
and attain peace. I need to be reminded of this continually —
for the background of my teaching these young people at Harvard
and Radcliffe. Although you would not wish me to, I thank you
for this bitter reminder."

He didn't allow himself the ease of improvising lectures, which
his platform experience would have made possible. Whatever the
group, whether or not he spoke from notes, each talk was outlined

in advance and reconsidered afterward in his journal. A "brief report" to himself on a speech to the Harvard Signet Society observed that

an audience's general expectation of me is that I must be very intelligent and as I am a novelist and dramatist as well as academic that my intelligence must be of a super subtle and devious character, full of latent second-intentions, innuendos and ironies. My liveliest proof (alas, to myself, and to those who have known me long) is that I am so unsubtle that I hurtle myself into remarks and developments which could be so interpreted without the faintest suspicion that such pitfalls are present. At the beginning of this speech, merely intending to "interest," I quoted Henry James as saying "the pompous little Club Houses [of Harvard]"; a few minutes later I was describing [these] clubs as "blackball snuggeries." I feel pretty certain that ultimately my real goodwill convinced my listeners that I had not risen in the Signet club to deliver a diatribe against its character and existence.

Another element had its part in rendering the first portion of the speech puzzling. The time has come when I can speak without nervousness, even when, as on Friday night, I am speaking without notes. My structure is well in my memory. To this extent all has been memorized and is recalled; that structure is now "outside me"; and as I am not at the moment thinking it through inside me, developing it as logical and as emotional sequence, *I forget to present the connections,* the *transitional matter.* In approaching a generalization I often forget to furnish the highly important qualifications under which a generalization must be made. The result is that I can be frequently heard talking *blithering idiocy.* The more discriminating in the audience cannot believe their ears; obviously Wilder is not an idiot — so he must be devious, or deep, or (charitably assumed) one of those difficult subtle thinkers whose material must be read to be grasped. The least discriminating, of course, merely hear the loud assured voice and see the "confidence" of an experienced speaker and take the material as all very authoritative and edifying, though "over their heads."

All these erratic efforts at speech-making represent for me a contribution in another category; they are a part of my deep interest in establishing myself in "community." As far as *they* are concerned it is my being obliging; as far as *I* am concerned it is my "having a part." If I talk nonsense occasionally, it does little harm. If a portion of every ten speeches I make is bewildering, my hope (and experience begins to assure me, my confidence) is that the distressing fact is finally overweighed by the evidence that I am not devious or malicious and that I am eager in as wide a circle within my "community" as possible to say Brother and Sister. I want always to make sure that my humanity is wider and more valuable than my brains, and I know damn well that whatever brains I have are of the sort which can only count for anything insofar as they are constantly fed from my humanity.

The teaching year was half over when Thornton went to Hamden for Christmas, "so over-fatigued that I just lay down nursing a cold and what the Southerners call a 'misery.' " He'd been having nightmares that he'd lost his lecture notes. Two months later, in Cambridge, he collapsed.

At first he had trouble walking any distance, his left leg "on the point of letting all Hell loose." By postponing engagements, he thought he might put up with the discomfort, except that he couldn't sit up to write. He'd been up the night before until after midnight, writing "with the fumes of a few highballs" in his head, woke up about seven, put his feet on the floor and felt sharp pains in his back, thigh and left leg. He managed to get through his ten o'clock class; the pain grew worse. At four o'clock he was taken to the Stillman Infirmary, then the Massachusetts General Hospital. He interpreted the breakdown as "a retort of offended Nature against my excessive exertions."

Between January 4, 1951, when he returned from New Haven, and his collapse March 9, he had delivered sixteen extracurricular lectures. That he was largely happy on the platform made him look further for the specific pressure that had brought him to bed. One was his correspondence. Mail and messages had risen to a minimum of twenty items a day. "I wrote letters copiously but that was simply not enough and the pilgrim's pack of unanswered mail followed me almost everywhere; as disheartenment and frustration and as psychological self-reproach." Then, too, he had been leading a flagrantly gregarious life, full of "false situations." He should have managed alternate long weekends in hideaways, "yet my engagement book shows how stern a self-governor I would have had to be to have accomplished that. How could I have said no to certain engagements which seemed to have involved so much obligation and constancy in support on my part and so much kindness and dependence on theirs?"

In the hospital, unable to sit up, drowsy under phenobarbital, he reread *Moby Dick* in clusters of fifteen chapters and made notes for class. Little by little he resumed walking and after four weeks was released from Massachusetts General, encumbered by a corset. He told Isabel that he would "never forgive" Harvard for the way he had aged in six months, but Amos pointed out that if he had been victimized, he was a willing victim. Might the explanation of his collapse, Thornton wondered, lie partly in the absence of the sort of friends he had had in Chicago, with whom he could relax offstage? Possibly, though there were Cambridge counterparts — Alice James, Edwin and Rebeka Cohn (Dr. Cohn had isolated the gamma globulin); Lucy Porter, who pounded the piano in her eighteenth-century house to demand general conversation; Mrs. Winthrop Chandler, an almost blind grande dame who had had a Henry Jamesian girlhood in Europe, translated the German poet Hölderlin, wrote two volumes of autobiography and made Thornton bourbon cocktails with a pestle and a Bunsen burner. They weren't young, but neither was he.

Nor was it the teaching that had worn him down. In front of a class, for all the sweat of preparation, he was like an aerialist doing the loops. What he found most taxing was working up essays on other writers — the nonnarrative form was uncongenial; his gift expressed itself best in the mythical tale and dialogue. And yet, once out of the hospital, he hobbled up the stairs to the third-floor stacks of the Widener Library to check some reference to Tolstoy or compare one critic with another, moving from English translations to original texts in German, Spanish, French. "Bowed down with work" and still not sleeping nights, he readied his remarks on vulgarization for the Harvard General Education dinner.

Having accepted so distinguished a professorship, Thornton was not going to neglect the research required for a survey of American characteristics as personified by Thoreau, Melville, Dickinson, Poe and Whitman.* He was "losing all sense of shame" about flinging himself unabashed into territories that presupposed years of specialization, not a little encouraged by seeing how poorly his colleagues did it. At bottom, he thought, they had no ideas, not even headstrong mistaken ones. "In their essays it's all too evident that they are scratching, scratching diligently to flush one real 'original' glowing idea; but they *do* have form — smooth presentational skill, where all I have is bad logic, bad transitions, and every vice of incomplete circumspections and bad digestion. However, let me remain shameless: *du courage;* let me trust that I have some good ideas and that the practice of discovering good ideas opens the channels to even better ideas and that with enough better ideas — real, full, generating, foliating insights — my presentational awkwardness will give place to something else — to my discovering *my* form, my way of expressing my notions."

Each of his American authors was replete with hidden questions. For instance, leaving aside whether Poe had a first-rate or a tenth-rate mind, Thornton probed to discover what kind of mind it was. Was gambling the basic temptation of his nature? "Gambling: the sign of intellectual energy that cannot find its focus, allied on the one hand to mathematical calculation and on the other to histrionic ostentation? Poe, who lost — was it $2,500 at cards in one term at the University of Virginia? And that he heroically mastered the temptation to gamble . . . and fell instead into the *lesser* vices of drug and drink." One did not demonstrate that a writer is great by showing how remarkably he achieved a little artistic success through overcoming fearful handicaps. But there was greatness in Poe. "My business is to explain our sense of his greatness where so much of the material is obviously manqué."

* Three of his six lectures, much revised, appear in a collection of his nonfiction, *American Characteristics and Other Essays,* published by Harper & Row after his death.

Why did Herman Melville hide behind screens of obfuscation? Could he make Melville's "My Chimney and I" — this "appalling exercise in concealment" — revealing? It was really an

> elaborate phallic fantasy — no, not a fantasy, not a reverie, because all is here also, right up in the conscious mind, a sly, conniving mind, outrageously confessional and no less outrageously ingenious in obfuscating. I dare to assert this because I had already been alerted to Melville's phallic preoccupation by that odd anti-climax (but to *him* a climax) to Billy Budd. . . . Billy, mysteriously, hagiographically, was exempted from a hanged man's ejaculation; and by the two chapters in *Moby Dick:* the Squeeze of the Hands (a swooning orgasm in sperm) and the next chapter, *The Cassock,* which D. H. Lawrence exaggeratedly calls the "greatest phallic chapter in all literature."

"My Chimney and I" seemed to him the *ne plus ultra* of slyness, bitterness, self-loathing. "Phallic auto-eroticism is the most selfish of all temperamental constitutions. This is the inhumanity. It cannot be idealized; it affords only the ashes at the bottom of the chimney."

The end of the academic year in June 1951 was not the end of Thornton's obligations to Harvard, for the university expected that his Charles Eliot Norton lectures would be published, and they were not in shape for publication. This expectation plagued him for years. At least at commencement, where he received an honorary doctor of letters degree, he considered that he could not be faulted, that his address was the best thing he had ever done in nonfiction and nondramatic writing. "We of the class of 1920," he told the graduates, "were appallingly provincial and parochial. The modern student is all alive to the complexity of man in himself and others. . . . He assumes that life is difficult, morally difficult. My young friends in Cambridge have shown me over and over again that to them it is as simple as breathing that all societies are but variants of another, that somehow all wars from now on are civil wars, and the human adventure is much the same in all times and all places."

He had wanted to do well at Harvard, to say something arresting, perhaps even original, about literature. His colleague, Professor John Finley, thought that he had succeeded, but only insofar as he "knew everybody, did everything, had marvelous social gifts, was very American, almost folksy, . . . cheerful and talkative as a village — and as isolated." Some of the Bright People, as at Chicago, put him down as less well trained or well informed than they, but most developed a respect for his intellect and integrity. He had dutifully met once a week with his twenty students in the course on the epic and the novel. His lecture on Emily Dickinson had been standing room only; at its conclusion the silence was broken by shouts and more shouts. One of the shouters had "never heard, no one else had ever heard any lecture received like that." Most "unbecoming in academic life," said Thornton.

It was the leftover duty to publish his lectures that helps us understand why, for sixteen years after his Harvard breakdown, Thornton produced no new novel or play, except *The Alcestiad* in 1955 and *The Matchmaker,* a rewrite of the earlier *Merchant of Yonkers*. Ten years later, the Harvard University Press was still inquiring about the status of the "Norton manuscripts."

As he mulled over his notes, trying to organize them for publication, he sought a form that would preserve the vivacity of the lecture. He was not a scholar, not an essayist. What was he to do? Was he too ambitious in trying to extract from the life and thought of nineteenth-century writers a picture of what the American was tending to be before the Industrial Revolution and the rise of the big city? He wanted to share certain assumptions: that the American is mistaken in feeling that he is a healthy, simple and uncomplicated nature; that, on the contrary, the traits inherited from the colonizing age and the problems presented by the succeeding age had placed him under extraordinary psychic tensions, and that he was in fact in a state of mental and emotional disequilibrium; that a study of the marked disequilibrium of Thoreau, Dickinson, Whitman, Poe and Melville might throw light on the nature of an American's psychic suffering; and finally, that this disequilibrium was not like an illness of degeneration but like an illness of growth, like puberty and pregnancy, and that to understand it was to gain confidence from it and aid it through its transitional difficulty. "These assumptions are, on my part, statements of faith and it is hard to say in what sense faith is transmittable.

Faith is an insight and insights are transmittable, but faith is more than an insight; it is an insight sustained by the will, and no one can coerce or even bestir another's will."

He tried again to express it at three o'clock one morning:

> The American we know — the American which we and foreigners so often laugh at and despise — the American in ourselves who is often the subject of our own despair — the joiner, the go-getter, the moralizer; the businessman with ulcers; the clubwoman who cannot remember one word of the morning lecture; the millions in the movie houses gazing at soothing lies — all, all . . . are very busy doing something of great importance. They don't know it and they often do it awkwardly and fall short. They are inventing a new kind of human being — a new relationship between one human being and another — a new relationship between the individual and the all. It is very occupying; it takes an immense toll in shattered lives and minds. It is not easy to be an American because the rules aren't made yet; the exemplars are not clear. It is like leaving the Known and Comforting and crossing an ocean into a trackless wilderness in which one must gradually set up a form of government and one must decide what should be taught in the schools and one must build a church. And one can't rely very much on those one knew before — over there, because, for us, those weren't quite right.

That formulation, too, was discarded.

Not long after the Harvard commencement, Thornton told Edward Weeks of the *Atlantic Monthly* that he had perhaps found a form to "catch the only vein in which I venture to approach these matters." The text of the lectures, themselves thoroughly rewritten, would be accompanied by a running commentary in italics, expressing what the lecturer thought about while he was lecturing. He was prepared for the fact that this presentation would look "unappetizing and merely bewildering in a review like yours," but the *Atlantic Monthly* would have the first right of refusal. Three lectures were refashioned in this form and printed by Weeks. But the further he moved into generalizations and abstractions, the more anxious he became; the words didn't "come right." After scores of unsatisfactory paragraphs about time and place, the American inheritance and language, the role of *things* in our lives, he doubted whether he was getting anywhere.

He might do better in France.

In a Fontainebleau hotel on October 2, a new start was made. "What I'm getting at is: Wouldn't there be in the Old World a tendency of the writer to feel himself vested with an Unanswerable Authority so that what he tells is The Truth; and in the New World, the author tells His Truth — that is, offers his testimony?" He pursued that inquiry for a while and concluded that it had been an almost total waste of time.

As he copied out sections of Emerson's essay on self-reliance his distaste for it deepened. "Not until I have read more of the essays will I try and explain this shortness of breath — the inability to hold an idea for more than a minute; this constant abuse of the 'sublime.' All is proffered to us as what we Wise Men know — we who, unlike the rest of you, are penetrated by Nature." The mystery of Emerson was how such an assumption of final wisdom could have been reached by him without the faintest evidence of struggle, of cost, and with such little happiness in its expression. "The array of gifts he received in life: a harmonious disposition, an unstrained family situation as a child, a formation within a society which he did not agree with but which he sufficiently agreed with to give him the sense of his superiority over it, an early first marriage of perfect happiness, then just enough money to be free from drudgery and anxiety, and yet not enough to trouble his conscience. And finally — best of all — a lack of imagination. He not only lacks any feeling for the tragic, but he can wiggle by any unpleasantness or stress." For weeks he wrestled with Emerson, sure that if he kept doggedly at it the key would emerge. "It is not that I wish to demonstrate how bad a writer he is, but that I may from the phenomenon Ralph Waldo Emerson deduce the principles as to how each American (a) must be the founder of a new religion; (b) shrinks from the operation which is art; and (c) is an autodidact and a bad one, i.e., is badly educated."

Approaching Thoreau, he felt a weight about his heart — so wonderfully endowed a man, on whom a curtain had fallen that cut him off from the human relation. "Here we come upon a damming up and a sealing down. It is precisely of Nature that he will ask something that NATURE unfortunately cannot awaken in us: the sensation that our love for her is a requited love." At some moment, Thornton observed, the "shut-up" gaze at the Medusa's head and a portion of their spirit turns to stone; the shut-up see the tragic background of life and recoil from some element of our human nature in themselves. "They have the sense that a pure relationship between the Inner and the Outer is not possible; that one cannot be understood; that one is OUTSIDE; that never, never, never can one tell one's story. Niagaras of words fall from their lips or their pews or their pens; they tell everything except the essential."

Was the shadow that fell across so many of these American writers simply the exacting New England conscience? Doubtless they lived under an ethical standard too big for them, the great admonitory thinkers of the Old Testament to which had been added the rigors of Calvinistic doctrine. "Under those counsels of perfection all of us are sinners, worms, poor stumbling inadequate sinners. But there are stern and lofty injunctions in the great Roman Catholic tradition; the Chinese formation is of extraordinary ethical elevations; and our Scots ancestors inculcated in their children a thorny, stoney path of virtue." Why, then, had our American ethics wrought such havoc? "Think of the ever-increasing role that psychiatry is playing in our life!"

Thornton never did shape the six Norton lectures into a book; they were the unappeasable eagle eating at his innards. Only after much travail had "Toward an American Language," "The American Loneliness," and "Emily Dickinson" been transformed into *Atlantic Monthly* articles. The rest he let go, and what we know of them is what we find in journal entries, many made in the fall of 1951.

He had not wholly recovered from the Harvard year on his return from Europe in November, and after reunions in New York with Mario Laserna, Monty Clift, John O'Hara, a meeting of the American Academy of Letters and Science and a short stay in Hamden, he went south for two hermit months in Florida. In Daytona Beach shortly before Christmas he dreamt of his mother:

I was walking along a street and thinking that I would read aloud the half-finished *The Emporium* to some friends. I said to myself: I'll ask Mother if she wants to hear it. She's heard it several times but she always likes to sit by, sewing and hearing it again. I seemed a moment later to be turning a corner — when suddenly two boys on bicycles collided and were flung to the ground. A crowd collected. The younger of the two picked himself up unhurt. The elder — about sixteen — lay curled up as though unconscious. Across the street stood a middle class old fashioned house with steps leading up to a veranda porch and a large front door which stood open. Some bystanders were picking up the wounded boy when he suddenly seemed able to walk; he bounded up the house steps and in the front hall he again fell and lay "curled up" and unconscious on the floor. At once his mother seemed to be standing beside him, leaning over and, perhaps, feeling his pulse. She seemed a relatively young woman and was completely calm. To myself I said: "It's good she happened to be at home. They almost always are."

Home was a dream, and it was uncertain when or how this "wounded boy" would rise and again find his course as a "wild fowl flying in the storm of the twentieth century."

23
Dead Ends

THROUGHOUT THE POST-HARVARD DECADE, 1952–1962, Thornton was interviewed, researched, honored — awarded degrees by Oberlin, the University of New Hampshire, Goethe University in Frankfurt am Main, the University of Zurich, on top of the six he'd previously received. He was decorated by the German, Austrian and Peruvian governments; given the American Institute of Arts and Letters' Gold Medal for Fiction, the German Book Sellers' Peace Prize, the Edward MacDowell Medal, a Creative Arts Award from Brandeis University and a medal from the Boston Arts Festival. He served as chief of the U.S. delegation to a UNESCO conference in Venice; Paul Hindemith put *The Long Christmas Dinner* to music; Louise Talma and he made an opera of *The Alcestiad*. He covered America by car and train and made eight trips to Europe, one lasting six months. But his output of work was meager — a three-act play, *The Alcestiad;* one of seven one-acts projected for *The Seven Deadly Sins;* two one-acts, *Infancy* and *Childhood,* for a series on the seven ages of man. When Malcolm Cowley suggested an anthology, he replied: "How little there is to choose from. My *oeuvre* is one-fourth of any other writer of my age."

The pattern was fixed. He registered at a hotel, met people, his privacy was breached, he moved on — in the winter of 1951–1952, from Daytona Beach to Winter Park and Sarasota, Florida. Twice Thornton lost and recovered the canvas bag that had been with him throughout the war and that contained two leather-covered looseleaf notebooks, one with his current writing and information that he had assembled on Lope de Vega, the other portions of his journal. He interpreted the loss in Freudian terms. "How clear it is! Even the dear Lope studies are an albatross about my neck. And the book [Norton lectures]! It's like some greedy improper self-deception that I can adequately write that kind of book."

Another motion picture assignment caught his fancy. Italian director Vittorio De Sica had shown interest in the forties in filming a Wilder script. He would be proud to collaborate with the "Italian Hans Christian Anderson," Thornton said, but had no idea at hand. De Sica persisted and in the summer of 1951 arranged a private showing of his latest film, *The Miracle in Milan*. The following April, at De Sica's prompting, they spent five days discussing a possible motion picture about Chicago, based on a story by Ben Hecht. For half of each week all the next month Thornton was in New York sketching plot and dialogue, only to abandon the project. A number of telling scenes had been mapped out, but he realized that De Sica was inclined to present Chicago as a loveless jungle of concrete, an image Thornton felt had been demanded of him by a small group of aficionados in Italy who were warning him in open letters in their newspaper not to be seduced from his neorealistic honesty by the deceptive optimism of the land of hamburgers and sanitary fixtures.

The De Sica script had been dropped, *The Emporium* and *The Alcestiad* were stalled and Thornton fell back on an idea that had been resting in his notebooks — a drama about a Christmas pageant in a Sunday school room of the Second Congregational Church in Sandusky, Ohio around 1912. The pageant would presumably have been written by the druggist, the hardware store man and their wives, and performed by children dressed in curtains and sheets. The audience would be assumed to be the townspeople, and from time to time the action would be transferred from the stage to the audience. Thornton visualized himself playing the town policeman. *The Sandusky, Ohio Mystery Play* got no further. He was stuck.

Again, civic duty stepped in.

He had twice declined to be a delegate to a UNESCO congress in Venice in September 1952, claiming he was an "imbecile" at edifying speeches about the liberty of the artist and distrusting writers who mouthed propagandistic abstractions. Moreover, he had promised himself that he would not speak in public for two years, though he had addressed the Oberlin College commencement, at which both Wilder brothers were given honorary degrees. But on August 23, while he was at the MacDowell Colony, Archibald MacLeish telephoned that Secretary of State Dean Acheson insisted that Wilder head the American delegation. Was it one's duty to do things that others mistakenly believed one could do well? Apparently yes. "Anyway, the American delegation at the Paris conference last year did so badly (Faulkner rose and said six words), so all I can do is to *try* to improve." It would be his first glimpse of Venice.

No sooner had the conference adjourned (it had been a "mess of incoherence" in his judgment) than Thornton was summoned to Florence by Marion Preminger, ex-wife of producer Otto Preminger, onetime actress, a flamboyant, inexhaustible talker and doer who was in Europe drumming up support for the hospital in Lambaréné, French Equatorial Africa, of Albert Schweitzer, the philosopher, musician and mission doctor. Of the good doctor, Thornton would say many years later in a letter to Hutchins:

> You speak of Dr. Schweitzer. . . . His *History of Modern Thought* — or whatever it's called — doesn't rise much above any *Dozent* [lecturer] Göttingen 1899. His hospital is remarkable only by location. You and I in Oberlin brushed shoulders with the children of doctors who ran hospitals in remote places that served more patients and diffused a wider radiance. His Bach-playing is unjust to Bach. The decision to go to Lambaréné gained its value from its incipient celebrity. (Many have gone to a "Lambaréné.") Then the little aphorism: *Reverence for Life.* A burr that stuck in the public consciousness. First we digested that you couldn't kill and eat immediate kinfolk, but you could kill the neighbors. Then that you couldn't kill in your tribes but you could kill your enemies. Then that you couldn't kill any human being (we haven't caught up to that yet). And then Old Albert says you can't kill anything that has bright eyes and reproduces its kind. Well, you and I could have thought of that on any rainy afternoon, but we didn't.

Then he ruled in Lambaréné. And, boy, that was ruling. Just as money and life insurance warp reflecting, so celebrity-in-good-works renders dizzy. I have not caught one vibration of an "inwardness" in any pronouncement or anecdote from Lambaréné for many years. His declaration about the danger of giving responsibility to the African tribes has its truth. But for him to say it — now — with all his celebrity — was stupid and cruel. His work has been among almost the lowest type of aborigine. He used to over-relish telling stories about their childishness. As though a Herr-Doktor-Professor *needed* to expatiate on the gulf. The sign of a spoiled great man is the tendency to deny independence to others — his doctors, his nurses, his aborigines — or even to envisage it.

Touring Florence with Marion Preminger was fatiguing. "You know what life with her is like," Thornton wrote Isabel; "we beat all records through the Uffizi and similar monuments and we ate in lofty halls. After all the externalization of myself at the conference and in this gadding about with Marion I am in dire need of tranquillity. The Italian towns and hotels cannot give me that." What could? He felt almost ready to attack *The Emporium* again. But where? He returned to Venice to think it over.

In the midst of this floundering, Ruth Gordon, "resolved like a lioness" to star in *The Merchant of Yonkers* in London, appealed to him to come to Paris to discuss the play with Tyrone Guthrie, the well-established British producer-director. How about Saint Moritz? Thornton asked. Wouldn't do, Miss Gordon said. So on October 15, unwilling to resist her "bulldog tenacity," he was in Paris conferring on a "revision" of *The Merchant*. Revision was Miss Gordon's and Guthrie's word; Thornton had in mind "a few retouches" that might take some time to work out. But he would do what he could. Guthrie's first impression of Thornton was of a "quite giggly" man who spoke incredibly rapidly and with a series of stabbing gestures. "If you sat opposite to him on a plane or train, perhaps you took him, with that clipped gray mustache, to be a slightly eccentric major on leave or an excitable country doctor or, noticing those strong incredibly restless hands, an artificer, a maker of precision instruments or, maybe, a piano tuner."*

Thornton didn't want to be in Paris and imagined that if he could have some long, lazy days somewhere else he could "fall in love" with that bothersome book of Norton lectures or with *The Emporium,* two "solid and good" scenes of which had been written.

> Oh! For quiet, for uninterrupted days. Not only for these tasks, but for the self. I must fight; I must be detestable. I have at least reached the time of life when I can fill a solitude, when I no longer pity myself for so missing the chance to "live"; let me profit by this. Let me build on it. The pressures of reputation have always tended to make me figure as larger than I am. If I can figure larger it will be via the small. I must say goodbye to collaborations and go hide myself. Saint Moritz is right, though lonely. I shall have no datelines before me and no promises. Let me see what I can do.

Half a million francs in royalties awaited him at the French Society of Authors. Thornton collected 100,000 francs, gave 100,000 to writers in distress and left the rest for Isabel should she decide to come to France. He went to Saint Moritz to work. Ruth Gordon and Garson Kanin, whom she'd married in 1942, came along. *Time* magazine interviewed him for a cover story. If *Time* phones, he wrote Isabel, "keep it clean. The great influences are Wager, Tinker and Gertrude Stein. Try and get the Légion d'Honneur in, it's not in *Who's Who.* Tell 'em I wash my own clothes because I hate to shop and haven't got enough to wait for the laundry. Give 'em the works." When the story appeared in the June 12, 1953, issue he bought a single copy of *Time* and threw it away.

Work to travel, travel to work. Saint Moritz, Zurich, Baden-Baden, Strasbourg, another three weeks in Paris. He wanted "the mother-peace of a good hotel in a town where no one knows you are there." Yet he didn't regret the perpetual motion or the obligations undertaken. "No, No! I still believe that all giving

---

* *Life in the Theatre* (New York: McGraw-Hill, 1959), p. 232.

of oneself, all hurling oneself into duty and conflict and contact can be productive." His danger was that he had been exposed to it too long. All could yet be saved, however, for works that would show that

> during these years I have been watching, listening and feeling in the loved presence of multi-faceted life. Let me at least prove that I have not fallen into the opposite peril (into which so many of my colleagues — the "preserve oneself," the shielded-studio "book follows book" writers — have fallen) of writing material increasingly based on memories of experience. The reason that I struggle and strain over the writing projects before me is that they belonged or are harking back to earlier stages of myself, now outgrown. These years, spent or misspent, have hidden from view changes in myself. The next things I write must have a new theme and form — a new theme in form. The supranational subject is mine — the individual in the all-time. Today I have put aside *The Emporium*. And I think I know why.

He had put aside *The Emporium* because a new idea had suddenly come to mind; a fresh line of thought had opened up in Baden-Baden, and in twenty-four hours he all but finished the first act of still another play. The locale of *The Heir* was to be Winesburg, Ohio; its hero, an existentialist man who's afraid that he doesn't hate everything enough; its theme, the eternal movement of social betterment. He got as far as the first scene of the third act when he discovered to his surprise that it was really about anarchists in Illinois around 1900. How strange that something that had started as a genre folk play had found its way toward "one of the subjects that so unfailingly moves me to tears — these tears which are curing my cold, the quiet, absurd, obstinate drive toward better things." The title was changed to *Illinois 1905;* it became a drama about the socialist Eugene Debs, and was dropped into the wastebasket.

It was out of season in Baden-Baden, Thornton's favorite season in all resorts, but, as everywhere, intellectuals of the theater and the university made known their presence. He switched to Stuttgart, then Tübingen. More false situations, more false starts. He looked forward to a quiet August and September at the MacDowell Colony, which he left with relief after the first month: "I look too much like a kindly Dean. So many insulin pep-talks I had to give. Won't it be great to eat alone?, to be able to work nights when one wants to? No, the very fact of change is enough to make it paradisal." He had turned fifty-six and said he couldn't shake off the sensation of being twenty-nine.

In a tower room of the Castle Hill Hotel in Newport, where he was the sole guest, he fought the third act of *The Emporium*, in between reworking his Harvard notes, writing a memorial to painter John Marin and an article on child actors that was to be printed in the August 1953 *Romance Philology*. He drew up a five-year plan for "work in comparative silence" and carried it with him in November to Key West. The nagging Norton lectures followed him. All he could say for his nonfiction labors was that he was learning not to shrink from the truism and the common-place, "maintaining the hope that from them — and only from them — will emerge certain just observations which will not be commonplace to me. I'm arriving so late in life at non-imaginative writing. Gray-haired, I must serve an apprenticeship which is appropriate to the twenties and the thirties."

Key West played itself out. He "got to know too many nice people." He could have gone to Wellesley, which wanted him in residence, or Smith, which had invited him for a semester, or Johns Hopkins for a lecture series. But he saw himself withdrawing from all that. "Saying No always cuts me; best to go where No is made understandable by distance," and since he disliked saying no in his own name, he would sometimes write a letter of regret and ask Isabel to sign it, or let her write some critic who had done a "terribly interesting" article on her brother, suggesting "very minor" corrections.

Isabel could do this because Thornton scrupulously kept her posted. Even in Hamden, if he left the house early for breakfast downtown, he slipped a note under her door to say he would pick up the laundry and buy Kleenex, ballpoint pens and fruit drops. When he was away, she forwarded urgent letters and awaited instructions. What about so-and-so's translating two of his one-act plays into German? Okay. Into Italian? Yes. Into

French? There was already an established translation in French. Another honorary degree? Sorry, can't be present; he'd write the university himself, if he could remember where it was.

No one was better informed than Isabel on Thornton's whereabouts and thinking, but she was careful not to presume. When asked to supply an adjective to describe Thornton Wilder's relationship to his writing public, she answered with eight hundred words, pointing out, however, that she was not speaking for her brother but about him. "My only contribution is in being able to furnish dates, names, and places." On the other hand, responding to a review of a book about him, she did call attention to the fact that she had been writing thirty-five hundred to five thousand letters a year on his behalf, "with the full responsibility of all Thornton's affairs." Agents, lawyers, writers, publishers had endless questions; she "had to decide something sometimes."

During the fifties Thornton made increasing use of his journal as a testing ground. Its primary purpose was to discipline his thinking, for he had noticed that his judgment on a work of art or his attempt to give reasons for his judgment ran off the track or fell into an elaboration that might bedazzle the innocent but left him despondent. He had likewise detected in himself a deep-rooted assumption that his thought must be farfetched, striking and original and yet sweepingly generalized and if possible sublime. He came to see that the practice of reflection alone — even on long walks — was fruitless. He needed a more exacting discipline and for that the written word was necessary: words written for precision, to prevent mere word-mosaic, words written to collect his notions into some system, a reservoir of more codified ideas on which to base the judgments so often demanded of him in conversation.

But he was blocked again and again, particularly in his efforts to compose the Norton book, by the sense that he was "incapable of theoretical thinking." He would become so flushed with pleasure at a glimpse of a half-truth, or an incidental auxiliary truth that might well have been erroneous, that only after many hours did he dimly perceive that "the road of real truth has gone off somewhere miles away, and that I am gayly dogmatizing in a swamp and a thicket." How often in those Chicago classes, attempting to explain or analyze, he had fallen into "faking," trying to whip up an idea that eluded him. Since none of his journal reflections were intended for publication, when he said that it was a repository for moving and gathering ideas, he was reminding himself that it would reward him only if the ideas in it were "snowballing." The nearest he would permit himself to a static idea was to "put down one which, as such, has just occurred and which by the very shock of its novelty gives promise of revealing its applications and consequences." In brief, the journal was an exercise in clarification, free of any writing for display.

To what end? Thornton understood better than his critics that his forte was not theoretical studies, essays or appreciations, but stories and plays. And where were they three years after Harvard?

In a 1954 Sunday column in the *New York Times,* Brooks Atkinson reminded his readers that Wilder in 1946 had said that he intended to have *The Sandusky, Ohio Mystery Play* ready for Christmas 1947. "More recently," Atkinson wrote, "the office seismograph has been recording tremors from *The Emporium,* which is to be a mixture of Horatio Alger and Franz Kafka, with a department store as the central theme. Nothing has come of this play yet. Mr. Wilder, one of our finest dramatists, has not been represented on the New York stage with a new play since *The Skin of Our Teeth,* put on in 1942." Thousands of young people "run after him in the hope that he will speak the magic word which will assuage their fears and order their minds. Perhaps they are not entirely mistaken, and this column is willing to join the throng with a devout wish that Mr. Wilder might take up in the theater where he left off twelve years ago. He is an enlightened man who is especially valuable at the present time. What he knows about the long, endless continuity of life, the basic decency of ordinary people and the eternal values of wisdom is a good deal more to the point today than political argument or social analysis."

The Emporium had been on Thornton's desk since the early forties and was unfinished because he could not "cope with the philosophical statement necessary in act three." In 1945 he had been far enough along to invite Jed Harris and Jean Dalrymple to New Haven to hear parts of it. Harris fell asleep. After reading two acts at the Brattle Street Theatre in Cambridge, Thornton turned to his audience and asked, "Where do I go from there?"

The concept of the play had come to him after rereading Kafka's *The Castle. His* castle would be an American department store like Wanamaker's or Marshall Field. The first act would open in an orphanage. Tom, about ten, runs away, is brought back, whispers that he wants to "belong." To whom? A scene on a farm would be followed by Tom's first interview as an applicant for a job in the department store, or show him in a boardinghouse in New York and his efforts to get near the Emporium.

The difficulty was how to convey the Kafka-castle character of the Emporium and Tom's agonized desire to belong to it as drama, and do it without leaning too closely on Kafka.

In one of twelve versions, members of the Retired Department Store Workers come onstage because they want to *see* and hear every word of the play, "so we're going to sit up here . . ."

> *Mrs. Dobbs.* We can't *act.* We can't *act* with all you people . . .
>
> *Mrs. Frisbie.* Why you're acting *splendidly.* Now, young man, you go right on with the play. We won't disturb you at all.

On board ship in 1948, after "another night of insomnia begotten by the play straining to be born," Thornton wrote a scene in which Tom overhears someone say that he might go far in the Emporium. Tom's girl is arrested by the store's policeman for submitting faulty accounts. Tom attacks the policeman. Would that work? "It is not impossible," he noted, "that most of the material that I've been thinking up during these feverish nights may turn out to be bad, but this is the way it's done. One becomes aware of the central idea of the play tearing around in one's head trying to find the clothes in which it must be dressed, or rather the concrete elements on which it must feed, picking up old motives and rejecting them or suddenly discovering that they will serve." Scene after scene was discarded, brought back. He couldn't visualize an ending. When the play seemed to be taking shape, another anxiety entered: it was all about one thing, the baffling search for "the right way." And what was that way? "What I want to write [about] is love under the conditions of *angst*. The subject must be finally the liberty found in the *angst*, the self reliance that is the only answer to the bafflement."

He was feeling confident enough by February 1949 to say that *The Emporium* had "advanced fine and back in Hamden I shall apply myself to finishing it in earnest." He hoped it was funny and heartbreaking, he wrote Alice Toklas.

> Gertrude's concept has coalesced with one of Kierkegaard; that in this world there are not only the Good and the Bad, as we wretched moralizers are always insisting; there is a third category: The Other. The Other is not interested in good or bad. It is a torment, an insult, a frivolity, a terror, a tyrant — and perhaps it doesn't exist. And in my play it's a department store, the A & J Emporium in Philadelphia about 1897. To its employees it's often inexplicably unjust, but never personally, never sadistic; they are rebuffed or insulted but are wildly loyal. It is a perfection, yet the oddest things happen. It demands all, and yet on some days it appears to its slaves to be just-a-store-like-another. My hero (this is the Horatio Alger play) hates (i.e., loves) it. He rises to the head of the other store, the good store, having married the boss's daughter (the good marriage always shattered by the fact that he loves the little midinette who wraps parcels in the basement of the rival Emporium). There's a boardinghouse scene that's meant to please you. Mrs. Carroway's. She is Rosa Lewis of the Cavendish in London, trailing a faded, brown velvet evening gown, a glass of gin in one hand and a fan in the other. "Now there are not to be any more suicides in this house. I won't have it. Nasty filthy business . . . laundress wouldn't wash the sheets, had to do it with my own hands. Mrs. Hobmeyer, are you contemplating suicide? Well, don't. If you want to do away with yourselves go and throw yourselves into the Schuylkill. Nice clean river put there just for that purpose."

In Portofino that year he almost "totally lost" the play several times, "but today's meditations have given it an extension of life.

I now have the first four scenes [orphanage, farm, boardinghouse, department store], but that may be merely dramatic vitality, not essential program." He kept trying to devise situations that would illustrate the mystery of the Emporium, jotting down dialogue in order to "agitate the springs":

People complain that the store is slow in delivering the goods. Why, a woman ordered a wedding gown. It arrived twelve years after the wedding.

She refused it!?

Refused it! — No, indeed. You should have seen the gown. She was the happiest woman in Philadelphia. Of course, the Emporium doesn't always send you the things you selected.

But that's not right!

Oh, it can be very sad — sometimes you pay your money and you don't get a single thing. I know a girl who ordered a wedding gown — the most elaborate you've ever seen. Really, three women must have gone blind making all that tiny, tiny embroidery. When she came to pay, they told her the price was $26.00. She was furious and refused the dress. She was sure that it must be a worthless rag. Sometimes I can't sleep nights for thinking of all the waste at the Emporium. If no one comes to buy the things then they throw them away. Why, every month they throw away dozens of diamonds and emeralds and rubies. If after a year or two nobody has bought them they simply throw them away. They say that they're wilted.

For three months after writing that passage he did nothing on the play. "Never have I had a work at once so far advanced and so far from completion."

Acting out what he had written was Thornton's method of testing audience reaction as well as how he, performing, felt about the integrity of the work. In Cambridge he read two acts to a small group at Lucy Porter's, an old house preserved with such fidelity it had no electricity. A June thunderstorm broke overhead, the room got so dark it was like night. As the Italian butler quietly moved from guest to guest offering additional candles Thornton went on reading. One of those present remembered how he some-how evoked the department store, an old-fashioned early steel construction with mahogany walls, rather dark, and all the bustle that went on. "He just talked and there you were, half in the department store and half in this equally bizarre atmosphere of Mrs. Kingsley Porter's house."

Like the Norton book, *The Emporium* could neither be brought to life nor got rid of. But when the play seemed mired in the abstract, it found itself momentarily in the concrete:

> *Hobmeyer.* Sometimes I think that *this* — all this we see — isn't the Emporium at all.
>
> *John.* (*Breathlessly*) What? What do you mean?
>
> *Hobmeyer.* All this selling — all this buying and selling.
>
> *John.* Well, it's a store, isn't it? The Emporium's a store.
>
> *Hobmeyer.* Yes, but . . . maybe it's only a front. A front for something else that it's doing.
>
> *John.* Why that's crazy. Of course it's a store.
>
> *Hobmeyer.* But you've noticed yourself that it's not interested in selling — not interested in the same way that Craigie's [the rival store] is.
>
> *John.* (*Stopping for a moment*) Then what is it interested in?
>
> *Hobmeyer.* That's hard to say.
>
> *John.* If it's not a store, why are all of you — you work here — so crazy about it? That's what I don't under-stand about it.
>
> *Hobmeyer.* Come, it's time to lock the doors. Go down that corridor.
>
> *John.* Well, I know one thing: I'm never going to come here again. I don't want to work in a place that you don't know what it's doing. I'm going to stick to my job at Craigie's. At Craigie's you know where you are.
>
> *Hobmeyer.* You're perfectly right about that boy. At Craigie's you know where you are.

"Yes, yes," Thornton added, "I think it can be done." A week later it was all in a ferment. "My will-to-work slackens, my faith fades when the pages I am working on do not bristle, sparkle, dance, with representations of life's diversity, time's anachroneity." He could go no further; the play lacked passion, which in *The Emporium* was "the *movement* of the passion of people seeking the 'right way.'"

He had boxed himself in. "You could paper a house with what I've thrown away." He had been writing about the universe, symbolized by a department store where everything is to be had. He could not follow through dramatically on that idea. The third act was never finished.

24

Throwing Out Lifelines

BROOKS ATKINSON was not to be left with nothing to report. The revision of *The Merchant of Yonkers* that Thornton had promised Ruth Gordon and Tyrone Guthrie was completed, and Miss Gordon was to play the role of Dolly Levi that had been written for her originally. Under its new name, *The Matchmaker,* and after a tryout in Newcastle, the play was scheduled for the Edinburgh Festival, the Haymarket in London, then Berlin. Thornton's spirits revived, and when he sailed for England in July 1954 he was feeling "simply mad about life!"

It was not apparent from the start that *The Matchmaker* would catch on. At Edinburgh's Royal Lyceum, the houses were nearly full, but the play met what director Guthrie termed "a fanfare of bewildered and superior criticism." Hugh Beaumont, the producer, was even doubtful about bringing it to London. That it became a boisterous success in time was due in part to Guthrie's brisk direction, to sets designed by Tanya Moiseiwitsch, and to skillful casting. Eileen Herlie as the milliner Irene Molloy gave what was described as a "deliciously modulated performance"; Sam Levene was a forceful Horace Vandergelder, the merchant; and Miss Gordon, racing about the stage, never missed a step or a funny line. But the frisky farce, so lackadaisically received as Reinhardt's *Merchant of Yonkers,* had also been brightened by Thornton's touch-ups. For example, toward the end of the second act, Mrs. Levi, the matchmaker, takes merchant Vandergelder away from the millinery store, leaving behind Mrs. Molloy, her assistant, Minnie, and Vandergelder's two young clerks, Cornelius and Barnaby. Cornelius and Barnaby are broke. Unaware of that, Mrs.

Molloy browbeats them into escorting her and Minnie to an expensive dinner at the Harmonia Gardens Restaurant on the Battery. In *The Merchant of Yonkers* the scene ended with:

Mrs. Molloy.   (*Turning to Cornelius and Barnaby*) There are some carriages at the corner. First you're going to take us for a drive up to the park; then we're going to Piccardi's for a glass of sherry, and then to the Harmonia. Start along. And when we come back tonight you will be pulling our carriage instead of the horses, and I'm not a girl to spare the whip.

In *The Matchmaker:*

Cornelius.   We want you to come with us more than anything in the world, Mrs. Molloy.

Mrs. Molloy.   No, you don't! Look at you! Look at the pair of them, Minnie! Scowling, both of them!

Cornelius.   Please, Mrs. Molloy!

Mrs. Molloy.   Then smile. (*To Barnaby*) Go on, smile! . . .

Barnaby.   My face can't smile any stronger than that.

Mrs. Molloy.   Then do something! Show some interest. Do something lively: Sing! . . .

Cornelius.   Barnaby, what can you sing? Mrs. Molloy, all we know are sad songs.

Mrs. Molloy.   That doesn't matter. If you want us to come out with you, you've got to sing something. (*The boys turn up to counter, put their heads together, confer and abruptly turn, stand stiffly right of table . . . and sing "Tenting Tonight; Tenting Tonight; Tenting on the old Camp Ground." The four of them now repeat the refrain, softly, harmonizing.*)

Mrs. Molloy.   We'll come! (*The boys shout joyously.*)

Mrs. Molloy.   You boys go ahead. Minnie, get the front door key — I'll lock the workroom. (*The boys go out, whistling.*)

Minnie.   Why, Mrs. Molloy, you're crying!

> Mrs. Molloy. (*Flings her arms around Minnie.*) Oh, Minnie, the world is full of wonderful things. Watch me, dear, and tell me if my petticoat's showing. (*The curtain falls.*)

The sentiment and the music are vintage Wilder. Act one of *The Skin of Our Teeth* closes with:

> Sabina. (*To audience*) Will you please start handing up your chairs? We'll need everything for this fire. Save the human race. Ushers, will you pass the chairs up here? (*Singing starts — "Jingle Bells"*)
>
> Henry. Six times 9 are 54; 6 times 10 are 60. (*In the back of the auditorium the sound of chairs being ripped up can be heard. An Usher rushes down the aisle with chairs and hands them over. Sabina takes the pieces; tosses them on the fire.*)
>
> Gladys. And God called the light Day and the darkness he called Night.
>
> Sabina. Pass up your chairs, everybody. (*Voices in background rise in volume.*) Save the human race.

At the end of the second act of *Our Town,* in the wedding scene, Thornton creates the same effect this way:

> (*Stage Manager mutters, "the ring." George takes it from pocket, slips it on Emily's finger, then steps to embrace and kiss her. The kiss is held throughout the following speech, Emily's ecstatic face uplifted against George's left shoulder.*)
>
> Stage Manager. . . . Well, let's have Mendelssohn's *Wedding March!* (*The organ picks up* The March.)
>
> Mrs. Soames. Aren't they a lovely couple? Oh, I've never been to such a nice wedding. I'm sure they'll be happy. I always say: *happiness,* that's the great thing! The important thing is to be happy.

The Matchmaker's shaky opening in Edinburgh may have had something to do with Miss Gordon's mood. Two incidents had upset her. When Thornton, accompanied by Isabel, went backstage to pay tribute to the cast (he called it "the perjury of the Green Room"), he inadvertently spoke to the lesser lights before calling on the star in her dressing room. He was met with cold hauteur. The next evening he took Isabel and Tanya Moiseiwitsch to supper; at a nearby table, Ruth and Garson Kanin were entertaining actor Michael Redgrave, who had no part in the production. "As we left," Thornton recounted, "we stopped at their table a moment. Ruth's face was ravaged. She mentioned a minor cut in the text as so harmful to her role that she could 'give up her part.' She had so threatened a week ago and two weeks ago. Now Michael . . . had thrown Ruth's confidence in the play."

Redgrave's upsetting intervention had not been intentional. At supper, he had made some minor suggestions on stage business, responding to "a very urgent appeal from Ruth . . . a bundle of spiny nerves, you know." He had said no more, he wrote Thornton, "than what I said later to you and I'm sure that Ruth and Gar would not have said anything if I had not been one of the first, so they assured me, to bring the matter of Guthrie's direction up." He was glad Thornton had succeeded in calming Ruth that night. "I still can't believe that it was I that uncalmed her. . . . I *very* cautiously — as I always do with theatre friends who are in the middle of playing something — avoided any reference to things which could not be helped."

The Kanins were among Thornton's best friends. He saw them often in New York, New England, Europe. He was Ruth's "Thornton dearie," guide, mentor. They had had many festive evenings and his remarks were remembered and quoted by them. But Ruth had not entirely approved of how *The Matchmaker* was staged. She thought Sam Levene was wrongly cast, that good lines had been cut. On his last evening in Edinburgh, Thornton was still writing a new scene, "mostly to please Ruth, who wanted to get off the stage quick after her first entrance in act three. I wrote some stuff and then just felt bankrupt and carried it unfinished to their room. I came near yelling, '*Play* what's written and it'll go.'"

Miss Gordon perhaps thought, and had a right to think, that she had a special relationship to the author. There were weeks when she was with him almost constantly. He had the highest respect for her acting ability; she had been his first choice to play Dolly Levi. In time she would disappoint him; he would feel that she had become careless, too interested in popularity, money. All the same, Thornton enjoyed her company and that of her husband, though he didn't look forward with pleasure to the possibility that Kanin might someday write about him. Leaving a dinner party with the Kanins, Thornton said to Isabel, "You certainly noticed how I keep repeating my best stories to Gar." "Yes," she said, "you certainly do." "I'm doing it so he'll get them straight, God willing."

American audiences made *The Matchmaker* seem like a different play. They were more quickly onto its intrigue, quicker to take jokes about money and sex, but, Guthrie noted, almost "totally blind and deaf to the fact that the best jokes were not just laughs but had a serious undercurrent; that the best situations were not funny, but pathetic, even poignant. Poignancy had gone for good."* The play may have suffered a loss of poignancy in America, but it didn't suffer at the box office, and the notices couldn't have been better if Guthrie had written them himself.

The most interesting notice, indeed what Thornton called "the most perceptive words I ever read about myself," appeared in *Il mondo* of January 31, 1955. Nicolà Chiaramonte, reviewing an Italian production of *The Matchmaker* (*La sensale di matrimoni*), termed Wilder "the only contemporary American writer who is literate in the European sense . . . the humanistic sense"; one who evidenced a "more or less serious tolerance of the world, as though he were disgusted by the fact that the world is real rather than imaginary. What better way to do this than to idolize and imitate the forms of the past or the past itself." Wilder, wrote Chiaramonte, "is not one of the great, nor does he presume to be. He is a moralistic *pasticheur* [and] his morality is exclusively related to the imaginary world that he likes to create by realistic means. Such an attitude cannot be maintained without gifts of sophisticated subtlety or without excellent culture."

"He [Chiaramonte] thinks the *kind* of literature I make is bad,"

* *Life in the Theatre*, p. 234.

Thornton commented. "I assert that the kind is all right — has been so and will be so again — only that I don't do it well enough. I find myself struggling to ask why this dependence on the art of the past, or on form itself, cannot be looked upon as a mode for the transmission of the real."

He was en route to Paris in late September, then on to Aix-en-Provence, where his only acquaintances in five weeks were the result of "assiduity at bars." He thought of renting a cottage in Aix. "Isn't it awful the way I plan to go into SECLUSION?" And wasn't it absurd to be considering an invitation from Ian Hunter, director of the Edinburgh Festival, to furnish a new play for their problem hall — the Assembly Room — high council chamber of the Presbyterian church? The absurdity lay in his having already before him so many unfinished projects. Nevertheless, he promised to answer Hunter by November first.

Something he'd been "tearing to tatters" *might* support a play. A space drama. A father will not let his daughter marry because the world is about to come to a cataclysmic end. He gathers his family about him, and while awaiting doom in a cave sees a flying saucer descend. For a month, Thornton played around with his "Martian play," science fiction in the manner of Aristophanes. Should he call it *The Bats?* He visualized the father as a bitter misanthrope who has put in his application to leave earth on the first conveyance. News comes that a spaceship for Mars is almost ready; seats are available for two people. End of part one. Part two: Three little furry men emerge from a flying saucer. "But you speak English?" "Yes, we hear everything you say on the radio and see everything you do on television."

He'd see what came of it when he got to Fontainebleau. Dozing on the train, he "invite[d]" portions of the play.*

At the Hotel Legris et Parc in Fontainebleau he was met by messages from Miss Gordon and Hugh Beaumont calling him back to England for more *Matchmaker* rewrites. His man in the cave went with him. "The minute I start thinking about him I see that my Part One has not enough forward movement. Alright,

* "He sleeps in berths more than he does in beds," Alice Toklas remarked, which was not true, at least in Europe. Thornton couldn't sleep well on trains and traveled by stages, stopping off for a night's rest in hotels.

when the play opens he has merely decided to retire with his family into a cave because of the H-bomb. He has sent for his sister-in-law; to her he announces his second decision, to embark for Mars. Photographers and press are there. Anyway, what I got this evening was a picture of the sacks of mail that arrive daily at the cave. And why is the larger world so concerned because he announced that he would not allow his daughter (daughters?) to marry, adding that it was dishonest to bring a child into the world in our time? And where is the spirit of Aristophanes now?" It was more TV cartoon than Wilder.

No more was heard of *The Martians* or *The Bats,* for toward the end of November another play was getting born, *The Alcestiad.* It had been getting born since 1939. Sections of it were with him in his bag throughout the war, a new draft of the first act had been written in May 1945 and a draft of the second and third acts was ready by the end of the year. Then it went dead. But in 1954 in Geneva, where Thornton and Isabel were spending Christmas, it came to bloom and he was "working like a marijuana-drunk."* Each day it changed, for the better he thought, "the bigger, the crazier, the funnier, the more poetic"; it was going to "level the walls of Jericho; such a hymn to life and love." He wrote the last lines in Switzerland.

Before following *The Alcestiad* as it made its way toward Edinburgh, we pause to inquire how its author was expressing himself not in literature but in the drama of personal relations. In his younger days, Thornton had been convinced that the only people he could not incorporate into his life were the malicious. To them he had since added those who are the enemies of themselves. "One is always thinking one can do something for them — one's sympathy proceeds from the very fact that one defines elements of a similar self-destructive operation in oneself, but their self-preoccupation is so intense that however phosphorescently gifted, they cannot build, warm, love, nor benefit." Their company was "intolerable," but the intolerable were few. He was almost always willing to listen and counsel as friends and strangers who became friends told him their stories.

* The fullest account of the genesis of *The Alcestiad* is Isabel Wilder's, in her foreword to the printed version of the play (New York: Harper & Row, 1977).

"Suppose I had a friend," he wrote John Tibby, married to Emily Foresman, daughter of the master of Davis House when Thornton first went to Lawrenceville,

> who was going blind (I know her) or deaf; who had lost a leg (Charles Bolté) or several limbs (I worked for awhile in a paraplegic hospital in Atlantic City); or who had lost his voice through cancer in the larynx (Freud when I last saw him in London; now Walter Camp III in New Haven). What do you say? How do you meet her? How do you meet him? You tell her, you tell him, that you understand the dark valley. You remind them of all the skills that science has developed and urge them to avail themselves of that knowledge. But chiefly remind them that *they* are the persons you value — and that they must be the persons *they* value. It's not a burden to have a friend who has a handicap; it is a burden to have a friend who feels himself obscurely degraded by a handicap.

This hard-edged, almost clinical compassion gave no quarter to regrets or self-pity. So many griefs seemed to Thornton to reflect a lack of grit: "When the ills of life begin to strike me I shall probably be a difficult S.O.B. but I don't think I shall take the line that I am a victim of destiny." Had he not, then, been victimized by the punishing Harvard schedule? He seems to have thought so, but with a qualification, as his brother understood; he had been a *willing* victim. In general, Thornton's attitude was Caesar's in *The Ides of March:* "I not only bow to the inevitable, I am fortified by it." Fortified because he willed to be fortified. Thornton threw out lifelines, but he expected the one at the other end to take hold and hold on. He didn't argue with the sufferer, seldom criticized or, if criticism was called for, didn't dwell on it. And although he thought that his heart got colder with the years, the testimony to his constancy and helpfulness is so abundant that his self-deprecation has to be questioned.

His advice to the troubled had an overriding objective: prod him or her to face and accept necessities and find satisfaction in them. He didn't murmur that every cloud has a silver lining or that a stiff upper lip is a cure-all; his exhortations were not banal pep talk. Each was a realistic response to a particular problem of a particular person. A young man he'd just met was commanded to "get up at six in the morning and *walk.*" A former University of Chicago student was permitted "one year of sheer rest and mindless well-being. After that one year it begins to be evasion. So the second year you must resume reading and resume solving the questions of the intelligent young man in the Twentieth Century." Not "one more word about worry!" he admonished Isabel. "The mastery of anxiety consists of turning the eyes inward on the true subject that causes the fear — the very thing one does not wish to contemplate — and taking it out into the realm of reason and proportion and acceptance." He could sympathize with small troubles but not big ones. "Those Big Ones I lived through. They are deeply embedded in life, and nothing can be done about them and they have to be fought out and lived through alone. And it's a privilege and a necessity. And they're there to weed out the weak from the strong."

Reading in a magazine that John Sweet, a member of the *Our Town* cast in London in 1944, had decided to give up the stage, he wrote him a four-page letter urging him to think carefully about leaving the theater (Sweet carried it with him for thirty years), and when Sweet came to New York he was taken to the Century Club and given notes to five producers. Thornton did the same for scores of young artists.

A twenty-nine-year-old with girl trouble wrote, "I want you to show me how 'life can be such a wonderful thing.' I'm going to make you glad that you met me and proud of what you've done for me. I'm going to be one of your better nephews." The "nephew's" next letter was more feverish: "You won't forsake me, will you? You won't just say 'to hell with him'? What'll I do? I don't want to lose you. The words and thoughts just don't come out when I'm not looking directly at you; when I don't hear that machine-gun reaction; when Wilder's eyes aren't searching mine, out from under those shaggy eyebrows; when there's no fantastic outpouring of thoughts and emotions." When Thornton felt that the young man could stand on his own, the relationship ended; there was always another to bring out and up.

A woman with a talent for decoration was sent detailed instructions on how to create a salon, because he surmised she would

do it well. First, she had to discourage bores and undesirable fre-
quenters: "The more brilliant and talked-about your salon, the
greater the number of butterflies, horse-flies, and plain house flies
that will come." Her salon must be a place where a man could
talk three minutes without the peep of an interruption, even from
a charming woman. "Second secret: 'I'm at home every afternoon
at 5:00.' And she always is. Never goes to other people's 5:00
o'clocks. She can *never* fail to be there. She must have a man or
maid to pass drinks and tea. She mustn't *bustle about* being hospitable. The soul of a salon is conversation, and the soul of *that* is
the hostess' undivided attention. When latecomers arrive and *le
cher maître* is talking, she doesn't even rise from her chair. She
puts her fingers to her lips and the guests glide into the nearest
chair — hushed and privileged!"

When five o'clock rolled around, Thornton was on the prowl
for anyone's news, anyone's inner weather. He asked strangers
what they did, "No, not where you work, you can do that anywhere, what are you really doing. Are you studying French, what
are you reading?" The avuncular manner put them at ease; they
told all.

A pub crawl with Sally Begley, daughter of his Harvard friend
Mrs. Edwin Cohn, ended up in one of the lower circles of Newport,
where Thornton got into conversation with a chief petty officer,
the terror of any ship. Bewildered, the CPO turned to Sally, all
the stuffing out of him, and said, "I don't know what's the matter
with me, but I'd rather talk to him than to you." What did they
talk about? The CPO's daily life, why he didn't have eighteen
grandchildren, what he was doing in this bar, how he got to be
a chief petty officer.

Thornton had known Sally since her childhood, and had written
her then that he was going to like her more and more and was
going to torment her by urging her to "enrich all your vital endowments by work, work, work." She must learn to dress her natural
beauty with great art, overcome her shyness not by energy but
by repose, and enroll him among her friends. Long after, when
she was discouraged about the world, he told her that "the *bêtise*
of our human community is everywhere; recognize and accept it
once and for all. It can only really harm us when we ourselves

are in states of self doubt and dejection." When she married, had children and was divorced, he said that she was passing through "one of those seasons that our grandparents use to call 'trials' — how I hate the word with its theological connotation of a stern God testing his loved ones. Few escape 'em. In the meantime, fortitude, courage, and even gaiety. The very sufferings you are going through are making you a wonderful reader of the great books. Read *War and Peace* again. Watch yourself in Natasha. You were a Natasha once — privileged, endowed with great vitality. Get yourself a new hat; shake up a choice martini and recall me with a grin."

From Key West, he wrote her an "Old Polonius" letter. "Do set aside three-quarters of an hour — late afternoon's best, just before joining the family at dinner. And do what? Sit in your room and STOP THINKING. Don't lie down, sit up; but don't slouch. Let your fingers fiddle in your lap, at most, as though you were a poor Ophelia weaving garlands. I don't mean be an Idiot Girl — but just be *ABSENT*. Breathe beautifully as Zen has taught you. The thing is not to think (cultural thoughts or personality thoughts or personal-problem thoughts). If you do this correctly you will feel stealing back into you something as simple as the life-force or as animal fate or as yes-to-life — all that to which you have a right, your right. After ten minutes of blank I shall permit you, for a few seconds, to smile at me, for I shall be smiling at you."

Hundreds of counseling letters had this overflowing gaiety, admonitory zeal, emancipating confidence and a concentration of affection. The British publisher Hamish ("Jimmie") Hamilton came across Thornton in 1935 in Paris. Depressed at the time, Hamilton asked if "cheerful, loquacious and philosophical" Thornton had a recipe for happiness.

Dear Jimmie:
1. Wouldn't one of the things that give existing a sense of value be the watching of the unfolding of an activity of which oneself is the principal willer — i.e., work. Work to be rewarding must have three factors; the work must be felt to be a good activity; oneself must be felt to be a singularly suitable energizing force in it, willing to risk one's responsibility in

the daily adventure of its potential failure; one must see this work not as static in time, but as always mounting.

2. One must "know thyself." This (with "nothing too much") was the favorite dictum of the Greeks and yet their greatest thinker fell short of outlining a technique whereby we go about to fulfill it. Something of going about to catch oneself in one's inevitable evasions of self-candor. Something of experimenting in the possibilities of one's traits. Something of frankly taking pride in one's merits. In cases where one seeks a special conditioning for good or ill, especially when one feels a recurrence in the pattern of life of some more than usual fear-element, the reading of Freud has been a startling clarification. It is a strange law in that realm but true that to "see" the difficulty is to cure it.

3. The thousands of contacts of the day, the conversation, the lunch, the dinner — we swim in the sea of a daily life. It has two possibilities of enhancement: The intellectual fascination that watches, comments, analyzes this unremitting panorama, and, the fact that these multitudinous contacts are heightened by the constant recurrence of friends. I'm writing to a natural born befriender, and befriended, or I should let myself out into a lot of material.

4. The making-sure that no day goes by without a conscious admitting into it of the great and the spacious. We must consciously seek the lofty by reading, hearing and seeing great work at some moment everyday. Especially in our time when there is very little of it about (the last great book written at the death of Tolstoy; the last great music at the death of Brahms; the last great picture at the death of Cézanne). We are in an interregnum and must compensate artificially for this lowering of the spiritual water-level. "We are all exiled heirs and princes of a remote country; there we learned our loyalties; there we learned our admirations and we cannot depart from them now; that is our language and there is our home."

Naturally this paragraph wishes to be extended into the religious, but Religion is shy of being talked about.

The more I think, Jimmie, of your splendid endowments for all four, the more surprised I am at your ingratitude to Life that gave you so much and to which you say you have

fallen into listlessness. However, except in an occasional sad-
ness in your face in repose, I saw no evidence of a real spiritual
inertia and I feel this diagram is merely a letter to a convalescent
who will soon be able to read all the lessons back to me and
then we can try and race each other in affirmations about the
significance of living.

Notable in this prescription is the omission of any mention of
love, which in *The Bridge of San Luis Rey* was "the only survival,
the only meaning." Love also was "shy of being talked about."

When a South American confided his marital infidelities, Thornton reminded him of a Mediterranean legend of Roman women
weeping over the unfaithfulness of their husbands. "So don't be
sorry. You're no exception. You are of the Mediterranean and
Puritanism kills what you have. Don't accept Puritan values." Yet
they were, by and large, values from which Thornton could not
disentangle himself.

An Oxford student was told that if required reading robbed
great books of their "power spontaneously, richly and as-though-
you-were-the-first-reader to glory in them (glory in spite of a constant running disagreement)," then the Oxford system was tepid.

Between 20–30 I read all the great books in the French language; between 30–40, all the German; now it's been Spanish
and Italian (the English went on all the time). Waves of excitement have gone over me continuously, all the more exciting
because I found no one really to discuss them with. . . . It's
your business now not to be "eager" about the thousand and
one things in the nightsky of knowledge, but to be enthusiastic
about the one or two constellations that you have marked down
for your own, and the enthusiasm should have a legitimate
portion of pride in it, because they are matters about which
you are certain that you know a good deal. Count that month
lost in which you have not been swept up in an enthusiasm.

Richard Carlotta, manager of the Stockbridge Inn in Massachusetts, was one of the disciples who "loved him for what he taught
me." A gathering place for jazz lovers, the inn had a beery atmo-

sphere congenial to the working class as well as to visiting bohemians. In the late afternoons Thornton was often at the bar, combining drinks with a three-hour dinner (sneaking in an occasional whiskey sour), after which he and Carlotta might talk until daylight. If he left before the closing hour of one, he handed Carlotta $100 to "take care of my friends." One evening, a gang of tough motorcyclists strode into the inn and Carlotta, apprehensive, told them to cool it, he didn't want his other customers scared away. Before long Thornton had joined the Warlocks and was conversing with them as casually as he did with young actors who drifted in from the local summer theater.

To children, he was "Uncle Thornt," unforbidding as a rag doll, a compatibility that may have owed something to his never having had children underfoot. "Even down here I seem to collect 'em," he wrote from Daytona Beach. "The other day I gave little Patty Gibson, age 11, a little demonstration of how to make an 'abstract' picture, and I started Bobby, my landlord's son, age 10, on a postage stamp collection which has swept him up into a sort of fury."

Unmarried, he could rhapsodize about parenthood. To a mother in California who requested some sentences for a hospital benefit auction on "how to treat children," he unhesitatingly replied that

the important thing is that when you give your attention to the child you give your entire attention. Then you mark off clearly when you have withdrawn your attention, returning the child thereby into a child's world and a child's thoughts. I have known homes where for months at a time a child receives only a partial, or a condescending, or an irritated, or a doting attention (which is not a "listening" to the child at all). The child has great need of this intermittent entire attention — therein lies his assurance of security, both material and emotional; yet he cannot sustain it for long; it is dazzling and disconcerting; from it he can return with reassurance to his child's world. A large part of a child's nagging questions are not questions at all (are not the opening mind seeking information) but are the long-frustrated effort to obtain a moment's entire attention. The happiest evidence that all is well with a child is that it can sit for hours in the presence of a loved adult without demanding any attention.

Having mailed this advice, he wondered if it applied to young men and women in their relation to older people.

Recent experience with many students over here [in Europe in 1953] tells me it does. In the last few years in America — before, during, and after the Harvard year — I found myself to be bored by the young. I had heard it all too often, the growing pains, the same assertions unsupported by information, the same philosophical wheezing, the same "problems" envisaged always in the light of a self-centered egocentric spoiled child. They do not really listen; they are not really outward oriented. That is all changed here; without claiming oneself to be all-wise, one can have an enormous influence. Part of it is due to their stupefication that an Old Man is not stiff and "final," that he listens to them.

Let us be clear what counselor-healer Wilder was doing. Would-be actors and writers, well-bred college girls, small-town waitresses, discontented matrons, alcoholics (one of them wrote, "I thank you for my sobriety") were not being challenged to conform to some general expectation, to "shape up." Thornton's authority was bred of singular frustrations he himself recognized and had gone beyond. He was saying: make a virtue of the unalterable, make the best of *yourself*.

The will and the ability to help another may be at variance, as illustrated by the well-intentioned but blundering narrator of *The Cabala,* whose object of charity becomes his victim. In Thornton's case, the will and capacity were joined, aided by a sensitive ear that picked up what was meant behind what was said. Scores of writers were the beneficiaries, not all of them equally deserving. One whom he scolded for not working hard enough defended himself by pointing out that he had typed his manuscript three times! Thornton didn't respect writers by coddling them. "Pay attention! Steel yourself! I talk tough." That was to the Canadian playwright-novelist Timothy Findley, who had had a small part in *The Matchmaker* in 1954. "I hope to heaven he knew what he meant as a man and as an artist to thousands like me," Findley said. A sample of letters Thornton wrote him between 1954 and 1970 explains Findley's remark.

Hold your hat and tighten your belt. Have you confidence and trust that I'm saying this as one adult to another — as one serious worker to another? I only say these things because I'm sure *you know them already*. That is the Socratic method: You never teach anyone anything; you merely *recall* things to them that lay sleeping just below the level of consciousness. You — as dramatist — gazing deeply into the problem of mankind's agonized straining under the problem of original sin should have placed on the stage not a discussion of original sin but a living, suffering example of original sin. That's what the theater's for. That's what the theater *is*. It has a far more glorious function than the lecture hall and the discussion forum: It is where you *show* the human situation. Don't be so at-a-distance meditative. Come down onto the hot stage, and involve [your characters] and yourself in the shock and clash of situation itself, not in intellectual commentary.

You are crazy about the big feeling inside of you, to quote Gertrude Stein, but you're not also crazy about the challenge and excitement and progress and sheer learning which is craftsmanship. Less yearning, striving emotionalism and more alert, happy, proud intellectual growth into *how* these dreams are brought down from the abstract to a concrete expression on the page. Be content to be a clown, a misfit, or whatever you are. I urge you to continue to explore the right kind of self-centeredness. Objectify more and more your understanding of the reason why you are so driven. A progressive understanding, not a repetitious luxury in self-contempt, not a beating of the breast, not a grain of self-pity.

Young writers have several ways of pushing their way of writing too far: Some strain their will power ("I will write eight hours a day without leaving my room"). Some induce a sort of will-to-the-sublime (Thomas Wolfe). I can imagine the latter would be encouraged by that something that is in the air in greater Los Angeles (where there's such a cult of the Beautiful and the Soulful, as though there were things that could be acquired merely by the wishing). You are a very emotional man: Never ride on it for too long at a time.

As to your question of sex in the novel, I'm a Freudian. I think it's intermingled with everything. But it easily becomes a prison and a sickroom and a morphine-parlor (not *doing* it, but brooding about it). But I shrink from advising Mankind on the matter. I'll be very interested to see what develops from the hippy generation: Does an uninhibited promiscuity at fourteen and fifteen "clean the psyche"?

Select your subject carefully. One very real and close to you — not autobiographically but inwardly. Take long walks, view it from all sides, test its strength, its suitability for the stage. Then start blocking out the main crisis or stresses. I suggest (though all writers are different) that you don't begin at the beginning but at some scene within the play that has already begun to "express itself in dialogue." Don't hurry. Don't do too much a day. In my experience I've found that when I do a faithful, unforced job of writing every day that the material for the next day's writing moves into shape *while I'm sleeping.* Never hesitate to throw away a week's good hard-won writing, if a better idea presents itself.

"What's this about a tape recorder?" he asked James Leo Herlihy, who wrote the script for the film *Midnight Cowboy.*

That's the tool of the social scientist. You have a perfect ear for colloquial speech — and a memory which retains *what it can use.* If you're writing non-fiction, collect data from outside; data from outside that a novelist can use are those that life dumps in his lap, and not what he goes out to seek. Haven't you known young men (from Creative Writing Courses at Ann Arbor, for example) who borrowed $400 from grandma in order to go to Tahiti or Labrador to acquire some experience to write about — when what they really should have written about was grandma and the town where they grew up? Don't go to *observe* the Eskimos, to record the hippies, or as you say "live with them." Open a bookstore, become a reporter on a newspaper.

Herlihy's gratitude triggered a warning: "You want to make me into a guru of some kind. More and more I see the harm that's made in life by *over evaluation.* After over evaluation there's always a bitter disillusioned morning-after. Marriages are wrecked by it; father-and-son relationships are wrecked by it. Its popular name is idealization."

Thornton's address to his thirtieth class reunion in 1950 was covered for the *Yale Alumni Magazine* by undergraduate John Knowles, who would later write *A Separate Peace.* As a way of scraping up an acquaintance, Knowles brought his article to Deepwood Drive for checking before it was printed. He also just happened to have with him the manuscript of a first novel. Over the next five years Thornton read and assessed everything Knowles sent him.

When I saw you in New York I had read up to page 92, I was not ready to make any comment. Now I am at page 151. It is agreeable, fluent but I cannot read further — because it is hard to read a work in which the author is not *deeply engaged.* Now you have many a qualification for writing, and perhaps for writing a novel, but the qualifications rest in you really unactivated until you find a subject which you are deeply moved about, very much absorbed in. Then every fragment of conversation, every bit of description, all the characters primary and secondary, will come into an acuter focus. This problem is a character problem before it is a literary and artistic problem. It is from our most vital subjectivity that we write — not primarily from the field of observation and reading and our ever-shifting environment. Nevertheless, there is much that is attractive in this book; I hope you find a publisher for it [Knowles didn't] — but it is to you as the author of your next book that I address this letter.

Knowles said that Thornton's severities were crucial to his locating the theme and approach of *A Separate Peace.*

At the MacDowell Colony, Edward Albee, then writing poetry, was gently advised to work in another form: "Why don't you try writing plays?" On request, Thornton submitted a young lady's novel to several publishers, all of whom rejected it. He wrote the author cheerful reassurance that he hadn't given up and was approaching another publishing house. A book editor received a letter on behalf of Geoffrey Hellman, "one of the brightest pens in Yale for many years; if you could find any task for him, you would be catching a very gifted person and catching him early." An inquiring high school junior playing Mr. Antrobus in *The Skin of Our Teeth* was instructed to "pick out a few places where you'll be *real loud.*"

One didn't have to be an author or actor to engage Thornton's desire to instruct. When Gladys Campbell, one of the joys of his "best years" in Chicago, retired and didn't know what she would do without the sustaining routine of teaching, he suggested she *"continue to be Gladys Campbell* — only more so. Come out of the bushes. Begin with recognizing the fact that you've always been goodlooking as hell; and with a most knowing sense of how to dress. You have always been independent in judgment, but you've masqued it out of accommodation for other people's feelings. You don't have to do that anymore. Be stoutly ringingly all yourself — yourself — to the edge of eccentricity and scandal. With that new note you can also shape, build, teach, and create, so sez your devoted old friend, Thornt."

After a reunion in Chicago with the Goethe Street gang, he wrote Charles Newton that the

> role of Inspiritor is my role and God gave it to me and I have no business being ashamed of it; but every once in a while I don't dare sail into it for fear that people will think I'm doing it out of hypocritical pity for the Patient. But no! No! (Let Frank Harding read this solemnly.) You are both endowed beyond ten thousand and I, for one, will never absolve you from doing twenty times more than you're doing now with your brains and your charm — and if you drag

through your middle twenties with any concessions to fatigue or Need of a Change of Atmosphere and so on, I shall be forever indignant. You are to resume your diary in French and write it much more detailed, too, by-god. And learn German or Greek. . . . You are not to be a charming, cynical, tired newspaperman at forty.

A wartime friend, alone since her son had been sent off to school and her husband gone to teach in Africa, wrote Thornton of feeling at loose ends. "You may remember," he answered,

that each time I've seen you since Caserta, I found a moment to tell you of my conviction that you are an extremely capable woman and that being a schoolmaster's wife didn't draw from you ONE TENTH of your proven gifts and talents. (I was a schoolmaster for six years in a similar school and could see the wives — more than most — relegated to routine domesticity and general "sweetness," like clergymen's wives.) Do you remember my teasing you about this — and seeing that my teasing had a touch of earnestness too? Because unemployed talents disquiet me — and their possessors. Here's your chance! Unless you got rusty — or unless the long repression has made you timid — strike out! Get a job. If necessary go back to school and get the certificate to obtain a job. I've been reading all the "Situations Offered" in the back pages of the *New Statesman.* I can see you as a receptionist in a hospital, as interviewer in an employment agency. You have organizing ability, you have quick clear judgment. It's bracing to be occupied; it's doubly bracing to feel that you're being of service to your fellow citizens.

There are kindly gestures that cost little — flowers on Mother's Day, a birthday check, a store-bought get-well card, blithe avowals that the-problem-will-solve-itself-if-you-ignore-it. Thornton's gestures were not of this cheap sort. Learning that John and Emily Tibby's marriage had broken up, that Tibby had remarried and the second marriage had collapsed and that Tibby was having difficulty writing his own name, he responded instantly.

I divined that you were in trouble. It took some divining because you professionally strong Argonauts are ashamed of suffering, and you write elliptically, half-jaunty, half-frightened.
There are several kinds of mental anguish, but the most frequent and the most woeful is the fear of not-being-the-master-
of-one's-own-house (not domestic house, but one's house of
thought and will). So the instance of not being able to write
one's own name is a signal — like the red light of GAS or
GEN on the dashboard of one's car. Would you wish me to
come down now — at once and sit a few hours with you?
Say on the inner porch-veranda of the Century Club? (I'm
not doing anything at present, to speak of.) Keep a sober,
mature watch on yourself. Watch that red signal. Absent yourself from the office, when it seemeth best to you. Go to the
Bronx Zoo. Buy a sitar. Smoke banana peel. Ransack your
memory for some friends of long ago — especially girls who
were fond of you and wouldn't know an anxiety if they saw
one and who are funny. Do you know any place in the woods
where you can *smash things?* Go to the Brooklyn Bridge and
have sweet consoling thoughts about throwing yourself off it
("they'd love me when I'm gone") but don't throw yourself
off, because you have an engagement with me on or about
August 3 and you are a man of honor.

After they met in New York and imbibed two fifths of whiskey,
Thornton wrote Tibby:

You are an *Atlas* and a *Perseus.* It is essential to your very
nature that you aid, sustain, and support a number of human
beings. You've done that, and I can believe that you've done
it very well; YET, somehow things haven't worked out very
well. Well, now, I suspect that part of the trouble — only part
of the trouble — is in you. You expected gratitude. You are
confused and hurt that your beneficiaries take your magnanim-
ity — your service — for granted. That comes with the John
Knox heritage. But, Atlas, your beneficiaries are dimly aware
that you have already derived a large satisfaction from your
function. *You've been paid already.* They can't understand your
uneasy moods and (am I right) dim expectation of rapturous

gratitude. You want to be loved for what you do! But none of us are loved for what we *do,* but for what we *are.* I'm sure you're eminently loveable, but you "cloud" it all up by obscurely asking payment. Service is joyful or it's nothing. So cease those probings as to "what-do-I-do-wrong." Self reproach and remorse and fingernail biting and sackcloth brooding (with a bottle of Scotch) are unworthy of heroes. Don't look back. Be Argus. Be St. George. Grasp your happiness in your myth. . . . Anxiety is not a Christian virtue. Don't get down on your knees to *pray* to be a better man, get down on your knees to thank God for all you have and are. And then rise and do a little Charleston and Tango and Frug around the room.

The letters to Tibby arrived almost daily for a week. John and Emily later remarried.

Humorist and cliché slayer Frank Sullivan, near death in Saratoga, was the target of a battery of joking missiles, none mentioning illness.

Dear Frank, Was on the road by 6:30 A.M. Got into the Algonquin well before 11:00, followed by a cloud of State Troopers, like Keystone Kops. Put 'em off the scent, though, first by unfurling some bunting that said JUST MARRIED and slowing down. They dashed by me like a school of minnows. Then I started off and accumulated some more cops. Eluded them by raising my superstructure YONKERS DIAPER SERVICE. I didn't have to employ my *third* camouflage. Saw Dotty [Dorothy Parker] at the Academy session [where she, Truman Capote and Arthur Miller were honored]. Never did I more wish for a mind-reading radar than when she stood up and bowed to the assembly. So who do they place me between at lunch? Lucky Wilder! Between Carson McCullers and Djuna Barnes. "You're not eating that good roast beef, Carson" I said. "I can't cut it up," she said. So I — synchronizing with the television cameras — cut her meat very nicely. "I just saw that exhibit of your work in the Paris show about American-Expatriates-in-the-Twenties, Miss Barnes." *"Mustave been horrible!"* "No — very attractive. I went with Miss Toklas." *"Never liked her!"*

"Really, and Miss Stein?" *"Loathed her."* "I was especially interested also in the Joyce exhibit." *"Detestable man."*

It takes courage to write you a letter. You are constantly exposing the hidden traps of flatulence that lie under our homely give and take. But I've decided I'm not going to be afraid of you. I'm not going to flinch when I tell you that I've spent years trying to make two ends meet and holding my head above water and paying the piper and draining the dregs. Nor am I ashamed that I am — until the cows come home — yours, Thornton.

Vincent Sheean was barely scraping along in the fifties, bereft of money and recognition. Thornton, apologetically, gave him both. Sheean "shuddered and crimsoned" for days over a letter from Thornton expressing shame that a check had been sent via a lawyer. "Oh, my poor dear Thornton!" Sheean wrote his wife; "no letter containing $300 could ever seem repellent to me — I thought it was a perfectly normal lawyer-like letter — and my pardon is probably the one thing on this earth that Thornton, or anybody else, can have without even asking. But is this not characteristic of this odd boy that *he* should beg *my* pardon? For what, I rise to inquire? For saving my life twice over in a single year?"

What did Thornton receive in return for these acts of consideration? Inner satisfaction, probably. Gratitude, certainly. "Without your marching along in the world how much poorer *my* life would have been," Dinah Sheean wrote him. Frances Steloff of the Gotham Book Mart credited him with having had no small part in getting her started. His letters were "the greatest inspiration of my life," Leslie Glenn said. R. Buckminster Fuller, grateful for Thornton's advising him to delay publication of his mathematical findings, "made his advice my life's policy."

The key question is whether or to what extent the role of Everybody's Uncle diverted Thornton from his central task — "the bringing to light of the successive images and myths and promptings that move the masses of men, for good or ill." If he had been asked that question, he probably would have replied that his life and art could not be divorced.

25

The Legend of Alcestis

THORNTON HAD SAID that *The Alcestiad* would be ready for production at the Edinburgh Festival in August 1955, and it was. The first two acts were typed by Isabel in Switzerland in January and the third mailed within the month, before Thornton left for Aix-en-Provence. Thereafter, until July, he covered more ground than an American presidential candidate. A week in Aix was followed by forty-eight hours in London, seven days in Paris, Marseilles to hear *The Barber of Seville,* Genoa, Rapallo, Villefranche, Arles, Saint-Rémy-de-Provence. "Maybe next week I'll go to Spain." Málaga was reached via Cannes ("Brighton with Arabs"), Gibraltar, Andalusia, Granada.

In July, in London for rehearsals of *The Alcestiad,* he was disheartened by what he saw and heard. Neither producer nor director was optimistic about the play's chances and persuaded Thornton to retitle it *A Life in the Sun,* at least for the Edinburgh Festival. "These people seem to think that because it's all about people in Greek legends that the average audience will be sort'a cool," Thornton remarked. He couldn't understand it. After all, the legend was timeless.

Alcestis has only one wish, to be a priestess of Apollo at Delphi. She marries Admetus, king of Thessaly. Admetus sickens and is near death, Alcestis gives her life for his but Hercules brings her back from the dead. Admetus is later assassinated, a plague strikes, the new king's daughter dies and the king begs Alcestis, now old and in rags, to intervene with the gods and restore his daughter to life, because she loved him. Alcestis replies that "love is not enough," that "the last bitterness of death is not the parting. . . .

it is the despair that one has not lived . . . that one's life has been . . . nonsense." Now Alcestis faces her own death, but Apollo takes her to his grave and into immortality: "The grave means an end. You will not have that ending." Alcestis asks whom she should thank for this happiness. The play ends with Apollo's reply: "Those who have loved one another do not ask one another that question."⌐

Catullus in *The Ides of March* had recited the story of Alcestis and her ambition to become a priestess of Apollo at Delphi. The *hetaira* Chrysis in *The Woman of Andros* was akin to Alcestis in wishing to be remembered "as one who loved all things and accepted from the Gods all things, the bright and the dark."

The play had been conceived at Hamilton Field, California in October 1942, when Thornton "felt the need of literature." But he was in no position to get it, he had written his mother, "and I wouldn't even like to read it if I had it. So — as simply as falling off a log, I found a solution: I started making my own. I began *The Alcestiad*. I write only about ten speeches an evening. If I find that it moves into the center of my interest, or keeps me awake at night, I'll have to give it up. But so far it contributes its fragment of tranquillity every night. And on Sundays I can do a larger portion. As I see it now, it's very Helen Hayes. Anyway, so far it's still a secret."

The Alcestiad rested half-finished in a bottom drawer of his desk until the fall of 1954, when he picked up pages he had brought with him by accident to France. He had been reading Kierkegaard's *Philosophical Fragments,* and "from the first *The Alcestiad* reposed on the same group of ideas that S. K. treats so beautifully in the allegory of the King in love with the Fishermaid — God as the 'unhappy lover.' " All but the rewriting had been finished by mid-December. Was it "a great welter of grandiloquent 'emotionality'?" he asked. "Maybe, maybe, maybe. Remains the hope that with a cooler head I can trim and de-rhetoricize a great deal of this material without weakening its power — a doubly difficult task when one is writing an English text which is both immediately colloquial and yet adequate to these Gods and lofty beings."

Thornton had considered Montgomery Clift to play King Admetus, and the director, Tyrone Guthrie, had been agreeable, pointing

out, however, that Clift's accent was "different from all the others,"
and that it would harm a later London run if such a star withdrew
early from the cast. At that point Thornton had not lost confidence
in Clift as an actor or in his genuine interest in *The Alcestiad.*
Had he not written "Dearest Avuncle" in early 1955 begging
for a copy of the script? "Monty will play Admetus," Thornton
said in April. By June, Clift had become obsessed by little changes
in the part; "can't say that, can't play that," Thornton told Isabel,
"tries to draw me into arguments about the characterization of
Admetus, vaguely threatens to give up the part if I don't change
that. He hasn't signed a contract yet. Yet there's no doubt that
he wants to do it. It's just all nerves and terror, and the need
for mother mother." Soon after, Clift resigned the role: "He didn't
tell me at once, all very gradual and roundabout. He didn't like
to say that he found the role unsuitable for him. I tried a little
persuasion, but I couldn't long stoop to weedle and cajole. I
showed little exasperation. We 'parted friends.' He won't change
his mind and I don't want him to. I don't think it was actor's
nerves — like Ruth [Gordon]'s resignations. I think he found the
role insufficiently starry, 'only four scenes.' "

With Irene Worth as Alcestis, *The Alcestiad* opened August 22,
1955, for a three-week Edinburgh run. Up to the last minute
Thornton had been revising the third act, worried at rehearsals
by the heavy, operatic tone of the play. Even Guthrie's direction,
which had so pleased him in *The Matchmaker,* seemed dead; he'd
"lost the ear and eye and sense for direct emotion." He feared
that Guthrie would underlight it. "I'm back at that old difficulty:
The directors who think that half-lights are mood inspiring."

At the premiere, Irene Worth had an attack of nerves and slowed
everything down. Jed Harris showed up and hated the play. Kenneth Tynan, who as an Oxford undergraduate had been dazzled
by Wilder, hammered it, calling the author "a schoolmaster who
would like to be a poet" and the play a "dramatic nullity." "The
Sunday paper's disapproval throws such weight against [it],"
Thornton wrote, "that I'm drawing all British rights back into
my own hands September 11. This puts an end to any discussion
of a London production." That the entrepreneurs in London had
insufficient confidence in *The Alcestiad*'s drawing power to lay on

a post-Edinburgh production was accepted with equanimity. What, Thornton asked himself, would *he* have had to say about it if it had been written by someone else? "That Wilder has again tried to succeed in a vast undertaking and has fallen conspicuously short." His intention had been prodigious — "to exhibit in drama a series of actions in such a way that we could never be certain that the supernatural was truly speaking, hovering — nay, existing; to devise an intrusion of The Other in such a way that it could be interpreted as accident, delusion, mirage ('some said it thundered; others that a god spoke')." What in fact had he produced? His answer:

A play of faith which is not a very good or radiant or convinced play of faith. I have an elegiac ballad about episodes which require faith in order to lift them out of the category of mere picturesqueness. What I should have written is a play of skepticism which is continually shot through with an almost violent and demanding invocation to interpret the actions in the light of faith. I fell short of doing this for two reasons: The silly life I have been leading since the war has dulled and dimmed my capabilities for intellectual passion. It would not have been necessary to have had faith to have written *The Alcestiad* which I should have written; all that was needed was to have been decades-long urgently at grips with the problem; I should have been passionately aware of what can be done with faith and what can be done without it. Also, as an artist, I have been so lazy these last years that I can no longer assemble repeatedly my total concentration — that which alone can hold the whole of a play under attention at each moment of writing, so that the Whole is reflected in each of the parts. To achieve that one must write all the time; that is a matter of practice — and the only comfort I derive from the thoughts contained in this paragraph is that I feel that I can now go on and write others and that the *practice* in having written *The Alcestiad* will help me in its successors. The second reason why this play is not what it should be is that the old TNW-pathos, the human tug, entered it so largely. There is a large place in this legend for precisely that human tug, and woe to the dramatist who approaches it without that pathos, but I have allowed it (though not in act one) to get out of hand. What strength it has would have been all the more compelling in the framework of clear, harder intellectual structures.

It couldn't be unwritten, but he needn't dwell on it. He quit Edinburgh for Paris.

The French left Thornton alone. They had no interest in *The Alcestiad* and not much in anything else he had written. Only now was *The Cabala* available in translation; it was the first book of his he'd ever seen in a Paris window. Yet he had taught French for seven years, knew its literature, studied Romance languages at Princeton, visited France regularly. It should have been a love affair, but the French never found him *chic*. He now returned the disparagement by finding them incorrigibly frivolous; they "never have anything 'self-forgetting,' but they can imitate it, the frog trying to blow himself up to the size of the bull." The French theater of the fifties seemed to him a savage attack on the nature of woman, and French excitement about the sins of the flesh only a subterfuge to conceal their subjection to a more deforming obsession — avarice. Albert Camus's *La chute* struck him as "the stale laundry of departed masters." André Gide was "hollow, full of *mauvaise foi.*" Sartre, he now thought, was writing from a deep personal resentment against the cards that life dealt him. Colette's *La chatte* was shocking, not for the reasons that would have offended Queen Victoria, "but because of her hot, immodestly close relations to her characters, the candor of her hatred of the heroine; the greediness of her love of her hero . . . anti-intellectual . . . anti-human." He had even lost his admiration for Proust's *Remembrance of Things Past*: "Over half of it is dreary self-indulgence."

An afternoon with his French publisher sharpened his displeasure. "Someone persuaded old Gallimard that he should sign up Wilder for life. Wilder was imposed from above on *ces messieurs.* I arrive in Paris and call at the Maison. How they hated me. They barely rose from their chairs. They let the conversation fall to the floor. They made me uncomfortable and gloated over it." But Paris wasn't a working town anyway, and after drinks at Harry's Bar with Sally Begley, lunch with Alice Toklas at La Pérouse and dinner with Marie Bousquet, he packed his bags for "adorable Saint Moritz," where the first snow was falling and he could isolate himself in an empty hotel. The maharajas and film stars wouldn't arrive until Christmas Eve.

"Damn and double damn!" Three transatlantic calls. He must leave Saint Moritz at once for Philadelphia and more rehearsals of *The Matchmaker,* scheduled to open there on October 27. "Crisis, flap . . . I'd better go." Two weeks later he was back in Europe, having idled his days aboard the SS *United States* dictating a translation of Samuel Beckett's *Waiting for Godot* to Alan Schneider, who, on Thornton's recommendation, later directed the play. From Cannes he drifted to Naples, Rome, Venice — "every Italian a 3-volume novel" — Salzburg, Vienna, the Alpine passes. Semmering, Verona, Granada and gypsy dances. It wasn't that he liked living abroad, he explained, but "it keeps me from dissipating my life in the thousand and one things that assail me when I'm in Hamden or New York."

When he got home in March 1956 he was confronted by a project that was "sheer horror." Someone had dreamed up the idea of presenting him with a biographical bouquet on television. "Blazes!," he wrote Hutchins. "What a compliance with marketplace values. If I dig my heels in and declare I won't have it, they say suavely 'but you're not in it, it's merely about you.' If my friends and relatives say they're too busy (I hope they do) they may-might think that it would get back to me and that I'd be terribly hurt. But the worst of false situations is that of producing a flower of friendship on demand. The whole thing goes back to our age's belief that every man and woman is absolutely mad to get his name in the paper." All he could do was disclaim responsibility and not watch the program.

Days at Deepwood Drive divided roughly into four parts — two sleeping, two waking. Weather permitting, Thornton drove into town for breakfast about seven, read the newspaper or fell into conversation with the waitress or someone at the counter, then dropped by the Yale library before returning to his top-floor study with its stacks of papers, magazines, manuscripts and mail. Books were piled up on tables or shoved into cases around the wall, sideways, upside down. On his desk were two or three looseleaf notebooks with fake leather covers, the left side of each page reserved for corrections. Whole sections of a book or play were copied by hand from one notebook into another.

After a morning's writing, he lunched on a good-sized bowl of soup, a juicy sandwich and a bottle of beer; went to bed, often in his pajamas, and slept two or three hours. Then it was cocktail hour with Isabel or friends, at home or out. If he was absorbed in some project, he climbed upstairs to his study after dinner for anywhere from a half hour to two hours; or he might take another nap until around eleven, join Isabel for a nightcap and return to his desk until two or three.

The Hamden routine worked well for three months; then it was time for a change. On June 9 he drove 525 miles without mishap to Roanoke, Virginia; continued on to New Orleans and the border at Laredo, Texas; entered Mexico and after four weeks in the Hacienda San Miguel Reglas got restless. "Tomorrow I drive for three days at the Capital." From noisy, dusty Mexico City he moved on to Acapulco. "What on earth made me come down here when I had the world to choose from? Oh, I remember: It was my hope of acquiring — incidentally, as it were — spoken Spanish. Well, that dream is as far off as ever. There's no one that can beat me for *having no plans.* How happy I'll be when I cross the border." The drive through Texas was long and hot. He revived in an air-conditioned hotel in New Orleans and slowly made his way north to Hamden, where he lost three teeth in three weeks and came down with a cold. "To bake out a deafness," he escaped to Florida and on his sixtieth birthday, April 17, 1957, was in Paris with Isabel, telling columnist Art Buchwald that henceforth he would not be kind to strangers, would dump all letters from schoolchildren into the incinerator without reading them, either keep, sell or give to the New Haven library any books sent him, erase the foolish misconception that he was a "Thinker with a Message for our times" and not allow himself to be drawn out as a critic or attend conferences.

Things were going to be different, and he had foreseen that they would be different. At twenty-one he had written his mother that those "last periods into which authors fall when they begin their third score of years or near it are often very wonderful times.

They begin to write for themselves then, in a new and different sense. Inner values float up. Beautiful patterns become clearer in symbol, allegory and fantasy."

But the twenty-one-year-old hadn't foreseen the consequences of becoming venerable. Even the indifferent French press took note of his sixtieth birthday, allowing that "one of the greatest contemporary American novelists and playwrights" spoke French perfectly, knew Paris like the back of his hand, and that *The Matchmaker* was "an amusing piece." In Zurich, a concert in his honor featured Mozart and readings from *The Ides of March.*

He and Isabel were in Europe primarily to see *The Matchmaker* performed in French at the National Theatre in Brussels and a German production of *The Alcestiad* in Zurich at the Schausspielhaus. While awaiting rehearsals of *The Alcestiad,* Thornton divided his time between a new one-act and a preface to a collection of his three full-length plays. The stimulus for the one-act had come during an all-day train trip to Saint Moritz when he wasn't feeling well and kept trying to take his mind off the pain by inventing material harking back to undeveloped journal entries on the *Life of Tom Everage.* Two other play ideas had been "lost in the baking"; perhaps he could pull this one off. The Tom Everage one-act was lost as well.

The draft of his preface went better but bore little resemblance to his final text.* "My notion or question or search was this," the draft read: "How can we justify a validity for any one moment in the homely daily life? Is that more difficult than to justify even a high experience of passionate love or loss or hate? As readers of these plays will see, I stake my wager not on the supreme crisis of the soul; I have wanted to save, for dignity, what is humble."

None of this appears in the published preface, which ends with a disclaimer: "I am not one of the new dramatists we are looking for. I wish I were. I hope I have played a part in preparing the way for them. I am not an innovator but a rediscoverer of forgotten goods and I hope a remover of obtrusive bric-a-brac. And as I view the work of my contemporaries I seem to feel that I am

---

* *Three Plays by Thornton Wilder: Our Town, The Skin of Our Teeth, The Matchmaker* (New York: Bantam Books, 1958).

exceptional in one thing — I give (don't I?) the impression of having enormously enjoyed it."

Now it was the Germans' turn to pay birthday homage, and they brought forth their best brass bands. At ceremonies in Bonn, Thornton was introduced by President Theodor Heuss, who awarded him one of West Germany's most coveted decorations, *"pour le mérite."* Speakers referred to the profound political significance of *The Ides of March*. At a lunch in his honor, Thornton was seated to the right of Chancellor Adenauer, from whom he expected only the barest civilities. Instead, the eighty-one-year-old head of state and he chatted about Harvard, families, graphic arts, Goethe, *The Bridge of San Luis Rey;* "we even kept looking into one another's eyes and laughing," Thornton wrote Isabel. In the evening, he was taken to a student performance of *Our Town* and afterward to a beer hall with the cast. They parted at one in the morning shouting *Hochs*.

Celebrations continued in Zurich, where *The Alcestiad,* revised, had a warmer critical and popular welcome than it had had in Edinburgh. In Milan, Thornton worked over a speech to be given in Frankfurt in October; he was to be the seventh recipient and first American to receive the German Book Sellers' Peace Prize. But before that he was due in Berlin for an American cultural festival.

The occasion for the festival was the dedication September 19, 1957, of Congress Hall in West Berlin, for which the secretary of state's sister, Eleanor Dulles, had raised the money. Thornton was to speak along with the lord mayor, Clare Boothe Luce, Robert Dowling and the American ambassador. A lively series of entertainments had been planned: Martha Graham's dancers; Virgil Thomson conducting the RIAS (Rundfunk im Amerikanischen Sektor) orchestra; seven one-act plays, three by Thornton who would appear in two of them as well as in one by William Saroyan. Burgess Meredith would have the lead in Thornton's *The Wreck of the 5:25* and Ethel Waters in his *Bernice*. Production was under the general management of Gertrude Macy, Lamont Johnson directing.

All was chaos six weeks before the festival. Ethel Waters announced she couldn't go to Berlin, Ruth Gordon decided *she* wouldn't go. Lillian Gish was recruited. Ethel Waters then changed

her mind but complained there was no God in *Bernice.* Somehow
it came off. Miss Waters was appeased; after the last act of the
last play she was allowed to sing "His Eye Is on the Sparrow."
Miss Gish was magnificent, "notes of dramatic power," Thornton
said, "that we have never seen in her, as well as the pathos. Astonishing." He wandered about, hat on, smoking, speaking a few
words in German to the house, staying up with his fellow actors
until three in the morning. He was still "catnip" in Germany
and thought it awfully funny. "They all behave as though any
minute I might bite — from big shots to head waiters — as though
I might give some abrupt sign of displeasure. So I get more and
more bland, like a pudding."

In Bad Homburg, before going on to Frankfurt for his Book
Sellers' address and an honorary degree from the university, he
got his first full night's sleep in weeks and there finished his speech
on culture in a democracy. At first reading, he wrote home, it
might sound like a thousand tired typewriter ribbons, but "by
the time Baby gets warmed up to it, all hell's let loose; all anti–
T. S. Eliot — who drearily believes that there can be no flowers
of the spirit when those high-born elites are gone. Whitman to
the rescue!"

The address did set off a few rockets. *Die Zeit* ran a full page
of pro and con comment. Eliot called it "a piece of hysterical
nonsense." There were phone calls and letters, some indignant,
others asking for clarification.

Some old-style *hoch Deutsch* may have been disturbed by Thornton's remarks, but nothing in them could have startled the postwar
generation. The address was latter-day Jeffersonianism, an attack
on the assumption that "leadership is transmitted in the chromo-
somes; and that only communities enjoying these mystical privileges can produce and encourage and maintain all that is excellent,
true and beautiful." He associated himself with the common, the
ordinary, the vulgar. "Can't we say these words? The evil that
I'm bringing to your attention is not so much that there were
coteries of persons in high places, but that their jealous protection
of their undeserved and unjustified privileges robbed the rest of
the world of spiritual dignity — not only social dignity, but spiritual
dignity." He asked his audience to remember the many thousand-

year-old lies that were gradually disappearing: "that a woman is incapable of responsibility in civil life; that a woman in marriage has no rights in property and no rights in regard to her children; that a man — under God and the state — may own and buy and sell total ownership of another man; that children, because of the accident of their birth in needy families, may be made to work from dawn to sunset; that a man because of race or color or religion is an inferior creature." Hardly hysterical nonsense.

In late October, Thornton, the Kanins and Terrence Catherman, a young American working for The State Department, were in Vienna for *The Alcestiad* opening and more salutes. "There's an old law at the Burg," Thornton wrote Isabel:

> The Doyen of the house (Otto Tressler, 85, covered with decorations) comes out at the end of act two before the curtain: "I have the honor to express to you the thanks of the author" (only for living authors). If the author is present, he then comes forward, makes a little speech. . . . Ritual is ritual. Ruthie said I did the bows just right — she was "proud of me." Afterwards a *souper* at Sacher's. Forty people. The Burgermeister had received me in the afternoon and given me a beautiful book about Vienna. So I've now had that kind of festival reception in the city that does it best. Fun? Fun? Oh, Lord, yes.

There was more acclaim ahead — the Austrian government's Medal of Honor for Science and Fine Arts, the MacDowell Colony Medal (he would be its first recipient). Sauntering down an avenue in Paris and about to take the boat train for Le Havre, he told Sally Begley that he had never been happier, not even in Chicago.

26

Opera

AT THE PERUVIAN EMBASSY in Washington on February 27, 1958, three decades after publication of *The Bridge of San Luis Rey,* a beribboned medal was draped around Thornton's neck, the ambassador made a decorous speech, Thornton courteously responded, an elegant lunch was served, the honored guest toasted, and after the ceremonies he said privately that it was "just one sample of why I'm always off in far places — I can't keep my work hours. And why I'm going off to New Mexico." But Taos in early March had too many artists, feuds, cliques; "wouldn't stay here for anything." His sixty-first birthday was celebrated with the Sol Lessers in Palm Springs; he found the desert stifling and tried a Santa Monica motel. No good. Likewise the Knicker-bocker Hotel in Hollywood; the spunk had gone out of the town. Aspen in May was postcard beautiful, but the upper-class socializing got in the way of work. Where to turn? The government wanted him to go to Russia or Mexico or Greece as an ambassador of goodwill. Not interested. President Eisenhower suggested he come to Washington and lobby Congress on behalf of international cul-tural exchanges. Wilder a lobbyist? No. So he settled that summer for the familiar terrain of Amherst, Williamstown, Stockbridge, Peterborough, Cambridge and finally New York. But New York was too hectic; he'd return to Italy.

Italy was strikebound. Badgastein beckoned. Badgastein never heard of a room with bath. Salzburg. Not right. He would *not* go to Vienna. "I think Sunday that I'll go to Semmering, an old-fashioned spa and ski resort, where I've been before — about two hours away — until January 1st." After two weeks in Semmering, he was in Vienna.

Why not be a gypsy? Thornton had no binding home ties, no wife or children, no nine-to-five job, no lack of ready cash. He could carry his work in his head and a briefcase. He was free. Yet none of these circumstances explains why he chose the path of perennial wanderer. Some travel because they're bored; he wasn't. Or they imagine the grass is greener in the next pasture; he'd been to the next pasture and knew better. They flee to escape company; he attracted company wherever he went. They're on the run from a tax collector, a mother-in-law, a jilted miss. Or they feel alien in their native land. Not he. Was he seeking furtive pleasures risked only in anonymity? Where was he unknown? The South Seas? Tibet? He never went there: "I return only to old nests." Was he getting away from Isabel? But Isabel was a guardian of his privacy, and it was he, knowing that she often felt unwanted, who urged her to accompany him to Saint Moritz, London, Paris. True, there was an afternoon in Paris when Thornton telephoned a journalist friend and said, "Take me somewhere where Isabel can't find me," but that was a rare occurrence.

Questioned about his wanderlust, Thornton said that he simply liked moving around, that he had an "unceasing appetite for change," but that when he got where he was going, he couldn't stay long because "they" always caught up with him, even though he instructed hotel managements to say that nothing was known of Mr. Wilder's whereabouts.

Did he really want to be cut off and alone? Yes and no and never for long. No one forced him in a single day in Germany in the fall of 1959 to entertain a scholar who was writing a thesis on him, have five people to tea, visit the American seminar at the university in Hamburg and attend a reception of the Congress for Cultural Freedom. Tranquil days are of one's own making. He could have had them in Cologne, but he was no sooner there than he was "TORN, TORN, TORN as to where to go next." It was, he said, "very wearing to be so indecisive."

He was not indecisive that fall on one subject. He made up his mind to close down his study of *Finnegans Wake* for five years.

From his research on Joyce and Lope de Vega, Thornton had derived more satisfaction than many an academic scholar gains in a lifetime. But he had also lost almost all memory of what it was like to be swept up by the making of something that was his own. He was writing from the peripheral area of his will and imagination — "the small area left half-alive beside the bewitched devotion to Lope and Joyce." It might, he thought, take a long time to refire the center of his mind, and he was nearly sixty-three. He regretted his "cricket-like fiddling while remorseful life was moving on," and with dismay recognized that it was not merely a matter of finding subjects and presenting them as literature; it was a matter of "reawakening the fields of observation and reflection that alone nourish and give significance to the fictions. I return as one from an illness or from a long journey into a remote territory to make my house and hearth again."

Thornton's intent to return to creative writing made news. Arthur Gelb in the *New York Times* of November 6, 1961, announced that "the first segment of what is expected to be [Wilder's] artistic summing up" had been completed. "He has already devoted three years to the project, a double cycle of fourteen one-act plays with the over-all theme of 'our lives and errors.' As Mr. Wilder completes other plays of the two cycles [*The Seven Ages of Man, The Seven Deadly Sins*] they will be added to the repertory of the Circle in the Square. José Quintero, the Circle's director, and Theodore Mann, its producer, anticipate that the fourteen plays will be presented over a period of six years." Thornton had told Gelb that some of the one-acts were on the stove, some in the oven, some in the wastebasket.

Only three plays in the two cycles — *Someone from Assisi, Infancy* and *Childhood* — ever reached the New York stage, and were performed at the Circle in the Square January 11, 1962, under the title *Plays for Bleecker Street*.

Infancy and *Childhood* are statements about the imaginativeness of the very young and the obtuseness of their elders. In *Infancy* two babies in carriages converse. The adults understand nothing the infants say, the audience understands a great deal. In *Childhood*, it is again the very young who are wiser than grown-ups. At home, says Caroline, age twelve, "everybody says silly things they don't mean one bit . . . nobody treats you like a real person." Dodie, age ten, says that the reason he doesn't like older people is that "they don't ever think any inneresting thoughts. I guess they're so old that they just get tired of expecting anything to be different or exciting, so they just do the same old golfing and shopping."

Acting editions of *Infancy* and *Childhood* were printed by Samuel French, but not the dramatization of the sin of lust in *Someone from Assisi*. One critic hoped the author would find it as easy to dismiss that play as did the audience. Of the projected series of fourteen one-acts, Thornton completed six, although his notebooks were filled with situations and dialogue for the remainder. In addition to the three plays for *Bleecker Street,* he finished *Bernice* (pride), *The Drunken Sisters* (gluttony) and *The Wreck of the 5:25* (sloth), none of which was published in English. *Bernice* had been salvaged from the Vittorio De Sica film script.

Youth "all but finished" in the spring of 1960, was to show us a fraternity initiation at some Ohio college in 1912. "I'm going to have the president of the fraternity wear a mock white beard on his mask. Shall I have the initiate drink blood?" It never got beyond draft form; nor did a second and third version. *Adolescence* was to have been set in ancient Babylon, where we would see the children as adolescent, then their parents as adolescent, then that epoch in history as adolescent. "It'll be scrumptious," Thornton wrote before throwing it away.

Simultaneously, he was casting his net for a plot that would dramatize *High Noon* — that self-sufficiency of one's prime, which he placed at age thirty-three.

He lost interest.

How might he handle extreme old age? Perhaps the audience could be told by an announcer that certain ancient Greek societies put the old to death by giving them powdered poppy seed and a cup of hemlock. He might bring this custom up to date: "We see . . . some delightful people in their late forties, at most, in evening clothes. They seem to have accepted the convention [of death] — no protest, not even resignation." The idea was scrapped.

Hanging over Thornton the winter of 1961–1962 was not only Arthur Gelb's premature story of the forthcoming *Seven Deadly Sins* and *Seven Ages of Man* and the anticipations that arose from that announcement, but also a request that he write "a big piece" with which to open a new theater in Frankfurt. What could he offer? *The Emporium* had no third act. He had nothing else.

"Begin with an individual," F. Scott Fitzgerald wrote, "and before you know it you find that you have created a type; begin with a type, and you find that you have created — nothing."* Thornton had listened to hundreds of individual histories ("Now, tell us the story of your life" was a frequent conversational opener), but for him they were not the stuff of literature. "The sheer data — the abject truth — does not interest me," he said. He was looking for clues to the universal; his characters were carriers of timeless messages: Emily in *Our Town* ("Oh, earth, you're too wonderful for anyone to realize you"); Mrs. Antrobus in *The Skin of Our Teeth* ("Too many people have suffered and died in order to make my children rich, for us to start reneging now. So we'll go on putting this house to rights."). The small incident had to embody the big subject, some useful, abiding truth about humankind, translatable into character and plot.

His literary garden in the early sixties seemed littered with plants that did not root. Yet something did flower, and it grew out of Thornton's passion for music.

In a memoir, composer Mabel Daniels recounts that from the day he rather haltingly confessed that music was the real love of his life, she had known that Thornton was more than the ordinary amateur. In Cambridge in 1950, after dinner at her home, he had at once made for the piano bench, sat beside her and "from then on we forgot all about time while he played faultlessly at sight on the piano the bassoon part of my 'Three Observations for Three Woodwinds.' I filled in the oboe and clarinet parts. Then we sang any number of things, including that exquisite 'Vergine Madre' from Verdi's "Four Sacred Pieces," with those superb words by Dante. One could hardly call it singing, but with Thornton, who has an excellent baritone voice, improvising a duet to my none-too-accurate soprano (for I was completing the harmony on the piano at the same time), we went on and on enjoying ourselves immensely."†

* "The Rich Boy" in *The Stories of F. Scott Fitzgerald* (New York: Charles Scribner's Sons, 1951), p. 177.
† "Thornton Wilder — A Musical Memoir," *Radcliffe Quarterly,* May 1964, pp. 16–19.

As a boy in Berkeley, Thornton had saved up money to buy the score of *Tannhauser* and had it bound in blue gingham. At Oberlin, he played the organ. At Yale, he took scores from the Music School library into the practice room and "heard" them by reading them. In Princeton in 1923, he often dropped by undergraduate John Kirkpatrick's room to go through his musical library.* Nearly every Friday night in Chicago in the thirties, he played four-hand piano at the home of Professor and Mrs. Ralph Lillie. In New Haven, he sang German lieder.

Substantial sections of Thornton's journal are devoted to musical notation and commentary — the piano concertos of Beethoven, Stravinsky's handling of time. Off to a concert ("God be praised, I'm starved for noble strains"), he eagerly looked forward to Brahms's Piano Quintet, "wildly curious to hear whether those noble Italian players can somehow purify and elevate it." Having taught himself after long practice to read music with the inner ear, he studied the Masses of Palestrina in the early hours of the morning. It never occurred to him that music would ever professionally engage him, and when Edmund Wilson in 1940 suggested the possibility of his writing an opera libretto, he replied: "After the age of forty, no. After the age of forty opera librettos are like driving a car: *Let George do it.*"

In the early fifties, however, he met Paul Hindemith, then teaching composition at Yale, who proposed collaborating on an opera. Thornton gave him *The Long Christmas Dinner*. Nine years passed before Hindemith drafted an outline of the musical form, and since Thornton's words did not fit neatly into Hindemith's musical structure, some compromise between the poet's and the musician's vision had to be found. "Are you still willing, after this?" the composer asked. Thornton was. The opera was completed in three months and performed December 26, 1961, in Mannheim's Kleines Haus of the National Theater, Hindemith conducting, the librettist absent. "I've never attended the premier of my plays," Thornton told Catherine Coffin. "Shucks, it's the public that's on trial, not the authors. Hindemith's opera is a jewel; it will appear everywhere; I shall be catching its 500th performance some-

* Kirkpatrick became curator of the Charles E. Ives Collection in the John Herrick Jackson Music Library at Yale University.

where." He was wrong. The opera was heard only once in America, March 1963, at the Juilliard School of Music. Wilder had "done his work skillfully," Peter Hayworth wrote in the *New York Times,* but the music failed to attain eloquence.

A second opera, the more exciting one to Thornton, opened in Frankfurt two months after the Mannheim premiere of *The Long Christmas Dinner. The Alcestiad* had been set to music by Louise Talma.

Miss Talma, who had studied with Nadia Boulanger and at the Juilliard School and taught for a number of years at Hunter College, had met Thornton at the MacDowell Colony in 1952. As with Hindemith, the idea for collaboration was the composer's. Two of her friends carried Miss Talma's proposal for an opera to the Edinburgh Festival, and Thornton sent back word: "Tell her [*The Alcestiad*] is hers. Let's pull out all the stops — full orchestra, chorus." What emerged was an entirely new libretto in verse form. From beginning to end, Miss Talma said, Thornton was sensitive to what voices could do. She nicknamed him "the panther"; he was absolutely still only when listening to music.

She devoted three years to composition, two more to scoring and throughout Thornton was quite sharp about not interfering. "No, no, from time to time I'll come and hear what you have done, but this is entirely up to you. I've given you what I hope is a viable libretto and from here on out it's yours to do." There was far too much text for a two-and-a-half-hour opera, so he cut and stitched and hoped the result would show "striking divergences from the play — all in the direction of higher color and singable effectiveness . . . very much a 'grand opera.'" Minor characters were deleted, but he added full-throated arias. Librettist and composer met for work on the East Coast, the West Coast, in Rome in 1955, and after hearing some of her musical passages at the MacDowell Colony in 1956, Thornton complimented himself on "what a good picker I am — she's a superb composer, dramatic to her fingertips. It's in 12-tone system, but the 'dissonance' comes out as expressivity."

He wanted *The Alcestiad* to be performed first in the United States and to that end tried in April 1959 to enlist the support of Mrs. August Belmont, whose wealthy, horse-racing husband had had a prominent financial role in building New York City's subways. Mrs. Belmont's word was heard with respect in fashionable circles, including the inner circle of the Metropolitan Opera, which is why Thornton wrote that it was "a real satisfaction, Dear Mrs. Belmont, to know that we have your friendly good will. The acceptance of an opera lies ultimately in the intrinsic value of the musical quality and its meaningfulness for the audience at any given moment in cultural history. From now on that lies with the Metropolitan's Committee of Experts. Whether this work satisfies them or not, it is a smiling pleasure to know that you've expressed so kind an interest." Whether the experts seriously considered *The Alcestiad* is not a matter of record. In any event, its sole performance was in German on March 19, 1962, under the direction of Harry Buckwitz in Frankfurt, where it inspired a nineteen-minute ovation but fared less well critically. The *New York Times*'s correspondent, Paul Moor, politely avoided any judgment on the music or libretto.

Thornton was sixty-five, retirement age for many. Was his writing life, like *The Emporium,* to have no third act? He had turned out a respectable number of playlets, one-acts, essays, five major novels, four long plays. He'd won three Pulitzer Prizes, and, if it was any comfort, none of his peers produced anything of lasting value after sixty-five. Quite a few of them were dead — his Yale friends Philip Barry and Steve Benét; Thomas Wolfe at thirty-eight; Fitzgerald at forty-four; Hemingway a suicide at sixty-two. Robert Sherwood wrote no plays after the age of forty-four; Eugene O'Neill, nothing in the twelve years before his death at sixty-five. William Faulkner, the same age as Thornton, had only another year to live. John Steinbeck, awarded the Nobel Prize for Literature in 1962, published his last book that year, at age sixty.

There was to be a third act. It opened the second half of 1962, catching the critics and perhaps Thornton by surprise.

27

Retreat to the Desert

THE WANDERER was going to break with precedent by hiding
out in some desert town in the Southwest and staying there. Not
for a week or month, but a year, or maybe two. He wanted to
live for a long stretch as if he were eighty-five: "Not to go out;
not to frequent cultivated company; above all not to speak, talk,
open my mouth; not to ask How are you? Not to reply I'm well,
thank you." He was "weary sick" of automatic gestures, but admitted, "Of course, just while I've been bewailing the emptiness of
social gatherings I must — with staggering inconsistency — say that
I look forward to dinner tomorrow night at the Whit Griswolds'
with Lillian Hellman and Dorothy Parker; and after dinner I'm
going to read aloud some of my new stuff, which manages to
draw laughter from a turnip and tears from a stone at the same
moment. Known as Wilder's Last."

All Thornton's experience supported his confidence that guests
would welcome his performing, but that night at the Martha's
Vineyard home of former Yale president A. Whitney Griswold,
he came up against a nonconforming spirit. Informed that Thornton was to read his play, Dorothy Parker threatened to walk out
of the house. She was kept in her seat by Miss Hellman.

One can slip off to the desert unnoticed, but not if one talks
about it to the *New York Times,* which on March 3, 1962, gave
Thornton's departure thirteen paragraphs, quoting him as saying
that he was heading out for somewhere in Arizona to be a bum
for two years, "without neckties, without shoelaces and without
cultivated conversation." He pictured himself in a little white frame
house with a rickety front porch, where he would "laze away in

the shade in a wooden rocking chair, rising occasionally to put out a saucer of milk for the rattlesnakes."

He was on the road at dawn on May 20, and when his car broke down in Douglas, Arizona he went no further.

Douglas was a tacky, on-and-off mining town of about ten thousand, almost half Mexican-Americans. It had a main street, twenty-six churches, a couple of old-time bars, blue-plate-special cafés, and the Gadsden — a high-ceilinged, half-empty, fifty-year-old hotel with a large lobby and ample armchairs in which to doze. Thornton took a room.

The temperature at noon was over a hundred. Anything that could move slowed down, including Thornton's correspondence. Letters went undated: "Shucks, that's for people who have engagements to meet." The locals called him "Doc."

The only vibration from the outer world, and it made little stir, came in July when the Douglas newspaper reported President John F. Kennedy's award of the Presidential Medal of Freedom to Thornton Wilder. Nothing else disturbed the calm. In the first five months, Thornton's one fixed appointment was with the dentist.

In late afternoons he drove into the desert and watched the thunderstorms play among the mountains. Every two weeks he went to Tucson to browse in the university library. The silence ("*my* silence") was soothing. A pleasure in work was returning. Only once did he admit to the blues, but "the elements for the 'miseries' are always around us in the air, even when we're at our most contented. The benefit of a 'misery' is that generally one rebounds pendulum-wise; and I've felt fine ever since."

Invited for a meal, he had a handy excuse: "Hermits Anonymous don't go out to dinner." They may, however, go out to drink. When the Gadsden's bar closed at one in the morning, Thornton and a local judge drove across the border to Agua Prieta, where the bars stayed open as long as there was one customer sitting upright.

Gradually, he began to mingle with the townspeople — with Eddie, who worked at the airport; with Gladys, who cooked at one of the eateries; with a gaggle of widows at the hotel. "Well, well, you can imagine what happened when Thorny began picking up reticules and holding doors and asking how they were," Thornton wrote Isabel. He met an engineer employed at the reservoir, a highway patrol officer, and the owner of the local radio station, who became a drinking companion at Harry Ames's bar down the street from the Gadsden. He was persuaded to come to a housewarming: "Oh how we drink in the West," he wrote. "One lady lost her supper (very good cold ham, buffet style). I had a headache until noon today." Another evening, when he arrived late at the policemen's ball and found that all the badges had been given out, the chief of police gave Thornton his. He passed along that fact to Isabel, to show her that "IN SPITE OF YOUR FEARS I'm in good standing in Douglas. I joined the table with Rosie and Angela who sells shoes and Dorothy Noyes, accountant at the Gadsden, and some traveling salesmen. Fun? Fun!" It was fun because it was undemanding; he could stand apart and observe, as if these Douglas acquaintances were characters in a play written by someone else.

He moved into a small apartment in August and ventured some elementary cooking. Janet had given him *The Bachelor's Cookbook* and on an impulse he turned to French toast but had no powdered sugar. The next day, he remembered that his sister-in-law had sent him a can of maple sugar. Result: more and better French toast, just like in *Our Town*.

> *Dr. Gibbs.* Why Julia Gibbs. French toast.
>
> *Mrs. Gibbs.* 'Taint hard to make, and I had to do something.

He cut his hand washing dishes, and the first two times he tried to light the oven it blew up in his face. But he was soon cooking three out of four of his meals.

The apartment suited him — a plump violet divan, an overstuffed chair, *art nouveau* lamps, a bed for sorting out manuscript pages and another for sleeping. No telephone.

Thornton was in Douglas when *The Ides of March,* dramatized and directed by Jerome Kilty and starring John Gielgud and Irene Worth, opened at London's Haymarket Theatre in June 1963.

The possibility of staging the novel had arisen after Thornton saw Kilty's play *Dear Liar,* which, like *The Ides,* is based on letters. Having known Kilty through their common interest in the Poets' Theatre and the Brattle Street Theatre in Cambridge, Thornton had suggested that he submit an outline of a possible dramatization of *The Ides* and notes on "tone." Shortly before leaving for Arizona, he had worked with Kilty for three weeks at the Claridge Hotel in Atlantic City, emphasizing, however, that he didn't want *The Ides* to be "a Wilder play." Kilty, the much younger of the two, would fall into bed exhausted after long evenings of talk and drink. Thornton would continue working through the night, pacing up and down, laughing at something he'd thought up for the script, eager to resume at ten the next morning. He was "like a child with a jig-saw puzzle," Kilty said.

Again, Germany was the first to offer its stage to Wilder, and *The Ides* had its initial showing in Berlin's Renaissance Theatre in early 1963. Unfortunately, the irony of the Caesar story was lost in German translation, and in view of poor notices it was doubtful whether the play would be seen again. However, John Gielgud and producer Hugh Beaumont, having attended the Berlin performance, wrote Thornton that with minor revision it could succeed in London. From Arizona he contributed a patch here, a patch there. A reputable British cast was assembled. Gielgud reported that he was trying to get Kilty "to put a few more dark shadows into my part, for I fear the one difficulty is that Caesar is too sympathetic throughout, and might turn into a benevolent sheep instead of an irascible tyrant." But the Caesar of Thornton's novel was not at all a tyrant.

The play faltered; "the news from London is not good," Beaumont wrote. Kilty was blunter: "We were slaughtered." One of the kinder critics, in the *Oxford Mail,* said that "it is not yet in perfect trim." The *Times* of London called it "grossly inadequate."

Thornton had been prepared for the worst. "Oh how awful to put Catullus in corduroys. Jerry [Kilty] alone would have put on a dull play; it took Gielgud to make a displeasing play." Perhaps it had been foolish to try to rewarm yesterday's porridge. If he had intended to write a play on that subject, he said, he would have "gone about it differently in every detail." But *The Ides* and London were quickly forgotten.

On March 31, 1963, Thornton wrote Isabel from Douglas: "Well, I won't stew about it any longer, but come right out with it that I've written what must be ninety pages or more of a novel." He wasn't sure what to call it. *Anthracite?* And he couldn't describe it except to say that it was as though *Little Women* were being mulled over by Dostoevski. It would be a long family saga, an adventure story, a mystery. Its locale was a southern Illinois town, 1902–1904, and if there was a real town called Anthracite, he'd change the name to Carbondale or Colsburgh or Coaltown.

By fall the plot lines had been nailed down, and he turned to biology-trained Janet for her expert opinion: "Does anyone know how nature arranges that there are eleven females born to every ten males? Or how it is that the male birth rate goes up so after many men have been killed in a war?" From biblically trained Amos, he sought "the exact rendering of 'Make straight in the desert a high road for your Lord' — highway? . . . the Lord? . . . our Lord?"

Thornton had planned to leave Douglas in late summer of 1963 ("such pangs for water and for green"), but each month it became harder to contemplate giving up the walk to the post office at noon, the homemade lunch of soup and a tomato-egg-cheese sandwich, the uninterrupted naps and the midnight meetings of the Little Group of Serious Drinkers at the Gadsden: "Smitty at the Bar, Rovina assisting — Milly, Eddie; we had to discuss the party that Rovina and Jim Cotton got up at Mike and Estelle's place last Friday night. Five dollars a couple, all the beer you can drink and sandwiches and chile con carne. . . . Would make a novelette, but not by me."

The southern Illinois novel, going "like an express train" by October 29, was derailed a week later by a White House telegram. Medal of Freedom ceremonies and a presidential luncheon were set for December 6 at noon. The honoree was expected to be present.

Three days before Thornton's intended departure for Washing-

ton, President Kennedy was assassinated and the ceremonies canceled. The death, Thornton wrote Isabel from Arizona,

> lights up an aspect of Douglas I haven't told you about. These
> South plains-and-desert states are bubbling with hatred, and
> a different kind of hatred than the Gulf States'. The Gulf States
> have a long history — war, defeat, bankruptcy, guilt — a long
> uninterrupted defensive retreat; but these states have no mem-
> ory of a past, ignorant and proud of it, sublimely certain of
> their being right. Examples:
> Discussing the assassination in the Gadsden bar: "Well, he
> had it coming to him, didn't he?" The idiom means: He was
> improperly provocative.
> Another small rancher, smiting the bar with his big fist:
> "Mrs. Roosevelt did more harm to the world than ten Hit-
> lers."
> You remember that ladies in the telephone headquarters
> tried to discourage my making long-distance calls for cash pay-
> ment [most of the nightly calls were to Isabel]. They have a
> nice appearance, could pass as P.T.A. mothers in Hamden.
> One of them asked Eddie Stiles: 'Who is that Mr. Wilder? Is
> he a Communist?' The train of thought is as follows:
>   A. He doesn't have a telephone.
>   B. He makes $8 and $10 phone calls.
>   C. He comes to this headquarters to make them, so that
>   they can't be "traced."
>   D. He has a funny accent.
>   E. He wears a necktie even in July and August. QED.
> It would not be surprising if there had been six assassins
> waiting for the President in the various cities of Texas, un-
> known to one another.

Thornton had meant to come east in December and saw no
reason to revise his schedule. He gave away books, phonograph
records, kitchen utensils and bade farewell to Douglas. He'd talked
for years about getting away from it all; now he'd done it and
was ready to put it behind him; the Arizona experience had run
its course. And since there was no longer any rush to get to Wash-

ington, he took the longer southern route home, through Texas and Louisiana.

When they saw him in Cambridge, his brother and sister-in-law were appalled by Thornton's appearance. He had a skin cancer on his face and a hernia so large his coats had to be altered to hide the bulge. At Deepwood Drive, everything was at sixes and sevens. Isabel was finishing up Christmas notes, putting Thornton's files into shape, then running to the attic to look for some article of clothing that might be serviceable for winter travel, for Thornton had decided they would go to Italy and was anxious to be aboard the *Cristoforo Colombo* in January.

A man can travel light, discarding books along the way, but he cannot travel cheaply, not if he's in his sixties, goes to Europe three times within two years (1964–1965) and intersperses those trips with excursions to Quebec, Stockbridge, Saratoga Springs, Newport, New York and Florida. And not if he puts up at grand hotels and treats his guests at fancy restaurants. Thornton had no investments; he lived off royalties. Moreover, his income was a roller coaster of dips and climbs. There were low years between Pulitzer Prizes, and the federal government's belated allowance of a five-year income tax carryover to lighten the artist's burden would come too late to benefit him. He needed to earn.

Philosophically speaking, Thornton believed, there is no such thing as luck. Practically speaking, there is no other way to explain the dollars that now filled his pockets from a brassy musical comedy that was based on *The Matchmaker*. "I never thought I'd end up with all this money from [Hello] *Dolly*. Imagine it!" He'd had no part in it, attended no rehearsals and was a bit shamefaced about its instant success. The music and lyrics were Jerry Herman's; Michael Stewart had done the "adaptation." Starring Carol Channing as Dolly Levi, it hit Broadway on January 16, 1964, while Thornton and Isabel were in Italy, and won ten of twenty Tony Awards. "One of those real gold mines that come along every five years or so," wrote Jack Gaver of United Press International. The musical would boom its way across the United States, "Hello, Dolly!" being sung by Miss Channing, then Mary Martin, then Ginger Rogers, and becoming almost as popular as "Auld Lang Syne." Of Thornton's income from writing in 1964 and 1965 —

$350,575.92 — *Our Town* and *The Bridge* accounted for $12,344.88. $202,085.25 came from *Hello, Dolly!*, plus an additional $5,312.76 from the sale of records.

Thornton didn't like to be asked about it, but he carried newspaper clippings in his pocket and exclaimed over *Hello, Dolly!*'s box office receipts. By the end of August 1965, the show was enjoying its eighty-fifth week of standing-room-only business, a touring company was playing to record grosses and profits, and the producer, David Merrick, was planning two additional road companies and a tour abroad. It was found money.

Could the same thing be done with *The Skin of Our Teeth?* The possibility flared briefly. Leonard Bernstein, whose *On the Town, Wonderful Town,* and *West Side Story* had been Broadway hits, proposed an adaptation of *Skin* with choreography by Jerome Robbins, a Bernstein score and lyrics by the successful writing team of Betty Comden and Adolph Green. Thornton said go ahead, Bernstein began composing, and then something strange happened. In Thornton's absence, Isabel was asked by Comden and Green whether they could audition their first act for her and Harold Freedman. She then learned that Robbins and Bernstein had pulled out. Comden and Green wanted rights to the play and would pick another choreographer and composer. "I'm now convinced," Thornton wrote his sister New Year's Day 1966, "that the Bernstein musical could never have been a success — but before it flopped you would have had a hundred conferences and rehearsals — torn in every direction by committee quarrels. They would have put in an atom-bomb sequence — then taken it out again. Tears, mounting costs, Rosalind Russell engaged as Sabina furious that so much attention is given to the Antrobus family, nobody speaking to anybody, and all would have been laid on the lap of YOU. What I hate about the whole thing is all the money that went to their and our agents and lawyers. We should be indemnified for Leonard Bernstein's changing his mind."

Thornton thereupon gave a two-year film option on *Skin* to Mary Ellen Bute, because of his admiration for a film of *Finnegans Wake* she had produced and directed.

Bernstein's one-line to the press was that "it didn't work out."

"The one way to keep us from harm is to fill our lives with the four or five human pleasures which are our right in the world," says Dolly Levi in *The Matchmaker*, "*and that takes a little money. Not much, but a little.*" Thanks to *Hello, Dolly!*, Thornton was making more than a little and paying as little attention to it as he had when he lived off a Lawrenceville salary. Over the years the management of his affairs had been left more and more to Isabel, who had no secretary, no fondness for bookkeeping, didn't want to pry into her brother's affairs and, Wilder-like, felt there was something slightly shabby about money talk. "In my house," Thornton had told his father in 1934, "no one will be permitted to mention MONEY." Nonetheless, someone had to pay bills, keep tab on royalties, maintain files, examine contracts and deal with Wilder play and book rights around the world.

In the late thirties, Thornton had turned over supervision of professional rights to his plays to Harold Freedman, head of the dramatic department in the Brandt & Brandt agency in New York.* Amateur dramatic rights were handled by Samuel French, Inc. Most of the other day-to-day business was Isabel's province, and it was she who had written New Haven attorney Dwight Dana in 1945 that she was being "swamped with requests from France, Italy, Spain. Thornton changes his mind so often, one can't do a job of it well. We need an agent to police Thornton's rights." Nothing was done. Sixteen years later, Isabel again wrote an attorney about putting her brother's financial affairs in order: "Thornton has to be helped. This kind of decision and planning has to be formulated clearly for him; then — not unduly persuaded or led — but definitely told this side and that of the issue. He is concerned but not really interested. He does not pretend to understand; nor can he *care* much about how or why. [His] patience is short on having to think about the material ends and details. He wants them in order and all going smoothly. He is only free to go on with his own work if the basic structure is settled and functioning. You would be truly shocked to know how little he knows or wants to know."

Finally, in 1962, with Thornton's permission, Isabel shoved all

* After Freedman's death in 1966, William Koppelmann of Brandt & Brandt took over.

his contracts into four shopping bags and dumped them on the desk of Carol Brandt in New York, asking her to straighten them out. From then on, Brandt & Brandt would act as his agent for all nondramatic literary properties. When Mrs. Brandt read the contract with the Bonis for *The Cabala* and *The Bridge of San Luis Rey,* she was scandalized; she thought it was the worst contract from an author's point of view that she had ever seen. The handling of motion picture rights had been so casual that Thornton benefited financially — $25,000 — from only one of three different films made of *The Bridge.* Isabel subsequently told Beulah Hagen, assistant to Cass Canfield at Harper & Brothers, of her relief "at having Mrs. Brandt at work for us. . . . I can't tell you how important it is proving. If we had gone along much longer without having [someone] to go through everything and been forced to bring order, we would never have known how much housecleaning was needed." Within months, Mrs. Brandt had handed over a huge file to Italian agent Erich Linder in Milan with the instruction: "Do something. Things are not right." Indeed they were not right. None of Thornton's prewar writing was in print in Italy. Linder arranged for publication of *The Bridge* by the Italian firm Mondadori, and when there was a falling out with Mondadori, found a new Italian publisher, Garzanti. But Linder soon learned that his author couldn't make head or tail of contracts. "He took pleasure," said Linder, "simply in being translated and well translated." After the Second World War, Thornton had given permission to stage his plays in Europe to almost anyone who asked, and when Isabel had admonished that he shouldn't, nor should he allow his essays to be available to all comers, he grumbled: "When is an author's work his own?"

Thornton was not anti-money. But money, as Dolly Levi said, was like manure, "not worth a thing unless it's spread around encouraging young things to grow." He loaned a young man five thousand dollars and years later, when the borrower apologized for not having repaid it, wrote that he'd "forgotten all about that 'advance.' I extend to you a 'remission in perpetuity.' " Money was handy because it allowed Thornton to work at his own pace, travel, give to needy individuals and institutions and support Isabel, for whom two trusts from royalties were set up, one in 1960 and a second in 1966. "So funny being well-to-do again," he had written Mabel Dodge Luhan in 1938. "The relationship between me and money has always been the oddest; keeps me laughing the whole time. I have a deep ancestral need to pretend to myself I'm poor, and a deep necessity to be effusively hospitable and lavish toward others. The result is that I never buy any clothes and take friends to the Trocadero dressed in one of the two suits that I was forced to buy in 1935."

Leather-bound books, antiques, silver, pictures, bric-a-brac, even a television set were not for him. And when he listened to the conversation of people who did care about possessions and money and had a lot of both, he was bored: you couldn't "keep your eyelids open with gum." Their talk could be "kind of soothing," he acknowledged, "especially in Chicago," or "briefly imposing in New York, like Harry Luce; briefly awe-inspiring in Europe, like Niarchos" — but it was never really interesting.

Some climb the money ladder without a backward glance and feel secure at the top, taking pride in their accomplishment. Thornton came of a family with no such pretensions. Theirs were the values of the honest, upright, educated middle class, which as a matter of taste has to appear indifferent or superior to the amassing of wealth. The young tutor-narrator in Thornton's last novel, *Theophilus North,* will bicycle around Newport from "cottage" to "cottage," rearranging the lives of their wealthy owners, as if saying to himself, "I'm much poorer than you, but I'm happier and smarter." It seemed to Thornton, so he told columnist Art Buchwald, that the rich had to be constantly reminded, mainly by newspapers and magazines, that they were somebody: "The rich may claim to detest the press, but without the reassurances of the society pages and columns that they are what they think they are, they would have a completely empty feeling in their stomachs." In his journal, he was more precise:

> Veblen missed the point about conspicuous waste; it is a repressive strategy. It is designed to cow the less fortunate into believing that the privileged rich are of a different order of man and are mysteriously entitled to their out-sized possessions. . . .

The man with an income far larger than he can employ must be left untouched because society would be crippled (its "progress" would come to a halt) unless individuals of exceptional administrative gifts were exceptionally rewarded (i.e. they would sulk or lose their genius without enormous personal monetary compensation). . . . Do not disturb or fret men with half-a-million annual income; any limiting of their rewards will discourage others from benefiting the community. They have a *right* to their earnings and if that right is questioned the incentive will be removed from those who would imitate them.

"I'm getting to be a crypto-Marxian," Thornton remarked in his sixties. "The unequal distribution of wealth vitiates against all exchange of ideas. Like the cuttlefish it exudes a black secretion."

Insofar as he enjoyed the milieu of the well-to-do, and he did, it was partly because he felt detached from it; he could appreciate it as an outsider, without needing or caring to know how it managed its affairs. Indeed, after *The Bridge of San Luis Rey,* Thornton took less and less responsibility for his own business affairs. If he didn't want excerpts from his plays, particularly *Our Town,* to be used or didn't want his plays included in too many anthologies, the word was passed along to Isabel, who followed through. Numerous practical questions were relayed to her from Brandt & Brandt. If they seemed important she consulted Thornton; otherwise, she acted on her own. Learning that someone had taken an option on Arabic rights to *Heaven's My Destination,* she asked Carol Brandt to find out whether the Punjabi language came under the heading of Arabic. Mrs. Brandt asked Beulah Hagen at Harper's. Mrs. Hagen replied that the arrangement did "not include the Punjabi language, only Armenian, Bengali, Malay, Indonesian, Persian, Peshtu, Urdu, and several indigenous languages of Africa." Mrs. Brandt then informed Isabel. Thornton wasn't bothered.

28
The Eighth Day

WHEN HARPER & ROW in late 1964 inquired about the novel Thornton had been writing in Arizona, Isabel replied that her brother, who was on a slow boat to France, said it was more than three-quarters done. He had been in and around New Haven most of the summer, undergoing a hernia operation, nine x-ray treatments for minor skin cancer and the removal of a small growth from under his eye. Now, in cabin 47 of the SS *Rossini* (he'd bribed the steward to let him keep his porthole open), Thornton felt fit and full of good resolutions. He would have small breakfasts and lunches, smoke little or none, read only excellent books (he had with him the complete works of Molière and Corneille), drink nothing but beer after ten at night, answer all the letters in his baggage except the ones that didn't deserve an answer and not apologize for being antisocial.

He couldn't, of course, be antisocial, he could only wish he were. For instance, there was that attractive young widow from Rochester, the polio invalid in a wheelchair whom he saw in a Cannes hotel restaurant. He had to invite her for a drink and chat with her until four in the morning and squire her around the Riviera for two weeks in a hired car with driver. It was all very proper, a squeeze of the arm or hand. He was so "silly and nonsensical," Bettina Hart Bachmann remembered, "full of games." But he paid for the late nights. He had a bad cold, he hadn't cut down on smoking, his southern Illinois novel was dragging. He packed his bags for Nice.

The much advertised carnival and flower battles in Nice — daily parades of bobbing papier-mâché ogres — seemed insipid ("even the children want to go home"), but there were opera and an organ recital and a concert by pianist José Iturbi. And a bar in the Hotel Ruhl. "And I, with my damned curiosity, get involved. And then the only thing to do is to RUN." He ran to Cannes. A month later, the unfinished manuscript in his suitcase, he was in the Netherlands Antilles.

In May 1965, Thornton was at the White House to receive from Lady Bird Johnson the National Book Committee's Medal for Literature and five thousand dollars. Five months later he was headed for Casablanca to "get away from kind phone calls and polite requests and well-intentioned invitations as the book [now titled *The Eighth Day*] draws to its very serious close." Approaching North Africa, he stumbled on an ending for his story, something that pulled it all together, an adaptation of some remarks of Stein. "It lay half recognized at the back of my mind the whole time, so that it won't require much touching up earlier in the book, but it makes writing the last chapter a very exciting daily task. All I need is a hotel room. It looks as if I may be able to finish the book by January [1966], but not the last finishing touches."

Published March 29, 1967, three weeks before Thornton's seventieth birthday, *The Eighth Day* starts as a murder mystery and grows into an extended meditation on the mystery of existence. It is nearly twice as long as *The Cabala* or *The Bridge of San Luis Rey*, as if the author had been driven to tell . . . everything.

Breckenridge Lansing is murdered May 4, 1902, in Coaltown, Illinois and his friend and neighbor John Ashley is convicted of the killing. While being taken to prison, Ashley is rescued, set free, makes his way to New Orleans, thence to Chile, where he works in the Andes mines. We know that John Ashley is not the murderer; we don't know why he was rescued, by whom, or the identity of the killer. When the mystery is finally solved we hardly care, for we have meanwhile been led through the vicissitudes of two generations of Ashleys and Lansings, from southern Illinois to Chile, Chicago, an island in the Caribbean, Hoboken. The flight of John Ashley to Chile ends with his death at sea, and we pick up the story of the Ashleys left behind. Mrs. Ashley runs a boardinghouse in Coaltown, her son becomes a successful journalist, one daughter a famous singer, another a saintly social activist.

The first working title, *Anthracite,* had been succeeded by *Make Straight in the Desert.* For hours Thornton had been listening to motets by polyphonic composers of the sixteenth century on the biblical verse "The voice of him that crieth in the wilderness, Prepare ye the way of the Lord, make straight in the desert a highway for our God." He settled on *The Eighth Day* because his subject was creation and "the part played in it by men and women of faith, and how the great design for the groaning multitude is passed down from grandparent to grandchild." To Pierre Teilhard de Chardin he was indebted for the concept of mankind's "second week," to Kierkegaard for the idea of the invisibility of the Knight of Faith: "I'm like a bird, I build my nest from other birds' feathers and bright bits of wool that once warmed others."

The novel is a cluster of appropriations. The "demon of contrariety" that hovers over the murder trial of John Ashley is a phrase of Edgar Allan Poe's. Will there someday be a "spiritualization" of the human animal? It is Teilhard de Chardin's question. Janet Dakin makes her contribution to the passage: "What stretches of time are required to complete the procession of a marsh to a forest. The professors have drawn up the time plan: So much for the grasses to furnish humus for the bushes; so much for the bushes to accommodate the trees; so much for the young of the Oak family to take root under the grateful shade of the Wild Cherry and the Maple, and to supplant them; so much for the White Oak to replace the Red; so much for the majestic Beech family." The references to tribal lore and the dances of Indians in Illinois, though "sheer invention," hark back to a creation myth memorized by young men in the Pueblo tribes of New Mexico, with which Thornton was familiar. Much of a Coaltown doctor's description of Earth before the appearance of life is culled from a discursive essay by Gottfried Benn. When the doctor says that education is "the bridge man crosses from the self-enclosed, self-favoring life into a consciousness of the entire community of mankind," Thornton is borrowing Thomas Mann's definition.

Kierkegaard's *Knight of the Secret Inwardness* is the model for John Ashley:

He did not know that he was a man of faith. He would have been quick to deny that he was a man of religious faith, but religions are merely the garments of faith — and very ill cut they often are, especially in Coaltown, Illinois. Like most men of faith, John Ashley was — so to speak — invisible. You brushed shoulders with a man of faith in the crowd yesterday; a woman of faith sold you a pair of gloves. Their principal characteristics do not tend to render them conspicuous. Only from time to time one or other of them is propelled by circumstance into becoming visible — blindingly visible. . . . They are not afraid; they are not self-regarding; they are constantly nourished by astonishment and wonder at life itself.

What do these "knights" have faith *in?* Creation. "And there is no creation without faith and hope. There is no faith and hope that does not express itself in creation. These men and women work. The spectacle that most discourages them is not error or ignorance or cruelty, but sloth. This work that they do may often seem to be all but imperceptible. That is characteristic of activity that never for a moment envisages an audience." Gertrude Stein is in the wings here, as she is again when Thornton mentions John Ashley's respect for superstition.

There is a barroom interchange between Ashley and a stranger in a pimps' café in New Orleans:

In his ignorance Ashley spent an evening at Joly's. Toward the end of it Joly approached him and asked him in a low voice, "Are you from St. Louis?"

"No."

"I thought you was Herb Benson from St. Louis. You're in the *tambour?*"

Ashley didn't know why he should be in any "drum," but he compliantly said that he was.

"Where did you work?"

"Up in Illinois."

"Chicago?"

"Near it."

"Great in Chicago, eh? Great?"

"Yes."

In the thirties, Herb Blumer, a criminologist on the University of Chicago faculty and a professional football player, had taken Thornton on a night tour of the Chicago underworld. The proprietor of a pimps' café had whispered that a certain girl had lost her protector and offered Blumer her services. "So," Thornton wrote, "it's found its way into my novel. Ashley as a hunted man — waiting for his smuggler's boat to South America — has to move among pariahs. He drops into 'Joly's' by mistake."

Thornton credited Goethe for the line "It is doubtful whether hope, or any other manifestations of creativity, can sustain itself without an impulse injected by love." A benefactor of Roger Ashley's remarks: "I don't believe in God, but I love the gods." Freud had said that to Thornton in Vienna. Gazing at the constellations above the Chilean mountain peaks, John Ashley thinks: "In infinite space, in infinite time, in infinite matter, an organism like a bubble is formed; it lasts a short while and then bursts; and that bubble is myself." The sentence is Levin's in *Anna Karenina*. A stranger in Chicago, Roger Ashley stops to stare at the throngs on LaSalle Street: "During his first days he thought he was seeing the same persons walking back and forth." Juan Gris had told Stein that he had exactly that sensation on the Place de la Concorde. Before the murder, John Ashley starts the day by singing loudly before his shaving mirror, raising a joyful storm in the house: "Bathroom's free, little doggies! Last one to breakfast is a buffalo." It was Thornton's father's phrase.

All these incidentals are derivative, yet the novel is entirely Thornton's, a narrative into which he draws whatever he chooses from reading, imagination and experience.

The only identifiable character in *The Eighth Day* is Mrs. Wickersham, who manages the hotel in Chile where John Ashley boards. In Peru on his State Department tour, Thornton had met Mrs. Tia Bates who ran the Quinta Bates Inn, and the resemblance between her and Mrs. Wickersham worried Thornton sufficiently that he prepared a disclaimer: "A number of enterprising travelers may recognize in Mrs. Wickersham, her *Lafonda* and her hospitals some allusions to the famous *Quinta Bates* in Arequipa, Peru. Mrs. Bates disdained any resort to cosmetics and it is certain that she never ransacked her guests' luggage, but those who admired and loved her may find some reflection of her generous heart and resourceful mind." Neither his agent nor Harper's saw any reason to include the paragraph and it was left out of the book.

Timeless creation and its transformations is the novel's leitmotiv: "Nothing is more interesting than inquiry as to how creativity operates in anyone, in everyone: Mind propelled by passion, imposing itself, building and unbuilding; mind — the latest appearing manifestation of life — expressing itself in statesmen and criminals, in poet and banker, in street cleaner and housewife, in father and mother — establishing order or spreading havoc; mind — condensing its energy in groups and nations, rising to an incandescence and then ebbing away exhausted; mind — enslaving and massacring or diffusing justice and beauty." All this forms the tapestry of life, and the hidden figure in the tapestry "transmits fairer messages than it is itself aware of."

Not only Gertrude Stein's notion of the continuous present, but the rhythms in her *The Making of Americans* are evoked in the last paragraph of *The Eighth Day:* "There is much talk of a design in the arras. Some are certain they see it. Some see what they have been told to see. Some remember that they saw it once but have lost it. Some are strengthened by seeing a pattern wherein the oppressed and exploited of the earth are gradually emerging from their bondage. Some find strength in the conviction that there is nothing to see. Some"

A new novel by Thornton Wilder, nineteen years after *The Ides of March,* was bound to be noticed. The Book-of-the-Month Club put up a $90,000 guarantee, 60 percent of it for the author. The book sold 82,000 copies in six months and was on the best-seller list twenty-five successive weeks. Edmund Wilson thought it was "the best thing he ever wrote"; most critics disagreed. Edmund Fuller's comments in the *Wall Street Journal* of April 19, 1967, were among the more complimentary. He surmised that the book's qualities "will not be widely or quickly understood. . . . A reader too thoroughly steeped in — even brainwashed by — some of the most critically fashionable or best-selling fiction of the moment may scarcely know what to make of its range, its values, its vocabulary." It was one of those old-fashioned things called novels, wrote

Denis Donoghue in the *New York Review of Books,* "stories with truth in them. The trouble with books of this kind is that they claim to tell All, and the claim is difficult to sustain." The *New Yorker's* Edith Oliver argued that there was no point in saying a weak ending doesn't matter: "In a murder mystery the ending matters. None of the characters, major or minor, is essentially credible to the reader."

The most censorious review was Stanley Kauffmann's in the *New Republic* of April 8, 1967: "The theme, as apprehended here, is sophomoric, although Wilder has dealt with it before with at least some immediate effect. . . . The art of the man who was once scolded for being too much of an artist has become simultaneously shriveled and bloated. The sad result is that, toward the end of his career, we have — from a man who has always meant well — a book that means nothing."

Kauffmann's thrust missed the mark. *The Eighth Day* may be overadorned with aphorisms and essays and too didactic, but nowhere is it empty of meaning.

Thornton put up no defense. At seventy, he said, "one is less elated or depressed by immediate things." The novel, he told Jay Leyda, was an "attempt to redeem some dreary stupidities in my life." He had never before written a long book, but he'd always thought it would be exciting to live in one, with "corridors and vistas and echoing galleries. . . . I simply *started* and themes and images that I had collected in a long lifetime that were waiting and eager to be given voice — they clustered about the rising structure; the self effacing 'man of faith,' the doctrine that civilization is borne forward by a remnant." A year after its publication, Thornton mentioned to Cass Canfield that he had been more reprehended than commended for introducing many short reflections, even essays into the story, but "the works of very young writers and very old writers tend to abound in these moralizing digressions."

Like all Thornton's work, *The Eighth Day* narrates the journey of pilgrims through adversities. Awkwardly, comically, naively, painfully, heroically, they "seek the light." The narrator in *The Cabala,* George Brush in *Heaven's My Destination,* the Abbess in *The Bridge of San Luis Rey,* Chrysis in *The Woman of Andros,* Caesar in *The Ides of March,* Mr. and Mrs. Antrobus in *The Skin of Our*

Teeth, the Ashley family in *The Eighth Day* — all endure the unalterable so that the unalterable becomes a source of strength. Each adapts to necessity as though it were a choice. This, Thornton believed, was the motif of Beethoven's last quartets: "es müss sein." He saw it in Kierkegaard's *Fear and Trembling:* "To transform the leap of life into a walk, absolutely to express the sublime in the pedestrian — that only the Knight of Faith can do." Goethe, too, had said it, in the fourth stanza of his poem *Urworte; Orphisch:*

> . . . "I will" yields to "I would"
> And chance desires are stilled before that willing;
> That which is dearest is harried from the heart,
> Will and caprice bow to the austere "Must."
> So we are seeming-free, after many a year,
> Nearer at least thereto than in the beginning.

Ought we then to classify Wilder as a religious writer? He did not claim that distinction. Moreover, it is a mistake to equate an artist's convictions with those of his fictional characters. In *Our Town,* he had written that there is "something in all of us that is eternal," but that was far from an avowal of personal immortality. He could only say, in a letter to James Leo Herlihy in 1968, that he'd be very embarrassed to say what his philosophy was: "I'm optimist and pessimist and religious and non-religious. I try 'em out for size. I'm tossed from pole to pole. I'm an awful wobbler. But I do (by act of will) take certain positions and explore them." A week before his death, he pointed out that he had been formed by the Protestant beliefs of his father, his school in China, and Oberlin — "and the very thoroughness of my exposure to dogmatic Protestant positions made me aware that they were insufficient to encompass the vast picture of history and the burden of suffering in the world."

Yet in his preoccupation with the preciousness of ordinary daily life, in his figurations of faith, love and hope — especially hope — Thornton was not outside the mainstream of Christian teaching. The Crucifixion seemed to him the most magnificent metaphor ever found for mankind's imperfection. On the other hand, he thought that Christianity's involvement in blood and murder "reawakens the latent anguish of the infantile life and fills the inner mind with such vibrating nerves and such despairing self-abasement that the spiritual values can barely make themselves heard."

This can be said: Whatever the well-springs of his outlook, and they were many; whatever his personal doubts, shortcomings, anguish, or those of the world, he resisted the temptation to believe that the human race is going to hell. Mankind is like the planet Earth in *Our Town,* "straining away, straining away all the time to make something of itself." A melancholy Christmas greeting provoked an exasperated response: "The first Christmas also came into a world of anxiety and distress, hence the summons to be joyful — 'rejoice, I say, rejoice!' " There were always sufficient pretexts in life for melancholy. "No, no — refuse that indulgence. Love life and be loved." The knowledge of imperfection was not to be carried on one's back like a load of stones.

Trusting in the invincibility of the saving remnant and in the will to survive, how could he not have been drawn to Jews? The attraction was not purely intellectual, an admiration for such superior beings as Freud, Stein, Claude Lévi-Strauss. By heritage, upbringing and schooling, Thornton was the quintessential white Anglo-Saxon Protestant, one of "the majority" in Madison, Chefoo, Thacher, Berkeley, Oberlin, Yale, Princeton. Nonetheless, a "different" boy early senses kinship with others who, for whatever reasons, sense they are outsiders. For most of his adult life, Thornton was at home within fellowships where Jews were familiar and welcome — literary, theatrical, publishing, academic. There are frequent references in his letters and journal to his concern for victims of bigotry and ostracism. He told Amos, who served on a commission of the World Council of Churches that discussed the relation of the Christian church to the Jews: "It's been absorbing to see that at last sense and precise thinking (in addition to charity) is breaking up that miasma cloud about the Jews. It must be bracing to feel yourself an agent." He wrote producer Cheryl Crawford in 1966 that "we are in a phase of the culture-climate of the Jews. A great jet-fuel of the human race. Thank God, I have some drops of Jewish blood. After centuries of contempt they are emerging into estimation and not only estimation but the *goyim*'s expectation of greatness." When someone alleged that Thornton had left the Bonis "because of anti-Semitism," he sighed, "Oh, Lord, what you have to take in life!"

29

"Not Bad . . . Wot?"

ONCE DELIVERED of *The Eighth Day*, Thornton suffered another brief breakdown of morale. There was nothing to be done for it but rest and read, underlining and annotating books and dropping the marked copies into wastebaskets for acquisitive hotel chambermaids or ship stewards. By the time he and Isabel got to Europe in the late fall of 1966, the dejection had been shaken off.

He was in Milan when he heard of Henry Luce's death in Arizona on February 28, and when Hutchins wrote that he had liked Luce, Thornton's reply was qualified: "Like is a word of wide spread. I've known too many in his empire." What he and Luce had had in common was their fathers, a "very special breed of cats, very religious, very dogmatic Patriarchs. They preached and talked cant from morning till night — not because they were hypocritical, but because they knew no other language. They were forceful men. They thought that they were 'spiritual.' Damn it, they should have been in industry. They had no insight into the lives of others — least of all their families. We're the product of those (finally bewildered and unhappy) Worthies. In Harry it took the shape of a shy-joyless power drive."

Thornton was no less driven, but in his case the propelling force was a quest for the Right Subject, and he thought he'd found it in the idea of a fictionalized autobiography. Before long it was "gushing like a Texas oil well, pages every day for a week," "funnier" than *The Eighth Day* and "very Marxist: the rich are dehumanized by possessions; the poor dehumanized by care. So I'll be lugging around another manuscript again. I'd thought I'd put that behind me." Maybe he'd call it *What the Children Did to Newark, New Jersey.*

The pressure to produce another book was not economic. Reviews notwithstanding, *The Eighth Day* had brought him a comfortable return, and the sale of motion picture rights to *Hello Dolly* had added $131,580 to his income.

On Thornton's seventieth birthday in April 1967, telegraph boys arrived in relays at Deepwood Drive with cables, including one from the president of West Germany. "Poor Isabel" was left to deal with phone calls and letters; Thornton removed himself to Martha's Vineyard, where he listened in Edgartown or Oak Bluffs bars to the young talk about the Vietnam war. "Do you know what would make me psychedelically happy," he wrote Isabel. "To have my book embraced by the young — as [J. D.] Salinger was. I want to be the next station after Salinger. It would make me delirious to read that there's a coffee joint on Bleecker Street called the Eighth Day. I want to be a culture-hero to the young and among the hippies. Shalom! Shalom! Shalom! If that happened I'd change my name, go around as a Tolstoy socialist, give up tobacco and alcohol — what wouldn't I do?" But the young hadn't heard of *The Eighth Day.* Thornton's writings had never lit the eyes of a younger generation or dictated their attitudes and emotions, as had Fitzgerald's bitter-sweet romances or Hemingway's bone-hard stories or, later, Jack Kerouac's descriptions of the "beats."

His "autobiographical" novel was taking curious turns, leading the author toward the Arctic Circle. All right, he would invent the life of a trader with the Eskimos. Then the locale shifted from the frozen north to the Amazon, where a Mr. and Mrs. Bonnefay are prisoners of a tattooed tribe ("Oh, no — nothing daunts me"). In Paris the fall of 1967, Arctic Circle and Amazon were forgotten and Thornton began writing from memory.

From his seventieth through his seventy-fifth year, he wrote almost every day for at least an hour. Fresh discoveries overwhelmed him — Claude Lévi-Strauss, William Empson ("my hero, my favorite critic"), Haydn's last dozen piano trios, new frontiers of microbiology and astronomy. The onetime schoolmaster told himself that he no longer understood what went on in the heads of the young, though he had "fine rapport with girls eighteen–twenty-two . . . oh, to be fifty again!" In Genoa in 1968, he had looked down from his hotel window on student demonstrations in the streets and placards proclaiming "Marx Mao Marcuse." He bought Marcuse's *One-Dimensional Man* and *Eros and Civilization,* and thought, "no wonder the students are indebted to him. He explains their *malaise* and their resentment against their parents, their governments and their professors." On Martha's Vineyard, the young men told him they were learning from *life.* He found them "insecurely boastful; great intellectual pretension and bone-ignorant. Here's 'Wilder's Law' — a man between eighteen and twenty-five who for several years has done nothing becomes a misery to himself and a bore to others. It is written into the human constitution that MALENESS means work." He was ready to believe that there had once been something idealistic and generous in their rebellion, but it had become a huddle-together in misery and defiance: "There is a despairing how-did-I-get-this-way anguish under that vagabond dress — stupefying conversations of lofty posing." It was hard to arouse their interest: "They are 'cocooned' in self-sufficiency. One is so totally a vegetarian that he can't even eat fish, and I defy you to make conversation pro- or anti-vegetarianism. Marijuana may not be harmful, but all-day Marijuana and all-day 'country rock' make for a regression toward infantilism. I call it the 20-year hiatus in civilization. Like everything else it's the result of two-plus-one World Wars — mind-shattering, belief-shattering; for another fifty years we can do little more than grope among the ruins."

Thornton's itinerary was now as predictable as the months of the year. Four trips to Europe from 1968 to 1971 — Paris, Munich, Innsbruck, Milan, Venice, Zurich, Cannes. If not in Europe, he was in Florida, New Orleans, New England, New York, Mexico, staying nowhere longer than a month. A European trip in June 1968 was cut short because he discovered a swelling under his right clavicle and suspected lung cancer. It was a false alarm.

Disciplined as he was to accept the unalterable, he chose not to accept age as a stop sign. Nature was on the side of pressing forward, assisting those who put their confidence in it. He had never had regular medical checkups. Only when he lost almost all vision in his left eye, in June 1970, did he call on a specialist, who told him that it was less an ocular than a circulatory problem. Pills, rest and restricted use of his eyes were recommended, which meant that he had to "hang around New Haven for a number of weeks." He had been saying for years that he didn't enjoy any company larger than four, and he had gladly let Isabel stand in for him when he was given the National Book Award in 1968. All the same, he was a boisterous participant at the fiftieth reunion of his Yale class in 1970: "What a Yalie, what a bulldog, what a noisy, back-slapping old grad am I."

Because Isabel was concerned about his health, and to make it easier for them both, Thornton drafted a form letter she could draw from and send under her signature:

> Mr. Thornton Wilder regrets that he is no longer able to: deliver lectures, read publicly from his works, take part in platform discussions, speak on the radio or television or into tape-recording equipment, or attend performances of his plays; send autographs or photographs; sign volumes, photographs, or theater programs; send objects to be sold at benefit auction; read material submitted to him; arrange to be interviewed or photographed. Mr. Wilder will have received expressions of appreciation of his work, but because of increasing deterioration of his eyesight is no longer able to answer these letters in person.

His hearing came and went. He got relief from shortness of breath by yoga exercises taken from a popular handbook he'd picked up from a drugstore rack ("more useful than anything my doctor said to me"). He still drove his car through the New England countryside, though from time to time he was aware of a perturbation in the vision of the other eye. "If that 'kicks up' — goodbye to reading and writing (which I limit strictly now anyway)." There were sleepless nights and resorts to mild sleeping pills. High altitudes, climbing, even long walks were ruled out. The sacroiliac pains returned, and for every hour of sitting up he had to compensate with several hours of lying down.

But the enthusiasms were bountiful. New material on Shakespeare, the prospect of unlocking the Etruscan script, the revelation that Schubert sometimes took a movement of a Beethoven sonata and used it as a sort of guide-grid on which to write one of his own. "I'd go crazy," he wrote Leo Herlihy, "if I weren't pursuing some hobby — absorbing, totally occupying train of inquiry. At present it's Greek vase painting. I've lived seventy-two and ten-twelfths years without giving it a thought. Also, for what I'm reading I felt I should know something about the Tibetan *Mandala*. Before that it was Lévi-Strauss and structuralism." He had lost none of his interest in theater. "For the present, movies have taken over the slice-of-life," he told Robert Penn Warren, "but the movies never never will take over the poetic *word*. The prose play is dead: The theater has only a future as mass ritual and as poetic drama. The older I grow the more I lean on myths and on prototypes in literature."

Routine inquiries went unanswered, but Thornton counseled E. Martin Browne on how to direct a performance of *Our Town* in England: "Actors — by selection and training — are highly suggestible; they will try to impose the mood (not the content) of the last act on the first two. They will grave-yard the whole play. . . . God grant you can find an actress who can say Emily's farewell to the world not as 'wild regret' but as love and discovery."

His new novel? "Oh, I know that you think I've been stringing you along," he wrote Hutchins in a letter dated "maybe July 29 or so, 1972," "pretending that a book is taking shape, wildly boasting that it's the best book since *Riders of the Purple Sage* and *The Trail of the Lonesome Pine*, putting up a raffish show to conceal from you my laziness — worse, my yawning vacancy of mind. Well, sir, you're mistaken. Nine chapters are completed. Four are well advanced. Contrary to your blackguardly suspicions, I have worked like a horse on a treadmill daily. No, that's not fair, like a flower bed in a greenhouse. I've had a second blooming."

At one stage, Thornton had had in mind a collection of memories: 1908–1909, China Inland Boys School; 1919–1920, Yale; 1937, Salzburg; 1943, Allied Air Headquarters in Italy. Each was to offer variations and commentaries on the question: "What does a man do with his despair (his rage, his frustration)? What does every different kind of person 'shore up' to evade, surmount, transmute, incorporate those aspects of life which are beyond our power to alter?" Since he wanted the freedom to invent, the book was not to be strictly autobiographical. Perhaps he felt that fiction was the only form for the truth he had to tell.

Work on those early chapters, which he later discarded, had been interrupted by a controversy over the right to use the title *The Skin of Our Teeth,* a controversy that had its innocent genesis in the spring of 1967 when Irene Worth, star of *The Alcestiad* in Edinburgh, came to New Haven to act in Robert Brustein's theater company at the Yale Drama School. During dinner with Thornton and Isabel, she had passed along a request from Sir Kenneth Clark, who wished to use the title *The Skin of Our Teeth* for one part of his BBC television series, *Civilisation.* Thornton and Isabel had the impression that it was to be a single program, an educational feature, and Thornton at once said that he had no objection. After all, the title came out of the Bible, anyone could use it. He asked Isabel to write Sir Kenneth to that effect, and after some delay, she cabled that "Thornton feels no copyright problem in sharing title since works are different literary forms. Sends greetings."

If Clark's request had been turned over promptly to Brandt & Brandy and Thornton's lawyer, as it should have been, the ensuing argument could have been averted, for it soon became apparent that Sir Kenneth's project was more ambitious than Thornton had presumed. *Civilisation* was not one or two BBC programs but a widely distributed series on film that was to be shown throughout the United States. Mary Ellen Bute, who was trying to raise money for her own filming of *The Skin of Our Teeth,* was upset. Thornton, committed to her undertaking and sharing her fear that the use of the title by *Civilisation* would jeopardize her chances of financing, took up the dispute. On July 21, 1970, he wrote his lawyer that he "did not give him [Clark] or the producer BBC permission for its multiple reproduction on film to be shown to audiences gathered in auditoriums — that is to say: *The motion picture rights.* . . . I want you to prepare to sue the British Broadcasting Company, producers, and assignees for a million dollars for breach of agreement and for the damage they have already done — and are continuing to do — to the property rights I hold in any motion picture production of my play entitled *The Skin of Our Teeth.*"

More lawyers were brought in, and after lengthy negotiations it was agreed that the title would not be used in advertising *Civilisation*. No suit was filed, and Thornton returned a $25,000 advance he had received from Miss Bute for her option on *The Skin of Our Teeth*. She was never able to raise the necessary financing, which was the fate of every effort to transpose his wartime play into another medium.

It was 1971 before Thornton returned to his autobiographical novel in earnest, and by then he had narrowed it to a few months in Newport in the twenties. Despite poor eyesight, recurrent deafness and high blood pressure, he was able to work about four hours a day in Florida the winter of 1971–1972. For three weeks in March there was an arid spell when he couldn't bear to glance at the manuscript; then he got "a ripping idea for another chapter" and with the aid of insomnia, bourbon and a phonograph record or two, he started again. By June on Martha's Vineyard, he could see the entire map of the book, but in November the last four chapters were causing him "no little sweat"; the stories were getting "more and more *costing.*" The following month he was on the last lap and *Theophilus North* was accepted for publication by Harper & Row. "Not bad at seventy-five, wot?"

He had set out to write a droll story to amuse an ailing Bob Hutchins, to whom he sent a copy of each chapter as it was finished, a book that would "hurt your sides — endanger your stitches and all that," but the "old Wilder-Niven inheritance" had taken over. He ended up with a book about Theophilus-the-fixer, the mender of rips and tears in the human fabric, and he had qualms about its reception, fearing that it might be ridiculed and thus embarrass Hutchins, to whom it was dedicated. "Maybe I've let you in for some derision in the market-place. Well, that may still happen, but I believe you to be Oberlin-proof against mere malice."

Theophilus North relates the Newport adventures of a bright and eager young man with a taste and talent for solving other people's problems. Is he Thornton? Or is he Thornton's twin brother who died at birth, Theophilus Wilder, referred to in the family as Pax? Or is he Thornton imagining a daredevil Theophilus within himself? The narrator-hero has something of each twin in him. The book is a sequence of episodes that Thornton experienced in Newport, dreamt that he experienced, wished that he had or might have had.

The twin relationship had been long pondered. Theophilus (the stillborn brother) and Todger (Thornton) were bound together in an unstable coexistence. Todger carried the burden of his father's New England ethos, whose watchword was duty — self-improvement and the improvement of others. Theophilus was eager to explore other roads — adventure, enjoyment. Todger was the excellent student, one who set an example to misguided fellows who bring grief and shame on their parents. "But it should be remembered at the same time," Thornton wrote, "that these twins were mixed-up young men." Todger had his curiosities, too. Nor was Theophilus a mere hedonist; he had his share of quixotic idealism. Identical twins, Thornton noted, are not just amalgamations of the characteristics inherited from their ancestors, as is everyone, but are one man's packet of characteristics in two editions: "If your name (say) is George, there are two Georges. Outwardly you and your brother George resemble one another exactly." Inwardly, too, you are identical but the ingredients are differently mixed: "In George One and George Two there are only the same inherited traits: distributed differently. One's not all saint and the other all sinner, sage or dolt." In his journal, Thornton remarked, "It was some time before the author of this book became fully aware that he was a mixed package."

The novel had an advance hardcover sale of around thirty thousand copies, a guarantee of $67,500 from the Literary Guild–Doubleday Book Club and Avon paperbacks, and stayed on the bestseller list twenty-one weeks. In the German edition, it was titled *Theophilus North: Saint against His Will,* which was its true subject. There were friendly reviews, though Brooks Atkinson had told Cass Canfield that "since a critic is supposed always to tell the truth, I regretfully report that I am disappointed in it. It starts out like an autobiography and I was hoping for more of the same. But I got lost later on in the book. Sorry. Please don't tell Thornton."

The *Times Literary Supplement* thought that "its atmosphere of benevolence, because incidental and unforced, never threatens to grow too sickly, while its air of expansive tolerance toward a world

of fools rather than knaves has no relish of humbug about it."
Malcolm Cowley said that if he was any sample of the public,
"it will be enthralled and held in chains until the last page."

A number of Thornton's admirers, however, detected a forced
tone in *Theophilus North* — not in its delightful description of past
and present Newport, which Thornton compares to the nine cities
of ancient Troy, but in the endeavors of bustling Theophilus, who
to many critics seemed affected. The bright-eyed narrator, they
felt, came across as an officious meddler, too confident of his ability
to straighten out the kinks in other's lives. There had been a touching innocence about George Brush in *Heaven's My Destination;*
one's sympathies were won by this soul-saving Don Quixote who
didn't know it all. Theophilus at moments seems a rather smug
manipulator. One wishes that he would fail, at least once. By the
end of the book, the reader has begun to suspect that at bottom
the hero is a sentimentalist, and it was Thornton who had defined
a sentimentalist as "one whose desire that things be happy exceeds
his desire and suppressed knowledge that things be truthful; he
demands that he be lied to. He secretly knows that it is a lie;
hence his emphasis, his elations and his heartlessness."

The last lines of *Theophilus North* had been written on Palm
Sunday 1973, and Thornton had awakened the next morning to
the discomfort of having nothing to do. On Easter a "*smashing
idea*" occurred to him — a rip-roaring, spine-tingling melodrama
under which would be hidden "the most affirmative clarion-call
for the meaning of existence since Beethoven's *Leonore* Overture
No. III." It came to nothing.

30

Last Days

"THE LORD hath laid trials after trials on thee — as our fathers would have said. But don't think of your predicament in those terms." So Thornton had written his ill friend Bob Hutchins. "I — and Goethe — acknowledge a God but we don't anthropomorphize him. We call him *die Natur* and we know He, She, It embraces this vast process and has fashioned it with a million marvelous smaller processes which betray an intense concern for how the whole thing works — a concern that much resembles love. All Nature strives to bring every detail to its truest expression of its function. All Nature is working *for* you. Rise above immediate things and feel that — get a-holt of that. Float in the teleological tide."

But at seventy-four, Thornton himself had slowed down, at least to a fast trot. Over the next three years he would be seen in numerous New England towns, and in New York, Florida, the Caribbean. There would be a last trip abroad and an award by Princeton of the James Madison Medal for contributions to American literature. Type had to be reset for a new Samuel French acting edition of *Our Town* — 295,000 copies had been sold, 100,000 more than the next most popular drama on its list — and Thornton cheerfully signed 2,000 colophon pages of the play published by the Limited Editions Club.

On Thanksgiving in 1973, in Amherst for family dinner at the Dakins', he was haunted by ghosts, "including the blessed ones; so many storms at sea, so many near shipwrecks and one shipwreck — my sister Charlotte at the Brattleboro Retreat an hour-and-a-half from where we were sitting." If he violated his rule of no more than two crowd engagements a day he felt depleted, though after a lively evening at Catherine Coffin's in New Haven that year, novelist Paul Horgan remarked what a great satisfaction it was to find Thornton so robust.

Nembutal sent him to sleep in a half hour but left him groggy, so he devised a sleep-inducing stratagem: "Turn out the light. Pick on something to think about. (I imagine myself going down a street in Oberlin or Tübingen or Aix en-Provence systematically — or almost — recalling details of a doorway, a shop, or crossing). Then deftly change the vision. I insert an irrational element. A minaret I knew in Constantine, Algeria. I explore that. Then I switch the train of thought again. These successive nonsequiturs throw the grimly set pride in the rational will off base. It throws the train-of-thought into the open seas of free association, which is the door into dream-territory." Three bourbons-and-water between midnight and one also helped.

A walk of more than five or six blocks was becoming painful. When his left leg wobbled, Thornton pulled himself together and determinedly *walked,* and felt better. His most recent New Haven physician, Oscar Roth, noted that he seemed bubbling with vitality in 1974, but any discussion of medical subjects laid bare an underlying melancholy. He was still having four or more drinks and seventy cigarettes a day. To counter his hypertension, emphysema and irregular heartbeat, Dr. Roth put him on digitalis, hypotensive drugs to lower blood pressure, a salt substitute and a diuretic. By November, Thornton had lost some weight, was less bloated and breathing more easily. He continued to answer about twenty letters daily and was excited about a sequel to *Theophilus North,* which was going in "starts and halts like an old jalopy. I disregard little matters like eyesight, hearing and respiration."

But *die Natur* could not be disregarded. Thornton had been hospitalized on Martha's Vineyard in August 1973 for a recurrence of a slipped disc. Twelve months later he was back in the same hospital after a terrifying afternoon of dizziness, vomiting and soaring blood pressure. A young intern worked on him for three and a half hours in the emergency room, fearing a massive stroke or heart attack. He slowly recovered, but it seemed to Isabel that he might continue to be the semi-invalid he had been during the past eighteen months. Then he rose out of his muddle into clear light, resumed writing and evaded his physician's advice on dieting. Each Saturday morning and Sunday afternoon in January 1975 he claimed his special table by the window in the New Haven Howard Johnson's. Breakfast, according to his favorite waitress, was oatmeal with sliced bananas, orange toasties, pancakes with sausages, coffee. Dinner: a double whiskey sour, veal cutlet, tea and a hot fudge sundae with lots of nuts and whipped cream.

On Sanibel Island in Florida that winter he became aware of a lurking tension above his left eye. Dreading that a potential stroke would announce itself, he refused any official dinner or any intellectual discussion. He would not be a wheelchair nuisance, an object of pity. Nor would he dwell on the past; he would "expunge it." Blessed are the forgetful, said Nietzsche, for they get the better even of their blunders. Yet the past could not be erased; its marks were indelible. Within the aged man was the wide-eyed Madison boy in a horse and buggy, and the boy on a San Francisco–bound boat with a dollar watch from Papa in his pocket. There, vivid as the jet streaking across the Florida sky, were the Berkeley Episcopal church choir, the Greek chorus, the dress-ups and playacting, the dawn on farms in San Luis Obispo and Berea, the Torreys' books and player piano, the missed catch in right field at Thacher, the ill-fitting coat and pants, the stage-struck Oberlin freshman.

So much had happened. In his lifetime Thornton had witnessed an extraordinary magnification of power — power to traverse the planet, soar through space, store knowledge, answer complicated questions at lightning speed; power to signal, produce, preserve, heat, cool, construct, annihilate. It had come about so quickly, leaving one unprepared. "The worst of having been brought up in the late foam-rubber phase of American Protestantism," he wrote Hutchins, "is that we don't have the daring even to think window-breaking thoughts. We should have had our savage thoughts earlier and have lived with them and tempered them."

In spite of not having "caught the vein," he continued writing hours each day, and with faltering eyesight reread Goethe's conversations with Eckermann, Madame de Sévigné's letters, Trollope's *Barchester Chronicles,* Darwin's *Voyage of the Beagle* ("splendid"),

Boswell's *London Journal* ("a little Scotch puppy and how he grew") and, most stimulating, the social anthropologist Claude Lévi-Strauss, whose thought in *The Naked Man* paralleled his own. "Man has to live and struggle, think, believe and above all preserve his courage," wrote Lévi-Strauss "although he can never at any moment lose sight of the opposite certainty that he was not present on earth in former times, that he will not always be here in the future and that, with his inevitable disappearance from the surface of the planet which is itself doomed to die, his sorrows, his joys, his hopes, his works will be as if they had never existed."

Was it a sign of partial recovery that in February 1975 he was frantic to cut short his stay on Sanibel Island and get to New York? "With my mania for constant change, I don't really enjoy staying in New York for more than three days, but I can't wait to descend on the Hotel Algonquin — and then do what? I don't know. Lost my relish in play-going, concert-going, gallery-going. I just like being *there.*" All the same, he and Isabel stayed in Florida until the middle of March. He was "not doing well," Isabel wrote Cass Canfield.

After their return to Hamden, Thornton made three trips to Manhattan to the bedside of Vincent Sheean, who was undergoing radiation treatments and dying. Under one arm he carried the essays of William Empson, which Sheean *had* to read ("don't get lazy!"); under the other a Milan newspaper and a copy of the *Nouvelle Revue Française.* Walking up Fifth Avenue with Dinah Sheean, he brought out a worn envelope and, mumbling something about hotel living's being expensive, hurriedly thrust it at her: "Don't tell Isabel or Jimmy." The envelope contained three thousand dollars in cash.

He was feeling well enough on his seventy-eighth birthday to suggest a dinner party at Deepwood Drive, thinking it would cheer up his sister: "Poor Isabel has been for long weeks under the cloud of my anti-social gloom." They invited nephew Tappan Wilder and his wife, Robin; his niece, Catharine Dix Wilder; the Herman Lieberts (former Beinecke librarian and president of the Grolier Club); and Thornton's literary executor, Donald Gallup. A friend who saw Thornton soon afterward thought he looked pale, nervous and overweight. On the contrary, Thornton maintained that his health had taken a turn for the better: "I shall go to Martha's Vineyard where I hope to get on with some writing. I'm pulling myself together for another piece of work. One becomes very severe on oneself at this time of life. I hope to overcome that and to write — as the great Gertrude enjoined us — 'as though nobody were listening.' "

Various proposals had been submitted for an adaptation of one of his plays or novels as a motion picture, a musical, a television series. Another reached him on Martha's Vineyard from Sol Lesser and Martha Scott (the original Emily), a remake of *Our Town*. Thornton replied that he was too old and had to save his energy for the "slow but steady progress I am making on a new book." More surprising was Leonard Bernstein's reappearance; he wanted permission to appropriate Sabina's opening lines in *The Skin of Our Teeth* for a song.

Thornton answered: "I did not want an opera to be made of *The Skin of Our Teeth*, but I admired and trusted you, and was persuaded. I trusted you and the fellow-workers you would select. When your chosen fellow-workers fell apart I felt relieved of my commitment to you. Hereafter while I am alive no one will write or compose an opera based on that play. . . I'm sorry to disappoint you, but my mistake was to say yes in the first place; yours to have not followed through with the original plan offered me."

He broke his stay on the Vineyard in July 1975 for several days in Boston, on the excuse that he wanted to buy a book, Lewis Thomas's *The Lives of a Cell*. Also, Ruth Gordon had asked him to reread Shaw's *Mrs. Warren's Profession* and advise whether it would be a good vehicle for her. He didn't have a copy and hadn't the strength to walk from the Copley Plaza to the Boston Public Library; Amos and Catharine brought the play to his hotel. He was standing in the hall waiting for them, and Catharine's first impulse was to take him to their house in Cambridge and look after him. Instead, he suggested they have a drink downstairs. They declined and left around eleven; it was the last time the brothers were together. When Amos and Catharine got home, they telephoned. There was no answer in his room. Thornton was in the bar.

Back on the Vineyard, he discovered a book of reproductions

of Chinese paintings: "I must hurry and get well and go to the great collections over there in China." But such enthusiasms were short-lived. In September he entered Massachusetts General for an operation on a cancerous prostate. When Sally Begley visited him in the hospital, Thornton was wearing a bathrobe and surgical stockings; it was not how he liked to appear. Afterward she went to the Chilton Club for lunch and saw Isabel eating alone. "Her face was such a mask of sorrow that I didn't recognize her, and then I watched her, and then I realized it had to be she and I spoke to her." The next day, Sally brought her children to lunch with Isabel at the Ritz: "I did what he used to do for me." Isabel was in tears.

Within two weeks Thornton was out of the hospital and contemplating a stay of three and a half months at the Hotel Royalton in New York! "The gap between your wishes for him and his following is still pretty wide but narrowing," Isabel wrote Dr. Roth. He had little vision in one eye; a cataract had developed in the other; his blood pressure had gone down somewhat but fluid escaping from the blood vessels into tissue made him bloated. He assured Dr. Roth that he had stopped smoking, whereupon the physician took from his desk drawer a recent issue of the *New Haven Register,* which carried a photograph of Thornton holding a lighted cigarette. The patient smiled.

Something almost as vexing as his health wearied Thornton greatly during his last weeks. He mentioned it in a letter of November 21, 1975: "The book by my self-styled biographer does not appear officially until next week but it's in the bookstores. We haven't read it nor intend to, and we sent back the copy the author sent us. Letters and phone calls of consternation and outrage have reached me."

The book, *Thornton Wilder: An Intimate Portrait,* by Richard H. Goldstone, had a distressing history. Thornton and the author had met in Miami Beach in 1942 when Thornton was in officers' training camp and Goldstone, a graduate student in English, was about fifty hotels down the shoreline, in a student training corps. In Caserta in 1944 at Allied headquarters, the acquaintance had been renewed, and after the war Goldstone suggested an interview for the *Paris Review*. "I could see," Thornton later wrote Cass Canfield, "that he wasn't mature enough for the work. I wrote about all the questions and answers on separate slips of paper. Veterans were constantly called on to do favors for other veterans."

Having more material than could be printed in the *Paris Review,* Goldstone proposed a book. "There are always a few projects like that in the air," Thornton said; "you couldn't stop 'em if you wanted to. But I made it perfectly clear that it was a *critical appraisal* not a biography. No literary man of serious intention has a biography written during his lifetime — that's for athletes, mountain climbers and hack jobs about movie stars."

Goldstone seems to have had a different impression. After all, the two of them had had many conversations — in Caserta, Rome, Capri, and later in Princeton, New York, Stockbridge, East Hampton, Westport, New Haven, Williamstown, Cambridge and along the connecting highways. He presumably believed that he had been given a green light to collect further material, interview Thornton's friends and write a biography. "Isabel now confesses," Wilder told Canfield, "she made a great mistake in not making firmly clear to Goldstone and to Beulah [Hagen, of Harper & Row] the *limits of his project.* Damn it, I began hearing from Bob Hutchins and Bobsy [Goodspeed] Chapman and the Rev. Glenn that they'd received calls for interviews and requests to read my letters. . . . 'Thornton, do you *really* want me to dig out those letters for him?' There was nothing sensational about any of them, but inevitably [they] contained free 'play of mind' about living persons and mutual friends. But Goldstone — obtuse, pushing, half-baked — has now got the bit between his teeth." Thornton considered that he had been patient too long, from sheer indifference. "To put it in a nutshell, I don't want him *posturing on my grave."* He suggested that Harper & Row ask to see some chapters, "find out for yourself that he can't write, has no ideas . . . and slowly, courteously deflate his balloon. If he wants to run up another book with another House I shall find ways to discourage it."

Goldstone was in an awkward position. Isabel had cooperated with him after Thornton, reluctantly, told her she could go ahead, "so long as I don't know anything about it; all that's in your department." Harper & Row, meanwhile, had given Goldstone a letter stating that he had a contract for the book and that the project "is being undertaken with the knowledge of Mr. Wilder's family. They agree with us that Mr. Goldstone's professional training and his long association with Mr. Wilder will make his approach to the subject an appropriate and interesting one." That letter was never seen by Isabel, and Thornton claimed that he didn't foresee that Goldstone wanted to give the book a biographical character: "I thought it would be principally a discussion of my writings. But you can't stop these energetic young professors. I don't wish my letters to be published during my lifetime."

As early as September 1967 Isabel had informed Harper & Row that Goldstone was "merely, under the auspices of Harper's, collecting material 'toward' a future work and material for others to use." But she'd been uneasy: "He [Goldstone] seems to have lost his head a little." When Louise Talma discussed the matter with Thornton, she found him "very distressed, extremely upset by it; he disliked the prying into family relationships."

The publisher, too, was in a frustrating position. Harper's first loyalty was to Thornton, and Goldstone, now convinced that nothing he said or wrote would have Thornton's approval, was asked to come to the office for a frank talk. "I wish we were out of it," Beulah Hagen told Canfield. Thornton wrote Goldstone that he would not open his last two letters, "because the preceding letters were so foolish and so superficial (and incidentally so uncomprehending of my fields of interest) they made me very angry and disturbed my working day. . . . I wish to be plain-speaking, but not rude. Can you understand the difference? Drop me. You've grown narrower and I've strained every means to grow wider."

There had then appeared in the *New York Times* of September 3, 1969, a story from London by Gloria Emerson that quoted from "117 revealing and affectionate letters, written between 1928 and 1950 by the American novelist and playwright Thornton Wilder" to Sibyl Colefax. The letters had been purchased by Goldstone from Lady Colefax's son; the story also quoted Professor Goldstone. Thornton was outraged. So was Harper & Row, who took the matter up with the *New York Times,* questioning their right to quote Thornton's letters without permission.

According to Goldstone, it was he who suggested to Cass Canfield that he would not be unwilling to withdraw from his contract with Harper & Row, realizing that Thornton's goodwill was more important to the house than his. The biography was thereupon accepted by Dutton and the "intimate portrait" was published shortly before Thornton's death. When Malcolm Cowley wrote that he planned to review the book for the *New York Times,* Thornton replied: "I found out long ago he was stuck in the perpetual graduate school student's mind. I gave up answering his greetings or letters. Poor Isabel carried the burden for awhile (in order to make sure that he got a few facts right — his insights were beyond one's guidance)." Goldstone might well have concluded that he had been misled or was the innocent victim of a misunderstanding.

It couldn't be helped. "I try to rise to the level of resentment," Thornton wrote Carol Brandt, "but (as with Doctor Johnson's friend) 'cheerfulness is always breaking in.'" He would get out of town. It had been a month since the prostate operation and he was fed up with confinement. He would return to New York for two weeks, not to "tear up a few cobblestones" this time, but simply to stroll down Fifth Avenue to the public library at Forty-second Street.

He and Isabel were driven to the city in November by Jim O'Neill, one of his Harvard students and "nephews." Thornton put up as a guest at the Harvard Club, which promised, if not anonymity, fewer chance encounters than the Algonquin several hundred yards away, where Isabel stayed a few days. He urged her to extend her visit, out of kindness she thought. They could not always be frank with each other. Dr. Roth had been consulted and had advised against this trip. "But I can't stop him," Isabel had said; "it wouldn't be fair of me, a sister can do only so much, I can't go on nagging."

The effort to enter the dining room of the Harvard Club left Thornton breathless. He gave up cigarettes for two days and was "in perfect hagony." He walked with a cane to the movies, to the French library at Rockefeller Plaza, to the Gotham Book Mart, where he asked for a chair, which he had never done before. He had long been encouraging the owner, Frances Steloff, to write the history of the bookstore. "Did you do what I told you?" he asked. She said she had begun. "Then let me see it." He took what she had written and returned her draft the next day with corrections and advice on how to proceed.

Isabel and Thornton had Thanksgiving dinner with the Kanins, after which she returned to New Haven. He taxied to Sutton Place to call on his old Chicago hostess, Bobsy Goodspeed, now Mrs. Gilbert Chapman, and they reminisced about the happiest years and their mutual friends — Fanny Butcher, Kate Brewster, Hutchins, Stein. It was "just like the old days, wonderful talk," she said.

He walked five and a half blocks on a gray, cold December day from the Harvard Club to Brandt & Brandt, where he hadn't been for years, greeting everyone from secretaries and office boy to William Koppelmann, his agent for dramatic properties. He told Koppelmann that he was going to say yes to a request that he allow *Our Town* to be made for television. That hadn't been his intention, but just before he entered the office he had changed his mind. "You tell 'em that Wilder has capitulated."

Thornton had not been keen on television drama ("the actors look like divers walking at the bottom of the sea"), and when Saul and Selma Jaffe and television director George Schaefer drove to Hamden to discuss a possible television serial based on *Theophilus North,* no conclusion had been reached. On the drive back to New York, Jaffe talked with Schaefer about adapting *Our Town* instead, making it a running family show. Schaefer thought it couldn't be done, but he did want to direct a single television performance of *Our Town*. The Jaffes and Schaefer put the idea to Thornton, who turned it down, but Schaefer brought it up again at lunch that last week in New York. Thornton replied that he didn't much care for the revivals of *Our Town* that had been put on recently, and that perhaps the time wasn't right for his work to be seen. Shortly after that lunch, Jaffe had a telephone call from Brandt & Brandt: Thornton had been to the office and said go ahead.*

As planned, Isabel sent a car and driver to pick him up at the

* *Our Town* was produced May 7, 1977, on NBC.

Harvard Club on Saturday morning, December 6. When he entered the house on Deepwood Drive, he put his arms around her: "All the way up the wheels said, 'I'm going home, I'm going home, I'm going home.' " He was tired and went immediately to bed. She brought him soup and crackers, he had a long nap and that evening was feeling better. Before retiring, he complained of an upset stomach; he had eaten too much in New York. She gave him a laxative and in the morning found a note under her door. "I slept well and had a good evacuation, and will be all set to go to Catherine's tonight." They were to have dinner with Catherine Coffin and her son, the Reverend William Sloane Coffin, chaplain of Yale.

He took it easy Sunday morning, had a light lunch, then his usual nap. Isabel said she would call him at five. "No, I'll be up. I won't be sleeping that long."

They were not due at the Coffins' until seven. Isabel went to his room about half past five, heard nothing, assumed he was still asleep and didn't open the door. She returned at six and found him in bed, on his side, facing the wall, dead. His hands and feet were still warm.

Bob Hutchins had had a letter from him that week: "I am temperamentally undiscourageable." People said, "God is dead." Well, "What a dreadful God it was." People viewed with alarm sexual promiscuity at sixteen. Well, "After some decades of adjustment (woeful adjustment), we shall be freed of this omnipresent prurience." People complained of labor unrest, of strikes. "The sacred character of PROPERTY will be unmasked for what it is: atavistic domination by the strong and the guileful." Nations threw their weight around, distrusted each other, fought; it was only "the last spitting of parochial self sufficiency as Other Worlds hove into view." And death?

He had had a dream when he was teaching at Harvard:

> In all dreams in which my mother appears she is still alive, so alive that on waking I go through a highly conscious moment of bewilderment, like this: "Now let me see . . . she . . . she . . . no, she is dead." In this dream she is across the room, sewing or somehow occupied in domestic work. I am

sitting on my father's lap, facing her; yet I somehow seem also to be behind myself and seeing, as it were, the backs of my mother's and my father's head. I think I see myself as full grown. Yet I have no sense of being a weight and encumbrance to my father. The mood of the scene is that of tranquil conversation, but one part of my mind is saying to itself: "We must not say anything that would remind my father that he is dead; it would embarrass him." Thereupon I woke up and rose to a level of consciousness nearer to waking and the following words rose spontaneously to my mind: "How wonderful it is that people die."

This astonishing sentence was propelled from me, from that atmosphere of contentment, as a joyous moment of illumination, and of course without the faintest shade of resentment or repudiation of the life represented.

When finally awake and considering what I have just described, my thought was: Is it possible that in aging we all receive just such intimations, such "animal" reconciliations with the fact of dying? I — who have never had any revulsion against the thought of dying — then hoped that that was so: Not from weariness of life, not from a tragic protest against life's difficulty, not from a dread of the declining years, but from some deep purely natural acceptance of the given assignment of youth, maturity, age, and death.

Acknowledgments

My indebtedness begins with the Wilder family. Thornton's sister Isabel Wilder was unstintingly helpful throughout the writing of this book, as were Thornton's brother, Amos, and his wife, Catharine, and Thornton's sister Janet Wilder Dakin.

The Beinecke Rare Book and Manuscript Library at Yale University, repository of major Wilder documents, gave all possible assistance, as did Thornton Wilder's literary executor, Donald Gallup. I owe much to my publisher, Chester Kerr; my editor, Katrina Kenison; Carol Brandt and William Koppelmann; Cass Canfield and Harper & Row, and my typist, Denise Mahrle.

The following institutions made valuable material available: American Academy of Arts and Letters, American Academy in Rome, Archives of American Art (Smithsonian Institution), the Walter Hamden–Edwin Booth Theatre Collection, the Lawrenceville School, Library of Congress, Newberry Library, New York Public Library, New-York Historical Society, Minnesota Historical Society, Pack Memorial Public Library of Asheville, North Carolina and the State Historical Society of Wisconsin.

In addition, I have benefited from information supplied by libraries of the following institutions of higher learning: Syracuse University, University of Houston, Stanford University, University of Delaware, Southern Illinois University, University of Illinois, University of Chicago, University of Iowa, Indiana University, St. Mary College (Leavenworth, Kansas), Berea College, Clark University, Harvard University, University of Michigan, Colby College, University of Minnesota, Cornell University, Columbia University, New York University, University of Rochester, Princeton University, Kent State University, Oberlin College, University of Oklahoma, University of California (Berkeley), Washington University and Boston University.

I am grateful to many who were willing to talk with me in many places — Berlin, Paris, Milan, London, Rome, Oxford; Connecticut, California, Arizona, Massachusetts, Illinois, New Jersey, North Carolina and Washington, D.C.: William Nichols, Charles Newton, Sally Begley, Therese Lewis Robinson, James Leo Herlihy, Malcolm Cowley, Jerome Kilty, Samuel M. Steward, Richard H. Goldstone, Glenway Wescott, John Evarts, Thomas Quinn Curtiss, Harry Levin, John Finley, John Morton Blum, Bettina Bachmann, Gertrude Macy, Lillian Gish, Seymour Lawrence, Tony Scott, John Marquand, Jr., Bruce McClellan, Donald Windham, Dinah Sheean, Mrs. Harold Kelly, George Schaefer, Eileen LeGrand, Julian LeGrand, Herman W. Liebert, Regina Fadiman, Marjorie Fasman, Patricia Bosworth, Susan Weininger, Richard Carlotta, Marietta Tree, Paul Weiss, Robert Penn Warren, Harriet Welling, Hamish Hamilton, Alison Henning, Eric Bentley, Emmet Lavery, John and Barbara Hersey, William Roerick, Dr. Carl Cassidy, Andrew J. Townson, Lillian Hellman, Mrs. William Aspenwall Bradley, Anna Valle, John Knowles, Terrence Catherman, Carol Channing, Mrs. Erwin N. Griswold, Jean Dalrymple, Rex Burbank, Edward Weeks, Louise Talma, Lewis M. Isaacs, Jr., Joseph W. Martin, Lillian R. Miller, Mario Laserna, W. Herbert Allen, Daniel Aaron, Dr. Hugh Dwyer, Leon Depres, James Greene, Donald Haberman, Lamont Johnson, Albert and Frances Hackett; and to the late Archibald MacLeish, Winthrop Dakin, Wilmarth S. Lewis, Anita Loos, Alfred Hitchcock, Mrs. William Sloane Coffin, Wendell Wilcox, Mrs. Gilbert Chapman, Sol and Fay Lesser, Dr. Oscar Roth, Erich Linder, R. Buckminster Fuller and John Tibby.

The biography has been aided also by correspondence with Edward Albee, Arthur Schlesinger, Jr., Mary B. Wallen, Frank Harding, William Jay Smith, Robert K. Patch, Timothy Findley, Waldo W. Greene, Gore Vidal, James Laughlin, Dr. Joseph Still, Miriam Beer-Hofmann-Lens, Clark Andrews, William Merchant, Robert Stevens, Mrs. Lila Tyng, Sir John Gielgud, Sir Michael Redgrave, Donald Hardie Fox, Anne Morrow Lindbergh, Vesta S. Hutchins,

James Hayden Silver, Milton Mayer, Katharine Hepburn, Elia Kazan, Louis H. Engel, Roy Anderson, Robert Lambert, Sarita Van Vleck, Alan Schneider, John L. J. Hart, Raymond Donnell, Mateo Lettunich, Walter Engel, Fitzroy Davis, David Weiss, Brooks Atkinson, Dr. George H. Pollock, Mary Lasswell, H. E. Patrick, Kenneth M. Price, Sister Ann Edward, James Carney, Mrs. Gordon K. Chalmers, Gladys Campbell, Orin Tovrov, Mrs. Harland H. Fraser, Dorothy Horowitz, Jean Stock, the Reverend Alfred W. Swan, E. Martin Browne, Douglas Wilson, John Malcolm Brinnin, Arthur Macy Cox, Bernice Palmer Beasley, Walter Carroll, I. E. Clark, Dr. Jean Gentry, Ralph Griswold, Mrs. Walter Paepke, Marshall Sprague, Leon Edel, Lynn Tufts, Paul Schlueter, Eleanor Lansing Dulles, Luciano Rebay, Peter DeVries, Katinka Loeser, Margaret Lang, Bill Mauldin, August Becker, and Nancy W. Kleinbord.

Index

The Enthusiast

GILBERT A. HARRISON

"Oh, earth," cries the heroine in Thornton Wilder's *Our Town*, "you're too wonderful for anyone to ever realize you!" The sentiment sprang straight from the author's heart; Wilder had a never-ending love affair with life.

From boyhood in Wisconsin, California and China, his imagination was fired by books and the theater, though he showed little early promise of becoming a three-time Pulitzer Prize winner and the celebrated author of *The Bridge of San Luis Rey*.

In this first full-length study of the man and the writer, Wilder is seen as an eager, desperately literary Oberlin and Yale undergraduate, as an explorer of ancient and modern Rome, as a schoolmaster working odd hours at his first novel, *The Cabala*. There are hilarious weeks in Hollywood, fights with producer Jed Harris over the staging of *Our Town*, contretemps over the acting in *The Skin of Our Teeth*. We follow Wilder's search for tranquility aboard ships, at resorts in Switzerland, Austria, France and Italy, and on brief escapes to hideaways in Florida and Arizona.

Wherever he alighted, Wilder picked up friends—waitresses, bartenders, a world-renowned boxer, a nightclub hostess, as well as such luminaries of his day as Ernest Hemingway, F. Scott Fitzgerald, Gertrude Stein, Tallulah Bankhead, and Montgomery Clift.

He was a paradox—solitary and gregarious, serious and clowning, peace-loving yet a